The Truth of History

When historians describe or explain past events, is there any sense in which those descriptions and explanations can be said to give a true and fair account of the past? Cultural relativism and postmodern writing on the nature of language have cast doubt upon the possibility of written history being true. *The Truth of History* by C. Behan McCullagh considers the question of how modern historians, confined by the concepts and forms of argument of their own cultures, can still discover truths about the past. Through an examination of the constraints of history, the author argues that although historical descriptions do not mirror the past they can correlate with it in a regular and definable way.

The Truth of History presents a study of various historical explanations and interpretations and evaluates their success as accounts of the past. C. Behan McCullagh argues that the variety of historical interpretations and their subjectivity does not exclude the possibility of their fairness and truth. He also offers a fresh analysis of causes and causal explanation in history, and defends the value of historical knowledge in helping us to appraise our social and cultural inheritance.

C. Behan McCullagh presents a thorough examination of the practice of history and debates the important issues commanding the attention of philosophers and historians today. The author argues that historians achieve a measure of truth which recent critics have ignored. He defends a position between the two extremes of believing that history perfectly represents the past and that history can tell us nothing about it that is true.

C. Behan McCullagh is Senior Lecturer in Philosophy at La Trobe University, Australia. He was formerly Lecturer in History at Melbourne University. He has published many articles on philosophy of history, and the book *Justifying Historical Descriptions*.

81731

The Truth of History

C. Behan McCullagh

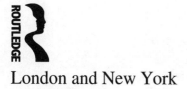

London and New York

First published 1998
by Routledge
11 New Fetter Lane, London EC4P 4EE

Simultaneously published in the USA and Canada
by Routledge
29 West 35th Street, New York, NY 10001

Typeset in Times by
Ponting–Green Publishing Services,
Chesham, Buckinghamshire
Printed and bound in Great Britain by
TJ International, Padstow, Cornwall

British Library Cataloguing in Publication Data
A catalogue record for this book is available from the
British Library

Library of Congress Cataloguing in Publication Data
McCullagh, C. Behan
     The Truth of History/McCullagh.
     p.   cm.
     Includes bibliographical references and index.
     1. History–Philosophy.   2. History–Methodology.
     I. Title.
     016.8.M386   1997   97–8185
     901–dc21   CIP

ISBN 0–415–17110–5 (hbk)
ISBN 0–415–17111–3 (pbk)

Contents

Not to us, O Lord, not to us,
but to thy name ascribe the glory,
for thy true love and for thy constancy.

Psalm 115, v.1

Introduction

There are two important issues commanding the attention of philosophers of history today. One is the question of the truth and objectivity of history. There have been three major lines of attack upon the truth and objectivity of history. First, the facts of cultural relativism, and postmodern writing on the nature of language have cast doubt upon the possibility of written history being true. Every culture views the world differently, through the lenses of its own concepts and interests, so how can any account of the world be thought true? According to the postmoderns, language has no important or regular relation to the world, so we should not expect descriptions of what has happened in the world to reveal reality. Second, the fact that interpretations of past events and societies vary with the cultural prejudices and personal interests and convictions of historians seems to imply that none of them can be true or objective. Certainly many have drawn this conclusion. Finally, historians often describe patterns of historical events in metaphorical terms, for example, as the growth or decline of something, as a revolution or contest, and some philosophers argue that metaphorical descriptions cannot be true or false. Rather, they say, such descriptions merely suggest ways of viewing the events involved.

The second question being discussed today concerns the reality and importance of social structures and general processes of social change. With the failure of Enlightenment theories of progress and Marxist theories of emancipation there is a general scepticism about the reliability of any accounts of social structure and process. Instead, some historians believe they should focus on the particular, the unique, and account for historical change simply in terms of individual decisions and their sometimes unpredictable consequences.

These are the two central issues to be addressed in this book. I shall argue in Chapter 1 that the facts of cultural relativism and of the relation between language and reality require historians to give up any naive assumption that historical descriptions correspond exactly to the events which they describe in the past. Nevertheless there is a sense, which I shall define, in which historical descriptions can be true of the past, allowing that they are always couched in the concepts of a particular culture.

I shall also show, through a careful analysis of historical practice in Chapter 4, that although historical interpretations reflect the interests and ideas of historians, they are not entirely subjective. Historians require that interpretations of past events, people and societies be true, fair and of an adequate explanatory scope. These constraints are seldom if ever sufficient, however, to determine that just one interpretation of an historical subject is superior to all others. It is normal for there to be more than one true characterization of an event or historical period. The variety of historical interpretations does not exclude the possibility of their truth.

As for the metaphorical descriptions of the past, I shall argue in Chapter 2 that they can indeed be true or false. The assertion that they cannot rests upon an inadequate theory of metaphor.

Turning to the importance of general knowledge in writing history, several chapters explain and defend it. Chapter 2 defends the possibility of historical generalizations being true; Chapter 4 illustrates their importance in providing summary interpretations of historical subjects; Chapter 7 shows how important general knowledge is in identifying causes; and chapters 9 and 10 discuss the use of generalizations in explaining collective actions and social changes. The last chapter, Chapter 11, directly addresses arguments that we should privilege the individual both in explaining and describing the past, but presents reasons for rejecting this proposal. To confine our knowledge of the past to knowledge of particulars would be to deprive us of an enormous amount of information and understanding, and leave us helpless victims of the forces of society and culture which condition our lives.

THE PRESENT DEBATE

In the last few decades philosophers of history have increasingly attacked the idea that history can present a true and objective account of the past. Although this literature has had little noticeable effect on the practice of history, it has thrown into doubt the significance of what historians write. This has concerned many historians, some of whom have expressed their anxieties in print. A vivid example of this concern is to be found in the encounter in *The American Historical Review* (Harlan, 1989) between David Harlan, using the work of Derrida and Lyotard to deny that history tells us anything true or meaningful about the past, and David A. Hollinger, who resists Harlan's scepticism in the name of historical practice. Hollinger ends by referring to historians' hope 'to preserve in the old historian's craft a cognitive element, which some of these theories invite us to give up as a lost prodigal'. He goes on: 'Perhaps someone will develop a theoretical account of the "cognitive element" able to command the respect of the men and women currently in the thrall of philosophies that reduce historical knowledge to a tissue of remnants and fabrications concealing, as Harlan summarizes the challenge, "an essential absence"' (Hollinger, 1989, pp. 620–1).

The case against objectivity in history is most famously made by Peter Novick in *That Noble Dream: The 'Objectivity Question' and the American Historical Profession* (1988). Having described the variety of interpretive approaches adopted by American historians, he concludes that history is clearly not objective, although objectivity has served the profession as an inspiring myth (pp. 3–6). I agree that historical interpretations are, to a large extent, subjective, but I will argue that nevertheless they can be true, fair and moderately comprehensive.

At a popular level, Keith Jenkins has denied the objectivity and truth of history in his popular little book *Re-thinking History* (1991). He admits that historians study sources, but remarks that

> the historian's viewpoint and predilections still shape the choice of historical materials, and our own personal constructs determine what we make of them. The past that we 'know' is always contingent upon our own views, our own 'present'. . . . Epistemology shows we can never really know the past; that the gap between the past and history (historiography) is an ontological one, that is, is in the very nature of things such that no amount of epistemological effort can bridge it.
>
> (pp. 12,19)

Jenkins says that historians only retain the idea of truth to add weight to their preferred accounts of the past:

> 'truth' and similar expressions are devices to open, regulate and shut down interpretations. Truth acts as a censor – it draws the line. We know that such truths are really 'useful fictions' that are in discourse by virtue of power (somebody has to put and keep them there) and power uses the term 'truth' to exercise control: regimes of truth.
>
> (p. 32)

There have been a few attempts to defend the truth and objectivity of history against attacks like these. Keith Windschuttle wrote *The Killing of History. How a Discipline is being Murdered by Literary Critics and Social Theorists* (1994) to explain the present predicament, and 'to defend the integrity of history as a properly scientific endeavour' (p. 3). Windschuttle seriously believes that failure to defend history will see the demise of the discipline. The same year saw the publication of *Telling the Truth about History* by Joyce Appleby, Lynn Hunt, and Margaret Jacob (1994). 'We are arguing here', they write, 'that truths about the past are possible, even if they are not absolute, and hence are worth struggling for' (p. 7).

Why is there such a strong division of opinion about the truth and objectivity of history? I suggest that it is because each side is focused upon one aspect of writing history, and not attending sufficiently to the other. Historians are generally aware of the rationality of their procedures, of their critical evaluation of evidence, their careful checking of inferences drawn from it, and their critical comparison of alternative explanations and interpretations, so they are naturally convinced that on many occasions they have uncovered something true of the past. Philosophers, on the other hand, attend closely to the assumptions which historians make, the conceptual schemes, beliefs about the world, and standards of rationality which they employ, some of which differ from culture to culture. They have also become conscious of how tenuous seems to be the relation between language and the world, and how much our words make sense only in the context of a discourse. The world itself seems to them to play no part at all in the construction of history, and so they cannot see how history could possibly be true of it. Furthermore, following the work of Kuhn, Foucault and the New Historicists in particular, they are aware of the important role played by people's social and cultural context and interests in determining which interpretations of the past they will promote. It seems that history is created for ideological purposes, rather than constrained by evidence to reveal what actually happened in the past.

In some cases, one side has made a few concessions to the other. Most historians will agree that their syntheses of historical events reflect their interests, that they pick out those patterns in the past which they think to be of historical, ethical or political importance. They do not all conclude with Novick, however, that this fact renders their accounts of the past entirely subjective. Then again, some philosophers have conceded that historians can discover true particular facts about the past. Even Jenkins allows this in an unguarded moment (Jenkins, 1991, pp. 32–3), though he soon denies it, saying that the basic facts of history represent 'a congealed interpretation' (p. 34). Nevertheless, other philosophers like Hayden White, who clearly allow that the basic facts of history can be known, insist that the patterns of events which historians present, and which give meaning to individual events, are pure constructions which cannot be said to represent anything that really existed in the past.

In effect, each side is attending to different constraints on the production of written history. The historians are very conscious of being constrained by the need to provide rational justification of their historical descriptions, interpretations and explanations, to show how they follow rationally from the evidence available to them. The philosophers are fascinated by the personal, cultural, social and linguistic constraints upon historians, and see their work as a function of these.

For progress to be made in understanding the truth and objectivity of history, each side must attend more closely to what the other is saying. In recent years the two sides have just opposed one another, affirming their own position and lamenting the other. Windschuttle and the authors of *Telling the Truth about History* have attempted to rebut the sceptics, but have not done justice to their arguments. (See the reviews of the latter book in *History and Theory* 34(4): 320–39 (1995).) On the other hand, the philosophers have not looked closely enough at the process of interpreting historical evidence. Historians' descriptions of evidence are not simply a product of their preconceptions, but are partly determined by the material nature of the evidence itself. In this book I will consider the constraints upon historical writing in the hope of achieving a balanced assessment of the truth and objectivity of historical accounts. Prominent among those constraints are the historian's conceptual frameworks and beliefs about the world, acquired largely from her culture, the historian's personal interests and concerns, and the conventions governing historical inquiry, maintained by professionals in the field.

CONSTRAINTS UPON HISTORICAL SYNTHESIS

In the first chapter of this book I examine the more important arguments for scepticism about the truth of historical descriptions. In a previous book (McCullagh, 1984) I have set out the patterns of argument by which historians justify their descriptions of the past, but I did not there consider these reasons for being sceptical of their conclusions. First there is the question of what can rationally be inferred from evidence. It is tempting to suppose that because historians sometimes disagree about the implications of the evidence available to them, the evidence never warrants certain conclusions about the past. I argue that although historical conclusions are always fallible, when they are well supported by evidence they deserve to be believed very probably true, that is, as telling us something true about the world. It is reasonable to regard reliable observations of evidence as true, for their reliability is best explained by saying they are caused by something in the world of a kind regularly correlated with such experiences. Furthermore, it is reasonable to accept as true conclusions inductively inferred from observable evidence, not because one can prove that inductive inferences regularly yield the truth, for one cannot do that without vicious circularity, but because we all conventionally and successfully believe that they do. To deny faith in well supported descriptions of the past simply because the rational justification of those descriptions cannot be completed, is to introduce scepticism where it is not needed. We should be sceptical of descriptions which are not well supported, but accept as true those which are. In that way we are most likely to act successfully in the world. Blanket scepticism is disastrous.

Second, I consider the implications of cultural relativism. As I said above, if different cultures perceive the world differently, one cannot reasonably say the world is just as we perceive it. But we can say that our perceptions, when they are accurate, are caused by something in the world which would normally produce perceptions of that kind in people of our culture. I suggest that historical descriptions are true if they are part of a coherent account of the world, and if the observation statements implied by that account either were or could have been confirmed by people of the appropriate culture and with the appropriate interests. Finally I look at some arguments of Barthes, Derrida and Lyotard, all of which deny that our language represents the world. Barthes and Derrida, following Saussure, look for the meaning of words and texts in their relation to other words and texts, denying that they have any regular relationship with the world. Lyotard's attack is upon the capacity of words to capture the unique features of events in the world, remarking upon their tendency to force the facts into frames of thought which suit the purposes of the writer. None of these reasons for scepticism is found compelling.

Philosophers have responded to the attacks upon the correspondence theory of truth in history in different ways. Some, like Goldstein, seeing history as a construction from available evidence, have denied that it is true of the past at all. Others, like Oakeshott, have said it can be true in a coherence sense, true when it coheres well with our other beliefs about the world. And yet others, like Habermas, have more recently suggested that descriptions of the world are true when they are agreed upon by people who have considered them in a rational manner. These alternative responses to problems of historical scepticism are considered, and declined, in the second section of Chapter 1.

Just as important as the truth of historical descriptions is their fairness. Historians try to avoid giving descriptions which are misleading. A misleading description might truly describe part of a subject, yet leave the reader with an impression of the whole which is in fact false. I analyse the fairness of historical descriptions in the third section of Chapter 1. In Chapter 6 I note some particular problems of ensuring the truth of historical descriptions which have arisen in ethnographic history.

Historians are well aware of the need to verify the particular facts they report about the past, but they are sometimes less familiar with the constraints upon historical synthesis. This is why some are prone to think that the patterns which they discover in the past are simply the product of their own interests and preconceptions, and represent nothing about the past itself. H. Kellner, for example, has attacked the idea that the patterns historians find were really there. He wrote: 'Historians do not "find" the truths of past events; they create events from a seamless flow, and invent meanings that produce patterns within that flow' (Kellner, 1989, p. 24). He is suggesting, I think, that historians simply pick out events to fit some preconceived idea about what was happening, and are not at all concerned whether they are fairly representing what happened or not. Implicit is the idea that you can usually find some evidence for any general description you care to make about the past. This is not the practice of professional historians, however, as Kellner would have realized if he had studied the constraints on historical synthesis more carefully. In particular he would have noticed that there are truth conditions for general descriptions of the past as well as for statements of particular fact, and that historians are anxious to find generalizations and interpretations which are both true and fair. In the second chapter I discuss the truth of historical generalizations, and in the fourth I demonstrate how historians look for true and fair interpretations of events, of people's lives, and of past societies. These are common forms of interpretation in history, and by examining the constraints upon them, I provide good reason for thinking that historical interpretations are not as subjective as Kellner and others suppose.

Studying historical accounts of events, lives and societies led me to discover a difference between explanations and interpretations of these subjects. Although explanations in history are normally thought to refer to causal explanations, it is useful to broaden the concept of explanation to refer to any answer to a question. This acknowledges the wide range of common uses of the word 'explain'. We can explain *what* happened during the First World War, *how* parliamentary democracy was established in Britain, *who* Gladstone was, and *what* was the structure of society in Victorian England, as well as *why* the Labour Party was formed. Explanations are constrained by the questions they are designed to answer, and so their adequacy is theoretically not very difficult to assess.

Sometimes historians set out to explain what a particular subject was like, providing a comprehensive account of it, guided by their preconceptions of its general structure. This is what is normally required by a request to explain what an historical subject was like. Thus, in explaining an event they will describe and account for all the main stages of the change it involved, in a systematic way. To produce a comprehensive biography, historians begin at the subject's birth and end with their death, and give a more or less chronological account of all they did and suffered in between. Selection can be a real problem for such biographers, especially when there is a lot of information available about their subject. The criteria they commonly adopt to guide their selection are designed not just to provide a comprehensive account of the subject at a certain level of generality, but also to allow the historian to mention facts about the life which are of historical and present significance. Finally, there are different ways of conceiving of a society, but an historian trying to give an overall picture of a society will select one, or more, framework of analysis and apply it in a systematic way. I study examples of these kinds of descriptive explanation in Chapter 3.

Some historians take a different approach to the description of historical subjects. Instead of providing a methodical account of the subject guided by a preconception of its structure, they provide a summary description of it which will bring together a lot of information about it in an intelligible way. These summary descriptions are not explanations, for they are not designed to provide information of a predetermined kind, but are designed to draw together salient facts about a subject by means of a relatively high-level description of it. It seems appropriate to call them interpretations of the subject, as an interpretation is one of several possible accounts which can be given of a subject, which usually gives significance or meaning to its parts.

Heidegger described interpretation as a way of understanding the world, which is a product of our involvement in it. Interpretation involves preconceptions, and a practical point of view. When we articulate what we perceive, we state its meaning (Heidegger, 1962, section 32). My analysis of interpretation builds upon Heidegger's remarks. The interpretations to which I refer are not just perceptions of the world but are accounts of something. One interprets music by playing it; one interprets a character by acting it; one interprets a law by saying how it applies to the case in hand; one interprets a text by saying what it means in one's own language. Historians interpret past events by describing them. If an interpretation is a function of people's preconceptions and interests, it is certainly possible and even probable that different people will interpret the same thing differently. Sometimes a difference in describing something will be a result of a mistake, for example of seeing an object inaccurately, or using a concept wrongly. Then we have, not an interpretation but a mistaken description of the object. I suggest that an interpretation of something is one of several, more or less equally justified accounts which can be given of it. Because there are usually many ways of interpreting a subject, it appears that interpretations are quite subjective, just personal impressions with no truth value at all. This is not the case, as I will demonstrate.

The question which arises is, are descriptive explanations interpretations too? There is at least one sense in which they clearly are. In describing what an historical subject was like, historians are guided by a preconception of the general nature of such a subject. This is usually a general idea of the parts of the subject and how they normally relate to one another. In asking herself what the subject X was like, an historian already has a concept of X which subsequently guides her inquiry, and provides a standard by which the adequacy of her descriptive explanation is finally judged. The explanation is structured in accordance with the historian's general preconception of the subject, and sometimes, notably in social history, there are several general concepts of the subject for an historian to choose from. These general concepts help organize detailed information about the subject, and suggest its meaning. It is quite appropriate, therefore, to call descriptive explanations interpretations of the subject too. So descriptive explanations of a subject provide both an explanation and an interpretation of their subject, whereas the interpretations discussed in Chapter 4 are interpretations pure and simple, and are not explanations, guided by preconceptions of the subject, as well.

Occasionally historians will begin to explain an event using a well-known general analysis of such an event, such as a Marxist analysis of a political revolution, but find that the detailed facts about the event do not warrant that general account of it. In such cases the historian abandons the task of exemplifying a preconception of the subject, and looks for a new general interpretation of it. Thus what begins as a process of providing a descriptive explanation can change into a search for a new interpretation.

The contrast between higher and lower levels of description proves particularly useful in analysing the way historians establish the meanings of a text, which is the subject of Chapter 5. It is possible to distinguish the basic meaning of a text, which is not quite its literal meaning, from higher interpretations of what the text, basically, says. Fish has denied that the literal meaning of a text can be fixed, but I argue that the basic meaning can be fixed, very often, on the basis of some widely respected criteria of meaning which are set out in the first section of the chapter. Secondary meanings of a text are interpretations of what it says, and although these are much less determinate, like all interpretations they must be both true and fair of the text they are describing.

To make the past intelligible, historians spend a lot of time explaining why events happened as they did. Not a lot has been written about explanation in history since the debates between Hempel and Dray a few decades ago. The brightest philosophers still find it difficult to specify the relation between cause and effect, as recent anthologies reveal. Causal explanation involves further problems, for it has not been clear whether historians explain events by mentioning just any causes which interest them, or whether there is a particular set of causes which is generally thought to explain events adequately.

One common analysis of causes, which I previously defended (McCullagh, 1984, ch. 7), is that causes are events such that, had they not occurred and other things remained the same, the effect either would not have occurred at all or would have been somewhat different. This theory has to be modified to allow for indeterminacy in human affairs: one can only say that had a cause been absent and other things remained the same, the probability of the effect would have been significantly less. Even so modified, this theory of causation needs to be augmented, for it does not capture the way in which causes bring about their effects. In Chapter 7 I present an account of causes in terms of causal powers or dispositions of things to produce certain outcomes in certain circumstances. Causes are events which trigger such dispositions, creating an active tendency to produce the relevant outcome. This analysis of causes proves immensely useful in capturing historical practice.

Chapter 7 considers not only the nature of causes, but also the nature of causal explanations. To understand the latter it is vital to distinguish causal and contrastive explanations, both of which are common in history, as they have different structures. Causal explanations describe a causal process or sequence of events by which a certain effect came about, each event affecting the probability of the outcome. I describe them as a genetic form of explanation. Contrastive explanations, on the other hand, simply show why one outcome was more probable than another in the circumstances. The analysis of causal and contrastive explanations reveals the patterns of causal explanation which it seems that historians generally try to exemplify in their explanations of past events. The chapter concludes with a careful consideration of functional explanations, which argues that events are not ever caused by their effects.

The analysis of causal explanations in Chapter 7 is illustrated and extended in Chapter 8, on historical explanations of individual human actions. They can be caused by desires, beliefs and principles which to some extent also justify them, but they can have other causes as well. I suggest that an explanation of an action is misleading if it does not go back to the cause which first made the occurrence of such an action much more probable than it otherwise was in the circumstances. In the case of human actions, this can mean tracing the causes back to the social and cultural setting of the action.

The next chapter, Chapter 9, is about explanations of collective actions. It is largely a response to those who would explain collective behaviour by describing the reasons which the individuals involved had for acting as they did. An explanation along these lines leaves an important question unanswered: why did so many people behave in the same way? The answer is that they were all subject to the same influence. Sometimes they all follow the same convention, which they have learned; sometimes they have all accepted a common set of ideas, an ideology of some kind, which is directing their behaviour; and occasionally they are all responding to a common situation out of self-interest. This shows that people are more subject to social and natural influences than is always acknowledged.

Chapter 10 considers explanations of social changes, and theories about the social conditions which cause them. At first it was hoped to find laws of society as regular as the laws of nature by which to explain social changes, but people do not act in as regular a way as billiard balls. Some researchers, like Theda Skocpol, have favoured a comparative approach for identifying the causes of social changes, but I argue that these are only of use in testing and refining causal hypotheses already arrived at on the basis of a theory about the causal processes involved. What social theories reveal are certain dispositions set in train by certain social conditions. For instance, in a capitalist economy, the owners of industries will tend to maximize profits on every occasion they can; and the employees will tend to improve their wages and working conditions whenever they are able. Historical explanations trace the interaction of such tendencies in bringing about historical events, allowing that the pattern of interactions could be different in every case. This model of social explanation is not widely appreciated yet, but it fits historical practice like a glove.

Some historians feel very uncomfortable about general causal theories, doubting their truth, and prefer to describe and explain history at the level of the particular. Chapter 11 begins with a discussion of methodological individualism, which draws upon Pettit's discussion of the issues in *The Common Mind* (1993). Pettit shows that explanations using social generalizations are very useful, but he denies that social facts actually cause anything. I argue that it is reasonable to think that social facts exist and have causal powers, which can help to explain changes in society. Pettit thinks that changes are brought about by individual actions, and that any explanation in terms of social facts is true in virtue of the behaviour of individuals. I note that while causal explanations of social changes employ generalizations which are true because of individual actions involved, many contrastive explanations of social change do not. The victory of one organization over another in some contest, such as armies at war or businesses grabbing market share, might well be due to its superior resources, communications, management structure and strategy, for it is well known that these affect the chances of success.

Historical synthesis, then, is not just a matter of arranging information about the past in any pattern which pleases the historian. It is generally governed by one of a limited range of questions (what was it like? how did it happen? what does it mean? why did it occur?) or by a desire to produce a true, fair and adequate interpretation of the subject. These tasks severely limit the range of patterns available to the historian, though they often leave some room for alternatives. History is not entirely objective, but it is much less a product of subjective preferences than philosophers sometimes assume.

LEARNING FROM THE PAST

Jean-François Lyotard is best known for his denunciation of grand theories of historical change. All promises of progress, emancipation, freedom and prosperity associated with the historical theories of Hegel and Marx, with the theories of liberal democracy and with post-Keynesian economic theories, have been proved false in this century.

> Auschwitz is an abyss in which the philosophical genre of Hegelian speculative discourse seems to disappear, because the name 'Auschwitz' invalidates the presupposition of that genre, namely that all that is real is rational, and that all that is rational is real. Budapest '56 is another abyss in which the genre of (Marxist) historical materialist discourse seems to disappear, because this name

invalidates the presupposition of that genre, namely that all that is proletarian is communist, and that all that is communist is proletarian. Nineteen sixty-eight is an abyss in which the genre of democratic liberal discourse (republican dialogue) seems to disappear, because this name invalidates the presupposition of that genre, namely that all that concerns the political community can be said within the rules of the game of parliamentary representation. The crisis of over-capitalisation that the world economy has been suffering since 1974 and will suffer for some time to come invalidates the presupposition of the discursive genre of post-Keynesian political economy, namely that a harmonious regulation of needs and the means to satisfy them in work and in capital, with a view to the greatest enjoyment of goods and services for all – that this regulation is possible and on the way to being achieved.

('The Sign of History', Lyotard, 1989, pp. 393–411; p. 393)

Elsewhere Lyotard explains that grand theories, like Marxist ones, are disproved by narratives about the fate of individuals. 'Thousands of uncomfortable little stories have recently been brought back by Solzhenitsyn's books, by eye-witness accounts from dissidents and by travellers' ('Lessons in Paganism', ibid., pp. 122–54, p. 127). The grand 'meta-narratives' were only believed, he said, while the witness of individuals was suppressed by those in power. Lyotard advocates the telling of little stories: 'because they are short, because they are not extracts from some great history, and because they are difficult to fit into any great history' (p. 132).

Many historians today prefer to tell 'little stories', which focus upon the activities of individuals, rather than upon rather abstract social structures. The everyday world of individuals is more familiar, and their attempts to cope with the contingencies of life often resonate with our own. It is easy to empathize with individuals as they struggle through life, and it gives us a vicarious pleasure to do so. A lively presentation of the fortunes of individuals is much more fun to read than a dry account of social abstractions. It sells better too.

In the last two sections of Chapter 11 I consider Lyotard's appeal for historians to write only about particular, even everyday things. It can be fascinating to see how others lived, but to confine our study of history to particulars is to deprive us of much of its value.

There are truths to be learned from the past. The grand theories which Lyotard denounced might be false, but there are many generalizations about human social behaviour and about our institutions which are vital for our well-being in historically derived communities. It is only on the basis of historical knowledge that we can judge what institutions and arrangements will promote freedom, justice and prosperity in our communities, and what will threaten them. It is only from a knowledge of why our institutions were created, and how they have functioned, that we can judge what use they might be to us in the future.

Those who would confine history to the particular would deprive us of the knowledge we need to protect and improve our communities. That knowledge is the peculiar and precious contribution which history makes to our civilization.

Acknowledgements

My thanks to the School of Philosophy at La Trobe University for allowing me leave to prepare this book. Also to the Research School of Social Sciences at the Australian National University in Canberra for a visiting fellowship which enabled me to work with staff there. I am particularly grateful for the useful conversations I had with Philip Pettit and Barry Hindess. I thank John Alcorn of Trinity College, Hartford, for his comments on parts of the first chapter.

Parts of Chapter 2 of this book are taken from my articles 'Metaphor and truth in history', which was originally published in *Clio* (1993) 23: 23–49; and 'Can our understanding of old texts be objective?', which was originally published in *History and Theory* (1991) 30: 302–23.

Finally, a note about pronouns. The use of 'she' in this book to refer at times to 'an historian' is a piece of reverse sexual discrimination. That it jars on some ears suggests it is still needed!

1   The truth and fairness of historical descriptions

In practice, professional historians have little hesitation in saying that descriptions of the past for which there is abundant evidence are true. There are thousands of basic facts about the past for which there is so much reliable evidence that no one doubts their truth for a moment. In theory, however, several philosophers have argued that such confidence about the truth of historical descriptions is misplaced, indeed is irrational.

Attacks on the truth of history have been mounted on three fronts. First there is a critique of the historical inferences which historians draw from evidence available to them, showing that they rely upon historians' personal epistemic values, and that even when the inferences are widely accepted their conclusions are not necessarily true. Second there are arguments from cultural relativism, which point out that historians' descriptions of the world are largely determined by the concepts and language of the culture in which they live, and so cannot be regarded as simply representing the world as it was. It is therefore naive to think that historical descriptions correspond to what happened. The third attack on the truth of historical descriptions comes from postmodernists who say that such descriptions pretend to describe the world, but really only represent people's concepts of the past, concepts which are essentially linguistic and which have no particular relation to reality.

These three lines of attack have each justified a measure of scepticism about the truth of historical descriptions, and together their effect upon many philosophers of history has been overwhelming. The idea that historical evidence does not prove the truth of any descriptions of the past seems to be supported by the fact that historians sometimes are unable to agree among themselves over what happened. Keith Jenkins, for example, cites uncertainty about Hitler's intentions after gaining power as evidence of the unreliability of historical descriptions. He was probably referring to the debate over the significance of the Hossbach Memorandum, in which Hitler outlined his plans to acquire extra territory for Germany. Some have interpreted it as an honest declaration of intent; and others, notably A.J.P. Taylor, have doubted its sincerity, suggesting that it was a plan which Hitler hoped would justify increased expenditure on armaments. (See my discussion of the document in McCullagh, 1984, p. 121.) Jenkins argues that if distinguished historians disagree over the significance of the same data, you can conclude: 'whilst the sources may prevent just anything at all from being said, nevertheless the same events/sources do not entail that one and only one reading has to follow' (Jenkins, 1991, p. 13). In fact this statement is not entirely true. In many cases inferences from historical evidence are so reasonable that there is no dispute about them at all. For instance, there is no dispute among historians that the Hossbach Memorandum is a record, more or less accurate, of a speech made by Hitler on 5 November 1937. When Jenkins declares 'Epistemology shows we can never really know the past' (p. 19), he exaggerates. Indeed even he goes on to admit, inconsistently, that some historical facts, such as dates of events, are '"true" but trite' (p. 32). Generally, however, scepticism about historical knowledge pervades his book. To explain why historians believe their descriptions are true, sceptical philosophers like Jenkins refer to their professional interests in adopting a certain line about their subject, or to their preference, often reflecting the attitude of their society, for a certain picture of the past. Indeed Jenkins calls history 'an ideological construct' (p. 17).

The facts of cultural relativism have also produced considerable scepticism about the truth of historical descriptions. Different cultures sometimes describe the same things differently. Descriptions of the world vary with the writer's world-view, their standards of rationality and their practical interests in the subjects of their descriptions. Thus an illness which a person in one culture might attribute to an evil spirit, a person in another might describe in terms of a medical theory. Even advanced western scientific world-views change from time to time, with changes in the prevailing paradigm, as Thomas Kuhn explained. If we are entirely trapped within our own culture, some have argued, we cannot have knowledge of a world which exists independent of that culture, far less knowledge of another culture altogether.

What is the significance of the fact that our perceptions of the world are a function of the conceptual framework we have acquired through living and being educated in our culture? Some are inclined to say: the world we live in is constructed from the concepts and beliefs of our culture, and we have no idea of what exists independent of our beliefs. Paul A. Roth asserts this to be the case:

> past events exist, qua events, only in terms of some historically situated conception of them. The notion of a historical truth for events, that is, a perspective on happenings untainted by human perception and categorization, proves to be incoherent. There exists a world not of our making, but any subdivision of it into specific events is our doing, not nature's.
>
> (Roth, 1991, p. 185)

Roth denies that historical facts can be true in any correspondence sense. 'My rejection of . . . "historical truth" is no *denial* of reality; what it does rule out is invidious distinctions between our view of events and some God's-eye perception of states of affairs' (p. 186). (See also Roth, 1988.) So far Roth has strongly denied that any description of the world can be independent of its author's point of view, which is entirely reasonable. However, he takes this to imply that descriptions of the world cannot tell us anything about it. Roth endorses a proposal of Murray Murphey, that historical descriptions are like the theories of physics, theoretical constructions designed to account for some available evidence. He adds: 'There is no warrant for maintaining that there is some static past world which diligent research in the archives . . . uncovers' (1991, pp. 186–7). Indeed he applauds 'ridding oneself of a notion of historical truth' (p. 187). Roth's view is that 'events' are given shape by the language we use to describe them, so that it is unintelligible to speak of events other than those postulated and described in historical writing. 'Events', he writes, 'are not natural entities and exist only under a description' (Roth, 1988, p. 10). So there are no events in the past for historical descriptions to be true of. The events which historians describe are merely constructions of their historical theories. This sceptical 'constructionist' theory of history has become quite a popular alternative to a realist interpretation, which is generally regarded as naive.

There are three major attacks on the truth of history which can be called postmodern. The first two depend largely upon Saussure's theory, subsequently developed by Derrida (1982), that the meaning of words and sentences depends upon their relation to other words or concepts, and not upon their relation to the world. Roland Barthes has said that although historical descriptions apparently refer to things in the world, they are really about the historians' ideas or concepts of the past. He said that historians mistakenly assume that their descriptions of the past are about the past itself, and heighten that impression by providing vivid, detailed accounts of what happened (Barthes, 1986, pp. 138–9). In fact he thinks that the relation between what happened and historical descriptions is entirely problematic.

The second postmodern ground for scepticism is the argument that since historical descriptions are derived from evidence, which usually consists of other texts – letters, newspaper reports, official documents and the like – they are not really about the past at all. Historical descriptions on this account are merely texts (descriptions of the past) inferred from other texts (written evidence) whose significance is purely linguistic. Like the first, this argument really depends upon the theory that the meaning of texts is provided by other texts, and that texts have no regular relationship with the world.

Finally Lyotard and others, while not doubting that historians can describe the past, have argued that their descriptions are always general and so inaccurate, designed to force the past into concepts which suit the historian's interests. Consequently it is wrong to imagine that they accurately portray the past.

Historians have commonly responded to these attacks upon the truth of historical descriptions by trying to ignore them, reaffirming the adequacy of their own procedures for reaching the truth about the past (e.g. Elton, 1991, ch. 2). I know of no practising historians who admit that they cannot discover anything true about the past. They may admit to being fallible, but they do not deny that a lot of the basic facts they present are very probably true. Some philosophers of history have suggested other responses to these challenges to historical credibility, but historians have not. For if they seriously doubted their capacity to uncover facts about the past, why would they continue to practise history? They may as well write historical fiction.

One historian who has expressed concern about postmodern denials of the possibility of historical truth is Lawrence Stone. He wrote:

> My only objection is when they declare not that truth is unknowable, but that there is no reality out there which is anything but a subjective creation of the historian; in other words that it is language that creates meaning which in turn creates our image of the real. This destroys the difference between fact and fiction, and makes entirely nugatory the dirty and tedious archival work of the historian to dig 'facts' out of texts. It is only at this extreme point that historians have any need to express anxiety.
>
> (Stone, 1992, p. 193)

If historians cannot answer these attacks on their credibility, their whole profession remains under a cloud. Are historians offering us what they cannot in fact supply, namely information about what has happened in the past? Are they now performing some sort of academic ritual, which does not have the significance they have so long imagined? Should we just adopt those accounts of 'the past' which suit our aesthetic, moral, political or other preferences?

In this chapter I consider the various attacks upon the truth of history, and argue that they are not as devastating as their proponents have thought. Although historical descriptions are not necessitated by the evidence for them, I shall argue that when they are well supported by evidence it is reasonable to believe that they are very probably true. In reply to the cultural relativist I shall argue that although different cultures conceive of the world differently, their descriptions are all true if the world is such that the truth conditions of their descriptions of it are satisfied. Finally, against the postmodernists I shall argue that both the meaning and truth of our descriptions of the world depend not just upon other texts, but also upon personal experiences which are produced by things in the world. That is why they can be said to refer to things in the world, and can be true of them. I agree with Lyotard and others that our descriptions of the world are always somewhat general and abstract, but disagree that they are therefore false. I shall argue that descriptions, no matter how general they are, can be true.

These conclusions fall short of what a very naive realist would assert. Rather than say that well supported historical descriptions are true without qualification, I say that they could be false, even when there is no reason for believing that they are. Rather than say that our ideas of the world mirror it precisely, as we normally assume, I say that a description of the world is true if possible experiences of the world correspond to those implied by the world view of which it is part. An adequate world view allows that different cultures perceive the world in different ways, while denying that perceptions of the world are the product of nothing but culture. Finally, a naive person might imagine that if a description of the world is true then it is absolutely precise, whereas I admit that this is not the case. All descriptions, even true ones, are vague, though not necessarily so vague as to prevent their truth from being decidable.

The concept of truth which I recommend is what I call a 'correlation' theory of truth, a close cousin to the correspondence theory which we all use unreflectively in everyday life. The correspondence theory says that a description of the world is true if there is something in the world which resembles one of the conventional truth conditions of the description. For example it is true that a river runs through London if there really is something in the world which resembles what we would normally envisage as a-river-running-through-London. Along with this theory there normally goes the belief that we can check the truth of a description by perceiving the world, and directly observing whether part of the world resembles or 'corresponds to' the truth conditions of the description or not.

There are numerous problems with the correspondence theory, but three seem particularly important. First, scientists tell us that our perceptions are caused by things in the world stimulating our sense receptors (eyes, ears, nose and so on), which in turn produce electrical impulses carried by nerves to the brain, which finally produces the perceptual experiences with which we are so familiar. This being so, our perceptions are best described as providing us with information about reality, but not necessarily mirroring it precisely. For instance, our brain does not contain the colours and sounds and smells which it causes us to experience. These are characteristic of our experiences, but not of the medium which supplies them. Scientists deny that they characterize the light waves, sound waves and chemical reactions which produce them either. Thus our experiences provide us with vivid information about the world, but do not seem to mirror it. Second, our perceptions are influenced by our culture. People from different cultures perceive the same things differently. One person sees a leaf, another sees it as a herb, a third might see it as a botanical specimen of a certain kind. A trained botanist might even discern features of the leaf which others would not notice, which enable him to classify it as of one species rather than another. So our perceptions of the world are not pure sense impressions of it. They include information about what is before us, and they include different degrees of perceptual detail. Finally, our perceptions are influenced by our needs, interests and desires. These direct our attention, so that we scarcely notice what is not relevant to them. Recall the experience of searching for a friend's face in a crowd; you hardly notice the others. Interests do not necessarily distort our perceptions, but they help to focus them. For these three reasons, at least, it is wrong to say that our perceptions simply correspond to the world.

Although our perceptions do not correspond with the world, we nevertheless believe they provide some informaiton about it, as they are partly caused by it. If we see an apple we immediately suppose an apple is present. If asked to justify that assumption, we could say that we think an apple is present to explain our perception. The beliefs we have about the material world can thus be considered explanations of our perceptual experiences. These explanations normally imply further observable facts. For instance, if it is true that we are seeing an apple, then from our general knowledge about apples we can infer that it would be sweet and crunchy to eat. Our explanations are true if they cohere with our other beliefs about the world, and if all the observations they entail would be verified in the experience of anyone who tested them. If we had not really seen an apple, but only a plastic replica of an apple, then it would not taste sweet and crunchy when we bit it. In which case, it would be false to say that we had seen an apple, assuming that our general knowledge about the sweetness and crunchiness of apples was true.

The descriptions of the world we develop to account for our perceptual experiences are clearly charged with all sorts of observable implications. These implications are based upon general knowledge of the things we assume to exist, such as general knowledge of the sweetness and crunchiness of apples. So when we test the observable implications of even quite a simple description of the world, we are really testing the whole collection of beliefs from which those implications were inferred. That is why we say that for a description of the world to be true, the world view of which it is a part must be confirmable by observation. The world view in question includes all those beliefs about the world from which the implications were derived.

Occasionally the very concepts used to explain what we perceive are rejected because they are inconsistent with other facts based upon other perceptions. Thus, for example, scientists no longer allow that our perception of the sun climbing in the sky is caused by movement of the sun because the theory which best explains our observations of the planets has the sun stationary and the planets turning instead. Once again, the truth of a description depends upon the truth of the whole theory of the world of which it is a part.

People's perceptions are couched in the concepts of their culture, and focus upon the features of the perceptual field which interest them. In deciding what observations a true theory would imply, we have to frame them for observers with a particular culture and set of interests. Usually the implications are described using concepts of the theory being considered, on the assumption I suppose that those who test a theory will be familiar with its concepts. To test special scientific theories it is often necessary to learn how to identify the perceptions they imply. Thus only trained pathologists can detect the presence of a disease by studying a blood smear under a microscope, as they have learned to identify the cells which are evidence of the presence of that disease. Even descriptions of everyday events can be verified only by people familiar with the concepts used to describe their implications. Some terms common in one language do not translate neatly into another.

In practice it is not always possible to check all the implications of an explanatory description of the world, especially the implications of those descriptions inferred by historians. Although the evidence available and the inferences drawn from that evidence often warrant firm belief in the truth of their descriptions of the past, because the past is inaccessible to present observation we cannot check out the truth of those descriptions ourselves. They are true, nevertheless, if we could have had the perceptual experiences they entail, had we been present at the time of the events being described. Notice that for any description of the world there is normally a range of possible alternative perceptions which would confirm them. Imagine, for example, the variety of perceptions which would establish the truth of the statement that Caesar's army crossed the Rubicon. It could have crossed by bridge, by boat, even by wading, or all of the above.

Suppose a theory of the nature of the world were confirmed by all the perceptions which it implies. What can be said about the relation between that theory and the world? If all the perceptible implications of a description of the world were confirmed, then we could reasonably accept that description *as if* the objects, properties, events and states of affairs it describes had counterparts in the world. This is consistent with there being other adequate explanatory theories, produced perhaps by people in other cultures, also being true. It does not mean that things in the world do correspond to our descriptions of it. It means just that all our possible experiences of the world are such as they would be if the world had those features we attribute to it.

We can also say, perhaps, that there is a correlation between the causal processes at work in the world which can produce human perceptions of it, and the theory which implies such perceptual experiences. The correlation is between their functions, if not their content. The world is such as to yield precisely those experiences which a true description of it predicts for people of a certain culture. This claim assumes that things in the world do cause our perceptual experiences, but this assumption is common to all popular and scientific theories of the world, and accepted by all.

It is logically possible that more than one explanatory theory could explain all observations possible of the world. In that case the truth of a description would be relative to the truth of the theory to which it was related, since a sentence true in one theory might not be true in another. The practice of always preferring the simpler theory, when there are two or more theories of equal explanatory scope, might mean that only one theory would be preferred in the end.

How can we call our best explanations true when we have no idea whether they will be part of the ideal explanatory theory? Either we do so in the faith that they will be part of that theory; or we call them 'true' in an analogous sense, for they explain observations in the same manner as the ideal theory.

This account of the correlation between true descriptions and the world accommodates Paul Roth's comment that objects and events are individuated by language. There is no suggestion here that the objects we describe correspond to objects in the world. All that it requires is that there be something in the world which correlates with them. Since we have no independent way of discovering what that 'something' is, we simply take the descriptions which we judge to be reliable and true and act *as if* the world is as we describe it.

The theory of our knowledge of the world which has just been sketched resembles in many ways the defence of 'scientific realism' recently presented by Charles Landesman (1997). He argues that since scientific theories are the best explanations we have of the observations we make, they should be regarded as pictures of reality: 'the evidence that shows that our theories are warranted actually establishes that they mirror nature in an approximate, if provisional way' (p. 159). I am inclined to regard scientific theories as internal to our knowledge of the world, in addition to those perceptions which those scientific theories are designed to explain. After all, scientific theories employ scientific concepts which change from time to time, so they seem better described as representations of reality, of whose real nature we remain mostly ignorant, rather than a mirror of its essential nature.

Some philosophers would clearly regard even such a correlation theory of truth as inappropriate to historical descriptions. Some like Paul Roth and Leon Goldstein have denied that historical descriptions are true of the world which exists independently of them, saying rather that 'the past' is constructed by historical descriptions. Others, like Michael Oakeshott, have said they can be true in a coherence sense, when they fit well with our beliefs about present evidence and past events; and some, notably Jürgen Habermas, have defined truth in terms of rational consensus. These alternative theories of the truth of history will be considered in the second section of this chapter, which will show that none of them satisfactorily catches the sense in which historical descriptions can be true.

When historians describe past events and periods, they have to be selective, and they are normally anxious not to misrepresent the subject of their description. Just as important as the truth of historical descriptions is their fairness, and the third section of the chapter explains and illustrates this concept.

THE TRUTH OF HISTORY

The constraints of evidence

When historians want to discover what happened in the past, they feel constrained to find evidence which will enable them to draw inferences about the people and events which interest them. This constraint seems perfectly reasonable, because it has long been thought both the necessary and sufficient means of discovering the truth about the past.

The arguments by which historians draw conclusions from evidence are of kinds which are entirely familiar to us in everyday life. We readily discover facts about currently unobservable features of the world by drawing inferences from observation. I am not talking about creating theories which refer to unobservable particles or forces to explain scientific observations. I mean we can often infer everyday facts about the world from what we observe. For instance, if I see that an orange is green and mouldy, I infer that it will not be pleasant to eat. If a hen's egg has been boiled for ten minutes, then I know it will be firm inside. And so on. Similarly, we draw inferences about the past. If I come across the blackened remains of a house in a forest, I infer that there was a fire there. If I notice a charred top and teddy bear, I may infer that children lived there, though I am aware that some adults keep childhood mementos, so it is possible that there were no children there. These inferences are so common and familiar to us, that we take their validity for granted. It is not at all surprising that historians take the results of such inferences for granted too.

If asked to justify our faith in these everyday inferences, we would probably say something like this. We have discovered that observations of the world give us reliable information about the world, so long as they are made under appropriate conditions. For instance, to identify things in the burnt-out house, we would need good eyesight and good light, and they should not be so damaged that we could not categorize them unambiguously. Under suitable conditions, however, sincere reports of what we perceive provide true information about the nature of the world. Then again, inferences based upon well-attested generalizations about the world can also be trusted to yield true descriptions of what has happened. Philosophers have identified conditions under which generalizations are reliable, and the forms of inference which can be trusted to yield truths, such as arguments to the best explanation and statistical inferences (see McCullagh, 1984).

You might ask what is meant by 'true', when we say that the conclusions of these inferences are true. Once again, the answer is not surprising. For any descriptive sentence, there is a range of possible truth conditions. Strictly speaking it would be true that a child lived in that house, for example, whether there were one or more children, and whether they were boys, girls or both. The sentence is true if the world was such as would normally produce a perception in an observer of one set of the sentence's truth conditions. That is what we mean by saying that an historical description is true. Suppose a young boy had lived in the house. That is one of the truth conditions for 'a child lived in that house'. It means the boy ate and slept there most of the time, played with his toys and watched the TV there, and so on. A consequence of this fact is that, if you were there at the time, you would have seen him doing all these things. That is what is meant by saying the truth conditions existed: they were such that you could have checked them out by observation, if you had been in a position to do so. Of course the criterion for saying a sentence is true, is that it can be inferred from available evidence. But the criterion for calling something true is not usually what we mean when we say it is true. We mean, not that it can be inferred from available evidence, but that one set of its possible truth conditions actually existed.

There are sometimes constraints which limit the ability of professional historians to arrive at the truth, and historians generally make allowances for these. There might not be very much evidence, and what there is might have several different implications, so that an historian cannot be quite certain of its significance. As I mentioned before, the charred top and teddy could have been the property of an adult, who had kept them for sentimental reasons, so that, on that evidence alone, one cannot be quite sure that children lived at the burnt-out house. Historians allow for degrees of probability, and would hope for confirmation from other evidence, say from a newspaper report of the fire, before being confident in saying that children lived there.

Also, historians are aware of the constraints of personal bias. Both our interests and our preconceptions guide our search for evidence, and the inferences we draw from it. For example, consider the different descriptions given by Gananath Obeyesekere and Marshall Sahlins in their debate over whether or not the people of Hawaii thought Captain Cook to be a manifestation of their god Lono. Sahlins has claimed that they had indeed thought Cook was Lono, and had used this hypothesis to explain their behaviour towards him (Sahlins, 1981). Obeyesekere denies that the evidence warrants Sahlins' hypothesis, and is generally keen to deny that Hawaiians would confuse humans and gods (Obeyesekere, 1992, pp. 20–2). At one stage, Cook had a red tapa cloth draped over his shoulders by a priest called Koah. Obeyesekere remarks: 'We know that Koah was a priest of the Ku cult and red is Ku's color' (Obeyesekere, 1992, p. 65). So perhaps they saw him as representing Ku, though Obeyesekere is inclined to think they did not regard him as representing any god at all. Sahlins had thought the red cloth signalled their honouring him as the god Lono, but Obeyesekere says:

> There is not a trace of evidence to suggest that 'priests clothed him with sacred cloth worn only by the god,' except on the assumption that because Cook was Lono, and because he was draped in a red cloth by a priest, that cloth must be the god's own vestment.
>
> (p. 158)

In response, Sahlins offers a lot of evidence for thinking the red cloth was used to adorn sacred things related to Lono (Sahlins, 1995, pp. 223–4). There is no doubt that each is looking for evidence in favour of his preferred hypothesis, and paying little attention to that which conflicts with it.

Debates like this one provide sceptics like Keith Jenkins with evidence for their conviction that reason cannot decide between truth and falsity, and that any conviction about the truth of an historical description must in large degree reflect a personal interest and presupposition. What Jenkins scarcely notices, however, is that there are thousands of historical facts which are not contested at all, because the evidence for them is large and unambiguous. These are often the basic facts of history, about what happened at certain places at certain times. The descriptions which are contested are usually those about what people thought or intended, where the evidence is quite often open to alternative interpretations. Whether the Hawaiians thought Cook was a god or not is a case in point. Historians also disagree about descriptions of the activities of gods and spirits, on which subjects their presuppositions differ radically. The fact that some historical descriptions are disputed does not imply that none can be proved true beyond reasonable doubt. In fact thousands can.

The debate between Sahlins and Obeyesekere raises the problem of bias in history. It seems that historians are naturally biased, that they prefer some interpretations of historical evidence to others for all sorts of cultural, social or personal reasons, so why should the public believe the conclusions which they draw? An historian's preferences are more likely to prevent fairness, a balanced account of an historical subject, than strict truth. The fairness of an historical description is discussed in the third section of this chapter. Personal preferences only affect truth when the implications of available evidence are uncertain, as in the discussion of Hawaiian beliefs about Captain Cook. Otherwise, when the evidence overwhelmingly supports the truth of one description rather than any alternative, an historian's colleagues will correct any inadvertent mistakes which bias might produce. There remain problems of pervasive cultural bias, which are discussed in the next subsection on the constraints of culture.

There is an argument for historical scepticism which Jenkins did not consider, that can be derived from some observations by Thomas Kuhn. Many historical descriptions are rationally justified by saying that they best explain certain available evidence. To judge which is the best of several different explanations of evidence, an historian takes into account several different features of the available explanations, especially their explanatory scope, their explanatory power, their plausibility, their *ad hoc*ness, the extent to which they are disconfirmed, and the degree of relative superiority of one with respect to the others (see McCullagh, 1984, ch. 2). Kuhn noted that in comparing scientific theories, natural scientists take into account a similar list of virtues: 'accuracy, simplicity, fruitfulness, and the like'. He went on to remark that different people are liable to weigh these virtues, to judge their relative importance, differently. For example, if two people 'disagree about the relative importance of fruitfulness and, say, scope in reaching a choice, neither can be convicted of a mistake. Nor is either being unscientific. There is no neutral algorithm for theory-choice, no systematic decision procedure which, properly applied, must lead each individual in the group to the same decision' (Kuhn, 1970, pp. 199–200). Kuhn points out that in fact it is communities rather than individuals that decide which theory to adopt, and their decision depends upon their values and experiences.

Do these remarks imply that all historical inferences to the best explanation are irrational? They do not, because often one explanation explains so much and such a variety of evidence, and does so much better than any other on all the criteria that there is good reason for accepting it as probably true. For example, some have wished to deny the existence, or at least the extent, of the Nazi Holocaust, but the evidence for it is irrefutable. Indeed in our culture, to accept the conclusion of an argument to the best explanation under these conditions is one criterion of acting rationally. Differences in the weight people give to the various virtues of explanations only matter when no one explanation is clearly superior to all others.

The conclusion which historians generally adopt is that if an historical statement is well supported by abundant evidence, and much better supported than any alternative account, then the statement can be rationally accepted as very probably true. It is always logically possible that the evidence is misleading, or that their beliefs about it and the other beliefs on which they base their inference are mistaken. Indeed sometimes there is reason to think this is not just a logical, but a real possibility. At any rate, even when it is entirely rational to believe an historical description is very probably true, historians must admit that it could possibly be false. Historical knowledge, like all our knowledge of the world, is fallible.

The constraints of culture

Traditionally historians have not thought it necessary to question their basic assumptions, notably their assumptions that (1) under appropriate conditions they can perceive their evidence as it really is; that (2) with appropriate care they can draw inferences whose conclusions, though not logically necessary, are nevertheless entirely certain; and that (3) with methodical checks, they can make allowances for bias, so that it does not prevent them arriving at the truth about the past. The facts of cultural relativism cast doubt upon all these assumptions.

(1) Consider first the assumption that historians can perceive evidence accurately, under appropriate conditions. It is a fact that people of different cultures see the world slightly differently. It is partly that they perceive different things: Innuits can see gradations in the colour and texture of snow which those who live in tropical climes do not. But it is mainly that they conceive things differently. Some see leaves as herbs or as medicines, which others know nothing of. Some think of an illness as the work of an evil spirit, whereas others think of it as a purely medical condition. Our perceptions of the things in the world are a function of our culture, of its practices and concepts.

Even within our own culture, there are differences in the way people see things. We see the sun rise over the horizon, but the scientist thinks of the earth turning toward the sun instead. Religious people might see a cure as God's answer to prayer, whereas an atheistic doctor would see it as nothing but the effects of good medicine. How we see things depends upon the framework of thought we bring to our perception. Our perceptions are not clear windows onto the world. We shape what we see according to the concepts with which we have learned to structure the world.

The thesis that our perceptions and descriptions of the world are partly determined by our conceptual schemes must not be misunderstood. We are familiar with the way people sometimes redescribe everyday events in terms of some special theory. Chemists refer to water as H_2O; as more people lose their jobs, economists talk of a growth in unemployment; a doctor will proclaim our child's spots to be a case of measles. These are cases in which the expert uses theoretical concepts to redescribe what we have already identified in everyday terms. To say that our perceptions of the world are mediated by a conceptual scheme could be taken to imply that when we perceive the world, there is some uninterpreted information, perhaps sensory experiences, which we then interpret according to whatever concepts we think appropriate. This, however, is false to our experience. Our perceptions are fully conceptualized from the start. To say that they are a function of our conceptual schemes is simply to offer a causal explanation of why they have the form they do. People who share a conceptual scheme tend to perceive things related to that scheme the same way; and people who have acquired different schemes perceive things correspondingly differently.

When Donald Davidson considered the suggestion that people interpret the world according to different conceptual schemes, he argued that the differences between schemes could not be very great, else we would not be able to judge the differences between them. If another culture's description of the world was entirely different from our own, we would be unable to translate it into our own language. It is only when we can understand other languages that we can see just how their concepts differ from our own (Davidson, 1974). This is an interesting point, and readily accepted. To understand the concepts of another culture, we must generally assume that at some very basic level people in it perceive the world by and large as we do, though they may understand it differently. To understand that when we say 'there is a clap of thunder', and when someone from another culture says 'the gods are roaring', we are both referring to the same thing, we must assume that they hear the same noise as we do, though they describe and interpret it differently. If people of another culture actually discriminate differences which we have as yet not detected, we will not be able to understand them until we learn to make those discriminations too. Davidson also noted that the process of interpreting other accounts of the world is often difficult, and our conclusions are sometimes tentative, several different translations or discriminations being equally consistent with the evidence. He allows that descriptions of the world depend upon the words being used and the meaning given to them, in short that descriptions of the world are relative to language (Davidson, 1979a, pp. 238–40).

It is true but trivial to say that a description of the world is relative to language. The interesting fact is that people actually have different concepts of the world. The terms in different languages or different discourses cannot always be found to correspond precisely with terms in other languages and discourses. Thus in everyday discourse the word 'water' is associated with concepts like 'wet' and 'drink', but not with concepts like 'atoms of hydrogen and oxygen', whereas the reverse is the case with the term H_2O. Conceptual schemes differ from languages, in that they refer to fairly discrete networks of interrelated concepts which occur within languages. The simplest examples of conceptual schemes are the languages of theories, chemistry, biology, psychology, economics and so on. Everyday descriptions of the world constitute one vast conceptual scheme, though even within that one comes across sub-cultures with their own range of concepts for describing the world. If the terms of a conceptual scheme in one language translate precisely into the terms of another language, as perhaps the terms of modern science do, then I would say the two cultures share a similar conceptual scheme. The schemes would not be identical, because the words and sentences by which each is expressed would be different. One cannot imagine a conceptual scheme independent of language. To say that two sentences in different languages say the same thing means just that the one perfectly translates the other, not that both are representing the same linguistically neutral concept.

Some writers, like Paul Roth, think that because our knowledge of the world is constructed from the concepts and beliefs of our culture to account for evidence available to us, we are not warranted in calling such descriptions true or false. There are two reasons they have for this conclusion. One is that to call a description of the world true suggests to most people that it represents some objective, God-like view of the world, undistorted by cultural presuppositions, and Roth points out that such a culturally neutral view of the world is not available. So truth of this kind is not possible. This is a true, important point, which is now widely accepted. If historical descriptions can be true, it must be in some other sense than this. The second reason for denying that historical descriptions can be true is the assumption that if such descriptions are constructed from culturally conditioned concepts, they cannot truly represent the world. This is also widely believed, but it is not true, and needs to be examined.

The weakness of the assumption that culturally conditioned descriptions of the world cannot be true is that it takes no account of why people perceive the world the way they do, and not any other way given their conceptual scheme. The explanation we commonly accept is: we have the perceptions we do because the world exists in such a way as to produce those perceptions in us. In other words, our perceptions are a function of *both* our culture and the world.

This account of our knowledge of the world is consistent with one of those which Hilary Putnam has been espousing in recent years. He has pointed out that 'Our concepts may be culturally relative, but it does not follow that the truth or falsity of everything we say using those concepts is simply "decided" by culture' (Putnam, 1987, p. 20). Any description we give of the world 'is never a mere copy; it always is a joint product of our interaction with the external world and the active powers of the mind. The world as we know it bears the stamp of our own conceptual activity' (Putnam, 1986, p. 261). Putnam concludes that '*a statement is true of a situation just in case it would be correct to use the words of which the statement consists in that way in describing the situation*'. In that case 'a sufficiently well placed speaker who used the words in that way would be fully warranted in *counting* the statement as true of that situation'. (Putnam, 1988, p. 115. His emphasis.)

Let us try to unpack the ideas expressed here. There are two things which need to be distinguished. First, descriptions of perceptions are true if correct according to linguistic conventions. For example, it may be right to say that an object which we see is a cow on the basis of our perception of its shape, its size and the texture of its coat. A horse, for example, appears to be of roughly the same size and texture, but has quite a different shape. The appropriate concept must be warranted by the details of the object as we perceive them, according to our rules of language. Second, the interpretation of a perception, that is the description of the world which it implies, is probably true if it best explains what has been experienced. Thus the presence of a cow often best explains our experience of it.

So far I have more or less assumed that our normal perceptions of the world are caused by the way the world is, but as was said above, they are also a product of our culture. In fact I believe that cultural variation of people's perceptions of the everyday world is not great, but it does exist, especially as perceptions are to some extent limited by our language and concepts, and are often theory laden, that is, they are often interpreted in the light of some theory about the nature of the things being perceived. Once this fact is admitted, then the accuracy of perceptions of the world must be relativized to a culture. It must then be said that a perception of the world is accurate if there was some state of the world such that it would normally cause a person *of a certain culture* to have perceptions of that kind. If it turns out that most basic perceptions of the world are not constrained by language and theory, but are universal, then I think we could say that descriptions of the world could be universally true, implying perceptions which everyone could be expected to have in normal circumstances. The evidence, on balance, seems to favour cultural relativism however, so I will assume that doctrine to be correct.

The truth conditions of descriptions of the world are not just perceptions of a certain kind, but states of the world which cause perceptions of a certain kind. A description of a medium-sized object in the world is true if there is something in the world which does or would cause people in a certain culture to have one of the perceptual experiences implied by that description in that culture. For instance the sentence 'There is a cow in that field' is true if there is something in the world which would normally cause people in an English-speaking culture to have a perception implied by such a description, namely an experience which looks roughly like the experience you have when you look at this (a range of suitable pictures follows). There is usually a range of such experiences which would warrant such a description. How people see the paradigmatic pictures, and how they see the world depends, of course, on their culture.

Notice that this sophisticated account, unlike our everyday theory, does not presume that the world has any particular shape, certainly not that it is shaped according to our concepts. Ordinarily, of course, we assume that it is shaped as we perceive it, but we do not have to make that assumption, and if people of different cultures perceive the world slightly differently, then it is an assumption better dropped. In other words, we had better not say that the world corresponds to our perceptions of it in any literal sense. Perhaps a better word for the relation would be 'correlation', since two things which are correlated do not have to be similar. Let's call the sophisticated theory of truth a 'correlation theory', to avoid confusion.

In deciding the best explanation of a perceptual experience, we look for one which coheres well with all of our beliefs about the situation. In particular we check whether there are any known possible causes of distortion or illusion. Could the perception be distorted by the perceiver's colour blindness, or be an illusion caused by a plastic replica or a hologram, for example? We know from experience that the best explanation is most likely to be the true one, that is, the one which will be confirmed by subsequent investigaiton.

There are, of course, things in the world which we cannot normally perceive because they are invisible, like electrons and other subatomic particles, and magnetic, gravitational and other fields. The reasons for thinking they exist are not that we perceive them, but that their existence best explains certain scientific observations of what can be perceived. Descriptions of invisible things are true if there exist in the world things which have the functions ascribed to them, particularly the function of bringing about those observable events in the laboratory which scientists have ascribed to them.

Most people are naive realists most of the time, thinking the world is as we perceive it under normal conditions, and so historians naturally interpret their inferred descriptions of the past in a naive way, as corresponding to what happened in the world, and not merely as correlated to it. Strictly speaking I think the correlation theory is more correct, but the practice of taking the world to correspond to our descriptions of it is convenient and generally harmless, like our habit of talking of sunrise and sunset, when we all know that, according to the accepted theory of the solar system, it is the earth which is moving around, not the sun. In everyday contexts naive realism produces few false expectations.

Roth endorsed Murray G. Murphey's idea that 'the whole of our historical knowledge is a theoretical construction for the purpose of explaining observational evidence' (Roth, 1991, p. 186). Roth says there is no reason to think such knowledge portrays 'some static past world' (pp. 186–7). However, if our historical descriptions of everyday things are true, then it is the case that there *were* things in the world which would have appeared to us, had we been there, in normal circumstances in a certain appropriate way. If the absolute truth of our best explanatory theories cannot be tested, as we have no access to all possible perceptions caused by the world, are we really justified in believing them to be true? To believe them true is to believe they will be confirmed by subsequent observations. Perhaps that is why we are more reluctant to call scientific theories true, which are liable to relatively frequent change, than descriptions of the everyday world, which are relatively stable as they use concepts less affected by theory change. At all events, belief in the truth of our best explanations is indeed an act of faith.

This account of our perceptual knowledge of the world implies that the things which can cause us to have certain kinds of perceptions could exist when we are unaware of them. Indeed they could exist independently of anyone ever knowing about them, for ever unperceived. This is a doctrine of metaphysical realism. It is sometimes thought that cultural relativism is incompatible with metaphysical realism, and that is true if metaphysical realism is understood as implying that true descriptions of the world are not relative to any culture. However, that is an unreasonable assumption. What we believe is that our perceptions and descriptions of the world are related to our culture, but according to the strict correlation theory of truth, we do not believe that the things in the world which partly cause our perceptions are determined by our culture. Our knowledge of them is conditioned by our culture, but they themselves are not. They have an existence independent of our culture, though our perceptions and descriptions of them do not.

Reality itself can only be said to be relative to a culture on the everyday theory of naive realism, for that supposes that things in the world are as we perceive them. If our perceptions of the world are culturally relative, then on the naive correspondence theory so too must be the world to which they correspond. This has been the source of much confusion, as to say that the world itself is a function of our culture contradicts our deep and reasonable conviction that the world itself, which causes our perceptions, is independent of them.

In what sense can general and theoretical descriptions be said to be true? General descriptions are descriptions of classes of things and of the relations between them, for example general accounts of the causes of political and social revolutions. Theoretical descriptions are accounts of processes, involving theoretical properties and/or theoretical entities, which could have brought about some observable changes, for instance a process in which some unconscious psychological drives cause some strange behaviour. To see how generalizations and explanatory theories are related to one another and to observation statements, one must examine books on their justification. Roughly speaking, general descriptions are regarded as true when instances of them occur regularly. (See McCullagh, 1984, ch. 6 for a full account of their justification.) Theories are justified if they provide a good explanation of certain observed regularities or patterns of behaviour.

What does it mean to say that they are true? In the case of generalizations, one must decide whether classes of things or properties really exist. I am inclined to deny that anything exists outside our minds which corresponds to general classes. Rather I suggest that to say a general description is true means that its instances occur as the description indicates. I am a realist about theories, however. To say a theory is true means that some things exist having the same causal powers as the entities posited by the theory, which produce the effects the theory is designed to explain. If theoretical entities and their powers did not exist, they could not cause that outcome.

Let me develop the implications of these remarks by responding to some common questions asked by people aware of the facts of cultural relativism. First, if our perceptions of the world are filtered through the lenses of our culture, its concepts and beliefs, is not the impression we receive of the world inevitably distorted?

There are three things to be said in response to this question. First, if the question is contrasting a view of the world framed by a culture's concepts with a view of the world which is *not* framed by a culture's concepts, one can only say that the latter does not exist. Even God, we suppose, views the world via concepts (universals), though we do not know what His concepts are. Second, we allow that sometimes we *believe* our perception is undistorted by natural causes, when in fact it is distorted. In that case our perceptions are distorted, but not by our conceptual framework. Rather they are distorted by things in the world, things like the atmosphere, our poor eyes, our confused brain. Finally, sometimes the concepts in terms of which we perceive the world have implications, ultimately observation statements, which turn out to be false. For instance, we might assume that because we are looking at an orange it will have pips inside it, when in fact, being a navel orange, it does not. In that case our concept of an orange is not entirely accurate. Notice that the degree of accuracy of our concepts depends on the proportion of their implications which are true of the object, state of affairs or event to which they are applied. Distortion of perception can be caused by inaccurate concepts.

The concepts in terms of which we view the world are revisable. Close examination of natural objects sometimes leads us to change our concepts of them a little, to distinguish finer discriminations within our perceptions of them, or to add or subtract facts from their list of implications. Unfortunately the concepts used in the social sciences are often vaguely defined, and so hard to apply. Are modern democratically elected prime ministers autocratic? Or just strong leaders? It is not easy to distinguish the two, but the distinction matters as the first brings disapproval and the second admiration. In applying concepts to the world, we use whatever criteria we have learned. We usually observe enough of those criteria to warrant the application of the concept, rather than any alternative, but there may be some criteria we do not check which in fact do not apply. It is possible however for a concept to be entirely correct, to imply no false facts, ultimately no false observation sentences, at all. (Karl Popper explained what it means to say that one theory is closer to the truth than another in roughly similar terms, in *Objective Knowledge*, 1979, pp. 47–60.) I conclude that the lenses of our culture do not necessarily produce a distorted view of the world.

Does the fact that different cultures sometimes describe the same thing differently imply that our concepts are not accurate? Clearly not. Suppose I view a plant, say fennel, as a decorative plant; another person may see it as a herb; and yet another may see it as a certain medicine. The concepts of fennel differ because they refer to different properties of the plant, related to different interests. But if the plant has the properties in question, then all are correct concepts and truly represent it. Note that a concept does not have to be completely comprehensive to be accurate. My concept of fennel as a decorative plant is not false because it does not include information about its botanical structure. A concept, or a description, can be partial, referring to only some features of a thing, and yet not be false. It is not false to say that a prime minister is autocratic, just because that concept does not include the fact that he is a father.

Sometimes one culture will regard another culture's concept as mistaken. For instance, one culture might think an object or ritual to have magical powers which another culture denies. In that case each culture judges the concept of the other to be inaccurate, relative to its own concepts and beliefs. We judge descriptions of the world to be false if their implications are contradicted by observations.

It seems, then, that the facts of cultural relativism do not provide good reason for saying that descriptions of the world cannot be accurate, relative to the culture which offers them. A true description asserts the existence of things in the world which will regularly produce perceptions within an appropriate range of kinds, under normal conditions, within a specified culture. These things are the truth conditions of the description. When it comes to historical descriptions, they are true if there *were* things in the world which *would have* produced perceptions of the appropriate kind under normal conditions for the members of the culture which made those descriptions.

When historians draw inferences from their observations of evidence, they employ general knowledge about the nature of the world, and use forms of inference generally thought to be reliable means of reaching new truths. The adequacy of these assumptions must be questioned in the light of cultural relativism.

When Hans-Georg Gadamer described how historians draw inferences about the past, he said that they draw upon general knowledge of the significance of historical evidence which their society has inherited from the past (Gadamer, 1975, pt.11, sect.11, ch. 1). The traditional understanding of the meaning of texts, actions and artefacts, he said, provides us with an initial basis for interpreting evidence. He called that initial understanding 'prejudice', explaining that 'In German legal terminology a "prejudice" is a provisional legal verdict before the final verdict is reached' (p. 240). From our traditions we form hypotheses about the meaning of a text, which we judge and modify allowing for the particular features of the text, which usually says something new. When interpreting a text from the past, Gadamer said, we pay less attention to its truth than to its meaning. To discover that meaning we must acquire a general knowledge of the world-view of the people involved, which he called their 'horizon of meaning' (pp. 269–70). Clearly one builds up an understanding of another culture by interpreting its documents, deeds and artefacts, hoping to find some consistency in their meaning. In creating the horizon of meaning of another culture, we are actually extending our own horizon to embrace it (p. 271). How is it possible to acquire the world-view of another culture? Gadamer gestures rather vaguely towards 'the attainment of a higher universality that overcomes, not only our own particularity, but that of the other' (p. 272).

There is no doubt that the hypotheses we form about the significance of historical evidence are based upon general assumptions drawn from our own culture. If the evidence is from our own culture, or its immediate ancestors, we can expect our current understanding of the meaning of language, acts and artefacts, to put us on the right track. But if the culture is remote from ours, and we have inherited no general knowledge of its language and world-view, then we must use our very general knowledge of human nature to form hypotheses about it. This is the task of ethnographic history, which is discussed in Chapter 6. If our hypotheses fit the data neatly, and there is a lot of relevant data to fit, then we accept them as true because we trust the very general knowledge upon which our hypotheses were based, and because we also trust arguments to the best explanation to yield truths about the world.

Some cultural relativists deny the possibility of acquiring accurate knowledge of an alien culture, because they assume that the meaning of things in one culture cannot be accurately understood in terms of another.

What makes translation across cultures possible is often the fact that different languages frequently refer to the same things in the world, and to the same properties of those things, which people all perceive the same way. Although the meaning of some terms may be underdetermined by observable data, the range of possible meanings of a term in a discourse is usually quite limited, and often only one meaning will fit a particular context neatly. When there is no equivalent term in the historian's language for one in the culture she is studying, then she will usually use their word and explain its meaning as well as possible. Thus when Clifford Geertz wanted to explain Javanese concepts referring to a person's feelings and to a person's behaviour, he used their own words, and then explained their meaning in English as fully as he could.

> *Batin*, the 'inside' word, does not refer to a separate seat of encapsulated spirituality detached or detachable from the body, or indeed to a bounded unit at all, but to the emotional life of human beings taken generally. It consists of the fuzzy, shifting flow of subjective feeling perceived directly in all its phenomenological immediacy but considered to be, at its roots at least, identical across all individuals, whose individuality it thus effaces. And, similarly, *lair*, the 'outside' word, has nothing to do with the body as an object, even an experienced object. Rather, it refers to that part of human life which, in our

culture, strict behaviorists limit themselves to studying – external actions, movements, postures, speech – again conceived as in its essence invariant from one individual to the next.

(Geertz, 1976, p. 230)

Even when a neat translation seems possible, however, the ideas associated with some concepts can be difficult to understand. Cultural historians are sometimes quite tentative about their interpretation of the meaning of a word. (This and other problems of ethnographic history are discussed in Chapter 6.)

Although historians can often provide accurate translations of words and sentences in other cultures, it must be admitted that an historian's knowledge of another culture is seldom as complete as that of the people who belong to that culture. Some expert historians acquire a really intimate knowledge of another culture, thinking in their language and with their world-view, but few attain such familiarity. Students of language have reminded us how much the meaning of a word in a language depends upon the meaning of others, in short how holistic is knowledge of language. It follows that any translation of a sentence from another culture will miss many of the resonances which the text had in the original language. Nevertheless, a good enough account of its meaning can often be achieved for historians to know its truth conditions.

So far I have discussed the implications of the fact that our knowledge of the world is always filtered through our preconceptions and beliefs. I have argued that we must agree with the relativists that no culturally neutral knowledge of the world is possible; but that that does *not* mean, as some have supposed, that our perceptions of the world cannot be accurate, and our descriptions of it true.

(2) Our knowledge of the past relies not just upon our concepts and beliefs, but also upon our procedures of inquiry and standards of inference. These have changed a bit over the centuries. How can we justify the assumption that they yield true conclusions?

What procedures and standards of inference am I referring to? In my last book I described some of the forms of inference commonly used by historians. Consider two of those, namely arguments to the best explanation, and statistical inferences (McCullagh, 1984, chs 2, 3). I have listed seven conditions which must be satisfied before we accept an argument to the best explanation. The last was that the explanation in question must be much better, in terms of the other standards (explanatory scope and power, plausibility, simplicity and so on), than any other explanation that can be thought of. For this condition to be satisfied, historians must adopt the procedure of thinking of all the possible explanatory hypotheses they can. Then again, I said that the best explanation should imply fewer false statements than the other possible explanations. For this to apply, historians must adopt the procedure of testing their explanatory hypotheses by examining their implications. Suppose, for instance, that an historian explained the fact that a document seems to be a single continuous entity, written without a break, by the hypothesis that it was written by the one person. This hypothesis has several implications which can be tested. It implies that it was written in the same hand;

that it used the same range of spelling and phrases; that it was about the same issues, and presented a more or less consistent set of views and attitudes. Students of old texts, such as those in the Bible, have argued that some documents do *not* have the same author, because the hypothesis that they have is rendered doubtful by the fact that one or more of these implications is false. For instance, scholars refer to two different sources of Genesis, commonly named P and J, a priestly source and a Jahwist.

Then again, C.G. Hempel has shown that for statistical inferences to yield reliable conclusions, they must take account of all the evidence relevant to that conclusion ('the requirement of total evidence', Hempel, 1965, pp. 63–7); or more precisely, the inferences must 'be based on a statistical probability statement pertaining to the narrowest reference class of which, according to our total information, the particular occurrence under consideration is a member' (p. 398) ('the requirement of maximal specificity', pp. 397–403). Thus, I can infer that your sore throat will recover after a course of penicillin, because that usually happens, unless you add that your sore throat is caused by a type of infection resistant to penicillin, for that small class of cases does not usually respond to penicillin. Searching for the narrowest reference class is a procedure which must accompany the use of statistical inferences, if they are to be of any value. So to draw reliable conclusions from their evidence, historians must use reliable forms of inference and be conscientious in following the procedures associated with each.

We cannot prove that inductive inferences, conscientiously formulated, regularly lead us to the truth about the world, but we generally assume that they do. What we find is that experiences implied by their conclusions are regularly confirmed. That is why we prefer these forms of inference to other forms whose conclusions are based upon things such as auguries or tea leaves, which have been much less reliable in experience. We could only infer the general reliability of our forms of inductive inference from observations of instances of their success by employing the very forms of inference whose reliability we are trying to establish. It is a convention we all accept that sound inductive inferences regularly lead us to truths about the world, and it is a convention we take seriously, on faith.

(3) Finally, the facts of cultural relativism show that it is much more difficult to eliminate the effects of bias than historians have generally supposed. An historical description is biased in the perjorative sense if, on the basis of all available relevant evidence, it is reasonable for anyone in that historian's culture to conclude that it is either not true, or not fair, or both. An historical description is not fair if it implies something false about the subject. (The fairness of historical descriptions is explained in the third section of this chapter: see pp. 58–61 below.) As well as personal bias, which has been mentioned, there is systematic cultural bias to be reckoned with. This is manifest in common tendencies towards professional, gender, national and racial bias in historical writing.

The kind of cultural bias just described, namely bias which produces false or misleading descriptions of the past, can be largely overcome with the help of people from other cultures, who point out the logical implications of evidence which the biased historian has overlooked or misinterpreted. The way in which the Japanese government and people have come to acknowledge war crimes which had previously been ignored or denied is a good illustration of this process.

The bias which cannot be overcome easily, and which is just as worrying, is different. There are sometimes several quite different ways of describing an event, each equally justified, but implying quite different moral judgements about what happened. For example, some time ago white authorities took Australian aboriginal children away from their parents, when the parents were judged incompetent or unsuitable, in order to educate and civilize them in white families. That description of what happened truly captures the intention of the white authorities. But today we view the actions differently, as an expression of white disrespect for aboriginal culture, and an often inhumane disregard of the values of their family and community life. It may be that the aboriginals involved would not have judged the actions in precisely these terms, though there is no doubt of their distress. The judgement is certainly ours today, even if it was not theirs in the past. Each description of what happened implies a different moral assessment, the first one of general approval, the second of profound disapproval. There is no rational procedure for avoiding bias of this kind that I know of. Examples can be multiplied over and over again. Men who treated their slaves or their wives without respect in the past could be said to have been exercising their rights, though today many people would say that they acted inhumanely. Both descriptions are true, but each implies a quite different moral attitude towards what happened.

You might think that such bias could be overcome by requiring historians to describe all aspects of an event relevant to its moral value, the good sides and the bad. The trouble is that different historians have quite different moral values, so that what one will judge to be a bad aspect, another will regard as morally insignificant. For instance, the growth of industry has been accompanied by pollution, and people differ in their opinion as to how much pollution is bad. Then again, some will think that the wealthy have every right to all the money they can get, while others think that the benefits of wealth ought to be distributed more evenly. So there is no objective standard for judging the morality of many events.

Furthermore, differences in the interpretation of events are not always the result of different moral outlooks. They are just as often reflections of different social and political views and interests. Gene Wise was one of the first to analyse this in detail in *American Historical Explanations* (1973), where, for instance, he contrasted Progressive, counter-Progressive, and New Left versions of American history, relating them to the political outlook of the historians involved and more broadly to the culture of their time. Since then there has been widespread interest in the relations between historical interpretations and the social and cultural context of historians.

Some may try to overcome the problem of subjective interpretation by saying that historians should confine their descriptions to the perceptions of the people involved in past events, and not provide their own assessments at all. There are several reasons for rejecting this proposal, an important one being that historians often want to compare what really happened with what people at the time thought was happening. The relevant point to be made here, however, is that such a restriction would prevent an historian pointing out injustices which are recognized today but were not recognized in the past, such as injustices towards the rights of women and people of other races. It would surely be immoral to adopt a policy which prevented such morally important observations from being made.

I conclude that the cultural bias now being discussed, which does not involve false or misleading descriptions of the past, is inescapable, and provides the main reason for saying that history is subjective. In this way I agree that history is subjective. But this statement has been taken to imply that there is no truth in history, and that there are no objective ways of judging between historical interpretations and explanations. These implications are all false, as this book is designed to show. There are minimum standards of truth and adequacy which historians are expected to meet. The fact that once these have been met there is still room for radically different descriptions of the past is a fact which must be acknowledged, and the use made of historical descriptions for moral and political purposes should be fully understood.

The constraints of language

There are several philosophers who have been classified as 'postmodern'. They do not always agree with each other, but they share a common scepticism about the possibility of providing true and accurate descriptions of the world. I have selected for consideration just those who have presented the most forceful and well-known attacks upon the possibility of historical truth. More precisely, I have drawn upon selected passages from the writing of Roland Barthes, Jacques Derrida and Jean-François Lyotard. The language of these authors is not always easy to follow, so I have generally presented simple outlines of their arguments which are sufficient for present purposes, even though they exclude some of the subtleties which a full account of their work would provide. To make their arguments even more vivid, I will illustrate them by referring to a recent history book as well.

(1) The first argument begins with a point made by Roland Barthes. He affirms the theory of Ferdinand de Saussure that words in any language (which Saussure called 'signifiers') refer to concepts ('signified'), and not to things in the world. Evidence for this is the fact that we can often understand a text from a familiarity with the concepts it is presenting without having any acquaintance with the world to which it refers. To understand a text, he says, all you need to know are the concepts which the words signify.

Barthes argues that historians have not generally recognized that their descriptions of the past really represent a number of concepts about the past, and not the past world itself. William Sheridan Allen has written a fascinating history of the impact of Nazism upon the small German town of Northeim (Allen, 1989). In one passage he describes visits of Gestapo agents to the home of a Social Democrat named Hermann Schulze (pp. 198–9). Barthes would say that this description is really of Allen's concepts of what happened, arrived at from his investigations, and does not necessarily represent the world at all. Barthes calls the text 'the signifier', the subject in the world which it is about 'the referent', and the concepts it expresses 'the signified'. This is what he says:

> Historical discourse supposes, one might say, a double operation, one that is extremely complex. In the first phase (this decomposition is, of course, only metaphorical), the referent is detached from the discourse, it becomes exterior to it, grounds it, is supposed to govern it: this is the phase of *res gestae*, and the discourse simply claims to be *historia rerum gestarum*: but in the second phase, it is the signified itself which is repulsed, merged in the referent; the referent enters into direct relation with the signifier, and the discourse, meant only to *express* the real, believes it elides the fundamental term of imaginary structures, which is the signified. Like any discourse with 'realistic' claims, the discourse of history thus believes it knows only a two-term semantic schema, referent and signifier. . . . In other words, in 'objective' history, the 'real' is never anything but an unformulated signified, sheltered behind the apparent omnipotence of the referent. This situation defines what we might call the *reality effect*.
>
> (Barthes, 1986, pp. 138–9)

Historians do not say that they are describing just their ideas about the past. Rather, they write as though they are describing the past itself, and they heighten that impression by providing lively details. Thus Allen, for example, wrote:

> the Gestapo searched Schulze's house several times, very carefully. They cut open mattresses and thumped on the walls and even broke open a section of the wall that happened to be hollow. They confiscated Schulze's rifle, but Shulze hid the *Reichsbanner* flag [the *Reichsbanner* was a paramilitary corps for the defence of the German Republic] so carefully that they never found it. The Gestapo were very angry about it. They questioned him on that and related matters at least twenty times.
>
> (Allen, 1989, p. 198)

In writing like this, Barthes says historians produce an effect of describing reality, whereas in fact they are just expressing their concepts of what happened in the past.

Let us agree with Barthes that historians are presenting their ideas about the past. That is quite compatible with the possibility that their descriptions of the past are true, in the correlation sense explained above. Saussure cast doubt upon a regular relation between language and the world, claiming that the relation between words and the world is arbitrary. For instance, there is not a concept of a river which is regularly related to rivers in the world. Well, there is such a concept in English, where a river is larger than a stream. But the French conceptualize watercourses differently. They use the words 'fleuve' and 'rivière', but they are not equivalent to the English concepts of river and stream. A 'fleuve' is not necessarily larger than a 'rivière', but unlike the latter it flows into the sea (Culler, 1976, p. 24). These examples are supposed to illustrate the point that words refer to concepts rather than to things in the world. They also hint at the arbitrariness of the relationship between word and concept. This can be further illustrated by the way in which the meaning of a word changes over time. 'The English word *cattle*, for example, at one point meant property in general, then gradually came to be restricted to four-footed property only (a new category), and finally attained its modern sense of domesticated bovines' (p. 22). Not only is the relation between words and the world arbitrary, but so also is the relation between words and the concepts they express.

Even these remarks, however, do not exclude the possibility of descriptions of the world being true. They merely point out that the same thing can be conceived of in different ways in different cultures, and that the same word can have different truth conditions in the same culture at different times. The truth of a description is always relative to the meaning of the words (which includes their truth conditions) in the culture at the time.

To rule out the possibility of truly describing the world, one must accept yet another point made by Saussure, namely that words are not at all related to things in the world but only to concepts, and that the meaning of words and concepts is entirely captured by their relations with other words and concepts in the language. For instance, to understand what the word 'brown' means, one must know that things which are brown are not orange, green, yellow, etc. According to Saussure, Culler says, 'brown is not an independent concept defined by some essential properties but one term in a system of colour terms, defined by its relations with the other terms which delimit it' (p. 25). Compare the way in which Geertz defined the Javanese concepts of *batin* and *lair* by relating them to and contrasting them with other concepts in English, above. Commenting upon this theory, Terry Eagleton said:

Since the meaning of a sign is a matter of what the sign is *not*, its meaning is always in some sense absent from it too. Meaning . . . cannot be easily nailed down, it is never fully present in any one sign alone, but is rather a kind of constant flickering of presence and absence together.

(Eagleton, 1983, p. 128)

Jacques Derrida has been intrigued by this last assertion of Saussure's, and has developed it further. Saussure had thought the meanings of terms were fixed by their place in a language. Derrida, however, denied that the meaning of a term is fixed, but said that the meaning of a term depends upon all the different contexts in which it has been used. There is an indefinite number of these, and as they all add a little more to one's understanding of a term, one cannot say that the meaning of a term is fixed. Rather, he said, it is indefinitely deferred. As Eagleton explains it:

When I read a sentence, the meaning of it is always somehow suspended, something deferred or still to come: one signifier relays me to another, and that to another, earlier meanings are modified by later ones, and although the sentence may come to an end the process of language itself does not.

(Eagleton, 1983, p. 128)

If words have no regular relation with the world, then it seems they cannot truly describe anything in the world. If the meaning of a text is uncertain, it is impossible even to fix its truth conditions within a language at a time. Derrida said that the idea that language discloses the reality to which it refers is a 'white mythology', a piece of western metaphysics which should be demolished, deconstructed (Derrida, 1982, p. 213).

Derrida's expansion of Saussure's analysis of meaning certainly shows that the meaning of words and sentences is much less precise than has normally been assumed. However their meaning is often not so vague as to make it impossible to define their truth conditions. If it were, we could not communicate as effectively as we do. Historical descriptions, especially descriptions of basic facts about places, dates and events, are often precise enough to test against available evidence. Nevertheless, even if historical descriptions are often quite precise, they will not tell us anything about the real world if there is no systematic relationship between words and the world, as these philosophers have argued.

What Barthes and Derrida have overlooked is the way in which the concepts which many words express include the possibility of having certain kinds of experience. For example, the concept of an orange is not just of something which is orange, rather than yellow, blue, etc., and is round rather than square, and sweet rather than bitter. It is also the concept of something which can be seen to be orange and round, and can be tasted to be sweet. To assert that there is an orange on the table, therefore, is not just to produce a set of words related to other words. It is to refer to something in the world capable of producing the kinds of experience which the concept of an orange involves. The words arouse the belief in us that there is something in the world which, if perceived in the normal way, would yield such experiences. To learn what 'brown' means, one must be shown brown objects, and not just learn that brown objects are not yellow, blue, red and so on. The word is associated with the experience of a certain colour. It is not defined by verbal contrasts alone. (The same point is made by Michael Devitt and Kim Sterelny in *Language and Reality*, 1987, pp. 213, 218.)

So statements which refer to things in the world, like descriptions of historical evidence, assert that there are things which will produce perceptions of a certain kind in normal circumstances. These things constitute their truth conditions. A river is not just something which is bigger than a stream. It is something which if looked at will appear to be of a certain shape, size, and movement, and if touched will feel wet. To say that a river flows through London is not just to say there is something larger than a stream which flows through London. It is also to say that in London there exists something such that, if you look at it and touch it, you will experience the perceptual properties just described. Unobservable physical and mental states, like magnetic fields and personal beliefs, can only be perceived indirectly, by means of their effects. But all have either actual or conditional truth conditions which refer to what can, or could in certain circumstances, be perceived, directly or indirectly.

If this is right, then clearly the crucial premise of Barthes' argument fails. It was that descriptions of the world refer to concepts about the world, but not to things in the world. In fact descriptions of the world express our concepts about it, but they also refer to things in the world which can be perceived, directly or indirectly, in certain ways. Sentences about the past mean, among other things, that there was something such that, if you had been there to perceive it, you would have had experiences of certain kinds. So when historians refer to past events, they are not merely expressing a concept. They are telling us something about the real world. Historical descriptions are true if it is the case that, had anyone been present, then things in the world would have produced the perceptions which the sentences imply.

(2) The second argument against the possibility of historical truth can also be derived from the writing of Derrida. It also attempts to prove that descriptions of the world have no particular relationship to the real world, and so cannot reasonably be held true or false of it. There are traces of this argument in the works of other philosophers of history as well.

In its most extreme form, the argument is this: Although historical descriptions purport to be about the world, in fact when you question them their authors refer, not to the real world, but to other texts such as reports which describe people's experiences. So these descriptions are not related to the real world at all, even though they pretend to be so. They are just products of other texts.

For example, Allen based his vivid description of the Gestapo visits to Hermann Schulze, not upon his perception of those events, but upon an account of what happened given by Schulze and on other documents relating to it, which in turn were certified as authentic by a note from the British occupation authorities in 1946 (Allen, 1984, p. 357, n. 44).

One of the aims of the deconstruction of texts is to expose this fact, that although texts appear to be about the world, they are really just constructed from other texts. (See Eagleton, 1983, pp. 145–6.) Past events themselves, it seems, play no part at all in the construction of history. So although historical descriptions say they are about the past, it seems that they are not really related to it at all.

This argument is at the heart of Leon Goldstein's book *Historical Knowing* (1976). 'What we know about the historical past', he writes, 'we know only through its constitution in historical research – never by acquaintance – never as anything having a status independent of what is constituted in historical research.' Consequently, in history, he says, 'the distinction between facts and the description of facts . . . does not exist' (p. xxi). In other words, the facts of history are just those constituted by historians; they are not something else, which really happened in the past, which may or may not be correctly described by historians.

It is of course true that historians arrive at their descriptions of the past by drawing inferences from available evidence, which is often in the form of a written text, and not from observing events in the past. This would only imply that their descriptions cannot be true of the past if that evidence was not connected with what had happened. Derrida has been very interested to show how little one needs to know of the author and the circumstances of its composition in order to understand a text. Knowledge of the language alone can provide an immense amount of understanding, though in Chapter 5 below I argue that knowledge of the context and of authorial intent is sometimes necessary to clarify textual ambiguities and uncertainties of reference. The fact that one can sometimes understand a text without knowing anything about its author or original context does not mean the text can tell us nothing about those things. A text about what Hermann Schulze told British occupation authorities concerning his encounters with the Gestapo can reasonably be said to imply that the events he described took place, if such people reporting such events in such contexts generally tell the truth, and if the best explanation of his making the report he did is that the events happened as he described them.

Historians do not usually explain that their descriptions of the past are constructions based upon available evidence, though their footnotes witness to that fact. They normally write as though what they describe really happened, which is what they reasonably believe. It is not the fact that their descriptions are inferred from other texts which makes their truth suspect. It is suspect only if the evidence does not strongly entail their truth in the first place. When the evidence strongly supports the truth of an historical description, one is rationally entitled to believe it is very probably true.

(3) The third reason for denying that historical descriptions can be true has also been stated by Derrida (see Kevin Hart, 1989, pp. 122–5), though it has been developed by others, especially by Jean-François Lyotard, as well. They have noted that descriptions of the world always omit details. Historical descriptions use common nouns and verbs which pick out only general features of what they refer to. In the past we have naively assumed that our descriptions of the world can portray reality accurately, but, they argue, this is not the case. There is always much which any description fails to capture.

To understand the passion behind this argument, it is useful to relate it, as Robert Young has done, to the experience of French philosophers concerning official reports of the Algerian War of Independence (Young, 1990, p. 1). The French government presented the Algerians as just a problem, leaving them invisible as people, or if described, portraying them as an inferior race, dirty, stupid, lazy, and untrustworthy. In other words, the reports presented a picture of events which suited the interests of those in power, and ignored or distorted the details of what was really taking place. Such descriptions are manifestly unjust. Similarly, Roland Barthes wrote of a collection of photographs entitled *The Family of Man*, that they presented poverty as a normal human condition, remaining silent about the structures of exploitation which often produced it. They did not present the whole truth. Our representations of the world are always partial, in both senses, and so inadequate. Lyotard assumed it is wrong to describe the past if one cannot describe it fully. It is impossible to represent past events in all their particularity, so it seems that history is impossible (Readings, 1991, p. 60). I discuss Lyotard's hostility to general history on pp. 297–302 of Chapter 11.

Let us allow that historical descriptions cannot represent the past in all its particularity. It seems just self-evident to many, like Lyotard, that historical descriptions are therefore not true. In which case, should one stop attempting to describe the world? Different philosophers have responded to the problem in different ways. Edward Said, having deplored the way in which colonial powers conceptualize the world for their own purposes, recommends that historians try to avoid fitting facts into neat structures, but describe things in their plurality and particularity (Young, 1990, pp. 10–11). But as Young remarks, this does not address the fundamental problem of representation. No matter how detailed our descriptions, in that they use general terms they fail to capture all the details of the things being described. Emmanuel Levinas has developed an ethical stance of respect for things in the world, which leads him to gesture towards them but not to appropriate them linguistically (pp. 16–17). His views are difficult to understand, but it seems that he would allow we can refer to things in the world, but would judge any attempt to describe those things as a violation of them, an attempt to force them into one's own patterns of thought, misrepresenting them in the process. Lyotard's response has been, not to abandon history, but to urge readers to be constantly aware that the text and event are separate, different things. As Readings puts it, summing up Lyotard's ideas: 'Postmodernity rewrites history as anachronism: a kind of temporal anamorphosis [distorted projection], in which the present event of writing is not eliminated by the past event that is written about, or vice versa. Rather two heterogeneous temporalities are co-present' (Readings, 1991, p. 58). The text does not encompass the event, as historians sometimes appear to think. Rather the two are distinct, though related. We must respect the particularity of past events, and allow that they cannot be faithfully represented. In particular, Lyotard thinks historians should not attempt to describe things of great intrinsic significance, for in doing so they will trivialize them. For example, he thinks historians should never try to represent the horror of the Holocaust, for fear of making it banal. Readings sums up Lyotard's concern in these words:

> The task of historical writing is not to give voice to the silence of the oppressed, which would be only to betray that silence. . . . once we claim to represent the Holocaust as part of history, then it becomes just one atrocity among others in the long history of man's inhumanity to man, as West German revisionist historians have argued. In order to respect the impossibility of atonement, of coming to terms with horror by representing it, we have to write a history that will testify to the unrepresentable horror without representing it. We must not give voice to the millions of murdered Jews, gypsies, homosexuals and communists, but find a way of writing history that will testify to the *horror* of their having been silenced.
>
> (Readings, 1991, pp. 61–2)

Before considering how historians should honour the past, let us face the epistemological question. Does the fact that historical descriptions do not capture all the details of the events they describe imply that they cannot be true? There are two ways in which historical descriptions can be incomplete, which need to be distinguished. First, they might refer to only some aspects of the event or situation, and make no reference to others. This does not mean that the descriptions must be false. It simply means they are not exhaustive, and could possibly be misleading. What they say might be true nevertheless. Second, descriptions are incomplete in that they use general terms which refer to some general features of the event or situation, but do not capture those features in their singularity. For instance, no matter how detailed a description of deaths in Nazi gas chambers, one could never represent in detail the horror of each death. As was explained above, the descriptions tend to generalize what happened.

In response to this criticism we must honour the postmodernists for having exposed the limitations of descriptions so vividly. There is no denying that descriptions do use common nouns and verbs, and there is a range of sets of the truth conditions for any statement about the past. They do not capture every detail, though some can be very detailed indeed. But this has always been a feature of descriptions of the world. It means they do not mirror reality as we do or could know it, but it does not mean they cannot represent it with some degree of precision. The more general the description, the less precise it is. Nevertheless, very general descriptions can be completely accurate, in that they are entirely warranted by the known facts, even though they are far from precise. The precision and accuracy of historical descriptions have to be distinguished.

Lyotard's suggestion that historians remind readers of the difference between their descriptions of the past and the reality itself, seems a good one. It allows historians to gesture towards the past, to point to some of the things that happened without pretending to have captured them in their complexity. To give up all attempt at description, however, as Levinas suggests, is seriously irresponsible. Historians cannot capture the experiences of those in concentration camps, but they can analyse the circumstances which put people there, in the hope of enabling us to prevent such organized barbarism from occurring ever again.

Although postmodern writers have tried to divorce language and reality in the ways I have described, the two are intimately related. Language can successfully refer to and describe the world. The inferences we draw from our perceptions, according to our general beliefs about the world, often yield descriptions of the world which are proven true in experience. Historical descriptions are true if the world really was as they describe it, or more strictly, if it would have been experienced appropriately had the historian been there to perceive it. What postmodernists have pointed out is that our descriptions are much less precise than we had generally assumed.

SOME ALTERNATIVE RESPONSES

I have argued that the facts of cultural relativism and postmodern insights into the nature of language do not prevent us from saying that historical descriptions can be true accounts of what happened in the past, relative to the culture of the historian. They do, however, require us to qualify the claims we make about historical knowledge. We are now aware that when historians draw inferences from the evidence available to them, they bring with them a number of assumptions which might well be revised in time, assumptions about the accuracy of their concepts, the truth of their particular and general beliefs about the world, and standards of rational inference. Instead of saying that their well-supported conclusions about the world are simply true, historians should say that they are probably true, relative to the available evidence and to their culture at the time.

The postmodernists have made us vividly aware of just how partial and general are historical descriptions, and how little of the detail of actual events they are able to convey. The truth is always far fuller and richer than any historical account can represent.

There have been other responses to the facts of cultural relativism and to the writing of postmodern philosophers, however, and these should be examined before concluding. First, as has already been mentioned, there are some who have denied that we can know the truth about the past, and prefer to view written history as a rational linguistic construction which constitutes the past for us. Second, there are some who would like to retain the idea that historians tell the truth, but would provide a different account of truth from the one I have given. Some think of truth as coherence with existing beliefs; others view it as a consensus reached by rational inquirers. Let us look at each of these responses in turn.

The constructionist theory of history

Several philosophers have been struck by the fact that historians do not examine the past, but arrive at their accounts of the past by drawing inferences from present evidence. They conclude that history is not about the real past at all, but is just a construction created by historians.

R.G. Collingwood put forward this view as an answer to scepticism at the end of his essay 'The Limits of Historical Knowledge'. He wrote: 'historical thinking means nothing else than interpreting all the available evidence with the maximum degree of critical skill. It does not mean discovering what really happened, if "what really happened" is anything other than "what the evidence indicates"' (Collingwood, 1928, p. 99). He explained the sense in which historians could be said to know the past: 'not the past as it was in itself – for that is not only non-existent but unknowable into the bargain – but the past as it appears from its traces in this present' (p. 102).

Collingwood said that people are naturally sceptical of historical knowledge if it is interpreted in a realistic manner, as describing what actually happened. He said it is unreasonable to interpret it like this, for the two reasons given. First, the past does not exist: 'historical realism involves the absurdity of thinking of the past as something still existing by itself' (p. 101). This is false. Historical realists do not think of the past as still existing, but as having existed. He goes on to say that the historian 'does not want a real past . . . a reflection shows that he gets along very well without it' (ibid.). Historians do their work, not by examining the past itself, but by drawing inferences from present evidence. This does not imply that their conclusions cannot be about the real past, as we normally believe. Why deny that it is about the real past? Just to avoid the problem of scepticism?

Collingwood's reason for this denial seems to be a conviction that 'the past simply as past is wholly unknowable' (pp. 99–100). The reason which he offers is that we cannot know everything that happened in the past, but only those events of which there is some present evidence (ibid.). This is not a good reason for denying that the inferences which we are able to draw about the past cannot be true in a realistic sense. (In a discussion of this passage, W.H. Dray argues that Collingwood just overstated his view that historians can only discover what the evidence permits them to infer (Dray, 1994, pp. 64–7). I suppose this is possible, though Dray allows that in other passages Collingwood clearly expresses a constructionist view (pp. 67–70). The arguments stated here are common, however, and so deserve a reply.)

Leon Goldstein presented a similar defence of constructionism in his book *Historical Knowing* (1976). He referred to 'criteria of factuality, objectivity, and reference, which are rooted in perception', suggesting that because we cannot perceive the past, these criteria do not apply to history (p. xiv). He went on to describe history as involving another 'way of knowing' by which historians 'constitute the historical past' (p. xix). He concluded:

> To demand of historical descriptions that they conform to [the real] past is to demand what cannot be realized. . . . What we know about the historical past we know only through its constitution in historical research – never by acquaintance – never as anything having a status independent of what is constituted in historical research.
>
> (p. xxi)

The implication seems to be that our knowledge of the present world is reliable if it is confirmed by observation, whereas our knowledge of the past cannot be known to yield reliable descriptions of the past because it is inferred and cannot be confirmed by observation. It must be said that both of these suggestions are misleading. Direct observations can be unreliable, as those acquainted with visual illusions know; and many scientific descriptions of the present world are arrived at by inference from observations. For instance a statement of the temperature or pressure of a gas is normally inferred from the position of a pointer on a dial.

There is no reason to doubt the truth of historical descriptions simply because they cannot be checked by observation. Rather, our knowledge of the world, both present and past, is fallible because it is relative to our world-view and standards of rationality, both of which might be found unreliable in time. Also, as new evidence is discovered, our view of the past changes. But the fact that our knowledge is fallible is not a reason for saying that none of it can be true. It is reasonable to believe that most of our well-supported descriptions of the past are true. The chance of them being corrected in future is relatively slight, if past experience is anything to go by.

Rather than accept the fallibility of historical knowledge, philosophers like Goldstein prefer to deny that historians are trying to describe the past at all. Jack Meiland is another who is sceptical about the possibility of knowing the past, and prefers to think of history as providing a 'construction', rather than a description, of the past (Meiland, 1965, pt. V). He explains:

> The two main features of every particular Constructionist theory are: (1) a claim that the historian should not be regarded as trying to discover facts about an

independently existing realm of past events; (2) a claim that history is nevertheless important and significant because it attempts to deal with a certain class of present entities (which we will call 'documents'. . . .) in a certain way. . . . [The historian] tells a story that accounts for the existence and nature of those documents.

(p. 192)

Gadamer is another who presents what amounts to a constructionist theory of history in his book *Truth and Method*. He describes the process of fitting a hypothesis about the past to present evidence as play, a process of turning first to the data to see whether they fit the hypothesis, then to the hypothesis to adjust it to the data, then back to the data for more checks, and so on (Gadamer, 1975, pp. 91–3; 236–8). The logic of this process he likens to Aristotle's account of the way people make particular moral judgements by considering all the implications of different possible courses of action, a process Aristotle refers to as phronesis (pp. 278–83). What Gamader does not appreciate is the cognitive significance of this process when it is applied to the interpretation of historical evidence, for there it amounts very often to discovering the best explanation of the evidence (see McCullagh, 1984, ch. 2). Arguments to the best explanation are standard forms of inductive inference, whose conclusions we commonly accept as telling us truths about the world.

Gadamer says that the kind of truth which this process of inquiry reaches is a sort of subjective certainty, that the hypothesis finally really does fit the evidence. He likens it to the truth of aesthetic judgements about the beauty or meaning of a work of art, as analysed by Kant. A hypothesis about the past which an historian finds 'true' should not be thought to represent an independent past in any way, he says. Rather it constitutes the past we know. He writes: 'The world which appears in the play of representation does not stand like a copy next to the real world, but is the latter in the heightened truth of its being' (Gadamer, 1975, p. 121). Gadamer is here adopting Heidegger's account of the world as that which presents itself to us. The past which is disclosed to the historian from the study of present evidence is the only true past there is, according to Gadamer.

I shall shortly discuss Heidegger's reluctance to distinguish our perceptions of the world and the world itself, and show how the assumption that the world is as we perceive it is inconsistent with our scientific understanding of perception. Once the distinction between our beliefs about the world and the world itself is reinstated, then the question of the relation between our beliefs about the past and the past itself can be raised.

Constructionist theories try to avoid this question, and the problems of scepticism which it raises, by simply declaring the conclusions of historians to have no particular relationship with the real past. They uniformly ignore the cognitive significance of arguments to the best explanation. In everyday life we commonly accept that explanations of evidence reveal truth about the world. So why not do so in the case of history? If you park under a tree, and find some white splodges on your windscreen, you infer that a bird dropped them there. If a friend writes to you about her experiences on holiday, you infer that what she described probably happened. Arguments to the best explanation are powerful and common forms of inductive inference. The examples I've just given are of everyday historical inferences. If historians use inferences of the same kind, surely we should believe their conclusions.

The sceptic might ask for proof that arguments to the best explanation commonly yield truths about the world. But what would count as proof in this case? The observable conclusions of such arguments are often confirmed, which is a good reason for calling the arguments reliable. When it is possible to check the conclusions of such arguments by observation, people usually have the kinds of experience implied by the conclusion.

Do these confirming experiences tell us anything about the world? We believe that they are not a product of chance, but relate to things in the world which would regularly produce such experiences in people like us, with our senses and culture. So we rightly regard them as true of the world, in the only way we can make senses of that phrase.

Truth as coherence

Historians arrive at their conclusions about the past by considering what present data implies according to their present particular and general beliefs about the world. They do not reach them by observing the past world, which is impossible. These facts have inclined some to think that the truth of historical descriptions is a matter of their coherence with other beliefs rather than their correlation with what has actually happened. Indeed, if we assume that the meaning of a term is given by the conditions which warrant its use, then we can say that the word 'true' when applied to historical descriptions means 'rationally coherent with other beliefs'.

Michael Oakeshott believed that the truth of historical descriptions lay in their coherence with the historian's beliefs. This suited his idealism, his conviction that 'history cannot be "the course of events" independent of our experience of it, because there is nothing independent of our experience – neither event nor fact, neither past nor future' (Oakeshott, 1933, p. 93). But one does not have to adopt an idealist metaphysic to find the coherence theory of truth attractive. Oakeshott believed that 'a world of ideas is true when it is coherent and because it is coherent' (p. 48). He thought this particularly true of history: 'it is impossible to establish the truth of historical facts piecemeal. The truth of each fact depends upon the truth of the world of facts to which it belongs, and the truth of the world of facts lies in the coherence of the facts which compose it' (p. 113).

If one is a realist, and allows that the world exists independently of our thoughts about it, then the concept of truth is more complicated than Oakeshott allows. For then one can contrast conditions which warrant one saying that a statement is true, and what is meant by saying it is true. Your telling me sincerely that a car is in the garage might warrant my saying that the statement is true, for I know you are reliably informed of the matter. But when I say that it is true that a car is in the garage, I do not mean that I am warranted in asserting that statement. What I mean is that a car is indeed in the garage, that this state of affairs exists in the world. This is the state of affairs which would normally give me a perception of a certain kind, namely of a car in a garage, were I to visit the garage. It is that state of affairs which, if it exists, makes the statement true.

To make this assertion of the correlation theory more acceptable, let me admit that discovering the precise truth conditions of a sentence can be tricky. Quine made this fact vivid with his famous example of the anthropologist trying to understand the reference of the word *gagavai*, which could refer to rabbits, parts of rabbits, temporal 'slices' of rabbits, or parts of a mass of rabbits. Often ambiguities can be resolved by further inquiry, but it may be that some words and sentences remain ambiguous. Also, many sentences can be made true by a range of particular conditions. Just think, for instance, of how many states of affairs could make true the sentence 'There are two people in this room.' Any two people, in any position, would do. The vaguest set of truth conditions are those related to dispositions and powers, such as personal attitudes and beliefs, legal authority or economic power. These are only manifest under appropriate conditions, so that sentences describing these are true only if the relevant conditional statements are true. It is sometimes difficult to provide an exhaustive list of such statements, even in general terms. Consider the truth conditions of 'A loved B' and of 'Parents were responsible for their children', for example.

All I have shown to this point is that, assuming the world really exists, it is possible that historical descriptions are true in a correlation, and not just a coherence sense. One may judge their truth on grounds of coherence, but mean that they are true in a correlation sense. In fact if coherence means no more than logical compatibility, then the coherence of an historical description with our other beliefs about the world is not sufficient reason to assert its truth. Several different explanations of evidence could be compatible with it, yet one be much superior to the others in its scope, power and simplicity, and so alone be worthy of belief. Even in a case like this, however, to call the superior historical explanation true is not to say that it is well supported by the evidence. Rather it is to say that the explanation tells us about something that really happened in the past. Why should we interpret truth thus in these cases? The answer is the same as was given to those who denied the possibility of historical truth. Historical descriptions can be justified by arguments from observations of data, and these arguments are common, reliable means of arriving at truths about the world. The fact that we cannot observe the past to check whether our historical descriptions are true is no reason for denying their truth. You cannot see an electric current, but you do not deny its reality when you touch the wires which carry it.

Donald Davidson has suggested 'that coherence yields correspondence', that 'if coherence is a test of truth, then coherence is a test for judging that objective truth conditions are satisfied' (Davidson, 1983 in LePore, 1986, p. 307). The details of his argument are obscure, but its heart seems to be as follows. He asserts: 'the truth of an utterance depends on just two things: what the words spoken mean, and how the world is arranged' (p. 309). For Davidson, the meaning of utterances describing the world is given by the conditions of the world which are generally acknowledged to make it true, i.e. by its truth conditions, and so a description is true if there is an appropriate relation between it and the world. Davidson does not examine that relation closely, beyond saying that we must 'take the objects of a belief to be the causes of that belief' (p. 317–18). What emerges fairly clearly is this: if we judge that the world is as someone describes it, and that their belief about it was caused by its being as it is, then we are justified in regarding their description of it, which expresses that belief, as true. Davidson refuses to analyse the concept of truth, but presumably in this case the description is judged to be true in the 'correspondence' sense to which he had initially referred. Because the description 'coheres' with the world in this way, we judge it true in a correspondence sense.

A realist will not agree that because someone *believes* a description of the world portrays the way the world is, that the description is true. The belief that a description coheres with the world may justify *belief* in the truth of that description, but that belief could be mistaken. The truth conditions of the description might not, in fact, be satisfied. For example, if you and I have walked for hours in a hot desert, and you say 'There is an oasis in that valley', and I look and see it too, then if I am totally ignorant of mirages I would be justified in believing your description is true, though it is not. As this example shows, our perceptions of the world are not invariably accurate. They can be distorted by local conditions, as in this example, or by our preconceptions and interests. Indeed our perceptions are caused by stimulation of our sensory organs, and by electrical impulses in our brain, so that their relation to the world is quite problematic. As Davidson says: the idea of 'a confrontation between what we believe and reality . . . is absurd' (p. 307). The most we can do is compare what someone else believes about the world and what we believe it to be. Nevertheless, to make his argument work, that coherence implies correspondence, Davidson must suppose that we can perceive the world as it is. Otherwise the fact that we judge a description of the world to cohere well with the way the world appears to us will not guarantee its truth in some correspondence sense. So he writes of objects in the world: 'what we, as interpreters, must take them to be is what they in fact are' (p. 318).

Davidson says: a description is true if I judge it to cohere with a part of the world which caused it. I say: a description is true if the observations it implies correspond to those which could be had in experience. The conditions which warrrant belief in the truth of a description are not those which make it true, for warranted beliefs can be false. Coherence of a description with other beliefs about the world, even with some perceptions of it, does not guarantee its truth. The statement 'There is an oasis in that valley' might cohere well with our perception. But it is true only if all the perceptual experiences it implies can be obtained. If the perception were a mirage, we would not be able to enjoy the cool shade of the oasis when we reached the valley in which it seemed to lie.

Davidson relates the truth of descriptions simply to judgements; I relate the truth of descriptions to their relation with things in the world. Sometimes it seems that Davidson would accept my view, but it is not entirely clear that he does so, as he keeps shifting from questions of truth to questions of interpretation. In fact I see no reason why Davidson would object to my view.

Richard Rorty is one who has directly confronted realist and non-realist accounts of truth, and has opted for the latter. He writes:

> we should drop the traditional distinction between knowledge and opinion, construed as the distinction between truth as correspondence to reality and truth as a commendatory term for well-justified beliefs.... For the pragmatist ... 'knowledge' is, like 'truth,' simply a compliment paid to the beliefs which we think so well justified that, for the moment, further justification is not needed.
>
> (Rorty, 1989 in Krausz, 1989, pp. 38–9)

I suggested above that well-justified beliefs could possibly be false. Rorty queries this possibility in two ways. First, he doubts that sense can be made of such an assertion in terms of a correspondence theory. Once he has established the impossibility of comparing our knowledge of nature with nature itself, as we have absolutely no idea of nature itself independent of our knowledge of it, Rorty has no use for a correspondence theory which says that a description is true if it corresponds somehow to the way the world is. This idea, that our knowledge 'mirrors' reality, he argues, is unintelligible (Rorty, 1980). It makes no sense, he says, to say that our descriptions of the world are either true or false in a correspondence sense. I agree with this point. My realist theory of truth is a correlation, not a correspondence theory, designed to accommodate this criticism of the correspondence theory.

Second, Rorty queries whether we really do doubt the truth of well-justified beliefs. Like Davidson, he argues we can only judge that some of our beliefs are false by assuming that most of them are true, and detecting anomalies concerning the 'false' ones (ibid., p. 309). It is interesting to see a similar concern with scepticism, and a similar conclusion, in Wittgenstein's *On Certainty* (1969).

> 247. What would it be like to doubt now whether I have two hands? Why can't I imagine it at all? What would I believe if I didn't believe that? So far I have no system at all within which this doubt might exist.
> 248. I have arrived at the rock bottom of my convictions.
>   And one might almost say that these foundation-walls are carried by the whole house. . . .
> 354. Doubting and non-doubting behaviour. There is the first only if there is the second.

I agree that in fact we could not doubt that we have two hands, and that our doubts are built upon other certainties. These points would be significant if the only reason for preferring a correlation theory was a worry that even our best supported beliefs seem to be false. In fact in this context the realist concern is not with the evidential probability of our beliefs being false but with the logical possibility of this being so. On some occasions, as with our description of the oasis in the desert, it is useful to contrast justified belief with the truth, in a correlation sense. If truth were defined as justified belief, as Rorty and Davidson seem inclined to think of it, then this contrast could not be made.

Rorty, it seems, is quite happy to accept this consequence. So are there other reasons for retaining a correlation theory of truth? First, there are several consequences of Rorty's so-called 'pragmatic' theory of truth which are unusual. The truth of a description according to this theory is a function of the beliefs of particular people at a particular time, so that a description can be true for some people and false for others, and true for some people at one time and false for them at another. Rorty's response to this problem is to deny that pragmatists have a theory of truth at all ('the pragmatist does not have a theory of truth, much less a relativistic one'), and in effect to recommend that we drop the concept of truth from our discourse (1989, p. 38). Rather than pursuing truth, scientists could be seen as just seeking agreement about what exists.

The second and most fundamental further reason for preferring a correlation theory of truth is that it retains an essential intuition that there can be a significant relationship between our beliefs and the world outside us, a relationship worth discovering so that we can act more effectively in the world. This intuition makes sense of the importance we accord our perceptions in judging the truth of descriptions of the world. It gives point to scientific experimentation and to the historical investigation of physical data, documents and other artefacts. We want our descriptions of the world to be based upon reliable perceptions, those which are regularly produced by whatever is out there. Rorty and others have to regard this prioritizing of observational data as merely a cultural preference in accordance with the scientific theory we happen to respect today. They see it as having no absolute significance in determining the truth of our descriptions at all. One could say that by denying the possibility of discovering facts true of the world they are not taking that part of our current scientific and historical theory and practice seriously enough. Rorty says 'we must, in practice, privilege our own group' (1989, p. 44), but in denying that the truth of descriptions concerns their relationship to the actual world, and preferring to write simply of our beliefs about it, he does not do so.

Those who are sceptical of the truth of historical knowledge assume that there is a difference between our beliefs about the world and the world itself, and then provide reasons for denying that we can prove our beliefs about the world to be true of the world in any meaningful sense. Philosophers like Rorty, convinced that we cannot say anything meaningful about the relation between our beliefs about the world and the world itself are prone to deny the distinction, and to say that all that there is in the world is what we believe about it. This theory of 'internal realism' says that anything we say about the reality of the world is inevitably part of a theory about it which we believe to be true, a theory which projects or constructs the world we live in. In that case philosophical inquiry into reality, ontology, reduces to natural science, and inquiry into the relation between belief and reality, epistemology, reduces to the science of perception and the study of scientific inference. This position plays down the significance of that part of our theory of reality which says our perceptions are caused by things external to us, regarding that as a trivial fact which raises no deep philosophical questions. The traditional realist, on the other hand, argues that if our knowledge of the world is built upon our perceptions, and they are caused by the world itself without actually corresponding to it, then the relation between our knowledge of the world and the world itself is problematic and certainly deserves philosophical investigation.

The distinction between our knowledge of the world and the world itself has sometimes been expressed as a problem of relating what is in our minds, our perceptions and beliefs about the world, to the world outside which produced them. This way of putting the problem of scepticism goes back to Descartes, and it has been adopted by western philosophers ever since. Martin Heidegger was particularly aware of the problem, as it plagued his colleague Edmund Husserl, and he thought it could be overcome by a careful analysis of people's experience of being in the world. This analysis, presented most fully in *Being and Time*, is quite fascinating in its own right, though difficult to understand. The point most relevant for the present discussion is Heidegger's observation that in our experience we discover that things in the world appear to us as objective, real things, not just as shadowy appearances of the real, and that as we give them careful attention, they disclose their nature to us in all its detail. Here then is an ontological and epistemological claim: we do have immediate knowledge of what is real in the world, and we know it because we are capable of discovering its nature as it discloses itself to us. Heidegger added a further point, that our descriptions of the world express our knowledge of it, and can serve to disclose it accurately to others (*Being and Time*, sections 43 and 44). Heidegger found support for his analysis in the writing of ancient Greek philosophers, Parmenides and Aristotle. Parmenides had said that we discover the 'being' of things in the world in our perception of them (ibid., pp. 215, 256); and Aristotle said that the truth, *aletheia*, involves the uncovering of things, to reveal their natures (ibid., p. 262). Heidegger had a lot to say about attitudes which prevent us from discovering the truth about things in the world, and which prevent us from communicating such truth to others, but this need not concern us here.

From a study of Heidegger one emerges thinking that knowledge of the world is not so difficult after all. We are directly acquainted with the world in experience, indeed most intimately acquainted with it in our awareness of our own being, as people concerned about our future. Being is not a category which we attribute to some of the things we perceive; rather it is part of what we perceive about them. The world is not some mysterious cause of our perceptions, but is given to us in those perceptions.

Heidegger's interpretation of everyday experience ('hermeneutic phenomen-ology') is so compelling, it seems to overcome the problem of scepticism. The trouble is that the conclusions Heidegger draws are naive, and ignore the facts which create the problem of scepticism. We know that there are three things which causally contribute to our perceptions, and which render doubtful any claim that our perceptions truly represent the world. First, science tells us that our perceptions are mediated by light waves, sound waves or chemical changes, and then by electrical currents within our nerve pathways, to produce the sights, sounds and smells we perceive. It seems unlikely that our perceptions resemble the objects and events in the world which cause them. Second, anthropologists tell us that different cultures perceive the world differently, not so much perhaps in identifying different contrasts within it as in conceiving of the things they perceive differently. Some see a herb or a medicine in a leaf, and others do not. Finally, psychologists have shown that our perception of the world reflects our needs, interests and desires: we magnify what we desire, and sometimes what we fear; we overlook what is inconvenient or mildly offensive, and so on. So our perceptions are the products not just of the world, but also of our sense organs, our culture and our interests. It is very naive to suppose that they simply represent the world.

Heidegger was aware of the last two causes of variation in people's perception of the world, and argued that they could be overcome. He said that we first encounter things in the world in a practical context, and identify them as certain kinds of things, such as a hammer, related to certain uses. Thus our interests and our preconceptions of things are both at work in our first apprehension of things in the world. This is how we interpret their meaning and understand them (ibid., section 32). However, this form of acquaintance with things can give way to another, either when the objects refuse to work as we expect and we view them anew; or when we rest from a task, and view objects disinterestedly. Then things reveal their true nature to us: 'Uncovering is a way of Being for Being-in-the-world. Circumspective concern, or even that concern in which we tarry and look at something, uncovers entities with-the-world. These entities become that which has been uncovered' (p. 263).

There is something immediately plausible about Heidegger's claim that we see things more truly, or at least in greater detail, when we regard them in themselves, and not just as instruments for our use. However, I suspect that it is naive to suppose that even this inspection of things in the world is unmotivated and unaffected by preconceptions. When Heidegger writes of 'pure perception', we are back with the *tabula rasa* of Locke ('Being is that which shows itself in the pure perception which belongs to beholding, and only by such seeing does Being get discovered' (p. 215)). In beholding a tree, some will look at the colour of its trunk and leaves, others at its shape, its peculiar configuration, others at its health, and perhaps at its place in the local ecology. Even our most open perceptions of the world reflect our interests. Heidegger writes of being 'amazed to the point of not understanding' when contemplating things, suggesting that no conceptual-ization takes place, no preconceptions are applied to what is perceived. Can one really see a tree without identifying anything about it? Surely one sees, say, an oak, with its characteristically shaped leaves, and its acorns, and thinks of how they will all be shed in autumn. Our perceptions are inevitably shaped by our preconceptions as well as by our sensory experiences. In that case, even our purest contemplation is influenced by our interests and our culture, and so cannot be as pure as Heidegger supposed.

If Heidegger were a pure idealist, he might simply assert that the world is as we perceive it. In fact he is a realist, and allows that the things we perceive do exist independently of us, so the question of the relation between the things in the world and our perceptions of them can certainly be put and discussed.

The greatest failure of Heidegger's analysis is his refusal to take account of our scientific knowledge of the causes of our perceptions of the world. This seems entirely at odds with his naive faith in our ability to perceive the world as it truly is. As Frederick Olafson has remarked, Heidegger has not much discussed the problem of error (Olafson, 1987, p. 46). What he has said about it concerns errors which we detect and can usually correct in day-to-day situations. He rightly says that to identify these and correct them, we must assume certain other observed facts about the world to be true (ibid., p. 47). For instance we know the stick in the water is not really bent, because we know it was straight when we inserted it, and that water regularly produces such distortions in the appearance of things thrust into it. The accuracy of all our perceptions of the world cannot be challenged on the basis of occasional errors such as these. Their accuracy can be challenged, however, when one notes that perceptions are mediated by sensory organs and electrical impulses, so that the direct access we seem to have to things in the world is in fact absent. Heidegger does not seem to have discussed this fact at all.

How could he possibly respond? He might say that scientific theories are themselves built upon observations interpreted realistically in the manner he has described, and that if science is to continue we must continue to allow that these do indeed give us access to the nature of the world. The alternative I suggest is that while we remain confident about the content of our perceptions, we treat their interpretation as a matter to be investigated. Some we we will explain by saying that they were caused by objects like those they contain. Others may require a different explanation, as distortions or illusions. The vividness and detail of a perception is certainly no guarantee of its correctness. The truth of an interpretation of a perception, as has been said, depends not on how it was reached, but on whether its observable implications could all be satisfied.

Heidegger was wedded to a certain approach in his understanding of the world, that of hermeneutic phenomenology, and there is no room in this for a careful consideration of the impact of scientific discoveries upon everyday beliefs. It just analyses how the world appears to us in everyday perception. In this respect, his is an extraordinary achievement. It is just a pity he did not reflect more critically upon his conclusions. Instead he developed his theory of truth into a praise of poetry and an attack upon unbridled technology.

Truth as consensus

Some writers have noticed that when people assert that a sentence is true, they often seem to imply that it can be rationally defended. Historians certainly claim they can rationally defend their descriptions of the past. Defend them as what? It seems all you can defend them as is entailed by the evidence. How could you defend the claim that they describe what actually happened?

Several writers have espoused this theory of truth, namely that to call a statement true is to say that it would be agreed upon by people who rationally investigate it. Kuhn, Rorty and Habermas come to mind (Kuhn, 1970, p. 200; Rorty, 1991, pp. 129–32). One thing they all agree is that there is no final standard of rational inference which must be employed. Kuhn pointed out that people give different weight to the various virtues of theories, 'accuracy, simplicity, fruitfulness and the like', and that there is no correct way of judging theories (pp. 199–200).

Habermas has developed this approach to the analysis of truth most fully. He did so in the context of an inquiry into communication. When people communicate, they normally imply that what they say is true (McCarthy, 1984, p. 280). What they mean by this, he said, is not merely that there is a consensus about it, because that consensus might be achieved by some sort of compulsion or for some particular purpose. Rather, in calling a statement true, people mean that well-motivated rational people would eventually agree with what was said, if they investigated it freely and at length (p. 308). Such people, he said, are in an 'ideal speech situation'. Habermas allows that the investigators may even query the available frameworks of thought, belief and argument (pp. 305–6). He requires that the consensus be well grounded, that it be based upon evidence and argument, and not just, say, convenience (p. 307). Habermas allows that the statements people call true today might be refuted tomorrow. Our assertions of truth are fallible. It is just that in calling a statement true we mean that it will be accepted by rational inquirers in an ideal speech situation (pp. 291–310).

One useful feature of this theory is that it relates truth to justification. Metaphysical realists admit that things could exist of which people have no knowledge, but clearly we can know absolutely nothing about such things. True descriptions of the world are ones which would conceivably be justified on the basis of experience. To say that a description of the world is true does not mean, on this analysis, that it will be agreed upon by rational inquirers in an ideal speech situation, for they might always lack the evidence needed to prove it. For instance, it could be true that people exist in a remote part of the universe, yet rational inquirers may never be in a position to agree that they do. To say it is true that they exist is to say that were one to get to their planet, then one would perceive them; but if their planet is very remote that might never be possible for us.

The main worry with the consensus theory is that by identifying truth with rational consensus, Habermas and the others fail to capture all that is meant by saying that a description of the world is true. We mean, not only that people appropriately placed would rationally agree about it, but that it is true because of the state of the world. True descriptions tell us of the state of the world. They are not merely reports of rational consensus.

Habermas offers an argument against the correspondence theory that statements are true if they correspond to facts. On this theory, for instance, the statement 'snow is white' is true if it is a fact that snow is white. The trouble is, says Habermas, that facts are linguistically constructed, always hitched up to 'that' clauses. They are not related to things in the world (McCarthy, 1984, p. 302).

This, I think, misrepresents what is meant by corresponding to a fact. A 'fact' can be either a sentence which is true, or a state of affairs in the world. When it is said that 'snow is white' is true if it is a fact that snow is white, the word 'fact' is being used to denote a state of affairs in the world which could give rise to certain perceptions, and which is accurately described by the sentence 'snow is white'.

Habermas gives the impression that people think rationally in order to arrive at consensus. But that is not the chief aim of rational thought. Rather we think rationally in the belief that this is how we are most likely to discover truths about the world in which we live. We need to know how the world is, if we are to predict and control events successfully. Survival takes precedence over consensus. There is no good reason for Habermas to deny that well-supported historical descriptions are true, that is, are often very accurate descriptions of what has actually happened.

Supporters of Habermas might make two or three points in his defence. First, some might say that Habermas' account captures the aim of historical, indeed of all, inquiry quite admirably. For historians do inquire into the past by means of a rational conversation with their colleagues, and hope by arguing strenuously on the basis of evidence to persuade them to agree with their descriptions of the past. If some stubborn colleagues will not be moved, then does not the convinced historian think that eventually people will see it her way, so that the truth will be established? It thus seems quite right to say that historians aim at truth in the shape of ultimate consensus among rational people on the basis of evidence.

People who say this confuse what warrants us thinking an historical description true, and what is meant by saying it is true. As I have just shown, the two are quite different. We can imagine many descriptions of the world being true which will never be agreed upon for lack of evidence, and perhaps also because people adopt different epistemic principles. There are innumerable events which people witnessed in the past, of which we have no evidence, and there are also events which people could have witnessed but did not, for which there is no evidence. Descriptions of all these events could be true by chance, without any rational consensus. Furthermore, it makes sense to say that people might, on the basis of partial, inadequate evidence, all rationally agree upon a description of the world which is in fact false. Rational consensus might warrant belief in the truth of an historical description, but the doctrine of fallibility, accepted by me and many others, asserts that even descriptions which are commonly agreed could possibly be false. What makes a description true or false is a state of the world, which people may or may not have described correctly.

The repeated confusion between the truth conditions and the assertibility conditions of historical statements may be explained thus. In statements about the present world, we can often check out the truth conditions by observation. In that case, the conditions which warrant the statement are reports of its truth conditions, which are states of the world. Here it is easy to conflate the two, so that the assertibility conditions seem to be the truth conditions, though really they are just reports of the truth conditions. After a while it becomes easy to think that the truth conditions of a statement are just those conditions which warrant belief in it. But they are not. The truth of historical descriptions does not lie in agreement about their assertibility, but depends upon whether the world was as they describe it.

This brings us to the second point which a defender of Habermas might make. What precisely is meant by saying that a description of the world could be true even though nobody was ever in a position to verify the fact? The idea seems unintelligible. If there is no warrant for calling a statement true, what is meant by doing so?

The answer is simple. To call a statement about the world true means that if someone were in the relevant position, they could perceive the events it describes, or perceive evidence from which the events could be inferred. For example, suppose it is true that Caesar scratched his head before deciding to cross the Rubicon with his troops. There may be no evidence of this fact, so that belief in it will never be warranted. But if it were true, then had someone been near Caesar at the time she would have perceived him scratching his head. That is what is meant by saying the statement is true.

There is a third point which a supporter of Habermas might want to make. If truth is not a product of consensus, but can generally be reached by inference from adequate evidence, will that not open the way for self-styled experts to dictate our knowledge of the past, imposing their views on the community in a somewhat dictatorial manner? One of the attractions of Habermas' view, they might say, is that it encourages the participation of all in the determination of knowledge, and so offers some protection from tyranny.

One has only to study national histories, especially of wars, to see how history is misused in the interests of national power. Leaders often use a distorted history to justify their bellicose, economic or patriarchal ambitions. There is a constant need to prevent history being left in the hands of a few, who can turn it to their own advantage. Everyone should be free to examine what historians say, and to have their opinions taken seriously. An ideal speech situation is a vital condition of democracy and freedom.

But this does not mean Habermas' analysis of truth is correct. He offers it as an analysis of current practice, not just of how people decide what is true, but of what they mean by 'true'. It remains the case that when people call a statement true, they do not mean that it will ultimately be agreed upon. His account of the meaning of 'true' is mistaken. (For another critical discussion of Habermas' theory of truth, see Braaten, 1991, ch. 2.)

What conclusions can be drawn from this discussion of the truth of historical descriptions? Those who have written about cultural relativism and about the relation between language and reality have given us reasons to qualify the claims we make about historical descriptions. Even when they are well supported by evidence, they could be couched in rather inaccurate terms, and they certainly do not convey the full complexity of what happened. Nevertheless, we have reason to think that they often provide fairly accurate, if somewhat general accounts of what happened.

Those who remain sceptical of historical descriptions have focused on the cultural and linguistic constraints upon historical inquiry, but have not examined adequately the relation between descriptions of evidence and the real world, or between sound inductions and the real world. It is often reasonable to say that historians have correctly perceived and described the evidence before them; and that they have drawn sound inferences from those observations. They often do tell us what it is reasonable to believe really happened in the past.

Those who deny that historians can know anything true about the world, sometimes seem to think that that can be accepted and nothing will change. After all, historians have no access to the past, so they can continue trying to make sense of the evidence, as they see it, just as before, aiming at coherence or consensus rather than correspondence with reality. Since they cannot check what happened in the past by perception, they cannot know whether their descriptions of it are true or not.

I have replied to these opinions above. What I wish to add here is that were historians not to be concerned about discovery of the truth, then the rationale of many of their practices would vanish. Why search for evidence of an historical period if it cannot reveal the truth? Why weigh alternative implications carefully and rationally? Why distinguish plausible conjectures from well-supported facts? What is the significance of the carefully 'constructed' accounts of the past which historians produce, if they cannot be regarded as largely true descriptions of what happened?

Someone might reply: but you yourself admitted that well-supported historical descriptions could be false. Why should we hold them to be true? The reply has been given already: they could be false, but those descriptions which are well supported by evidence are probably true. (For a discussion of adequate support, see McCullagh, 1984, *passim*.) That is why they should be believed.

If they had not been based upon a careful and fairly exhaustive study of relevant evidence, if they had not been based upon well-established particular and general beliefs about the world, and been arrived at by sound inductive arguments, then they would not deserve to be believed. But those conditions generally do yield reliable beliefs about the world, and the conclusions drawn in accordance with them are generally true.

Methods of historical inquiry are designed to maximize the chance of arriving at the truth. If they do not serve that function, they may as well be abandoned.

FAIR DESCRIPTIONS OF THE PAST

So far I have discussed the truth of singular descriptive statements in history. Such statements are true if one set of their possible truth conditions actually existed. Historical descriptions, be they singular, general or causal, are all meant to be true. In the case of singular and general descriptions, however, there is an additional constraint which historians normally respect. The descriptions are meant to be, not just literally true, but also fair representations of their subject.

The contrast between true and fair descriptions is not much discussed, but is easy to understand. If I say that my dog has an ear, an eye, a leg and a tail, that statement would be literally true. It has got all of those things. But the statement does not give a fair description of my dog, which has two ears, two eyes, four legs and one tail. As a description of the dog it may be literally true, but it is also misleading for anyone who reads it as providing a fair description of the dog. Normally people do intend their descriptive statements about the world to provide fair descriptions of it, though occasionally that is not their intent. The context of the sentence usually makes the intention clear.

In the past (McCullagh, 1987, p. 40) I have called descriptions which provide a fair representation of their subject 'true' in a second sense, meaning reliable. It can be confusing to have two senses of 'true' at work, so here I will drop the second sense, and call fair descriptions of the past just 'fair'.

Precisely what constitutes a fair description of a subject? There are several possible answers to this question. So far, all that has been referred to is the assumption that when someone describes a certain kind of property of a thing, they will try to give a fair overall impression of that kind of property. So if one is describing a dog's bodily parts one will not mention just a few of them, but try to give a summary of them all, so that the overall impression of the dog's parts is not misleading. It is not required, in this case, to describe other characteristics of the dog, for instance its colour, size or temperament. Then again, suppose you said my dog had bitten the boy next door in a very aggressive manner. That could have been true, but a very isolated incident, when the boy drove my normally placid dog to distraction by beating it with a stick. The sentence itself, however, is not clearly intended to be a description of the dog's nature. One would have to search the context of the sentence to discover how it was meant to be taken. If the speaker concluded that the dog should therefore be muzzled or put down, for example, that would show that the incident was mentioned to give the impression that the dog was normally aggressive.

For a description of a certain kind of property to be fair, it must present the predominant feature or features of that property. For instance, if a dog is mostly black, one could call it black without being misleading, despite a flash of white on its forehead. However, if there are large patches of white on the dog, one should admit that it is both black and white. It would be positively misleading to say otherwise.

This kind of fair description involves finding a fair summary or general description of one kind of property of the subject, for instance a fair summary of the parts of the dog, or a fair generalization about its temperament or colour.

Because we expect historical descriptions to be fair, we call historical descriptions 'misleading' if they are not fair, for instance if they ignore major features of the property being described, and thus give a misleading impression of the whole. The most common cases of such distortion are those in which a friend or an enemy describes the character of another person or another nation or race. Friends highlight the good points and overlook the bad, and enemies do the reverse. Each implies what is false, namely that the subject is either wholly good or wholly bad. A fair representation is a balanced one, and historians are frequently at pains to correct the imbalance of previous histories.

An example of very biased history is discussed in a recent biography of

John Churchill, Earl of Marlborough. Marlborough was a brilliant general and charming courtier in the reign of Queen Anne, early in eighteenth-century Britain. By assiduous diplomacy he maintained a coalition against France during the wars of the Spanish Succession, and won several great battles. At home he rose from comparative poverty to become the wealthiest and most powerful man in the realm. J.R. Jones has explained how several historians disliked Marlborough, none more than Lord Macaulay.

> Macaulay's hostile interpretation embodied not only early Victorian moral values but also the political principles and expectations of progressive, liberal Whigs. . . . For him Marlborough as a courtier and patronage broker belonged to an evil system, the Old Corruption whose remains liberal Whigs were eradicating. As a soldier-politician Marlborough disquietingly resembled Wellington, the arch-reactionary, and it was contrary to the principles of reformed representative government for the entire destiny of the nation to lie in the hands of a single man, and particularly a soldier.
>
> (Jones, 1993. pp. 2–3)

Jones suggests that Macaulay also wanted a villain in his history, and chose Marlborough for that role: 'he unsparingly caricatured Marlborough as an odious careerist driven by ambition, avarice and an unbalanced wife who manipulated Anne without mercy' (p. 3). In a review of Macaulay's work, John Paget revealed his 'artful selection of evidence', but Jones says that 'the fully documented refutation came in Winston Churchill's four-volume biography published between 1933 and 1938' (p. 3). He showed that Marlborough did not generally act from selfish motives, but that he was a devoted servant of the Queen. Jones notes that Churchill was also biased, in that he 'failed to recognise Marlborough's declining physical and mental powers' towards the end (p. 4).

I have said that a fair representation is one which does not produce a misleading impression of certain properties of a subject, like the character of Marlborough, by omitting significant features of it. Notice that there are two ways in which an historian can describe something. One is with a summary statement: for instance 'Marlborough was a selfish, devious man'. This is not only unfair, but actually false, because the truth conditions of such summary statements are, conventionally, that they provide a fair summary, not an unbalanced one. A second way of describing something is to present a detailed account of it which gives a general impression of one sort or another. For instance, one could describe all of Marlborough's acts which could possibly be interpreted as bad, and ignore all the cases of honourable behaviour. Such a description might be literally true, in that every sentence in it might be true, but it would certainly be very misleading and so unfair.

A fair description of a subject in the second sense, then, is one which includes all the facts concerning that property of the subject under consideration. At once a problem arises, for historians surely do not have to cite literally all the facts concerning the properties of a subject which interest them. Rather, they must cite all of them at the level of generality and with the degree of detail which they have chosen for their work. Let me explain what I mean, by elucidating those concepts.

Some historical subjects can be ordered in levels of generality. For example, histories of individuals are less general than histories of groups of people, and they in turn are less general than histories of complex social structures. Similarly, the history of a single institution is less general than the history of a whole structure of institutions of which it is a part. Again, the history of a single hypothesis is less general than the history of a whole theory, and that less general than the history of a whole world-view of which it is part. In art history one can detect the same kind of order. The history of a certain technique is less general than that of a whole school, and that less general than the history of the whole cultural movement of which it is part.

The principle of ordering in all these cases appears to be in terms of a part—whole relationship (Porter, 1981, pp. 88–98). Many subjects can be described at any of these levels of generality. Thus a political history could be about the whole structure of power in a community; or about some or all of the political institutions it contained (political parties, the houses of parliament, the civil service, government corporations and so on); or about individuals who wielded political power. There is, of course, interaction between these levels which has to be mentioned, but a history can focus upon just one of them. Group behaviour, for instance, is usually affected by the policies and action of its leaders, and is constrained by the overall social structure of which it is a part. For example, the food riots by the *sans-culottes* in Paris at the end of February 1793 were partly provoked by the refusal of the Convention to control the price of corn, as they had been requested on 12 February, and they were partly directed by the leadership of Jacques Roux (Hampson, 1963, pp. 162–167). The present point is that if an historian begins by describing the history of a group of people, say the Parisian *sans-culottes*, he or she should keep recording the fortunes of the group as a whole, and not lapse into recording just the experiences of the individuals who composed it. The latter can be given as illustration of generalizations about the group, but should not become a substitute for those generalizations.

The second respect in which a narrative should provide a fairly uniform degree of detail, if it is to give a fair representation of its subject is that at whatever level of generality it is being written, the narrative should maintain the same degree of detail. Having chosen the level of generality at which he wants to write, the historian must decide which changes in the subject he wishes to record: small-, medium- or large-scale changes. A. Goodwin, for example, writing a brief, compressed history of the French Revolution, recorded only the largest changes in the groups involved. He noted the insurrections of the *sans-culottes* in Paris during February and March 1793 as follows: 'At the end of February and beginning of March a series of insurrectionary *journées* in the capital, organized by the extremists of *Enragés*, pointed to the growing seriousness of the class conflict. . . . The most important of these sectional movements occurred on 10th March' (Goodwin, 1953, p. 148). George Rudé, on the other hand, writing a longer history of the crowd in the French Revolution, provided much more detail of the riots in Paris between 24 and 27 February, spending pages describing precisely when and where they occurred, and which subgroups were involved (Rudé, 1959, pp. 115–17). He tells the history of the *sans-culottes* in much greater detail than Goodwin, though at the same level of generality. The experiences of that group remain the focus of his narrative.

So to give a fair representation of a subject, an historian should describe the subject at the same level of generality and with the same degree of detail. If the historian does this, omitting no facts which would give a misleading impression of the subject, then her description of the subject will be fair.

Is an historian ever justified in thinking that he or she has produced a fair description of an historical subject? The answer is, it depends how much evidence the historian has about the subject. If an historian's knowledge of a subject is scrappy, not at all comprehensive, then he or she is not in a position to say whether any particular narrative account of it fairly represents it or not. But if the historian has abundant evidence of the subject, so that it is reasonable to suppose that nothing of significance about it is unknown, then he or she is in an excellent position to judge the fairness of any narrative account of that subject. The comparison is made, not of course with the subject itself, but with what is known of it, it being assumed that the subject really had the properties believed true of it on the basis of available evidence. Sometimes new evidence leads historians to admit that a previously held belief about the past was false. Although historians believe that their well-supported conclusions about the past are true, they also believe that it is possible that they are false. It is not irrational to believe certain things true of a subject just because there is a slight chance that those beliefs are false.

2 The truth of historical generalizations and classifications

In the last chapter I explained how descriptions of particular historical events can be true. Some philosophers of history are willing to admit that descriptions of particular events can be true, but deny that generalizations and classificatory descriptions can be. They say that general terms do not refer to any particular things in the world, but just represent an historian's way of conceptualizing things that have happened. This is particularly the case, they say, when historians use metaphors to describe events, likening them to something else. They argue that metaphorical descriptions lack any particular meaning, and so cannot possibly be true.

This chapter examines the reasons which have been given for denying the truth of generalizations and classificatory descriptions, and shows that they represent a misunderstanding of what such descriptions involve. Generalizations and classificatory descriptions can certainly be true.

Before considering the arguments of the sceptics, it might be useful to point out the kinds of statements whose truth is being discussed. A general term is a term which can have more than one instance. Whereas proper names, like Melbourne, Australia, refer to just one thing, common nouns, like 'city' are general, in that they can have more than one instance. A generalization is a statement about the world which can have more than one instance. Here are four common kinds, and there may be more.

1 There are general summary statements about what existed. For example: 'There were Irish Protestant champions of Catholic interests in the British parliament in the early years of the Union; in particular Henry Grattan' (Boyce, 1990, p. 34). There must have been others, but Boyce only mentions Grattan.
2 There are statements attributing certain attributes to members of a reference class. For example: 'English and Irish members of parliament gave Emancipation support', meaning they argued that Roman Catholics should be given the right to vote (ibid., p. 34). This means that some of those who were English and Irish members of parliament (the reference class) had the attribute of supporting Emancipation.
3 There are general statements of a causal process which happened again and again. 'Britain stood by Protestant Ireland in opposing Catholic Emancipation

(or at least the Lords and Crown did), because the Lords and Crown were convinced that Emancipation would be dangerous to the British constitution' (ibid., p. 39). Since the upheavals of the seventeenth century, it seems that the Lords were anxious that the loyalty of Catholics to the Pope might conflict with their loyalty to the Crown. This statement means that the Lords and Crown repeatedly resisted moves to grant Catholics the vote because of their fear of the consequences.

4 There are statements attributing a class of activities to an individual. For example: 'Daniel O'Connell was a parliamentary reformer as well as a defender of the Catholics of Ireland' (p. 38). There were many things O'Connell did to promote parliamentary reform, and to defend the rights of Irish Catholics. I do not think that a statement of a person's disposition is a generalization, because I regard dispositions as psychological states (theoretical states) which cause the patterns of behaviour which manifest them. So when Boyce writes that 'O'Connell was a radical', I am inclined to say that is a description of his character, in this case of his commitment to mobilizing popular support for fundamental changes, such as the abolition of the Union between Ireland and England. It is not always easy to tell whether a description is of a person's activities or of their character, because the two are so intimately related.

Classificatory statements use general terms too. One can contrast two kinds of classification. The first kind names a property that a thing has. For instance, 'O'Connell had a large figure, a robust style, and a penchant for the wounding phrase' (p. 35). Such a statement classifies the subject by showing it to be a member of the classes named as properties. So O'Connell was a member of the class of large people, of the class of people with a robust style of talking, and of the class who used wounding phrases. The second kind of classification classifies something as a whole, taking into account a large number of its properties. They name the kind of thing it is, rather than some of the properties it has. For instance 'O'Connell was a lawyer' (p. 35), is one classification of O'Connell as a whole. Boyce also says he was portrayed as 'the very epitome of the priest-ridden, irresponsible Catholic' (p. 35). This is another description of the kind of person O'Connell was.

There are several kinds of classificatory description of this second kind in history, classifying something as a whole.

1 There is the classification of individuals, like those of O'Connell just given.
2 There is the classification of a pattern of behaviour as an action of a certain sort.
3 There is the classification of sequences of actions as an instance of a kind of role, ritual or routine. The 'trial' and 'execution' of Fenian rebels in 1867 (Boyce, 1990, p. 146) are instances of common rituals.
4 There is the classification of a pattern of events as constituting some common kind of change. For example, Boyce remarked upon 'the growing confidence and claims of the Catholic political leadership' in the early nineteenth century, when there was also 'a marked rise in agrarian crime and the proliferation of

secret societies' (ibid., p. 281). The patterns 'growing confidence' and 'marked rise in crime' are quite common patterns of change. He called the Fenian rising of 1867 'a rebellion' (p. 146); and later said that a change in the system of government which affected the elections of 1886 was called by some 'a revolution' (pp. 206–7). These words name kinds of change as well.

5 Finally, there is the classification of some social or economic or political structure as being of a certain kind, such as feudal, capitalist or democratic. In Boyce's opinion, Britain in the nineteenth century 'failed to create a homogeneous nation-state. As H.G. Wells put it, "Britain was not a state. It was an unincorporated people"' (p. 295).

Although statements which classify something use general terms, and so could be said to provide general descriptions, they are not generalizations because they are describing just one thing or collection of things. Generalizations can always have more than one instance.

Historians often sum up what they know about an historical subject in generalizations and classificatory statements. These summaries usually present a general view of the subject which the historian thinks interesting. Different historians frequently describe the same subject slightly differently, depending upon their interests and the concepts with which they are familiar. It is quite appropriate to call these summary general descriptions 'interpretations' of the subject, meaning that they are one of several equally justified accounts of the subject which could be given, which provides the reader with at least the historian's opinion of the meaning of what was happening.

Because general interpretations reflect historians' interests so closely, it is tempting to think that they must be entirely subjective and never true. Detailed descriptions of an historical subject, of observable features of the subject for example, can obviously be true or false. But general conceptualizations of a subject seem to be a product of the historian's preferred conceptual scheme, and not to correspond to anything observable at all.

In fact general descriptions can be true or false, so long as they have identifiable truth conditions. Admittedly some general terms are rather vague, so it is difficult to decide whether they have been correctly used or not, as we shall see. Whether there was a 'revolution' in Tudor government depends upon the meaning of that term. Most general terms have truth conditions, otherwise they would be meaningless. A general description is true or false depending upon whether its truth conditions were satisfied or not. For instance, if a rebellion is organized armed resistance of the government of one's country, then the armed attacks by Fenians upon police and jails in Ireland and England in 1867 constitute a rebellion. That description of those events by Boyce is a true one.

One philosopher of history, F.R. Ankersmit, has argued repeatedly that general descriptions of the past cannot be true, because they do not refer to anything real in the world. He thinks that particular events are real, but that generalizations are just conceptual constructions, created by historians but referring to nothing real at all. I shall address his arguments for this opinion in the first section of this chapter. Ankersmit has not considered the truth conditions of generalizations or of classificatory statements, and the historical convention that they be both accurate and interesting.

Ankersmit and others have observed that in describing the past, historians often use metaphorical terms. For instance to talk of confidence 'growing' and of crime 'rising' is to speak metaphorically. To describe a change as 'a revolution' is to use a metaphor as well. They believe that metaphorical statements in general cannot be true or false, so that descriptions of the past which employ metaphors cannot be true or false either. I shall examine this ground of scepticism in the second part of the chapter, disputing a theory of metaphor derived from the work of Max Black and Donald Davidson in doing so.

THE TRUTH OF GENERAL TERMS

Ankersmit's discussion of general descriptions in history concerns classificatory statements, but the points he raises often relate to all general terms, and so to generalizations as well.

Ankersmit first presented his reasons for denying that general terms refer to anything in the world in his book *Narrative Logic* (1983). In Chapter 5 of that book, he presents the following analysis of the use of such terms. Historians study available evidence and derive knowledge of many particular facts about the past; looking at these facts, they acquire an idea of one or more patterns in them, conceptual wholes which are sometimes referred to by general terms; they then describe these patterns in their writing. 'For instance, terms like "Renaissance", "Enlightenment", "early modern European capitalism" or the "decline of the Church" are in fact names given to the "images" or "pictures" of the past proposed by historians attempting to come to grips with the past' (p. 99). Ankersmit calls the ideas of such patterns 'narrative substances', and says that historians view the past through them, as they might view the world through binoculars. But he insists that 'the past itself has no narrative pattern or structure'; the patterns are simply ideas in the minds of historians (p. 110). At one point he says that these patterns are unique to the field of history to which they relate (p. 109), but he is not consistent on this point. Elsewhere he says that 'concepts such as "intellectual movement" ... "social group" ... do not form part of the past itself and . . . do not even refer to actual historical phenomena or aspects of such phenomena' (p. 87). These concepts are general terms, not individual ones. He writes: 'generalizations do not express any truths on the nature of (socio-historical) *reality*; they only reflect regularities in how we have actually *decided* to conceptualize reality (in terms of complete [narrative substances])' (p. 160).

So far, all we have seen are assertions. What arguments does Ankersmit offer for his sceptical conclusion? Scattered through the pages of Chapter 6, the following argument is to be found. Historical concepts like the Renaissance (pp. 163–4), and the Fall of the Roman Empire, are defined differently by different historians.

Indeed, there is no such thing as the 'Fall of the Roman Empire' – to mention only one problem: *when* did the Roman Empire fall? In 395 AD when the Empire was divided into two halves, in 476 when Romulus Augustulus [sic] was deposed by Odoacer, when the Empire became Christian or when the urban middle class, the so-called 'curiales', disappeared?

(p. 176)

Quite clearly, Ankersmit says, these concepts are defined differently in different histories. Consequently, it is absurd to say that they refer to facts in the world. Rather, they represent historians' ideas about the past, not the past itself. The situation is quite different with regard to physical objects in the world. Our ideas of physical objects are 'very precise' (p. 174), and there is no dispute about their application. The known properties of 'chairs, dogs, snowflakes, heaps of old iron etc.' are almost always found together in the world, which is why we can affirm their reality (p. 161). He adds that 'The (types of) individual things we discern in reality are not simply given to us along with reality itself: types form together an intricate, constructed, relational network' (p. 162). Finally, Ankersmit denies that we can detect common features among different states, revolutions and so on, to arrive at general concepts of these things (p. 164), presumably because each instance is so different that they lack sufficient common features.

Ankersmit's argument centres upon his denial that there are any truly general terms in history. He thinks that historians describe individual physical events in their uniqueness, but that any configuration they detect in these is nothing more than an idea they have about them, an idea which guides the construction of their narrative texts, and so, in a sense, is embodied in them. In Chapter 7, Ankersmit says that the configurations represent the historian's 'point of view', which presumably means the historian's interests as well as concepts.

A case can be made for regarding some interpretations of the past as unique. Ankersmit said that each account of the Renaissance is different, and undoubtedly that is true. As Jacob Burckhardt wrote in his Introduction to *The Civilization of the Renaissance in Italy* (1944): 'To each eye, perhaps, the outlines of a given civilization present a different picture; ... it is unavoidable that individual judgement and feeling should tell every moment both on the writer and on the reader' (p. 1). The period of the Renaissance, he went on, 'may be studied with advantage from the most varied points of view' (p. 1). The wealth and despotic government of Italian states, he said, fostered an interest in individual powers and opportunities for advancement (pp. 81–2), which made the world of classical Greece and Rome particularly interesting and attractive (p. 105). He remarked that 'the resuscitation of antiquity took a different form in Italy from that which it assumed in the North' (p. 105). Italians embraced classical culture as a whole, whereas northerners took just a few parts of it which interested them. It certainly seems both that Burckhardt's vision of the Renaissance is unique, and that the Renaissance he describes is unique as well, though Ankersmit would not distinguish the two.

What Ankersmit seems never to have acknowledged is that different instances of general terms are always unique in detail, but that that does not prevent them from also being classified. He allows that there are really chairs and dogs. But chairs and dogs differ enormously. Indeed it is quite difficult to think of the general characteristics of all chairs. Is an upturned packing case a chair, when you sit upon it? Not only are there numerous breeds of dog, but each individual instance of a breed is different in small respects as well. The fact that they differ so much does not prevent their being instances of chairs and dogs, because they all share the essential characteristics of chairs and dogs.

Precisely the same is true of the general concepts used to characterize the past. Individual instances of them differ in detail, but all share the same common characteristics. Ankersmit declares that this is impossible, because there is no fixed set of characteristics associated with these terms. Every attempt to define them precisely, he says, 'can be successfully challenged' (Ankersmit, 1983, p. 166). One can do no more than point to various instances of them. Is this correct? I think it is a matter of degree.

Consider some of the classificatory terms used above. Are there common rituals like court trials and executions? Are there many cases of 'an increase in confidence' and 'a rise in crime'? Of course each instance of such terms differs in detail, but they are quite common enough to be employed with complete confidence by historians. They refer to historical configurations less complex than the Renaissance. But even the Renaissance was found to be not entirely unique. The historian C.H. Haskins, in *The Renaissance of the Twelfth Century* (1957), wrote that 'the Italian Renaissance was preceded by similar, if less wide-reaching movements', referring not only to the Renaissance of the twelfth century but also to the Ottonian renaissance under the German Emperor Otto III and to the Carolingian renaissance under Charlemagne. Each involved a 'revival of the Latin classics and of jurisprudence, the extension of knowledge by the absorption of ancient learning and by observation, and ... creative work ... in poetry and in art' (pp. viii, 4–5). Certainly each renaissance had its peculiarities. The Carolingian renaissance was based almost entirely upon the study of classical Latin texts, and had biblical studies as its focus. Those in the twelfth and fifteenth centuries studied Greek as well as Latin sources, and that of the twelfth century looked at Arabic writing in philosophy and science as well. Another historian, George Holmes, saw striking resemblances between Florentine culture during the early fifteenth century and the European Enlightenment of the seventeenth and eighteenth centuries. So he classified the former period as one of 'enlightenment' in his book *The Florentine Enlightenment 1400–1450* (1969), noting that 'its resemblance to some of the attitudes commonly regarded as characteristic of the Enlightenment of the seventeenth and eighteenth centuries has been stressed: the preference for a common-sense approach in philosophy, indifference or hostility to traditional religion and metaphysics [and] artistic realism' (p. 266; see my article on colligation (McCullagh,1978) for further discussion of these points).

It may be that some terms do not have universal essential characteristics, but their instances have what are called 'family resemblances', a number of features in common. The concept of a 'game' is sometimes offered as an example of such a term. But most have clear enough criteria to be applied with ease.

Once it is admitted that there are criteria for the application of most general terms in history, then the possibility of their being true becomes plain. A general description of the past is true if the criteria for its application are satisfied. For instance, there is a rise in crime during any period in which the number of incidents of a more or less agreed list of crimes increases. It might be difficult to find reliable evidence about the number of crimes committed in some societies at some times, but the concept of a rise in crime is clear enough. The meaning of 'an increase in confidence' is also clear enough when it refers to the confidence of politicians in pressing their claims. The criteria for these descriptions constitute their truth conditions: when they are satisfied, the descriptions are true.

There is no doubt that some classificatory terms are quite vague, and their vagueness can sometimes lead historians to dispute their applicability. It was this problem of vagueness which was largely responsible for the debate over G.R. Elton's thesis that there was a revolution in the government of England between 1532 and 1540. The revolution, as he described it, had two aspects. There was a revolution in the constitution of the state, achieved by parliamentary statutes, which gave the king in Parliament authority over spiritual as well as temporal matters, thus making Parliament – king, lords, and commons – for the first time completely sovereign in the land. And there was a revolution in the government administration, for Thomas Cromwell set up a system of bureaucratic government which permanently replaced government by the royal household (Elton, 1955, ch. VII; Elton, 1962). Elton took the word 'revolution' to refer to 'any changes which profoundly affect the constitution and government of a state even when they do not involve the systematic and entire destruction of what there was before' (1955, p. 160).

This description was accepted by the other historians in the debate, who used the word 'revolution' in opposition to 'evolution', contrasting sudden substantial change with slow, piecemeal change (Harriss, 1963; and Williams, 1963, pp. 53, 56). But agreeable though this account was, in debate it proved disturbingly vague. How great had the changes in government to be to justify calling them a revolution? If a government's constitution and administration continued to retain many features which were not new, perhaps the changes which occurred in it should not be called 'revolutionary'. Furthermore it was not clear whether one could say that a revolution in government had occurred when constitutional and administrative principles had changed substantially, or whether it was necessary for constitutional and administrative practice to have changed substantially as well. It proved easier to show that the principles of parliamentary sovereignty and bureaucratic government had been accepted in theory than to show that they had been entirely accepted in practice.

Critics of Elton's thesis, especially G.L. Harriss, argued that the changes under Cromwell were not revolutionary because they did not constitute a sudden change in the nature of English government. During the Middle Ages the Crown had repeatedly exercised authority over Church matters, sometimes in defiance of the

Papacy. During the fifteenth century the authority of parliamentary statutes had already been affirmed, at least over common law. And finally, there were elements of bureaucratic administration to be found in the governments of earlier kings of England, especially between 1350 and 1450, and elements of household government remained even under Thomas Cromwell. That there were continuities between the government of England under Cromwell and the governments of previous centuries, Elton did not deny; but he insisted that the changes both to the constitution and to the administration wrought by Cromwell were so substantial and lasting as to be truly 'revolutionary' (Elton,1964, p. 27).

What I have argued is that general descriptions of the past can be both meaningful and true. I am not arguing that every case of historical synthesis is a case of classification. Suppose one was to interpret the activities of Hitler as driven by a desire to create a large purely Aryan state under his command. That would enable one to draw together a large number of his utterances and activities into an intelligible whole, yet that desire was, mercifully, unique, if only because it referred to Hitler himself. Indeed, by classifying a period one is drawing attention to features it has in common with other periods, and these might not be enough to make sense of many of the events in the period. To see Hitler's Germany as an instance of a Fascist dictatorship, for example, is to ignore the significant racial ingredient in his policy.

In a recent restatement of his theory, Ankersmit himself raises an objection to it. If the Industrial Revolution is just an idea about the past, and not a real event, how can one ask for its causes? Clearly the question is not intended to mean, what caused the historian to employ that concept? (Ankersmit, 1990, p. 285). His reply is that it is inappropriate to use causal language about such historical concepts. One can give a causal account of the course of the revolution, he says, but not find causes for the revolution as a whole. Despite saying this, Ankersmit quite naturally refers to 'the beginning of the revolution and the period immediately preceding it' in the course of his discussion, which makes sense only if the revolution was indeed an event.

Once it is understood that revolutions involve sudden and extensive change, then one can sensibly regard the Industrial Revolution as an event centred on the sudden and extensive development of modern industry, and ask how such a development came about, as historians have asked for years. If Ankersmit's theory entails that historians cannot ask and answer the questions that they do, and have done for ages, that in itself is reason for doubting its adequacy.

Does the fact that historians produce different classifications of a period mean that none of them can be true? If one historian sees early fifteenth-century Florence as a time of classical renaissance, and another sees it as a period of enlightenment, does that mean there is no truth of the matter? Different descriptions of the same thing cannot all be true if they are inconsistent, but otherwise they can all be true. For instance, the same person cannot be both a mother and a father, but she could be both a mother and a doctor. If periods of classical renaissance and periods of enlightenment were inconsistent, they could not both be true descriptions of early fifteenth-century Florence. But they are not inconsistent, they just emphasize different features of the culture.

Complications arise when a culture contains strong elements of two inconsistent traditions. Burckhardt distinctly opposed Renaissance culture with that of the Middle Ages. In the Middle Ages, he said, people saw the world through a veil of faith and illusion, and thought of themselves as members of groups: a race, family or corporation, for example. In the Renaissance, the veil melted and 'an *objective* treatment' of things in the world was possible; and people thought of themselves as individuals (Burckhardt, 1944, p. 81). These two sets of attitudes are clearly inconsistent. But some communities, at the end of the Middle Ages in Europe, included both. How then should they be described? The answer is simply that if one was very dominant the community could be described as holding to that culture; but otherwise the historian must say that both were present.

I think that Ankersmit's denial of the reality of historical configurations and the truth of descriptions of them stems from a conviction he has about the way in which historians arrive at their accounts of the past. He writes: 'the "historical landscape" is not *given* to the historian; he has to *construct* it. . . . [Its structure] is a structure *lent* to or *pressed* on the past and not the reflection of a kindred structure objectively present in the past itself' (1983, p. 86). It seems that Huizinga's (1955) writing contributed to this perception (1983, p. 86). He, for example, chose to see the fourteenth and fifteenth centuries in France and the Netherlands as marking the waning of the Middle Ages rather than the birth of the Renaissance. This may have suggested to Ankersmit that the structure is in the eye of the beholder, not in the past itself.

What Ankersmit has overlooked is that both singular and general interpretations are statements which have truth conditions, and that historians are assiduous in testing their interpretations to discover whether or not they are true. Consider Huizinga himself. Allow that the culture of the Middle Ages was unique, a time of religious faith and chivalry, a time of fixed hierarchies in church and state and little social mobility. To say that this culture dominated a society is to say that these conditions generally prevailed. If an historian detected just a few remnants of them, it would be wrong to describe the culture of the society as medieval, no matter how salient they were to the historian. Huizinga began *The Waning of the Middle Ages* by suggesting that whether you saw the history of fifteenth-century France and the Netherlands as marked by the end of medieval culture or the birth of Renaissance culture was a matter of choice (in his Preface to the first English edition, 1955, p. 7). In the text of the book, however, he argued repeatedly that the advent of the Renaissance was much slower in the north than it had been in Italy, and that France in the fifteenth century was predominantly medieval.

The fifteenth century in France and the Netherlands is still medieval at heart. The diapason of life had not yet changed. Scholastic thought, with symbolism and strong formalism, the thoroughly dualistic conception of life and the world still dominated. The two poles of the mind continued to be chivalry and hierarchy. Profound pessimism spread a general gloom over life. The gothic principle prevailed in art. But all these forms and modes were on the wane.

(pp. 333–4)

It would have been wrong to describe the period as one of early Renaissance, for it was 'still medieval at heart'. Medieval culture may have been unique in that there was only one continuous instance of it, but it had general characteristics which predominated for many centuries. The prevalence of these made it true to say that the period was one which was set in the Middle Ages, albeit at their end.

Ankersmit says that sometimes the interpretation of an historical subject will direct the historian's presentation of that subject, without being actually formulated in words. One could, for example, depict fifteenth-century France according to an idea of medieval culture without actually referring to the concept of medieval culture, without saying it was a period which saw the decline of the Middle Ages. If there was no statement of the interpretation, then there would be nothing which could be true or false, since only sentences can be true or false. This is quite logical, but beside the point at present. I am arguing that general descriptions of the past can be true or false, not that such unstated interpretations can be.

Historians using general terms to classify things in the past want them to be both accurate and interesting. Problems can arise in meeting these requirements, as the following examples show.

First there can be problems finding words in one's own culture to describe structures in another. A fascinating example is the Chinese concept *feng-chien*, which had originally been used 'to refer, first, to the system of regionally delegated political power instituted by the Chou Dynasty [roughly 1122–221 BC] and, second, to analogous systems, actual or ideal, when these were discussed in later centuries' (Wright, 1963, p. 53). According to Arthur F. Wright, Chinese translators early this century used this term as a translation of the word 'feudal', though it is now agreed that this was quite inappropriate: 'the differences in genesis and structure between Chou Dynasty *feng-chien* and western feudalism, however defined, are so great that they quite outweigh the similarities and make the terminological equivalence more misleading than otherwise' (p. 54). But that is not the end of the story. Twentieth-century Marxist historians, and Mao Tse-Tung himself, have since taken to describing those ancient centralized bureaucratic empires as 'feudal', so as to fit Chinese history to the Marxist model (p. 54)! So here we have two related cases of misleading general descriptions.

When there are no modern concepts to describe historical configurations, then historians are inclined to adopt the concepts used in the period they are studying, even if this involves using a word from another language, like *feng-chien*. Obviously the historian has to define the term to make it intelligible to modern readers. Even this move can have its problems, however. Sometimes the word used in the past is used today with a different meaning, and if the differences are not carefully stated, its use can result in anachronism. Robert R. Palmer has noted that people in the eighteenth century used the word 'democratic' to describe the revolutionary movements of that age. But the set of ideas they referred to by that word was quite different from its associations in the twentieth century. For them 'the democratic movement was primarily anti-aristocratic', and contained no suggestion of votes for all (Palmer, 1963, p. 69). Another example is the use of the word 'slave' to describe the institution called *douleia* in ancient Greece. We think of slaves in colonial America and elsewhere, whose status was nothing like that of the Greeks. Having noted that fact, M.I. Finley considered using the Greek word *douloi* to refer to the slaves of ancient Greece. The difficulty he then encountered was that it covers and obscures important differences. The word *douloi* was used to refer to the helots of Sparta, the slaves of Athens and the debt-bondsmen of pre-Solonic Attica and early Rome (Finley, 1963, p. 23). Finley concluded: 'One should insist on breaking the concept down still further, on using different words for helot, debt-bondsman, and so on' (p. 23).

The second problem facing historians is that of deciding how broad or narrow should be the concepts they use. As well as being true, historians are anxious that general descriptions of the past be fair, that is, not misleading. There are two ways in which a description of the past can be misleading, as was explained in the last chapter. It is misleading if it ignores significant features of the aspect of the subject that it is describing; and it is misleading if it ignores significant exceptions to the description it is giving. For example, to say that 'people supported the government' could be misleading in the second way. Suppose some readily identifiable sections of the people supported the government, say the Greens and the Democrats, but not the Liberals and Conservatives, then it would be wrong to say 'people' supported it, for that suggests that people across the whole spectrum of the political community supported it. Furthermore, suppose the opposition of the Liberals and the Conservatives had grown to the point where they were in a majority and likely to defeat the government at the next election, then although it is true that quite a lot of people supported the government (the remaining Greens and Democrats), it is misleading to say that 'people' did, suggesting that they all did, or at least that a large majority did, which was not the case. Notice that the general description 'people supported the government' is strictly true in this case, though it is very misleading.

Some very general terms are misleading because they suggest a homogeneity which does not exist, and obscure significant differences. That is why most historians of Victorian England object to using the simple classification of upper, middle and lower classes, even though this was the classification used by people in that period. These three classes have existed for centuries in England, if classes are defined simply in terms of people's rank and wealth. However, in Victorian England new occupations and lifestyles came with industrialization, but these are not distinguished if one uses the broad categories of upper, middle and lower classes. This is what J.F.C. Harrison was getting at when he wrote:

Most Victorian writers, when describing their society, divided it into the upper, middle and lower (or working) classes. . . . Unfortunately the convenient threefold division stereotyped a view of British society which has persisted down to the present day, but which is more a statement of ideology than a useful description of social stratification. The three class model is inadequate for comprehending early Victorian society because, amongst other things, it does not permit sufficient account to be taken of the very important group of 'middling' people who were distinct from both the more affluent middle class and the bulk of the working class; and because it obscures the great diversity within the working class.

(Harrison, 1971, p. 23)

Harrison went on to distinguish within the working class highly skilled artisans, who were masters of their craft, the less skilled artisans, then the labourers, some semi-skilled and others unskilled (pp. 24–5).

Similarly, G. Kitson Clark objected to the use of the term 'middle class' (Clark, 1962, pp. 5–7), and in his description of Victorian society preferred to write of the 'upper middle classes', with an annual income in excess of £200, and a 'lower middle class' who received between £60 and £200 each year (pp. 118–19). W.L. Burn has made the same point. Writing of 'the hazards of over-simplified classification', he remarked: 'The class hierarchy was a fact but the variations within a given class were scarcely less important' (Burn, 1968, p. 22).

Another consideration in deciding what concepts to use in describing a society is that an historian will want to identify those groups of people that were very active in the period, and perhaps brought about significant changes. The middle class as a whole did nothing much in Victorian England, but Harrison notes that sections of that class agitated for reform:

Two movements illustrate the potentialities for change via middle-class efforts. The first, the Anti-Corn Law League, was an agitation to secure changes which benefited, in the first instance, the industrial middle class. The second, temperance, was pioneered by members of the lower middle classes but directed primarily at the working classes.

(Harrison, 1971, p. 168)

Harrison also noted differences in the support for the Chartist movement among different groups within the working class.

Within the labouring population divisions were created by differences of skill and earnings. Chartism was directly related to these varieties within the labour force, and faithfully reflected them in its regional peculiarities. Wherever there was a substantial number of skilled artisans ... a Chartist organisation on the lines of the Working Men's Associations was to be expected, with an emphasis on self-help, independence, and propaganda for universal suffrage. But in areas where there were substantial numbers of distressed handloom weavers, as in Lancashire and the West Riding, Chartism assumed an altogether fiercer visage and adopted a more strident tone.

(p. 156)

One way in which a general description can fail to be reliable is that it fails to distinguish striking differences within its subject. Another is that it fails to take adequate account of exceptions to it. An excellent example of an historian correcting a generalization because it ignores evidence to the contrary is provided by Peter Mandler's book *Aristocratic Government in the Age of Reform. Whigs and Liberals 1830–1852* (1990). Historians have long been interested in the way the aristocracy of Britain continued to have an influence in the government of the land during the period of the industrial revolution without incurring popular hostility such as that which found expression in the French and other European revolutions. It had been thought that the British aristocracy survived and remained to some degree influential in government by adopting bourgeois liberal values, setting aside ostentatious displays of wealth and excessive self-indulgence for hard work and investment in new industries and services. By keeping their heads down, so to speak, they avoided having them chopped off. Mandler discovered, however, that in the 1830s and 1840s the high aristocratic Whigs did not behave as Liberals at all. So he begins his book with these words:

> This book challenges the view that there was a smooth and inevitable progression towards liberalism in early nineteenth-century England. It argues instead that England witnessed a reassertion of *aristocratic* power in the 1830s and 1840s, in part at least because *popular* forces rebelled against the forms in which liberalism had been presented over the previous half-century.
>
> (p. 1, his emphasis)

Far from adopting bourgeois practices, the Whigs who ruled in the 1830s and 40s were of the 'extra-ordinarily wealthy, fashionable, and politically tradition-laden families', such as the Cavendishes, Ponsonbys, Howards, Spencers, and Fitzwilliams (p. 16). These grand 'Foxite' Whigs believed that they were trustees for the people, bound to defend their interests through parliament (p. 19). Consequently they supported those people who agitated for constitutional and social reform through parliament. While Liberals 'privileged commercial and professional functions' (p. 23), the aristocratic Whigs promoted constitutional and social reform in the interests of the lower classes. Mandler shows that 'a high aristocratic identity and its political tradition did connect the generations, throwing up a bridge between the ages of Fox [in the eighteenth century] and [Lord John] Russell' (p. 45), who introduced the Reform Bill of 1832. He explains how moderate Whigs, like Lord Melbourne, preferred minimal central government, leaving reform to local authorities wherever he could (p. 172). Russell and his colleagues, on the other hand, suspected local authorities of furthering their own interests at the expense of the people, and preferred to rule from the centre. So new organs of central government administration were created to enforce social reforms (p. 173).

The careful examination of political life which Mandler's book displays is used repeatedly to correct generalizations about the scene which are not supported by the facts. For example, 'the Benthamite interpretation' attributes reform to the middle classes, trying to appease protesters so as to prevent social disorder. But Mandler objects that the Benthamite interpretation still does not give adequate scope to the influence of political forces. Both low politics – in the form of pressure exerted by popular movements – and high politics – the autonomy enjoyed by landed politicians – need to be taken into account. Both these influences were evident in the formation of social policy in the early 1830s, when they were in conflict.

(p. 172)

In this case, a generalization about the causes of the reform process was shown to be inadequate because it left out of account significant causal influences. It gave an unbalanced, and thus misleading impression.

Mandler's book is a good example of the way in which historians are constrained to find generalizations and classifications which fit the detailed facts as they know them. It shows that historians are not content with general descriptions for which they can find some evidence, when those general descriptions are misleading by being unqualified or unbalanced. The descriptions they seek must be both true and fair. Certainly the general concepts they use are drawn very largely from their own culture, though they sometimes use the concepts of the people they are describing. But historians do not merely impose any general term which takes their fancy. They are looking for both true and fair descriptions of the past.

In the attempt to ensure that their generalizations are fair, historians have developed useful procedures of inquiry. They have recognized the need to use general terms which are precise enough to be tested, that is to have instances which can be clearly identified. From the social sciences they have learned sampling techniques, to acquire data representative of the whole population they want to describe. I have discussed the nature and significance of these procedures at length before (McCullagh, 1984, ch. 6), so shall not do so again now. Instead I shall turn to the last line of attack on the truth of historical descriptions, namely the attack on those which use metaphors.

THE TRUTH OF METAPHORS IN HISTORY

Several philosophers have remarked upon the frequency with which historians use metaphors in describing the past. H. Kellner, for instance, has noticed

the middle-level, regulative metaphors of history, which generate explanations rather than adorn them: the organic figures of growth, life-cycles, roots, seeds, and so on; the figures of time with their rises and falls, weather catastrophes, seasons, twilights; the figures of movement (flow of events, crossroads, wheels); the technical figures of construction, gears, chains; theatrical figures of stage, actors, context.

(Kellner, 1989, p. 8).

The classifications might not be exact, but you get the idea.

Kellner is inclined to think that every general description of the past is metaphorical, but this is not the case. Most describe historical events in a straightforward non-allegorical way. Some literal descriptions may once have been allegorical, like the 'mouth' of a river, the 'neck' of a bottle, and the 'lip' of a cup once were, but with repeated use these and others have lost their metaphorical force. Their truth conditions can be designated fairly precisely. Similarly, when historians write of population 'growth', political 'pressure', and economic 'depression', they are using language which was once metaphorical but is so no longer. These phrases are well-worn and their meaning plain; metaphors must be fresh.

Both Ankersmit, in Chapter 7 of *Narrative Logic* (1983), and Kellner, deny that metaphorical descriptions can be true, and for chiefly the same reason. Both regard them as conceptual tools for creating order out of the profusion of particular facts about the past, an order which does not represent any reality but is a construction expressing the historian's point of view. Ankersmit concludes that metaphorical interpretations of the past 'are not descriptions but proposals' that the past be viewed a certain way, and 'proposals . . . according to their nature can never be empirically true or false' (Ankersmit, 1983, p. 217). Similarly, Kellner adopts the view that 'history is not "about" the past as such, but rather about our ways of creating meanings from the scattered, and profoundly meaning*less* debris we find around us' (Kellner, 1989, p. 10). Again, he says: 'Historians do not "find" the truths of past events; they create events from a seamless flow, and invent meanings that produce patterns within that flow' (p. 24).

I have set out and commented upon Ankersmit and Kellner's arguments in this connection quite fully elsewhere (McCullagh, 1993, pp. 36–49). Let me just remark here that their central argument, as stated above, applies to literal as well as to metaphorical descriptions. As descriptions of historical procedure and argument, it is plain from the cases described above that these accounts of historical writing are quite inadequate. They pay no attention to the truth conditions of historical generalizations and classifications, or the constraints that such descriptions be fair. Certainly historians find patterns in the past, using concepts familiar to them, but then they test their general descriptions to see whether they really are true and fair.

There is, however, a special problem with metaphorical descriptions which should be addressed. Metaphorical descriptions are literally false, so how could anyone say they are true? Kenneth Cmiel, for example, reviewing the discussions about what should be regarded as acceptable English which took place in America late last century, wrote of a 'fight' between conservative, academic purists and those willing to admit new colloquial language and technical vocabularies. At one point he wrote: 'Critics and scholars locked horns over the relative importance of expertise and liberal culture' (Cmiel, 1990, p. 162). These descriptions are literally false. There was no fight, or any locking of horns: these words are used metaphorically. In that case, is there any sense in which Cmiel's description of what went on can be true?

There is evidence that Ankersmit agreed with Max Black, who said that a metaphorical statement is 'a verbal action essentially demanding an *uptake*, a creative response from the reader' (Black, 1979, p. 29). Thus, by calling the discussions between the conservatives and modernists 'a fight', Cmiel is inviting us to see some resemblances between a fight and those discussions, to find salient properties that they have in common. The discussions took the form of an aggressive contest between two groups, each determined to suppress the other. Ankersmit's account of historical interpretation fits this theory of metaphor very well: historical interpretations suggest ways of viewing the events they interpret, but do not seem to state anything true of them.

It is difficult to explain which features of a metaphor we pick out when interpreting a metaphorical statement. The several contexts of the statement normally provide important clues as to what qualities are likely to be relevant. There is the context of the metaphor itself, for instance all we know about fights; and there is the context of the utterance, in this case the discussion about what should be regarded as acceptable English in nineteenth-century America. The relevant characteristics of the metaphorical object are often salient, immediately associated with it, but they must also be relevant to the context of the utterance. For instance, one might think that the salient properties of wolves are that they are carnivorous animals, but when one says 'Man is a wolf', these are not the properties one normally means. Rather it is the wolf's greed and aggression, always on the lookout for prey, which usually fit the context of such a statement (Tourangeau, 1982, p. 22; see also Cooper, 1986, pp. 245–7).

If the relevant salient features of a metaphor really do resemble those of the subject of the metaphorical statement, then we commonly say that the metaphorical statement is true. Just as metaphorical statements are true if the relevant salient properties of the metaphorical object resemble those of the subject, so too they are false if there is not a close resemblance between them. As W.C. Booth has pointed out, Plato did not think that Thrasymachus had correctly described the relation between a ruler and the state when he likened it to that between a greedy shepherd and his sheep. In *The Republic*, Book 1, 342–6, Socrates objects to it on two grounds. The first is that rulers in fact do not nourish their people in order to use them to their own advantage, but rather work for *their* advantage, as a doctor does for his patient, or a captain does for his crew. His second objection is that Thrasymachus had misunderstood the characteristic features of shepherds, which Socrates said were not selfish, but were concerned with the good of the sheep (Booth, 1979, pp. 64–5). The relevant salient features of the metaphor thus did not, in Socrates' opinion, resemble the subject of the metaphorical statement, and so he judged it to be false.

Donald Davidson has argued that metaphorical statements have no clear metaphorical meaning, and so cannot be true in a metaphorical sense. They usually have a literal meaning, he said, and this is the only sense in which he thinks they can be true or false. He remarked that 'there is no limit to what a metaphor calls to our attention, and much of what we are caused to notice is not propositional in character' (Davidson, 1979, p. 44).

I think that Davidson's position is too extreme. Take his first point that 'there is no limit to what a metaphor calls to our attention'. It is usually possible to provide a rough literal statement of the metaphorical meaning of a metaphorical statement in a particular context, even though it is difficult to capture all the nuances suggested by it. The basic relevant salient properties of the metaphorical object can usually be stated literally, even when those properties cannot be fully described. We can speak of a fight as an aggressive contest for power, even if we cannot precisely define its qualities. Again, to say 'the lake is a sapphire' is to say that it is a brilliant, translucent blue. It may also mean that it is sparkling in the light, and has the regular shape of a cut jewel. But it certainly means that the lake is blue. As Nelson Goodman has argued, this statement would be false if the water were a muddy brown (Goodman, 1979, pp. 175–6). In defence of Davidson, Richard Rorty has suggested that in this case what is being judged true or false is not the original metaphorical sentence, but a new literal sentence inspired by the metaphorical one (Rorty, 1991, pp. 171–2, n. 27). We could, however, say instead that a metaphorical sentence is metaphorically true whenever an approximate statement of its metaphorical meaning is literally true. This, I think, captures our practice accurately.

But what about the inexpressible nuances of metaphorical meaning? Can they be true or false? Davidson supposed that the only things which can be true or false are verbal statements, or beliefs and ideas which can be expressed verbally. But the advantage of metaphor is that it enables us to communicate information when literal speech fails. To call a discussion a 'fight' is to suggest attitudes and feelings of each side towards the other, which no literal description could capture. Davidson says that because some metaphorical meanings cannot be expressed in plain, literal language, they cannot be true or false. But surely he is wrong about this. We can identify and recognize properties of things which we cannot name. For instance, we can pick out two matching shades of yellow from a variety of yellow objects and say that one truly resembles the other without being able to describe precisely what colour they have in common. Similarly we can compare the salient relevant properties of a metaphorical object with the subject of a metaphorical sentence and tell whether they correspond, even though we cannot describe the common properties at all precisely.

Max Black has challenged comparative theories of metaphor, of which mine is one, by denying that there is always some similarity between the metaphorical object and the subject of a metaphorical sentence. Black's point is that the ways in which the relevant salient features of a metaphor are true of a metaphorical object normally differ from the ways in which they apply to a primary subject. For example, if we say 'Man is a wolf', then, Black says, that means 'he preys upon other animals, is fierce, hungry, engaged in constant struggle, a scavenger, and so on'. But the way in which men prey upon one another, though cunning and ferocious, is not precisely the way wolves attack each other, with tooth and claw. There is not an exact similarity between the two cases. Black concludes that the attributes of a wolf are understood in a different way when applied to men, so he concludes that the meaning of the attributes of a metaphorical object change when applied to another subject (Black, 1962, pp. 41–2).

This conclusion is mistaken. We often say that things are similar when they do not resemble each other exactly. We may say, for instance, that trees resemble one another in having trunks, branches and leaves, but the differences between them remain striking. Resemblance does not require perfect similarity: rough similarity will do. The points of similarity are often indicated by general classificatory terms, like 'trunk', 'branch' and 'leaf', which can be used of a wide variety of instances. Similarly the attributes of wolves which Black listed can be seen to be instances of general kinds, for instance of preying upon another, and men can be seen to exemplify those general attributes, in their own way, as well. Black has completely overlooked the importance of abstraction and generalization in the interpretation of metaphors. If he had understood it, he would not have introduced the suggestion that metaphors involve a change of meaning.

Perhaps there are other examples which support Black's thesis. He has listed the following relations between metaphorical objects and the subjects of metaphorical sentences: '(a) identity, (b) extension, typically *ad hoc*, (c) similarity, (d) analogy, or (e) what might be called "metaphorical coupling" (where, as often happens, the original metaphor implicates subordinate metaphors)' (Black, 1979, p. 30). The statement 'The Lord is my shepherd' is an example of the latter. Let me consider a really difficult example for a comparative thesis, St John's frequent assertion that 'God is light'. What does that mean? The metaphor is used a lot in the first chapter of his gospel. In that context it seems to mean that just as light reveals the truth about what is in the world, so God, in Jesus, revealed the truth through his words. It could also mean that just as light brings life to the world, for plants cannot live without it, so Jesus' words bring life to those who receive them. For St John, Jesus is the Word of God, the revealer of important truths, whose words are a source of divine life, whom those who 'preferred darkness' rejected.

Here is a straightforward case of analogy, known as analogy of proportionality: just as light reveals truth about what is in the world, so Jesus revealed truths about God and humankind. Each reveals the truth in its own way, according to, or in proportion to, its own nature. Describing this form of analogy, E.L. Mascall explained: 'an analogy of proportionality implies that the analogue [predicate] under discussion [in this case 'reveals the truth'] is found formally in each of the analogates [the subjects, here light and Jesus] but in a mode determined by the nature of the analogate itself.' Mascall said that this kind of analogy is indeed involved in metaphors, where 'there is not a formal participation of the same characteristic in the different analogates but only a similarity of effects' (Mascall, 1966, pp. 104, 103).

So even in a difficult case such as this (the assertion that 'God is light') there are common predicates which are applied to both light and to God: both reveal the truth, and both give life, albeit in quite different ways. The metaphor is strained and difficult to interpret because the similarities between Jesus (God) and light are not easy to understand. But without them, the metaphorical statement would be meaningless.

Sometimes the similarities between a metaphorical object and the subject of a metaphorical sentence are between the relations which each has to something else, for example to the speaker. For instance, suppose you propose a plan to defraud a friend of mine, I might reply 'That plan stinks!' Then I mean that your plan affects me the same way as a bad smell affects me: it fills me with disgust and makes me want to move away from it.

There certainly are many different kinds of similarity between metaphors and the subjects of metaphorical sentences, but it is those similarities which give metaphorical sentences their meaning. Black's thesis that attributes of metaphors change their meaning when applied to primary subjects is false, as a careful analysis of the process of interpretation has revealed. Either there is a direct similarity, as between the quality of a good shepherd's love and God's, or there is an indirect similarity, which relies upon our capacities to abstract and generalize in comparing the two.

This is not to deny that metaphorical statements have other functions besides the function of conveying information about the subject. As F.C.T. Moore has pointed out, metaphors not only make us notice similarities between two things, but often suggest that our attitude to the metaphorical object should also be our attitude to the subject of the metaphorical statement (Moore, 1982, p. 5). If a good shepherd can be trusted, so too can God. This additional function is very important, but it is entirely compatible with the view that metaphorical statements have cognitive significance, and so are capable of being true or false.

Black has been unwilling to say that metaphorical statements can be true or false as descriptions of things in the world. At one point he defends this reluctance by explaining that he refuses to distinguish the world from descriptions of it. He prefers to think 'that the world is necessarily a world *under a certain description*', from which it follows that metaphorical statements 'constitute' new aspects of the world (Black, 1979, p. 39). At another point Black seems to identify the world with a person's perception of it, refusing to contrast the meaning of 'is like' and '*looks* like' (p. 38). In this case, to create a new perception of attributes of something in the world is to constitute a new fact about the world. All I can say is that most of us do distinguish the world from our descriptions and perceptions of it, so that for most of us it is reasonable to say that 'metaphors reveal connections without *making* them' (p. 37), a position which Black rejects.

Of course we have no independent access to the way the world is, but we do not equate its nature with our perceptions of it. Rather we say it has certain properties in order to account for our perceptions. Normally we assume a correspondence between our perceptions and things in the world, to explain why our perceptions have the characteristics they do. Given some scientific theories of perception, and the fact that perceptions are partly determined by culture, a naive correspondence theory is not acceptable. Nevertheless, we believe our perceptions are caused at least in part by the way the world is, and would deny that the world is itself constituted by our perceptions or descriptions of it. Only our beliefs about the world are constituted in this way.

I conclude that metaphorical statements can be true or false of the world. Cmiel's description of a discussion as a 'fight' is true if there is a resemblance between the salient features of a fight, and certain features of the discussion. There is no good reason for thinking that metaphorical descriptions of the past cannot be true, in a metaphorical, not a literal, sense.

In this chapter I have reviewed a number of objections to the assumption that general descriptions of the past can be true or false, and found them all unpersuasive. An examination of historical practice has revealed that historians are very conscious of the need to find evidence for their general descriptions, not only to prove them true, but to ensure that they are fair, not misleading, as well.

3 Descriptive explanations

Historians sometimes set themselves the task of providing a comprehensive, systematic description of some historical subject. Richard Pipes begins his monumental history *The Russian Revolution 1899–1919* (1990) thus: 'This book is the first attempt in any language to present a comprehensive view of the Russian Revolution, arguably the most important event of the century' (p. 1). Historians have described all manner of revolutions, not only political and social, but scientific, industrial and cultural as well. Other popular events for descriptive analysis are wars, both international and civil.

As well as events, historians sometimes set out to give a comprehensive account of the life of a famous person. Most biographies are designed to describe all the events in the life of their subject, at a certain chosen level of generality and degree of detail, from birth to death, though some confine themselves to the subject's public rather than the private life. Thus Alan Bullock wrote in the Preface of his biography *Hitler, A Study in Tyranny* (1952):

'I determined to reconstruct, so far as I was able, the course of his life from his birth in 1889 to his death in 1945, in the hope that this would enable me to offer an account of one of the most puzzling and remarkable careers in modern history. The book is cast, therefore, in the form of an historical narrative.'

(p. 7)

Notice that as well as offering a description of Hitler's life, Bullock plans to make it intelligible.

A third kind of descriptive explanation commonly found in history is of the structure of a society, and how it changed over time. In the Introduction to *A Social History of France, 1780–1880* (1993), Peter McPhee usefully summarizes different approaches to the subject. He says that Roger Price, in his book *A Social History of Nineteenth-Century France* (London, Hutchinson, 1987), 'adopted a thematic and structural approach, proceeding from the economic and demographic bases of society to a description of major social groups (élites, middle classes, peasants, urban workers) and the major agencies of socialization (religion, education) and, finally, some concluding remarks about politics' (p. 2). In contrast, Theodore Zeldin, in his two volume history *France 1848–1945* (Oxford, Clarendon, 1973–7), wrote 'about individuals and their idiosyncrasies: French history is presented by him as a kaleidoscope of stories, ideas and passions but not as a structured society experiencing broad changes and continuities' (p. 2). McPhee adopts yet another approach, 'focusing on social relations of power – the unequal bases from which people acted to change or consolidate their world', which he hopes will convey a 'sense of a past which people at the time experienced as the present' (pp. 2–3). He is particularly interested in the way different groups were involved in the French Revolution of 1789–95 and the Second Republic, 1848–51, and how they were affected by these great events (p. 3).

The three tasks I have just described, of providing detailed information about an event, a person's life and a society, are instances of what can be called 'descriptive explanation'. An explanation is an answer to a question. It is structured to provide the information which the question requires. Historians sometimes set themselves the task of providing a systematic, comprehensive account of an historical subject, such as an event, a life or a society. In responding to this task they draw upon some general preconception of the nature of the subject to guide them in selecting and arranging their history. One could say that the question they are trying to answer is 'What was this subject like?', and one answers questions like this by describing the subject. That is why it is appropriate to call histories of this kind descriptive explanations.

Although the avowed aim of descriptive explanations is to provide a comprehensive account of an historical subject, in practice historians seldom if ever do so. To begin with, they seldom know all the facts about their subject, because the evidence available to them, even when extensive, never reveals all. Nor do they even present all the facts they have discovered about their subject, for to do that would be very tedious, for them and the reader. Some biographies seem to get close to a complete description of all that the historian knows, and these are understandably condemned. The well-known verdict of Lytton Strachey upon large detailed biographies bears repeating:

> Those two fat volumes, with which it is our custom to commemorate the dead – who does not know them, with their ill-digested masses of material, their slipshod style, their tone of tedious panegyric, their lamentable lack of selection, of detachment, of design? They are as familiar as the *cortège* of the undertaker, and wear the same air of slow, funereal barbarism. One is tempted to suppose, of some of them, that they were composed by that functionary, as the final item of his job.
>
> (Strachey, 1942, p. 222)

Descriptive explanations are selective. They are structured to give a systematic account of their subject, but not an entirely comprehensive one. They are not designed to illustrate some theme or pattern which the historian has noticed in the subject: that is the function of higher interpretations described in the next chapter. Rather they are designed to cover all the main features of the subject, according to the historian's conception of it. This preconception is a general idea of the parts of the subject, of the normal relations between those parts, and includes an idea of processes which commonly cause changes in the subject. In describing an historical subject over time, the historian is expected to account for changes in it, drawing upon their preconception of the various ways in which such changes can come about. So descriptive explanations include causal explanations, which will be analysed in detail later on.

Because descriptive explanations are selective, it is reasonable to consider them as interpretations of the subject, as there is often more than one way of presenting the subject, even when the aim is to provide a systematic description of it. For convenience, let me call the facts about the subject which an historian infers from documents and other artefacts the 'basic facts' about the subject. In practice, historians collect a large number of basic facts about their subject, when they are preparing a systematic account of it. They are usually facts about what individuals and groups of people did, and the changes they brought about. These basic facts are, as it were, the raw material from which the historian will create the final product. The inferences which historians draw from evidence are, of course, couched in their own concepts, and usually reflect their interests. But that does not prevent their being true, as has been explained before. Historians normally discover far more basic facts about a subject than they finally use.

How, then, are descriptive explanations constructed? The general answer is that they are designed to illustrate some preconception of the structure of the subject, though the preconception will often be modified or replaced after studying the basic facts. Peter H. Smith has outlined some of the different approaches to political history.

> What constitutes political history is, partly, a matter of definition. It can be defined as the study of government: as the narration of laws and regulations passed by those in power. It can be construed as the study of institutions invested with authority. It can unravel ideas and conceptions about justice, order, and the role of the state. It can focus on the ways in which people choose their leaders, especially through elections and other analogous mechanisms. And it can deal with broad patterns of change, as in longstanding (but fast-fading) efforts to detect origins and levels of democratization or modernization.
>
> (Smith, 1982, p. 5)

After outlining some quite complex and sophisticated models of political change, of use in South American history, Smith said, 'I believe that political history will continue to develop new forms' (p. 27).

To judge the truth and objectivity of descriptive explanations, one must know how they are constructed. In this chapter I shall look at descriptive explanations of three different kinds of historical subject: events, lives and social changes. Each kind of historical subject is explained in different ways.

There are two strikingly different ways of referring to historical events which are the subject of descriptive explanations. Some events are referred to by means of a general, classificatory term, such as a war, or a revolution, for example the English Civil War and the French Revolution. Historians describing events like this will be guided in the selection, arrangement and summary descriptions of the basic facts by their preconception of the structure of a war or a revolution. Generally they will have a simple concept of these things. Wars are military conflicts between bodies of people in armies, navies and airforces, each side aiming to defeat the other. A systematic account of a war will describe the conflict in chronological order, at whatever level of generality and in whatever detail the historian has chosen. Similarly, revolutions are thought to involve a struggle by groups without power in a country to seize the power held by other groups, and once again the progress of a revolution can be followed chronologically. There is a certain amount of vagueness in these general preconceptions. For instance, should the civilian war effort be included in a history of a war; and should the role of intellectuals be explained in a history of a revolution? The answer is usually yes to both questions, because descriptive explanations are meant to make the events they describe intelligible, by explaining them. Occasionally historians have more theoretical concepts of wars and revolutions, such as those which are found in Marxist theory. They will then try to illustrate those theoretical accounts, but if the basic facts do not fit the accounts, they will abandon them.

The other kind of event which historians explain is referred to as a change of some kind, for example an increase in the power of a ruling dynasty. To describe events of this sort seems simple: the historian need only describe the main stages of the change, at whatever level of generality and detail chosen. There has been some uncertainty, however, as to how a major change should be explained. Michael Oakeshott and Maurice Mandelbaum have said that usually a detailed description of a change will explain it, and Frederick A. Olafson has said much the same. I shall demonstrate that this is not the case, if only because such descriptions would make no reference to external contingencies which often affect a process of change.

Descriptive explanations of a person's life sound simple enough, as they have a conveniently continuous, readily identifiable subject, which can be described in a chronological manner at a chosen level of generality and detail. Even so there is need for selection, as historians generally know much more about a person's life than they would wish to describe. Many everyday details are just too boring to be included. Those who are sceptical of the objectivity of history would doubtless think that selection depends upon the historian's personal interests, but a study of historical practice shows that this is not generally the case. Historians normally select events in their subject's life which they think will help to make sense of it, and also events that are of general or historical interest. These conventions have not been made explicit, and so are not always observed, but they are widely followed in practice nevertheless.

Finally, as has been indicated, descriptive explanations of a society are based upon some preconceptions of the general structure of the society. This fact raises two questions. Can such descriptions be comprehensive? They can, but only relative to a chosen preconception or theory of the nature of society. Second, can descriptions based upon preconceptions ever reasonably be judged to be true? I argue that they can.

DESCRIBING EVENTS

Defining events

Before an historian can describe an event, she has to define it, and this is not always easy. Even fixing the boundaries of an event can be difficult. Some, usually rather small-scale events, are readily defined. The proceedings of a meeting, of a trial, and of a football competition have easily identified beginnings and ends. Even some larger-scale events, such as election campaigns, strikes and battles are not difficult to identify. But very large events, like wars and revolutions, do not always have neat boundaries.

Take, for example, the Russian Revolution. Most historians write of two revolutions in 1917, that which occurred in February (according to the Russian old style of dating) in which Tsar Nicholas II gave up the government, and a provisional government of liberal and conservative men was set up; and that which occurred in October, when the Bolshevik soviets, led by Lenin, took power. It is possible to see the two revolutions as one, as Leon Trotsky does in the Preface to his book *The History of the Russian Revolution* (1980). As he put it: 'During the first two months of 1917 Russia was still a Romanov monarchy. Eight months later the Bolsheviks stood at the helm. . . . You will not find another such sharp turn in history – especially if you remember that it involves a nation of 150 million people' (p. xvii). Both those who identify two revolutions, and those who see one with two stages, can be justified on the common-sense assumption that a political revolution is the violent overthrow of a government.

Some interpret the word 'revolution' a little differently, and so give the Russian Revolution different dates. Sheila Fitzpatrick writes:

> In commonsense terms, a revolution is coterminous with the period of upheaval and instability between the fall of an old regime and the firm consolidation of a new one. In the late 1920s, the permanent contours of Russia's new regime had yet to emerge.
>
> This book therefore treats the February and October Revolutions of 1917, the Civil War [1918–1920], the interlude of the NEP [the New Economic Policy, 1921–27] and Stalin's First Five-Year Plan revolution [1927–32] as successive stages in a single process – the Russian Revolution.
>
> (Fitzpatrick, 1982, p. 3)

The main point is that historians first define events in terms of their general understanding of what such events are like.

Historians' preconceptions of the nature of an event, especially of those which belong to classes of events like revolutions, determine not only the boundaries of the event, but also its structure. Historians generally try to describe an event according to their beliefs about its structure, but these preconceptions are sometimes changed when the details do not fit them. It is notorious that Marxist theory of class conflict produced some quite mistaken views of the English Civil War, and the French Revolution. According to Marxist theory, progress in history is achieved through class conflict, and Marxists believed that feudal society would be replaced by a capitalist society when the bourgeoisie, the growing capitalist class, found feudal government and institutions too restrictive and tore them down, to replace them with a government and with institutions which suited their economic interests. Such a preconception led some historians to view the English Civil War and the French Revolution as such a class conflict. The point I want to stress here, however, is that subsequent examination of the details of those conflicts has led historians to abandon the Marxist model as inappropriate. This shows that if an historian's preconceptions about the nature of a society are clearly mistaken, on available evidence, they are abandoned for a more accurate account. When that happens, historians cease trying to exemplify a preconception of the subject, cease searching for a descriptive explanation of it, and instead look for a new general interpretation of it. Certainly any new account will be couched in concepts, either of the historian or of the people concerned, but if these fit the facts well, they will not be misleading, indeed they will provide a true description of that society. Christopher Hill's early work presented a simple Marxist account of the English Civil War, which both he and others have modified since. It has become plain that the war was not between two homogeneous classes, of an economically ambitious gentry and a decaying aristocracy. Rather, as Lawrence Stone put it, 'more and more the tensions within the society are seen to take the traditional forms of a political conflict between a series of local power élites and the central government, and a religious conflict between Puritans and Anglicans' (Stone, 1972, p. 30).

Similarly, the Marxist interpretation of the French Revolution by, for example, Georges Lefebvre, has been set aside in the light of detailed examination of the facts. He said that the bourgeoisie, having set up and dominated the National Assembly in June 1789, set about destroying the privileges of the nobility in the name of civic equality. William Doyle (1988, pt.1) has explained how subsequent research has undermined this picture of events. Alfred Cobban showed that the people in the National Assembly were not predominantly businessmen, but *officiers*, lawyers and other professionals. Robert Forster and others discovered that the so-called nobility were in fact capitalists interested in maximizing profit on their estates and in business investments, and were by no means exempt from state taxes. Even in the Third Estate, which Marxists assumed represented business interests, most of the wealthy derived their wealth from land, not business, so that they had some interests in common with the nobility. Colin Lucas thinks the revolution 'was a revolt against a loss of status by the central and lower sections of the élite with the approval of those elements of the trading groups which were on the threshold of the élite' (Lucas quoted in Doyle, 1988, pp. 23–4). If the nobility were going to confine them to the Third Estate, then they would destroy the privileges of the nobility. The debate goes on, but enough has been said to show that historians' preconceptions are not allowed to distort descriptions of past societies.

Notice that in these cases, the terms 'English Civil War' and 'French Revolution' are taken as referring to a series of particular events in England and

France which together constituted a civil war in the one case, and a constitutional and political revolution in the other. The Marxist preconceptions about them were about what general concepts should be used to summarize and explain what was going on. With the general recognition that it is mistaken to describe these conflicts as between two classes, the feudal aristocracy and the capitalist bourgeoisie, the search has been to find other general concepts by which to characterize the particular events which constituted the war and the revolution. It is not certain that only one general description of the events is possible, for reasons explained below. Several different analyses might eventually prove equally well supported by the facts.

Sometimes disagreements about the nature of a kind of event are not readily resolved. For instance there are several different ways of writing the history of science. One can describe a scientific discovery as the product of a course of scientific inquiry, including the false starts and failures of the scientists involved; or one can provide a cleaned up rational reconstruction of the process of discovery, rather like the reports in scientific journals; or one can explain scientific inquiry as a product of social and cultural influences bearing upon the scientists, who act in conformity to them. The basic disagreement seems to be between the 'internalists' and 'externalists': 'internalists imagine that knowledge and reason subsist independently of any social embodiment, whereas externalists see knowledge and reason as the epiphenomenal projections of social factors' (Fuller,1991, p. 234). The view of externalists has been promoted by those associated with what is known as 'the strong programme' in history and philosophy of science. Warren Schmaus has tried to bring the two sides together by pointing out that a scientist's 'cognitive and rhetorical values and norms' do explain their work, but that these themselves have been imparted by society (Schmaus, 1991, p. 198). While different conceptions of the process of scientific discovery continue, however, correspondingly different histories of it can be expected. Each should then be regarded as an interpretation of the event.

Sometimes the events which historians describe are quite simple changes in the property of something. The beginning of the event is the start of the change, and the end is marked by its completion. The causes of an event often precede its beginning, which is why histories of an event often begin with a background to it. The history of an event traces the stages of the change, and explains each of those stages. Its natural structure, therefore, is the structure of a narrative. As John Passmore observed, 'an event-description is a summary of a narrative' (Passmore, 1987, p. 73). (M.C. Lemon has given a similar analysis, 1995, pp. 70–77, 163–4.)

Many of the events which historians describe are simple enough to be described by means of a narrative, but some are so complex that the narrative form cannot easily accommodate them. It becomes more and more difficult to retain a narrative form as the number of agents involved increases. In some wars, for example, different armies are fighting each other more or less simultaneously; and in some election campaigns, different candidates are saying things which sometimes affect the result, simultaneously. Maurice Mandelbaum has made the point vividly:

In order to depict the political life of a society one cannot follow any simple narrative sequence. This is evident if one considers even a sharply delimited segment of political life, such as a single presidential election campaign. . . . Much that happens in a national election happens at different times and in different parts of the nation, and the ultimate outcome of the campaign, even in an age of rapid, widespread communication, may depend not upon what happens day by day, but upon where it happened, and by whom it is known to have happened, and how it relates to what the opposition had already claimed. In other words, an election, unlike a chess match, is not won or lost by a series of neatly arranged sequential moves and countermoves.

(Mandelbaum, 1977, pp. 30–1)

Comprehensive accounts of such very complex events would not easily fit a narrative form describing successive stages in the one subject. It might be possible to use a narrative, however, to describe those complex events which involved only two or three protagonists, interacting with each other. Most plays present such interactions in a coherent and comprehensive manner, and show how well it can be done.

Sometimes historians abandon a conventional concept of an historical event, not because the facts do not warrant it but because they come to see it in another light. In doing this they are providing a new interpretation of the event. Pipes, for example, saw the revolutions of 1917 as part of a process, a revolutionary movement which began in the 1860s and continued to find expression until the death of Stalin in 1953, when a counter-revolution began. 'Broadly defined, the Russian Revolution may thus be said to have lasted a century' (Pipes, 1990, p. xxii). However, Pipes went on, this process had 'its culminating period' in 'the quarter of a century extending from the outbreak of large-scale unrest at Russian universities in February 1899 to the death of Lenin in January 1924' (p. xxii). Even that period is going to take Pipes two large volumes to describe.

Reading a systematic comprehensive history of an historical subject, it can be difficult to tell whether the general conception of the subject is one which the historian has brought to the task without much investigation of the particular subject, or whether it is a conception she has developed afresh to do justice to the peculiarities of the subject. Sometimes the historian explains which she is doing in the preface to her work. At other times the reader has to compare other accounts of the same or similar subjects to see whether hers is novel or not.

Incidentally, critics might say that when historians apply concepts to the past in the ways we have noted, identifying events as revolutions or wars for example, they are not describing anything that is there but rather are figuring it according to a concept which they have defined. Some, as was noted in Chapter 1, think that history is nothing but text, and that complex events such as 'the Russian Revolution' refer to nothing real, but merely sum up a lot of detailed descriptions of the activities of Kerensky, Lenin and their followers. I have argued, however, that historical descriptions refer to things which could have been experienced. Accepting this position, a critic might still complain that in the world there were people and guns and acts of violence, but no such thing as 'a revolution'. A revolution, they would say, is an abstract concept in the historian's mind, by which the historian colligates, or draws together, a lot of facts into a familiar whole.

The response to this argument is that there is no reason to deny the existence of complex large-scale events, just because we do not perceive them with our senses as unified wholes. From the earth, no one can perceive the whole of a cyclone, just a succession of storms, but there is no doubt the whole exists, as satellites have confirmed. Consider the assertion that Australia is a very large island. The explorers who drew it as such were just making sense of a myriad of observations of its coastline. Of course they never saw it as a very large island, but that is no reason to deny that it is. Let me switch examples from objects to events. We do not perceive even medium-sized events as wholes. If you go to a dinner party, you can identify it as a whole, from the time the people arrive until they leave, even though you never perceive the whole duration, only instants of it. Similarly with a lecture, or a game of football. Some events have indeterminate boundaries, for example a public demonstration. Does it begin when, say, three people have arrived, or only when they all get there? Still, we can talk about 'the demonstration' even if we define its boundaries rather arbitrarily. All these events are sequences of observable sub-events, and they can be more or less definitely defined. It would be silly to say they do not exist because they cannot be observed as a whole. A revolution is just an event, of an even larger scale. All events are conceptualized as such in our culture, and other cultures might see things differently, though in most cases they do not. All concepts of events have their truth conditions, more or less precisely defined, and if the truth conditions are satisfied, then the event really occurred. The truth conditions of a few events are sometimes debated (they are a matter of linguistic convention), in which case an historian using such a term has to stipulate the sense in which it is being applied. There is no good reason to think that revolutions, as defined by the historians, did not really occur.

Explaining how changes happened

As well as describing each stage of the change which constitutes an event, the historian tries to explain it. There has been considerable discussion of the structure of explanations of historical change. Some philosophers have thought that if a description of the stages of a change is detailed enough, then it will provide all the explanation of the change that is needed. Michael Oakeshott, for example, writes:

> Change in history carries with it its own explanation; the course of events is one, so far integrated, so far filled in and complete, that no external cause or reason is looked for or required in order to account for any particular event. The historian, in short, is like the novelist whose characters (for example) are presented in such detail and with such coherence that additional explanation of their actions is superfluous. This principle I will call the unity of continuity of

history; and it is, I think, the only principle of explanation consonant with the other postulates of historical experience.

(Oakeshott, 1933, p. 141)

To understand Oakeshott's view, one must know something about his theory of historical knowledge. Oakeshott presents historical knowledge as quite different from practical knowledge, which has to do with means of achieving present desires, and from scientific knowledge, which is the study of general causes and effects. An important reason for Oakeshott denying that historians isolate causes of events, is that to do so would be to practise science, not history (ibid., pp. 127–9). He thinks that the historian's task is simply to describe the past world which the evidence obliges us to believe, trying as much as possible to make that world appear 'coherent' (pp. 93–124). Unfortunately Oakeshott does not explain what he means by 'coherent', but from the above quotation it would seem to entail the absence of contradictions and the presence of some sort of natural connections between events. For Oakeshott the task of explanation in history is simply to make a new piece of information fit into what is already known about its historical context, that is to make it cohere with what has already been inferred. It is not to identify causes of an event, because that is a scientific, not an historical, form of thought (pp. 125–33).

When it comes to explaining historical change, then, as the above quotation indicates, Oakeshott believes 'change in history carries with it its own explanation'. Once we know every stage of a change in detail, then there is nothing more we must know to explain it. He goes on to say:

the only explanation of change relevant or possible in history is simply a complete account of change. History accounts *for* change by means of a full account *of* change. . . .

The conception of cause is thus replaced by the exhibition of a world of events intrinsically related to one another in which no *lacuna* is tolerated. To see all the degrees of change is to be in possession of a world of facts which calls for no further explanation. . . . And the method of the historian is never to explain by means of generalization but always by means of greater and more complete detail.

(p. 143)

This is a plausible theory, because very often we explain changes in everyday life by giving a detailed account of how they came about. This must be recognized as a distinctive form of explanation. It is sometimes possible to explain a change by reference to a covering law: for example, to explain why the price of something went up as the supply dwindled by saying that that is what always happens when demand remains constant. But another form of explanation is that described by Oakeshott, namely one which provides a detailed description of the intervening process.

The main problem with Oakeshott's account is, as Dray has pointed out, that Oakeshott gives no clear idea of what is to count as a continuous process of change.

Indeed some would say that a natural process of change is one in which events are related as cause and effect, something which Oakeshott wanted to deny (Dray, 1964, p. 10; and 1989, p. 219).

Maurice Mandelbaum has endorsed Oakeshott's theory of the nature of explanations of historical change (Mandelbaum, 1977, pp. 118–19), but he qualified it in a couple of important ways. First, he admits that not all explanations of historical change take this form. He thinks it particularly suitable for general histories of society, but not for special histories of aspects of a culture.

> In special histories ... the explanation of the characteristics to be found in one or more works is through recourse to something lying outside these works themselves, for example, through an appeal to certain cultural traditions, or to the talent and temperament and unique experience of the person who made them, or to the impact of societal change. In general histories, on the other hand, the explanation of what it was that happened is given through deeper penetration into what did actually happen, just as Oakeshott and others have maintained.
>
> (ibid., p. 133)

Mandelbaum's second qualification is to argue that events related in explanatory sequences are normally related as cause and effect, but that this relationship can be detected without recourse to covering generalizations (p. 139). To defend this claim, Mandelbaum argues that the relationship between cause and effect is one which can be immediately perceived. Sometimes they are part of the one continuous event, he says, as when a tackle in football brings down a player (p. 54). Furthermore, he claims that there is often a correspondence between a property of the cause and a consequent property of the effect. Causal relations can be perceived, he says, by detecting that correspondence. The force and direction of the tackle moves the player to fall with a corresponding force and in a corresponding direction (pp. 58–9). When neither of these conditions is present, as in the case of flicking a switch causing a light to go on, then the repeated instantaneous succession of such events reveals their connection. Here Mandelbaum admits we need to recognize the events as being of a particular type (pp. 63–5). Mandelbaum sums up by saying: 'the cause of an effect is simply the process that terminates in the effect: the cause is the whole set of actual ongoing occurrences or events that resulted in this, and no other, particular effect' (p. 93).

Before looking more closely at the possibility of explaining changes by describing a continuous series of mediating events, it is important to note that historical changes can be explained another way. Suppose an historian were to ask why the royal Capetian house in France increased so tremendously in power between 987, when it ruled a medium-sized county, and 1328, when it governed, directly or indirectly, almost the whole of modern France. One way to explain such a change is to describe and explain the main stages in that change, and thus to narrate the growth of the house. But another would be to draw attention to the set of circumstances under which one would expect any house in feudal Europe to extend its power. Robert Fawtier mentioned some of these in the Epilogue to his book *The Capetian Kings of France. Monarchy and Nation (987–1328)* (1964).

Of the Capetian kings he wrote: 'all of them were intelligent hard-working men', who kept 'firm control of the succession to the throne', who 'were prudent enough to refrain from attempting revolutionary changes' but 'claimed from feudal society only what was their due'. They 'made good use of their numerous opportunities to increase their power and possessions; but they were never in a hurry and always had the good sense to employ force sparingly' (pp. 227–9). Similarly Martin Scott noted the general conditions of the Capetians' success in his consideration of their dynasty in *Medieval Europe* (1964). They were not led, like the German kings, to dissipate their force in foreign wars: 'Their frailty forced them to concern themselves with the affairs of France alone, or even more narrowly of the domain itself.' Again unlike the German kings, the Capetians developed their own administration, instead of relying upon the Church to act on their behalf, and this grew to become 'the highly specialized administration for the whole kingdom of France, which was to be the envy of other European rulers at the end of the thirteenth century' (pp. 155–6). General facts about the Capetian house such as these enable one to understand why its power grew so extraordinarily during the period. Any feudal monarchy which had these characteristics would be likely to prosper, so long as it did not encounter any insuperable obstacle either within or without its kingdom. This is a general truth about feudal government, and serves to explain the Capetians' rise to power.

The other way of explaining the growth of Capetian power is to describe and explain each stage of its development. It would soon become apparent to the historian, if she did not know already, that the power of such a dynasty depended upon its wealth, which meant the estates it controlled; upon the strength of its armies, which meant the number of vassals it controlled; and upon the efficiency of its administration, which largely meant the loyalty of its immediate vassals. So to plot the major stages in the increase in Capetian power means describing the significant increases in these things. How does an historian judge significance? It depends very largely upon the degree of detail which the historian wants to describe. A brief history would note only very large changes; a long history would have room to describe some of the minor stages in the process of change as well. As Mandelbaum put it, historians can describe the past on different scales (1977, pp. 15–17). A brief history would have to sum up a number of minor events, as Martin Scott did when describing the achievements of Louis VI (1108–1137): 'In a series of campaigns lasting for most of his reign Louis gradually subdued a turbulent baronage' (Scott, 1964, p. 161).

How should each stage be explained? Oakeshott and Mandelbaum's suggestion that changes should be explained by detailed description of a continuous series of events mediating them is inappropriate in this case, as it is to most historical changes. Historical changes are almost never continuous in space and time. They are not always physical, and they often occur in stages with temporal gaps. The increase in Capetian power is a case in point. The process by which the kings acquired new vassals and greater wealth and influence was not a smooth physical process, but the result of a sequence of very different and often quite separate events. Many vassals were acquired when their owners offered homage to the crown in return for royal protection. Eventually many of their estates were purchased or forfeited to the royal domain.

What is remarkable is that Mandelbaum was himself vividly aware of the discontinuities in processes of historical change, and was even reluctant to admit that they could be described by means of a narrative. He preferred to analyse complex historical events such as election campaigns as temporal wholes made up of diverse parts. Indeed he said: 'the model of historical accounts that narrativists propose is so over-simplified as to be radically misleading' (Mandelbaum, 1977, pp. 30–1). After describing the relation between cause and effect as one involving a continuity of some kind, however, Mandelbaum altered his account of general history. He was then prepared to say: 'The history of society . . . consists of a continuing strand of related events' (p. 115). In an attempt to reconcile these two views of general history, Mandelbaum went on to say that the continuing entity in general history is a society: 'In a society . . . one can . . . regard its parts as being the organizational structures that, together, compose it, and this structural way of viewing the parts of a society is wholly compatible with viewing it as the sequence of events that together form its temporal history' (p. 126).

This structural view of society, seeing it as some sort of unified whole, can readily be challenged, as it has been by those who see it as an arena of conflicting interests. But even if it is accepted, this view does not rescue the claim that explanations of historical change are provided by tracing continuities. Although the growth of the Capetian kingdom was fairly continuous, the causes of that growth were disparate events involving people outside the royal government. Now Mandelbaum is aware that sometimes historical change is the result of something happening outside the subject of that change. He allows, for example, that an earthquake or an invasion can alter the nature of a society. In that case, precisely what is his model of historical change? On the one hand he says that to explain an historical change one has only to describe that change in greater detail. This fits some cases, as when an historian explains a person's response to a situation by providing details of the agent's intervening deliberation about the best way to respond to it (p. 121). But sometimes the change is mediated by events which are external to the change itself. For instance, the impoverishment of a vassal might cause him to sell his estates to the crown; or the death of a relation without heir might result in their estates being bequeathed to the crown. Mandelbaum allows that 'in such cases the sequential structure of a historical account must be supplemented' by information of those external events or conditions which contributed to the change (p. 33). But he tries to minimize the fact that external events play a part in explaining historical changes.

Even when an earthquake or an invasion drastically alters the nature of a society, it is because the *society's* economy has been altered or the *society's* political autonomy has been overthrown that the effect has come about. When one seeks to explain *how* its economy was altered by, say, an earthquake, or *how* it was deprived of its political autonomy through an invasion, one gives further descriptions of these events: One traces the different ways in which the earthquake disrupted the economy, or one traces the outcomes of the battles that followed the invasion and the peace treaty that brought the war to a close. In all of this one has remained within the framework of the ongoing processes that make up the life of a society.

(p. 133)

Clearly the subject of an historical change remains continuous, but it is wrong to suggest that changes in that subject can be explained by staying within its framework. Historical change is almost always the result of external events, and has to be explained in terms of cause and effect. A continuous account of that change is simply not enough.

Another account of explanations of historical change which could be relevant here is that provided by Frederick A. Olafson. In his opinion 'historical narrative is to be understood as the reconstruction of a sequence of human actions within which one action and its consequences become the premise for a succeeding action and so on' (Olafson, 1979, p. 151). Olafson says that historians study human actions, and that narratives which describe sequences of human actions link those actions by showing how each action and its consequences provided a reason for the next. The relations between actions are thus rational relations, and these relations supply the continuity of the narrative. Like Mandelbaum, however, Olafson has to admit that historical narratives are not as continuous as at first supposed. Sometimes the actions of one person, group or institution are a response to those of another, not just a response to the results of their own earlier behaviour (p. 158). And even more damaging, Olafson admits that sometimes an important cause of historical change is not a human action at all, but a natural event. The example he considers is the explanation of the famine in Ireland of 1846–49, which was caused by blight, that is by the *philophthora infestans* fungus (pp. 152–3). He points out that the famine can also be explained as a result of the failure of the British government to respond adequately to the crop failure, but he cannot deny that the event was caused by a physical process resulting from a physical infestation. However, also like Mandelbaum, he attempts to play down the significance of this kind of exception to his theory.

> The specific scientific explanation which the historian borrows in this way will very likely have little or no connection with the rest of his narrative. . . . But in the main the occurrence of a potato blight is simply a fact that serves as an essential premise in the kind of explanation which the historian is really concerned to give. What has to be explained is what human beings did in the situation in which they were in their different ways confronted by this fact which was also a premise of their practical deliberations and of their actions.
>
> (p. 154)

Certainly rational explanations are important means of understanding human actions. But Olafson's initial claim that in historical narratives 'one action and its consequences become the premise for a succeeding action' is not always true.

Often actions are responses to events which are not actions, or even the consequences of actions, at all.

There is no escaping the fact that the continuity of narrative accounts of historical change is provided by the progressive stages of that change, and not by any explanation of it, either physical or rational. The causes of, or reasons for, each stage in a process of change are by no means always related to an earlier stage in that process. More often than not, they come from outside it.

The question which now arises is how are those causes chosen? In Chapter 7 I will argue that historical events are normally caused by a conjunction of people or institutions with certain dispositions and circumstances which trigger them. The outcome depends upon the tendency and strength of all the forces interacting at the time. Each stage of a change will require separate explanation, as each is often a response to contingencies. But often there is a continuing cause as well, a disposition such as the Capetian ambition to increase their power, or the desire of Irish people to survive a famine. Once such continuing causes are described, there is no need to repeat them in explaining each stage of a change. They can simply be assumed. Furthermore, if the reader also assumes the existence of conditions likely to have prevented a change occurring, then the historian will also have to explain why they were absent or ineffective.

Martin Scott's account of the rule of the early Capetians illustrates some of the points just made. First, it shows that the means by which the Capetians increased their power was not a continuous process. Louis VI, for example, not only subdued rebellious barons. He also exacted his right to produce, labour and rents from his subjects; offered protection to churches and towns outside his domain; replaced hereditary office holders with men dependent on the crown; and encouraged his son, the future Louis VII, to marry Eleanor of Aquitaine (Scott, 1964, pp. 161–5). Here is no continuous process, but a number of more or less contemporaneous policies which added to the power of the crown.

Second, the explanations for each stage of this growth illustrate the analysis just given. What explains Louis VI's victories over his barons? Why were his forces more powerful than theirs? The answer is that they had the support of the people, which the barons' troops lacked:

> In his struggle Louis was aided by the nature of his opponents, who seem to have resembled the bold bad barons of popular imagination. No great affection for the Crown was needed to support its cause against opponents like Thomas de Marle, who rejoiced in torture for its own sake. The royal cause thus gained not only popular sympathy from merchants and peasants, who saw the Crown as their safeguard against similar treatment in the future, but, what was more important, it gained the powerful aid of the Church.
>
> (p. 162)

So the crown had the support of the peasants, merchants, and the Church, and that, according to Scott, contributed to its success against the barons. To explain that support, Scott takes the causal chain back a link or two, by showing how wicked the barons were, and how fearful and opposed to them these groups were as a result.

To explain how Louis VI exacted his rights to produce, labour and rents, Scott has to inform us of the convention which made this possible in those days: 'the most tenuous claim could be converted into a firmly established custom by a judicious royal appearance on two consecutive occasions'. Once the reader knows what normally made it possible for the crown to collect its dues, the reader can then accept the explanation that King Louis VI gathered his by assiduously travelling around his domain (p. 162). Such travelling, by the way, is something one could not have assumed, given the comparative indolence of his predecessors (pp. 158–61), but once it is known, then we may assume that the king used his visits to enforce his rights over his vassals. I conclude, then, that historians explain how a change occurred in something not merely by describing the stages of that change, which gives an appearance of continuity, but in addition by accounting for each stage of the change in terms of causal processes which often refer to events external to the subject of the change being explained.

Finally, there remains the question of historical accuracy. How can descriptions of the past be considered true when they do not provide us with all the details of what happened, but just with more or less summary descriptions. Consider the sentence quoted above: 'In a series of campaigns lasting for most of his reign Louis gradually subdued a turbulent baronage.' Admittedly this is not a very detailed description. It does not mention the individuals involved, or what they did to each other. Like all general summary statements, it has a large range of possible truth conditions, and so is a bit vague. But the very fact that it has truth conditions shows that it can be true or false. If Louis did not fight and subdue his turbulent barons in a series of encounters during most of his reign, then the statement is false. The statement does not mirror the world in all its detail. But it does tell us something about it, which is useful for the purpose of providing a rough idea of how Capetian power increased.

DESCRIBING LIVES

Paul Murray Kendall, who has written some great biographies himself, writes: 'The serious biographer ... is confined within the adamantine limits of the biographic oath to tell the truth. ... [H]is mission *is* the unfolding of an entire life as it occurred in the real world' (Kendall, 1965, pp. 123, 136). Even Kendall is aware that this is an exaggeration, for he goes on to say the historian must follow separate strands in the life of the subject (p. 137).

It is, of course, quite impossible to describe 'an entire life as it occurred', for that includes more thoughts and actions than anyone could, or would, record. Mark Twain made the point vividly in the preface to his autobiography. The biographer can catch the words and acts of a person, perhaps, but never their thoughts, he said.

The mass of him is hidden – it and its volcanic fires that toss and boil, and never rest, night nor day. These are his life, and they are not written, and cannot be written. Every day would make a whole book of eighty thousand words – three hundred and sixty-five books a year. Biographies are but the clothes and buttons of the man – the biography of the man himself cannot be written.

(Quoted by Justin Kaplan, 1986, p. 73)

Criteria of selection

Historians have to select what to include in a biography. They will choose only those experiences and activities which they judge to have been important. Those who have written about biography have had little to say concerning principles of selection. They are inclined to say that historians either tell everything they know, in a big boring multi-volume life, or they pick out threads or themes in a person's life, and illustrate those. Leon Edel called the first 'the chronicle life', and the second 'a portrait' (Edel, 1984, pp. 176–7). He himself preferred a long life in which 'the biographer constantly characterizes and comments and analyzes, instead of merely displaying chronologically the contents of a card index or a filing cabinet' (p. 183). His multi-volume biography of Henry James was of this kind.

It is tempting for me to accept Edel's classification of biographies, because it fits my analysis of historical descriptions so well. The 'chronicle life' is a systematic comprehensive account of the subject, based upon some general preconception about the nature of a human life, which fits my analysis of descriptive explanation. The 'portrait', which picks out a few themes in a person's life, is a perfect example of an interpretation of an historical subject. There are indeed biographies of both these kinds, and my analysis is applicable to those.

However there are biographers who do something else, who aim at a true, fair and intelligible account of their subject without attempting to include all the events in their life. I note that many also include information about events which relate to issues of interest to readers today, and also events which illuminate some aspect of the society in which the subject lived which is of interest to historians of the period. These criteria of selection have not been stated formally before, and so are not well known or universally observed.

There are two things which historians notice about a person's life in order to describe and explain it adequately but not exhaustively.

1 They generally focus upon those experiences and activities which were important to the subject. If the biography is to be brief, this means choosing just the very important events; if it is to be longer, then others which were of some importance can be included as well. One can tell which events were important from what the subject said about them, and how much time the subject spent upon them.

2 Historians are also interested in the subject's personality, the attitudes and motives which influenced much of their behaviour. Assessing these is usually a matter of interpretation, as there is often more than one way of reading their life. Anyhow, historians normally describe activities which clearly manifest the subject's character. Furthermore, in order to explain the ideas and attitudes of the subject, the historian normally describes events in the subject's upbringing

which were of influence, even if the subject hardly knew of them, or thought them unimportant.

Historians also describe facts about their subjects which are of general interest. These also are of two basic kinds.

3 First there are facts which are of general interest today. The historian will include events in the subject's life which had important historical consequences, whether or not the subject rated them important at the time. They may include events of intrinsic value, acts of great courage, great insight, or great virtue. They also notice acts of intrinsic disvalue, manifestations of racism, sexism, and imperialism, for example.

4 Finally, historians frequently use a biography as a sort of window onto the world of the subject, to relate what was happening around the subject, and how those events were viewed by people like the subject at the time. Sometimes the subject is a major player in the scene, which makes their perspective on what is happening all the more interesting, partly because they understand it intimately, and partly in explaining their decisions and actions. Anyhow, historians frequently include an incident in the subject's life for what it reveals about the world, rather than because it was much valued by the subject.

To illustrate these points, consider some of the introductory remarks which Caroline Benn made to her biography *Kier Hardie* (1992). Benn was anxious to present the truth about Hardie (1856–1915). 'There are many records to set straight, including the fact that Kier Hardie was the first working-class Member of Parliament, the first labour MP, or even the first socialist at Westminster, when he was none of these' (p. xviii). She also wanted to produce a fairer description of the man: 'For in most biographies it is only the political Hardie we see. His family is invisible; his personality is one-sided, and there is total silence on several important relationships. Sylvia Pankhurst, for example, with whom he was particularly close, was not mentioned in any biography until the 1970s' (p. xviii).

1 Benn notices that Hardie's political life and work have been thoroughly investigated by previous authors, remarking that it 'inevitably, receives more attention, since the political dimension, and interaction with the public, was always the one most important to Hardie himself' (p. x). Biographers naturally focus upon the activities of value to the subject.

2 Benn judged that Hardie's determination to improve the lot of the working class emerges as the backbone of his life, the 'one thing Hardie believed in from first to last', his 'single purpose' (pp. xviii, xxi). She would, perhaps, not have explained the essay he published in 1908 called *From Serfdom to Socialism* in such detail, if it had not been related to the central passion of his life (pp. 242–5).

3 A number of Hardie's activities are judged of interest by Benn, not because Hardie achieved much by them, but because they continued to be matters fought for by others after he had gone.

No other activist of the left stamped humanitarian socialism so firmly into the political fabric; or saw the future so clearly, espousing changes in social provision, industrial practice and democratic representation, which came into common being, but at the time were treated as the 'lost causes' his *Times* obituary claimed he wasted his life supporting.

. . . people continue to fight for the causes he made his own: class equality, environmental protection, trade union rights, women's equality, popular democratic control of community services, production for need not profit, animal rights, food reform, equality of the world's religions, full employment, and above all, peace and disarmament.

(pp. xv, xvi)

Several of these causes are still matters of active concern, which makes his espousal of them particularly interesting. Benn later comments that 'Hardie, as the carrier of a unique and enduring strain of humanitarian socialism, has had less attention, despite the fact that the dilution of labourism and the failure of centralized communism has rendered his socialism more relevant today than at many times in the past' (p. xx).

4 Benn says that although she will re-examine Hardie's

early work in the trade union movement, his parliamentary campaigns and his role in the growth of the Labour Party . . . this account seeks to balance them with equal attention to the development of Hardie's religious and socialist beliefs, and his work for a wide variety of social causes, together with the ideological and practical struggles he encountered, and the agitation he conducted, in collaboration with (or in opposition to) a wide range of socialist, labour and progressive contemporaries. This is as much a story of a whole generation as of one man.

(p. x)

Although Benn wanted to produce a balanced account of Hardie's life, it is not easy to say what a balanced account means. It cannot mean balanced in the temporal sense of giving equal space to equal periods of time in the subject's life. Hardie's childhood is not described in the same detail as his adult years. It could mean balanced according to each of the principles of selection listed above: a balanced account of all the things the subject thought important; a balanced account of his main motives; a balanced account of all the activities which were of future significance; and a balanced account of his interaction with the major events and movements of his day. Perhaps Benn was aiming at all of these.

These criteria of selection direct and limit a biographer's task. Within them there is clearly room for both some selection and interpretation, so every biography will reflect the personal views of the historian to some degree. But the room for a personal perspective is much narrower than commonly assumed.

Explaining human behaviour

How objective are the explanations which historians provide of the activities of the subjects of their biographies? They usually adopt, quite uncritically, the view of human nature which is commonly shared. As people grow up, they acquire ambitions and attitudes which explain much of their adult behaviour. The following passage is typical:

> When Hardie was twenty-one over 100 men died in a neighbouring [coal] pit in Blantyre in one gigantic explosion, caused by the mine-owners' failure to enforce safety measures. Such disasters consolidated mining society in a way that those outside could never appreciate.
>
> Inevitably, improving matters began to absorb Hardie and he became interested in the collective associations which miners in Scotland had been attempting to organize since the early 1870s – the trade unions.
>
> (Benn, 1992, pp. 15–16)

Benn remarks that Hardie's experiences in an impoverished community in Scotland influenced him profoundly. They 'were the wellspring of Hardie's politics and personality. He identified with the poverty and misery of others to a degree that often provoked uncontrollable anger. His hatred for powerful figures who broadcast their Christian piety yet sweated their workers, was never assuaged' (p. 7).

Occasionally biographers use Freudian theory to explain some characteristic of a subject's personality. Hardie was raised at first by his mother alone, so Benn observes: 'if Freud be correct that the man who is his mother's favourite conquers the world, Hardie started with a stunning lead in the great oedipal drama' (pp. 4–5). Notice how tentative Benn is: she is aware that Freud's theory has been strongly criticized, and so cannot be applied without reservation.

Benn is aware that people acquire some attitudes from their associates. She notes, for example, the influence of Cunninghame Graham in weaning Hardie away from liberalism to socialism in 1887: 'to Hardie he was not only an ally but an important spur to Hardie's growth of outlook' (p. 47). Benn lists a number of Cunninghame Graham's views, critical of Liberals and Tories alike, which Hardie soon adopted. Contemporaries referred to the change as 'a conversion' (p. 48).

The assumptions upon which these explanations are grounded, with the exception of Freud's theory, are so well established as to be incontrovertible. People's attitudes are often emotional responses to life experiences; and are sometimes acquired from friends who hold them strongly. The historian's judgement is displayed in deciding which incidents and experiences were formative. Benn seems to mention all which could have influenced Hardie, and not try to weigh their relative importance. Her causal judgements do appear to be true. (For a full discussion of how historians explain individual actions, see Chapter 8.)

Some might disagree with the psychological platitudes just mentioned, because they believe people are free to decide for themselves what they will do, and are not moved by external forces. In my opinion we are much more influenced by our circumstances than such people allow. The extreme libertarian view is seldom adopted by historians, but occasionally it arises. An example is Richard S. Westfall's biography of Isaac Newton (1985). He objected to the Freudian framework adopted by Frank Manuel in his *Portrait of Isaac Newton*. Westfall confessed that he 'wanted to believe in the autonomy of the individual and the autonomy of the intellectual realm' (p. 184). Manuel's Freudian view, he said, 'seemed to attack my conception of Newton. Perhaps more deeply, it seemed to attack my conception of myself' (p. 184). Whereas Manuel interpreted Newton's ruthless suppression, as an officer in the Royal Mint, of those who counterfeited coins, as attacks upon surrogates for his detested stepfather, who had deprived him of his mother, Westfall 'treated Newton as the responsible civil servant, assiduously performing a significant task which was also his appointed duty' (p. 186). He concluded that his biography of Newton was, in a sense, 'a portrait of my ideal self, of the self I would like to be' (p. 187). It is strange that he defends his view of human nature simply as one he would *like* to be true. Perhaps he is aware that it is difficult to defend empirically.

DESCRIBING SOCIETIES

The way in which historians describe societies depends upon their preconception of what a society is like. The quotation from Peter McPhee's *A Social History of France, 1780–1880* at the beginning of this chapter set out three different views of society. One saw society as consisting of economically distinguished groups, plus agencies of socialization. Another saw it as just a collection of individual lives, so that to describe a society is to tell the stories of the people who compose it. McPhee looked at society as a place in which different groups have different power, relative to one another. Clearly there are several quite different general ways of conceiving of a society.

To reinforce the point, let me mention a fourth quite popular model of society, known as a network model. Historians generally describe societies by identifying the groups which composed them. Some historians, however, prefer to describe societies by pointing out the networks of relationship between individuals and corporations, for they say that these networks have great explanatory power. The experiences of a person, organization or nation are often a function of their place in a network, rather than the result of any other fact. For example, the fortunes of developing countries have been shown to be better explained by referring to their place in the world economy than by studying their internal characteristics (Friedmann, 1988, p. 304). And again, the persistence of dynasties of élite families within a society is better explained by reference to the relationships between their members than by looking at their individual characteristics. Members of the élite help one another retain their wealth and power; and they generally marry within the same class (Tepperman, 1988, pp. 411–12).

Networks are kinds of planned or unplanned social structures. They are usually described as relationships between individuals or organizations who intentionally interact with each other. The relationships themselves are not always intentional. Wealthy people might always give preference to their wealthy friends without ever being conscious of doing so. But some sort of regular intentional interaction seems to be necessary for two or more people or organizations to be linked in a network. There is no doubt that networks are important kinds of social structure, whose significance is still being revealed. But it would be wrong to imagine that they are the only form of social structure of interest (as S.D. Berkowitz is inclined to think: 1988, pp. 477–81). For example, the relative size of an occupational group can be very significant. If there are too many labourers for the work available, then in many societies the price of labour is likely to fall. Networks may explain some social facts; and other social structures may explain others.

Given the variety of models of the structure of society, can one say that one is superior, or that they are all true? The general function of such models is to enable one to understand social practices and social change. One could possibly compare them for explanatory scope and power, but I suspect that different models will be found to explain different aspects of society well, so that each is of value for certain purposes. I have already noted some of the particular uses made of the network model. In the following passage, William H. Sewell jr. explains very clearly how different ways of classifying people's occupations serve different purposes. He is considering how to describe 'the occupational structure' of Marseilles between 1820 and 1870.

> Functional classifications of occupations can be of varying degrees of elegance and elaboration, from a simple dichotomy of white-collar and blue-collar workers to the detailed and complicated schemes used by modern sociologists or census bureaus. Here again, two different principles of classification can be distinguished. The first is to divide occupations by industrial sector – whether into very broad categories like agriculture, manufacturing, and services, or into smaller and more refined industrial classifications like building, textiles, metallurgy, transportation, public service, and so on. The second commonly used principle divides occupations by the type of work performed, whatever the industrial sector. Thus, in a classification of this sort, proprietors, clerical employees, and skilled workers employed in a single firm or a single industry would be ranged into three different occupational categories. Generally speaking, the classification by industrial sector is more useful if the main concern is description of the economy and economic growth. But for description of social structure and social change, classification by type of work performed is generally preferable, because the economic interests, lifestyles, educational levels, and other social experiences of an individual or group are likely to have more in common with those who perform similar kinds of work in other industries than with those who perform very different kinds of work in the same industry.

> (Sewell, 1985, p. 45)

One kind of classification was more useful for economic history, and the other more appropriate for social history. The implication is, I think, that different ways of conceiving of society suit different cognitive interests.

Once an historian has chosen a general model of society to suit her interests, then the adequacy of the particular explanation she gives must be judged relative to this model. J.C.D. Clark was aware that differences between his history, *English Society 1688–1832* (1985), and others on the same subject reflected different presuppositions. Clark said that his purpose was 'to argue against the familiar picture of eighteenth-century England as the era of bourgeois individualism by showing the persistence of the *ancien régime* until 1828–32' (p. x). The traditional picture, he said, rested upon 'a profoundly positivist, and ultimately economic-reductionist, vision' of society, which assumed 'that society evolved along rails ultimately forged by an economic determinism' (pp. 3, 4). This set of assumptions, he said, was developed at the beginning of the twentieth century by such as the Webbs, the Hammonds, R.H. Tawney, Harold Laski, Graham Wallas, and G.D.H. Cole, and was repackaged by historians of the 1960s and 1970s, with their interest in the economic basis of society (pp. 1, 5–6). Here is Clark's summary of their view:

> The main trend of popular and semi-scholarly writing on eighteenth-century England has been to portray it as essentially modern: a society of earthy, ambitious 'new men' fighting their way to the top; a world of thrusting entrepreneurs, eagerly adopting new methods in agriculture, commerce and industry; increasingly interested in empirical, scientific enquiry and the spread of rational knowledge; men zestfully engaged in the enjoyment of a new-found material well-being; commercialising leisure; resentful of traditional authority in Church or State; provincial men, Dissenters or sceptics in religion; hard realists in politics, thriving on the spoils of power, the mechanics of corruption and influence being the analogues of their commercial motivations; men with a strong streak of vulgarity, acknowledged and skilful social climbers; men who planned and realized England's industrial-democratic future.
>
> (p. 42)

Clark argued that this picture of eighteenth-century England 'hardly ranks above a parody'. He went on:

> this picture omits most of the features which made men of that time, in their various ways, different from us. It misses the religious dimension in which all moved, whether Anglican, Roman Catholic or Dissenter. And it misses those traditional, hierarchical, deferential forms which were neither antiquated, tenuous survivals nor mere veneers or superstructures on a reality which was 'basically' economic, but substantive and prevalent modes of thought and behaviour in a society dominated still by the common people, by the aristocracy, and by the relations between the two.
>
> (p. 43)

He remarked that 'Historians have, as a profession, carried their own class-perspectives back into the *ancien régime* with a near-unanimity which has hindered them from recapturing the world-views of peer and peasant alike' (p. 95).

What we have here is a contrast of perspective: some historians study past societies through the eyes of modern theory, whereas others, like Clark, try to capture past people's own view of their society. He quotes innumerable statements from people at the time saying how they viewed society, and their relations to others within it. If one looks at another history of society for the same period, Roy Porter's *English Society in the Eighteenth Century* (1990), the contrast in perspective is quite plain. Porter views the society through the twentieth-century concepts which interest him. These are reflected in successive chapters: socio-economic structures; political structures; family, education and the churches; economic processes; culture, high and low; manners, taste and morals; and the growth of industries.

It seems entirely likely that people's view of their own society in the eighteenth century was quite different from our view of it. It is unlikely that eighteenth-century folk would have made much sense of this description of their economy, for instance, which uses so many terms from nineteenth-century economic theory:

> Long before the eighteenth century the English economy had ceased to supply mere subsistence. Their ability to harness the surplus wealth-creating labour of wage-earners had long consolidated propertied ruling elites dominating pro-duction. The business of family formation, and of instilling values through education and religion, the interlocking of family, ownership and labour, production with reproduction, individual with community – all these ensured regular inheritance of capital goods, skills, drills and know-how from gener-ation to generation. These self-adjusting mechanisms provided against cata-strophe.
>
> (Porter, p. 185)

The difference between Clark's picture of society and that of 'materialists' might be explained, therefore, as the difference between the picture of society of those who lived within it, and the picture to someone living today, looking at it from without.

A qualification is necessary. The distinction between past and present perspect-ives, while real, is not always quite as neat as might be supposed. Even modern social theory admits that some groups in society can be defined only in terms of their rights and responsibilities as these were understood by the community generally. There is a neat example in Christopher Hill's writing on seventeenth-century England. In that century, the 'freeholders' in the counties, and the 'freemen' in the boroughs, had the right to elect the House of Commons. So these groups had political significance, but how were they to be identified? To answer that question, Hill had to explain what the words meant at the time.

> *Libertas* in medieval Latin conveys the idea of a right to exclude others from your property, your franchise. To be free of something means to enjoy exclusive rights and privileges in relation to it. The freedom of a town is a privilege, to be inherited or bought. So is a freehold estate. Freeholders and freemen are a minority in their communities. The Parliamentary franchise is a privilege attached to particular types of property.
>
> (Hill, 1972, p. 48)

Clearly these groups could not be identified without knowing how they were viewed by people at the time.

That is not true of all groups in a society, however. Some can be distinguished by their wealth, status and power, whether contemporaries were aware of the distinctions or not. And certain social processes can be described in modern terms, like those in the quotation from Porter above, which people at the time could not possibly have used. So many descriptions of past societies can be made which do not reflect the social beliefs of the people within them. Up to a point, the difference between Clark and those he criticizes could be explained as a difference of perspective.

Clark would not be content with this attempt to resolve the conflict, however. His point is partly that previous historians have simply failed to notice really important elements of eighteenth-century society, for instance the close relations between Church and State, and the patriarchal character of the relation between social classes ('the essence of patriarchalism was hierarchy and divinely appointed, inherent authority', p. 74). Past historians, he says, have viewed the society 'from below', with an eye to liberal developments in the nineteenth century. To correct their picture, he says, it should be viewed 'from above', and attention paid to continuities with the past, particularly with 'the continued cultural dominance of Anglican and aristocratic ideals and norms' (p. 77). Porter, in turn, is critical of Clark for being 'myopic in his apparent lack of interest in, even distaste for, so many of the areas in which the ways of life of ordinary English people changed dramatically during the eighteenth century' (pp. xiii–xiv). Clearly, what both historians want is a full and balanced description of the society, from either a past internal or a modern external perspective, which has been difficult to achieve.

One thing which this debate clearly shows is that once historians have adopted a perspective, either historical or modern, and have chosen a general model of the society they wish to describe, then they are anxious to produce a true and fair description of it. By describing one aspect after another, chapter by chapter, Porter evidently hopes to provide a fairly complete and balanced account of it, though he admits that the society was complex and irregular, and that 'No single social scientific terminology captures that complexity in its entirety' (p. 5). Both Clark and Porter wanted to produce a comprehensive account of eighteenth-century England, though their interests drove each to emphasize different parts of the society, Clark the continuities, Porter the sources of change.

Should they have expected to produce a comprehensive account? I think that a history of a society can only be comprehensive relative to a chosen theory. Suppose one viewed society as essentially composed of economic interest groups, then a complete social history would be one which described all such groups, and how they fared over the chosen period. Clark viewed society rather in terms used by people at the time, and they saw it as composed of various orders, nobility, gentry and so on, and religious groups. On reflection it seems unreasonable to require historians to adopt all possible theories in describing a society. To do so would certainly make for a complex, not to say confusing picture of the society. In practice historians normally use just one theory, and try to apply it comprehensively.

Now a new question arises. If historians are guided by a preconceived theory, what reason is there for thinking that their descriptions of a society are true? The point to remember is that theories use terms with truth conditions. If the facts about a society fit the theory, then a description of it in the terms of the theory will be true. Sceptics would say that historians simply force the facts to fit the theory, or see the facts selectively, purely in terms of their preferred theory, so that rather than describe what existed in the past, social historians impose their concepts upon it. Against such a claim there is the evidence of historical practice. In practice historians check and revise their theoretical descriptions of past societies against all the particular facts about them which they know. Sometimes they judge a concept inappropriate to a society, and abandon it. We have already seen how Marxist historians have stopped thinking of the English Civil War and the French Revolution as class conflicts. Instead they have looked for other concepts, more appropriate to the social relationships of those times. Historians are constantly aware of the need to check their general descriptions of society against the facts. The famous social historian Fernand Braudel put it thus:

In my view, research must constantly move between social reality and the model, in a succession of readjustments and journeys ever patiently reviewed. Thus the model is both an attempt to explain a given structure, and an instrument with which one can examine it, and compare it, and test its solidity and its very life.

(Braudel, 1972, p. 33)

Sometimes historians are content that the concepts they are using are appropriate, but find preconceptions about instances of that concept need to be modified. A record of this process can be found in Peter Burke's discussion of the model he brought to the description of society in Renaissance Italy (Burke, 1974). He wrote:

The working model of the social structure which has been used throughout this book distinguishes five main social groups: the clergy; the nobles; merchants and professional men; artisans and shopkeepers; and finally, peasants. Three of these groups, clergy, nobles and peasants, are the traditional three Estates, and can be defined in legal terms; the other two groups are more like classes, simpler to define in economic terms. But the chief criterion for distinguishing these five groups is not legal or economic, but social: The Weberian concept of a typical 'style of life'.

(pp. 280–1)

Burke noted that although all men who had 'taken the tonsure' were legally clergy, not all led the life style of clergy, performing the roles of friar, monk, parish priest, bishop and so on, but some lived like laymen. He went on to characterize the life styles of each group, by which its members were identified. He considered dividing merchants and professional men into two groups, but noted that they had many social features in common, in particular they were both represented in 'the greater guilds' (p. 285). Notice that by stating the criterion for distinguishing the groups he was describing, namely their 'style of life', he could examine and justify the general distinctions he made.

A little later Peter Burke queried whether the ruling élites of Florence and Venice should really be called nobility. Using his criterion of life styles to define social groups, he had to create a new name for them.

> It is worth moving from types to reality for a moment to point out the difficulty of classifying the ruling élites of Florence and Venice. . . . On the one hand it is difficult to call these groups 'noble' because of their interest in trade and industry, their ethos of hard work and thrift, their calculating mentality. On the other hand, it is difficult to call them members of the merchant-professional group, since they ruled empires, engaged in conspicuous consumption, put their names in a golden book (as in Venice) or engaged in the occasional tournament (as in Florence). It is possible to create a new category and call them a 'patriciate', but to do this is not all that useful, because we have to do here not with a new style of life but with a fusion of elements in two others.
>
> (Burke, 1974, p. 286)

The process of criticism goes on and on, so committed are historians to getting at the truth. E.P. Thompson declared that a social class should be defined as something which comes into existence 'when some men, as a result of common experiences (inherited or shared), feel and articulate the identity of their interests as between themselves, and as against other men whose interests are different from (and usually opposed to) theirs' (1968, pp. 9–10). In his famous book *The Making of the English Working Class*, he described the growing awareness of common interests among workers in Britain between 1780 and 1832. Geoff Eley has not queried Thompson's concept of a class, but rather his assumption that there was a unified working class before 1820. Rather, he says, factory and detail workers felt united, but saw their interests as contrary to those of skilled craft workers; and artisans did not sense any common interests with unskilled or casual labourers. He suggests that because all these groups were exploited by their employers, and repressed by the State, Thompson just assumed they would recognize their common interests. Thompson's account, he says, 'moves by grand inference from the actions and beliefs of an articulate radical minority to the implied solidarity of the skilled trades and beyond to the ascribed consciousness of the working class at large' (Eley, 1990, pp. 23–6).

It is clear from these examples that although historians bring concepts to the analysis of past societies, their application of those concepts is very critical. They are rejected if inappropriate, and instances of them are critically scrutinized. Historians use these concepts only if they correctly describe the social relationships which existed between individuals in the society being portrayed.

So far I have examined how historians describe the structure of a society, but have said nothing about how they explain changes within it. Generally they describe the main changes in a society, at whatever level of generality and in whatever detail they have chosen, and explain them in turn. I will describe common ways of explaining collective actions and social changes in chapters 9 and 10.

THE OBJECTIVITY OF DESCRIPTIVE EXPLANATIONS

Descriptive explanations answer the question 'What was the subject X like?', and the answer they give is structured according to a preconception of the general nature of that subject. The question 'What was the French Revolution like?' employs a concept of a revolution; the question 'What was Hardie's life like?' uses the concept of a life; the question 'What was British society like in the eighteenth century?' refers to a society. One could say that a descriptive explanation exemplifies the general concept mentioned in the question. It describes the particular historical subject as an instance or example of the general concept which the historian has in mind, for example the concept of a revolution, a human life or a European society.

Explanations are generally judged for their adequacy, according to whether or not they provide all the information requested. This can usually be judged objectively: for example, either the description of a subject does exemplify the general concept of that subject or it does not. The general concept attached to a term like 'a life' is usually that which provides the common meaning of the word, and the meaning is known to all educated users of the word. Occasionally the meaning of a general concept is drawn from a social theory, such as a Marxist theory of revolution, or an economic theory of society. In that case the historian has to indicate the sense in which the term is being used for people to judge the adequacy of the descriptive explanation which is governed by it.

Where there are several possible meanings of a general term to choose from, historians are most likely to choose one which reflects their interests. In that case, the consequent descriptive explanation can be said to be subjective, in as much as it is designed to exemplify a concept chosen for personal reasons.

As was explained before, the preconception of an historical subject includes general ideas of its elements, their relations, and how those normally change. If a particular subject exemplifies these things, then a description of it in terms of these general ideas is true. If the preconception does not fit the facts, then a description of it in terms of that preconception is false. It was wrong to describe the English Civil War as a class struggle because the opposing sides did not represent distinct classes. Because historians value the truth of their descriptions, they modify or abandon those which are proved false.

If a preconception represents part of a subject but makes no reference to other parts of a similar kind, as Clark and Porter's preconceptions of eighteenth-century British society apparently did, then the general conception does not provide a fair description of the subject. The historian who recognizes such deficiencies will usually supplement her accounts of the subject to make them fair.

The requirements that descriptive explanations be adequate, true and fair puts severe constraints upon them. Indeed, once the question has been asked, if the evidence is unambiguous and it fits the preconception, then there is often little room for personal inclination significantly to determine the resulting description. The basic elements of the story are fixed by the preconception.

In practice, as has been seen, descriptive explanations have been most criticized for being either untrue or unfair. Unfairness can be difficult to detect when a whole community of scholars shares a particular bias. It is notorious that historians up until a generation ago overlooked the history of indigenous people in lands settled by Europeans; overlooked the history of women and children; and found it difficult to understand the point of view of their country's enemies. Communal bias is the most difficult to guard against.

4 Historical interpretations

Sometimes historians do not have a fixed preconception of what a subject is like, but examine details of the subject to discover what general description of it will both relate many of the facts they have discovered about the subject, and help to explain them. General descriptions arrived at in this way can be called summary interpretations of the subject. There are usually several different general descriptions which can sum up a lot of information about a subject, each more or less equally justified, and each showing how elements of the subject are related to one another, thus displaying their meaning or significance. That is why general descriptions can be called summary interpretations of the subject.

One way in which summary interpretations differ from descriptive explanations is that they are not imposed upon the subject in accordance with a preconception of its nature. Another difference is that interpretations do not always aim to provide a systematic analysis of the subject, according to its intrinsic general structure. They are designed to draw attention to patterns in the data about the subject, patterns which relate many of the elements of that data into an intelligible whole. Sometimes they do this by providing a new general analysis of the structure of the event, but often they do it by simply noting major trends that occurred within it. Sometimes, having provided a systematic descriptive explanation of an historical subject, an historian will then look for distinctive patterns in the history of the subject, and describe them as an interpretation of it.

The process of searching for an adequate interpretation of an historical subject has been well described by J.W. Ward.

> For months, I spent evenings at the desk in what my wife calls the 'shuffle, cut, and deal' stage of scholarship, sorting and resorting, trying to find some pattern, some lines of relationship around which to organize what one thinks one knows. This still seems to me the most important moment in the act of writing, the willingness to suffer the anxiety of having no clear sense of direction, confident that if only one soaks oneself in the material, one will find the way.
>
> (Ward, 1970, p. 212)

The outcome was his book *Andrew Jackson: Symbol for an Age*.

The contrast between descriptive explanations and summary interpretations of a subject can be clearly illustrated by comparing different histories of war.

Australians recall with pride and horror the apparently useless sacrifice of thousands of young men in a battle against the Turks on the shores at Gallipoli in 1915. The official history of this campaign has been told in the first two volumes of C.E.W. Bean's *Australia in the War*, as well as in the British official war history *Military Operations in Gallipoli* (North, 1936, p. 22). These provide a detailed, systematic account of all stages of the battle. In contrast to these descriptive explanations of the campaign are several books written by historians reflecting upon what happened, and looking for an interpretation which will both sum up what happened and help to explain it. E. Ashmead-Bartlett wrote *The Uncensored Dardanelles* to show that it was a story of 'muddle, mismanagement, and useless sacrifice' (North, 1936, p. 30). John North wrote *Gallipoli. A Fading Vision* to contrast 'the suffering and the heroisms of the "simple soldier" with the almost superhuman inadequacy of his political and military leaders – particularly on the home front' (p. 32). His interpretation is quite comprehensive, but not simply a methodical account of the campaign. He remarks: 'although this book does not set out to give a straightforward narrative of the campaign, I hope that it omits none of the significant facts' (p. 21). In fact North selected his material to illustrate his interpretation.

Sometimes an historical subject simply lacks sufficient coherence for a general interpretation of it to be possible. Edward Royle and James Walvin discovered this when writing their history *English Radicals and Reformers 1760–1848* (1982). They explained the situation with these words:

> To impose coherence on this evidently vague topic is misleading. There is no clear picture of tributaries feeding into a main stream which can then be followed to the estuary and the sea. Rather, there is a delta, with many streams and outlets and no single or clearly defined ending. . . . One object of this book is to try to indicate the variety of streams of radicalism which in their several and sometimes conflicting ways contributed to the reform movement in Britain between 1760 and 1848.
>
> (p. 10)

Notice the authors' concern, in the first sentence, that their interpretation of the subject not be misleading. This point will be emphasized shortly.

If the subject of a history is very large and complex, then a systematic description of its parts can be exhausting, both to write and to read (official histories are just like that). In such cases historians sometimes look for a summary account of the subject which will enable them to describe it systematically but at a high level of generality. Thus, in describing a war, instead of detailing the movements of every division in every battle, they might look for the main protagonists, and the main points of conflict between them. The general concept of a war does not identify the protagonists at such a high level of generality in a definite way. Consequently historians have to search for adequate descriptions of them themselves. The result is an interpretation of the general structure of the war.

A vivid example of this process is provided by the historiography of the Thirty Years' War in Europe between 1618 and 1648. For example, Gustav

Freytag, a nineteenth-century German author, described the war as a conflict between local rulers in Germany and the imperial house of Hapsburg, and also as between Protestants and Catholics. He wrote: 'The opposition between the interests of the house of Hapsburg and of the German nation, and between the old and new faith, led to a bloody catastrophe' (Freytag, 1862, p. 4). S.H. Steinberg, writing in the middle of this century, disagreed with this interpretation, and has presented the Thirty Years' War as a stage in 'the larger struggle for European hegemony between Bourbon and Hapsburg', which lasted from 1609 to 1659. The Bourbon government of France fought to break Hapsburg encirclement of their country (Steinberg, 1966, p. 2). Even more recently, Geoffrey Parker has seen four sets of opposing forces involved in the war: 'In 1618 there had been four major tensions within the European political system: the struggle between Spain and the Dutch; the confrontation of largely Protestant princes and estates with the Catholic Hapsburgs in the Empire; the enmity of Sweden and Poland; and the rivalry of France and the Hapsburgs' (Parker, 1979, p. 281). The narratives they present tell the history of the central conflicts they have identified.

The historian S.R. Gardiner did not interpret the Thirty Years' War as a war at all. Rather he looked for and found certain processes at work through the war which supplied a framework of interpretation. He wrote:

Every history to be a history, must have a unity of its own, and here we have no unity of national life such as that which is reflected in the institutions of England and France, not even the unity of a great race of sovereigns handing down the traditions of government from one generation to another. The unity of the subject which I have chosen must be sought in the growth of the principle of religious toleration as it is adopted or repelled by the institutions under which Germany and France, the two principal nations with which we are concerned, are living. Thus the history of the period may be compared to a gigantic dissolving view. As we enter upon it our minds are filled with German men and things. But Germany fails to find the solution of the problem before it. Gradually France comes with increasing distinctness before us. It succeeds where Germany had failed, and occupies us more and more until it fills the whole field of action.

(Gardiner,1889, pp. v-vi)

At first Gardiner looked for some continuous entity to form a backbone to his narrative, something like the continuing institutions of government in England and France, or a continuing 'race of sovereigns'. But the Thirty Years' War involved so many countries and so many leaders that no such central subject would encompass it. So Gardiner then found a general thesis to provide a framework of interpretation: those rulers, like the Hapsburgs, who refused to tolerate religious dissent had their kingdoms broken, whereas those, like the French King Louis XIV, who, in this case through Richelieu, promised religious liberty to religious dissidents, kept their kingdoms intact (pp. 113–14, 220). This interpretation provided a unifying theme for his narrative.

Given such a variety of interpretations of the War, the question arises as to whether any is superior to the others. Only someone with an extensive and detailed knowledge of the War could judge which of these is the best. But any reader of history can detect the criteria by which historical interpretations are judged. If they are formulated in general or classificatory sentences, then these must be true and not misleading. But there are further ideals besides these. Interpretations are preferred which relate to a large number of the major events in the detailed history of the subject; and they are preferred if they provide a general explanation of the changes in the subject. In short, interpretations are judged for their scope and explanatory power. Historians are constrained to find interpretations which satisfy these criteria: which are true and fair; which relate a lot of facts into an intelligible pattern; and which provide a general explanation of the events they correlate. An interpretation which does all these things is a good one; and if there are several different interpretations of the same subject, they can be compared to discover which, according to these criteria, is the best. Examples of such comparison will be given shortly.

Hayden White has suggested that historical narratives are structured according to literary models, namely comedies, tragedies, romances and satires. Such models might sometimes influence the structure of an historical narrative, but they seem much less important to historians than their desire to describe the subject fully, or to illustrate their interpretation of the subject. White also says that the form of narrative chosen by an historian does not represent any pattern that is really in the events being interpreted, but is just a way of viewing them. I will argue that historical patterns and trends are just as real as the events which constitute them.

White's opinion raises the main sceptical question about historical interpretations, however. These high-level generalizations really do seem remote from reality. Are the patterns they describe really there, or are they just warranted forms of description, referring to nothing real at all? Looking at cumulus clouds we might see bears and lions, but that is not to say they are really there. Is it the same with historical interpretations? Surely the fact that people see the same subject in so many different ways suggests there is no fact of the matter.

Before commenting further on Hayden White's views, and replying to the sceptic, it would be wise to provide a number of examples of historical interpretation. I shall begin, therefore, with examples of interpretation of historical events, people's lives, and past societies, the same three subjects considered in the last chapter.

INTERPRETING EVENTS

Interpretations of the English Civil War have been legion. Lawrence Stone has listed many of them. Clarendon thought it to have been a 'Great Rebellion' by landed classes against an unpopular king. C.V. Wedgwood saw it as the natural consequence of a collapse of central government. S.R. Gardiner described it as a Puritan revolution against the established Church; whereas Lord Macaulay thought it a struggle for liberty against royal tyranny. As we have seen, R.H. Tawney and C. Hill presented it as a bourgeois revolution against feudal institutions, and H.R. Trevor-Roper said it was 'a revolution of despair' by the gentry, trying to re-establish their independence (Stone, 1972, pp. 47–8). Each interpretation, notice, both sums up what was happening and suggests a general explanation for the events involved.

The chief point I want to make, however, is that historians have shown themselves passionately concerned to check the truth and fairness of these and other interpretations. They are true if there really were people fighting for the causes mentioned; and they are fair, not misleading, if there were no other issues of major significance dividing the combatants.

Almost every historian of the Civil War has criticized those who have preceded him, so one could illustrate the passion for truth from the writings of most of them. Let me report some of the arguments of Conrad Russell, a very distinguished historian of the period writing fairly recently. At the start of his book *The Causes of the English Civil War* (1990), he comments on several interpretations which have been put forward by other historians. What chiefly divided the sides according to Russell were beliefs about the Church, about whom it should include and how it should be governed. The War cannot now be said to have involved hostility between two social groups or classes, he said, because 'the fullest possible knowledge of men's social and economic background, if it leaves out the preaching available in their home parishes, tells us nothing about their likely allegiance in the Civil War' (p. 2). In every social group he found supporters of both sides of the War. Similarly, Russell said the opposition was not between a court and a country party (p. 4), or between the government and an opposition. 'Just because it was a struggle involving major issues of principle, it divided those who might be classified as members of a "government" along much the same lines as everyone else' (p. 5). Nor was it a fight between those defending the established order and those for change, said Russell, because Parliamentarians claimed to be defending that order 'equally loudly' as the Royalists (p. 7). Again and again Russell rejects an interpretation of the War because it is contradicted by the known facts. His own account of events, he said, 'will not produce a simple picture, but it may have some approximation to the truth' (p. 25).

Another famous critic of previous interpretations of the Civil War is J.H. Hexter. R.H. Tawney, presenting a Marxist interpretation, had said that the middle class was rising and the aristocracy declining at the time of the War. Hexter noted that Tawney had mentioned a few cases in support of his generalization, but that they were not nearly as representative of the whole society as he had supposed (Hexter, 1961, pp. 117–33). (I have discussed criticism of Tawney's data in detail in McCullagh, 1984, pp. 152–3.) Another pattern of historical change which Hexter discussed is a Darwinian one, involving the gradual evolution of social and cultural phenomena. A.F. Pollard, said Hexter, adopted this framework, and saw the seventeenth century as part of the process of 'emerging nationalism' and the 'rising middle class', which continued steadily from the thirteenth to the nineteenth century. This theory, Hexter remarked, 'is wholly *a priori*, a purely imaginary construction that does not set historical facts in order, but altogether escapes and soars above their dreary restrictions. It is the product not of historical investigations but of the spirit of Pollard's age, the age of historical Darwinism' (p. 39). Finally, Hexter finds H.R. Trevor-Roper's interpretation of seventeenth-century conflicts as motivated by economic self-interest, the court gentry defending their privileges against the country gentry who were jealous of them, to be totally inadequate.

> In the squalid setting of this farce there is not enough room for William Chillingworth or Richard Baxter, for Edward Coke or Francis Bacon, for Thomas Wentworth or Oliver Cromwell, for John Selden, or John Lilburne, or John Hampden, or John Pym, or John Milton. . . . What is worse, without some understanding of what such men stood for in their own minds and in the eyes of others, I find that age not very intelligible.
>
> (p. 142)

It is not so much that Trevor-Roper's interpretation is judged to be false, as that it fails to include most of the heroes of the War, and fails to explain what they were fighting about. In other words, it lacks adequate scope and explanatory power.

Another good example of the importance to historians of truth, scope and explanatory power in judging historical interpretations is to be found in a discussion by John Hiden and John Farquharson (1983) of three general interpretations of the development of National Socialism in Germany. The Nazi party grew in numbers and strength, especially in the 1930s, and it is impossible to describe every event involved in its growth. Historians, having studied as much as they can, look for an interpretation to provide a structure for their account of the party's growth. Hiden and Farquharson examined three such interpretations.

The first is the simple Marxist view that National Socialism was the tool of monopoly capitalism. It rests on Lenin's maxim 'that free competition in the business world produces bourgeois democracy, whereas the monopoly stage of capitalism leads to political reaction' (pp. 154–5). The second theory is another Marxist view, called 'Bonapartism'. In 1871 Marx had explained the accession of Napoleon III in France as 'the only possible form of government at a time when the bourgeoisie had already lost its capacity to rule the nation and the working class had not yet acquired that capacity' (p. 156). This theory fits the history of Germany quite well. After March 1930, the authors remark, 'bourgeois government did break down, partly at least owing to the withdrawal of the SPD [Social Democratic Party] from government'; and 'the fratricidal strife between the SPD and the KPD [Communist Party, Germany] meant that the working class could not govern either. In 1933 the latter day Louis Napoleon was therefore able to come to power in the kind of vacuum that Marx had predicted' (p. 156). Although the new rule was supported by the bourgeoisie to protect their interests, it was seen to be capable of developing in such a way as ultimately to endanger them. This latter point explains why Hitler could order the destruction of Germany's industrial infrastructure in March 1945.

The authors criticize these two Marxist theories, first as rather implausible, and second for not explaining important features of the history of the growth of

National Socialism. The theories are implausible for two reasons. If they were true, one would have expected other developed capitalist countries such as Britain and America to have embraced fascism, but they did not. Second, it is incredible to suppose that capitalists would support a total war which destroyed their means of production (p. 159). The authors list several things which these theories could not explain, in particular 'the total collapse of organized labour in Germany in 1933'; 'the origins and significance of the basic ideology of Social Darwinism and race'; and 'why large sectors of the population ... should place devotion to their country and a spirit of nationalism above their own apparent class interests' (pp. 159–60).

The third causal theory which the authors consider is one derived from Barrington Moore's study of different routes to modernization. In Germany a rather fragile democratic structure could not cope with the loss of the First World War, and then with the acute economic crisis which developed during the 1920s, so the nation fell back upon semi-feudal political structures instead. Those who seemed likely to suffer most under growing capitalist industrialization, the lower middle classes, looked to National Socialism for protection and support (pp. 161–2). This theory can be extended to include Erich Fromm's thesis that people supported National Socialism because they were reluctant to assume political responsibility for themselves (p. 163). The authors are impressed with this theory. It explains why fascism occurred in Germany but not in Britain and France, where democratic institutions and ideology were much more firmly established. And, they say, 'it makes Hitler perfectly comprehensible as a man of the twentieth century rather than a latter day Attila the Hun' (p. 169). It does not account, however, for his mad and wicked anti-Semitism.

INTERPRETING PEOPLE'S LIVES

Many biographies provide no interpretation of their subject's life at all. They report the details of the subject's life, often at great length, in great detail, and leave it at that. Some historians, however, search for some theme which will give unity to their biography, over and above the unity provided by the subject whose life is being told.

In a lively Introduction to *The Historian's Lincoln. Pseudohistory, Psychohistory, and History* (1988), Gabor Boritt discusses some of the interpretations of Lincoln's life which have been made. Some, he says, have seen Lincoln's 'ultimate commitment' being to the Union, which he defended against the Southern acts of secession. Others have thought it was for liberty, especially the liberty of slaves. Boritt quotes textual support, from Lincoln's speeches, for both of these views. In fact, he says, Lincoln fought for both.

Then Boritt introduces a more serious problem. 'The need for a unified, believable portrait of Lincoln raised a second fundamental problem for historians. Ever since the moment of martyrdom in 1865 there have been two Lincolns: the man and the god. One was the crafty backwoods lawyer, ... the other, the immortal statesman' (p. xvi). Don E. Fehrenbacher (1987) had remarked on this dichotomy as well: up until his election as President in 1860, Lincoln is seen as a frontier hero, he said; and after that he is a national saint (p. 183). Boritt's own book on Lincoln, *Lincoln and the Economics of the American Dream* (Memphis State University Press, 1978) argues that in both his private and his public life Lincoln believed everyone should have the right to rise, both economically and socially. This conviction, it seems, is what unites his life.

There are several fairly obvious and common ways of finding a theme for a life. One is to identify an ambition, or a policy which is the goal of much of the subject's behaviour. Another is to detect a set of values and dispositions manifest in much of the subject's life. These could be said to constitute the subject's character. Finally, some historians attempt to find unity in an unconscious attitude, suggested by psychoanalytic theory.

Many distinguished people are driven by fairly precise goals, which give meaning to much that they do. Philip Magnus was able to sum up three stages in the political life of W.E. Gladstone by referring to both the policy he was pursuing at each stage, and to the convictions and values which they expressed. But underlying them all, Magnus said, were unquestioned Christian convictions, and the belief that everyone should spend their lives serving God. He gradually came to believe that people could only do this in freedom,

> and in that gradual discovery lies the key to all his changes. He came to repose his trust in the ability of individual men and women to hear, interpret correctly, and obey the voice of God using their private consciences to inspire and direct mankind. Gladstone fought for the second and third Reform Acts because he had acquired that trust.
>
> (p. xii)

In Magnus' opinion, Gladstone's sole purpose in life was to help others achieve the freedom they needed to serve God.

> Political life would have been meaningless to him without that purpose which attained its most outstanding public expression during three successive phases of his long career.
>
> In the first phase, when he was Chancellor of the Exchequer, Gladstone achieved unparalleled success in his policy of setting the individual free from a multitude of obsolete restrictions. He thereby implemented his creed that self-discipline in freedom is the essential condition of the mental health of men and nation, as well as of their material prosperity. The crowning moments were the great Budgets of 1853 and 1860. . . .
>
> During the second phase of his career, Gladstone achieved great success in arousing the moral indignation of the British people against Turkish misrule in the Balkans, and against what he regarded as Disraeli's blindness – typifying that of the great and cautious world – to the transcendental issues which are involved in all tyranny and oppression. The crowning moment was the Midlothian campaign of 1879. . . .

During the third and final phase of his career, Gladstone, in his magnificent old age, led a crusade against English misrule in Ireland. The crowning moments were the rejections of his first and second Home Rule Bills in 1886 and 1893.

(Magnus, 1954, pp. xi–xii)

Notice how different stages of Gladstone's career are each summed up by reference to a particular purpose. Then all these purposes are in turn explained by reference to his fundamental religious beliefs and values.

It is interesting to compare H.C.G. Matthew's interpretation of Gladstone, which is similar in some respects but not in others. While affirming the importance of 'his Christian faith, the preservation of the Church and the triumph of Christian values' in Gladstone's life, Matthew also noted the peculiar political attitudes which, whether he was aware of it or not, found expression in Gladstone's career: 'A radical conservatism, which fused at times with an advanced liberalism', which 'came to give Gladstone a curious position of great power in the centre of British politics, the power of surprise, of resource, of stability, and of an appeal, after the 1830s, that history and time were on his side' (Matthew, 1986, p. 1). Each historian was trying to make sense of Gladstone's life and career, and each chose slightly different characteristics to do so.

David Cannadine has reviewed several biographies in his collection of essays, *The Pleasures of the Past* (1991), and in most cases he surpasses the biographers in summing up the character of the subject. One review is of David Dilks' biography of Neville Chamberlain. He complains at the lack of theme to unify the work: 'By wandering from subject to subject – from butterflies to business, from orchids to organization – we may get a full picture of Chamberlain's life, but the result is an unstructured and chronological treatment, in which no theme is ever satisfactorily explored' (p. 310). Then, on the basis of Dilks' book, Cannadine offers his own interpretation. Notice that he uses some common-sense psychology in the process.

Although Dilks does not discuss this, it is clear from the evidence that for most of his life, Neville was dominated by somebody: as a boy by his father [Joseph], whom he idolized to excess; as a man by Austen [his brother], whose early career was so much more glittering than his own; and as a husband by his wife, who cherished political ambitions for him which he was too reticent or realistic to admit for himself. As a result, Neville was such a late developer, both psychologically and politically, that there was not very much to develop when the opportunities finally and unexpectedly came. . . .

By 1929 . . . he was set in a rut of self-righteous narrow-mindedness. . . .

As a person and a politician, he was just like his umbrella: drab, still, and rolled up tight.

(pp. 311, 312)

This is very witty, but does not explain his policies in any detail. That is the price of finding a theme sufficiently general to unify a whole life.

The need for an interpretation to be explanatory is of more concern in his review of Anthony Howard's biography of R.A. Butler. A summary of the man's character will not do:

> That he was donnish, sceptical, detached, intellectual, is true but trite: no attempt is made here to explore what he was actually thinking, nor to describe how his views change – which they did, very dramatically. . . . Nor is it altogether clear from this account quite why it was that Butler never got to the very top.

(pp. 334–5)

To say that Macmillan kept him down between 1957 and 1963 may be true, but 'explanations such as this do not go very deep' (p. 335). More promising is the explanation that Butler was a victim of the 'blue blood and thunder group' of Conservatives, the aristocratic and military element which condemned him as middle class and an appeaser. But Cannadine says 'the amount of evidence which can actually be marshalled in its support still seems decidedly thin' (p. 335). Cannadine attributes Butler's political failure to the fact that:

> In his early years, everything had gone too easily for him, with the result that he came to expect events to go his way, and never learned the arts of private intrigue or of public theatre to which any ambitious politician must eventually have recourse if he (or she) is to make it to the very top.

(p. 336)

Interpretations which appeal to psychoanalytic theory are not widely respected. Fehrenbacher has shown how varied and unconvincing are the attempts to interpret Lincoln's life this way (Fehrenbacher, 1987, ch. 16). As he says, the theory has not been satisfactorily confirmed, and those who use it often base their findings on inadequate evidence. Boritt is inclined to dismiss psychoanalytic interpretations as 'pseudo-history', though both he and Fehrenbacher are impressed with some of the insights into Lincoln's personal relationships provided by Charles B. Strozier's *Lincoln's Quest for Union* (1982) (Boritt and Forness, 1988, p. xvii).

The most convincing use of psychological theory is when it is appealed to in order to amplify an interpretation which has already been reached with everyday psychological insight. A useful illustration is provided by James Walter's analysis of the character of Gough Whitlam, the Australian Prime Minister (1972–5). He was elected with much enthusiasm as a man of great ideas, full of promise, but after three years he was out. First let me quote Walter's summary of previous interpretations of this man, and his reasons for dismissing them. These comments illustrate the importance of scope and explanatory power in an interpretation.

> On the one hand he has been depicted as narrow, arrogant, politically inept and essentially (almost villainously) self-serving – which does little to explain how he could have won the admiration and intense loyalty of many who followed his cause. On the other hand he has been shown as a talented, driving man of great vision and capacity defeated largely by unfortunate historical circumstances and the myopia of the Australian people – but this takes little account

of the maladministration and failure on an interpersonal level that were undeniably a part of his government. Then there are those who have assiduously and skilfully mustered both the positive and negative qualities of Whitlam as a leader, yet finally erect them in counterpoint as a baffling paradox.

(Walter, 1981, p. 31)

Walter hoped to find a personality type which would accommodate all of Whitlam's characteristics. The attempt, following H.D. Lasswell, to see his behaviour as ego-defensive came up against his expansiveness, his optimism and self-gratification (p. 33). Walter summed up Whitlam's character in these words:

> He is most simply described as a man who lacked any trace of self-doubt, demonstrated a strong urge to be in control, was intolerant of constraint, found great zest in exhibitionistic display, and showed limited empathy with others in interpersonal relations. This pattern . . . does not seem unfamiliar. Even so, it can be used to show the personal element in both his major successes, and most significant failures.
>
> (p. 33)

Walter found a theory which described just such a person, a theory of 'the narcissistic personality' in the writing of M. Balint, H. Kohut and others. It is explained as the result of not experiencing frustration when young, and having an overevaluation of self. Whitlam was protected as a child, and a brilliant scholar (pp. 33–4).

INTERPRETING SOCIETIES

When historians interpret social history they usually look for patterns of change or stability within their chosen period, and for explanations of the patterns they find. A good example is to be found in the Conclusion of Roy Porter's *English Society in the Eighteenth Century* (1990). The themes he identified not only relate a lot of facts about the period, but explain its stability as well.

> This book has highlighted three main aspects of eighteenth-century English society. First, the fundamental strength and resilience of its social hierarchy. . . . My second theme has been this: though the social hierarchy was inegalitarian and oozing privilege (some of it hereditary), it was neither rigid nor brittle. There was continual adaptiveness to challenge and individual mobility, up, down and sideways. . . . [T]he third main focus of this book has lain on [the] attempts [of the ruling order] to secure consensus within this acquisitive, restless society. . . . The hope was to win acquiescence and endorsement by influence and persuasion – bluster, grandeur, liberality, promises, show and swank, the open door held just ajar.
>
> (pp. 340–44)

The social fabric of England was not torn like that of France in the eighteenth century, but continued to withstand the pressures put upon it. Porter notes this fact, and explains its continuity in the three themes he has selected as the foci of his history. The magnates maintained their wealth, and their control of Church, State and the Army. They did not stop others making money and entering their ranks. They offered spiritual salvation to the poor, and material pleasures to the prosperous, thus keeping most content with their lot.

When Peter McPhee (1992) came to sum up the themes of his history of French society between 1780 and 1880, he did so by criticizing the interpretations of others.

Alfred Cobban had pictured France unchanged throughout the nineteenth century until the establishment of the Third Republic in 1877, with the land owners prospering under the protection of the state, but McPhee detected 'a revolutionary transformation' in the people's attitude to authority and sovereignty during that period. Before the Revolution (1789–95), few of those entitled to vote went to the polls, but after it, a large majority did. In times of political instability, as in 1799, 1815 and 1851, the people allowed a strong leader to seize power from above, supported by the army. But the big change was the growth of republicanism. 'The erosion of the awesome influence and symbolism of throne and altar was matched by the triumph of an alternative republican iconography' (pp. 264–6). In McPhee's eyes, Cobban left out a trend of major significance in suggesting there was no significant change in French life over the century. His argument 'remains fatally flawed in what it ignores' (p. 267).

Eugen Weber is the next historian singled out for comment. He too thought there had been no change, particularly in rural France, which he depicted as consisting of isolated, backward communities. McPhee comments: 'By singling out the most extreme examples of "isolation" as the rural norm . . . Weber has painted a picture of an archaic countryside. However, the changes which he points to after 1880 were already well advanced almost everywhere' (p. 267). Once again, Weber's interpretation is criticized as not a fair one. McPhee describes widespread schooling established during this period, and a network of new roads.

Robert Forster has argued that between 1800 and 1880, France was ruled by an élite class of notables, nobility and very wealthy men. McPhee observes that this is not the case. 'During the July Monarchy [1830–48], the social composition of the ruling élite became less aristocratic and more drawn from business and the professions. . . . Nineteenth-century élites, progressively more bourgeois in social composition and ideology after 1815, dominated a state apparatus which gradually widened its spheres of control over public life' (pp. 268–9).

McPhee summed up the changes of the century as seeing the transformation of a rural, pre-capitalist society, through 'an interconnected series of gradual transformations', into 'a capitalist society in which market-oriented agriculture and a disproportionately growing urban industrial economy were the source of the extraction of surplus value, by economic élites and the state, from the labour of urban and rural wage-labourers and the self-employed' (pp. 270–1). 'The most important transformation in rural society was that by which peasant polyculture became specialized small farming' (p. 272). Then, in the interests of increased accuracy, McPhee adds the following qualification: 'Of course, socio-economic transformations of such magnitude were infinitely varied in their specific nature, timing and intensity across the face of a large, diverse country' (p. 273).

So far McPhee has identified several important trends in the history of French society from 1780 to 1880. Finally he considers whether these can in turn all be interpreted in terms of an overarching concept, as a process of 'modernization'. In a careful consideration of the implications of the term, McPhee rejects it as misleading in several different ways. For instance: 'Central to the modernization model is the argument that the consolidation of liberal, parliamentary government was the triumph of political modernity over both autocracy and recurrent popular insurrections.' In fact, McPhee says, 'the victory of parliamentary democracy by 1880 was due more than anything else to deeply-held beliefs among working people that popular sovereignty implied manhood suffrage and electoral choice'. So it was not imposed from above by a dominant middle class. Then again, modernization theory suggests that with modernity comes secularization and 'grasping materialism', but on the contrary, religion flourished in France during this period (pp. 275–7). Not only is the concept of modernization misleading, but McPhee does not think it explains much either. 'Modernization theory . . . tends to be teleological, reifying into an inevitable process a whole series of social changes which need to be explained' (p. 275). These comments clearly reveal the standards of interpretation which McPhee, like other historians, respects. They certainly show how false it is to think that any interpretation of a period is as good as any other.

It is interesting to note how, once a dominant pattern has been detected in an historical subject, it is difficult to see other patterns or to set it aside. The history of Nazi Germany, for example, has been interpreted as a sequence of repeated conflicts between the Nazi Party and the old German government bureaucracy, conflicts which were won increasingly by the Nazi Party, with a corresponding increase in its power. Jane Caplan (1978), however, detected another process at work, namely an attempt by the central federal bureaucracy to resist administrative decentralization. It is noteworthy that in each case generalizations about changes in the social structures were suggested by high-level theories of social change.

The following extracts from Caplan's essay illustrate these points about the processes of interpretation. In particular they reveal the constant preoccupation with truth, as well as a desire for comprehensive understanding. Caplan begins by noticing that it has been common to represent the Nazi state as 'a conflict between a rational authoritarian bureaucracy, and an irrational totalitarian political move-ment', in which the bureaucracy is seen as a victim. This conception of the nature of the state was developed by political analysts such as Ernst Fraenkel and Hannah Arendt, she said. She goes on:

> If authors such as these have provided the theoretical framework for a particular kind of political interpretation of the regime, historians have in some cases applied it directly to their empirical observations. . . . More recent research has tended to retreat from this fundamental contrast between party and state,

but without finally evicting the dualism inherent in the rational bureaucracy–irrational movement pair, with serious consequences for the explanatory capacity of the interpretations proposed. A distinction of some kind may well be validly drawn, but it ought to be sustained by theoretical clarity and historical evidence, not by the weight of pre-given assumptions. Only in this way will it be possible to achieve a comprehensive analysis of the Nazi state.

(Caplan, 1978, 236–8)

Caplan then suggests a new 'thread of continuity' by which to interpret much government activity at the time.

It is easy enough to see the organisational continuity in the state apparatus that spanned the dividing line of 1933 – the extent to which particular offices, procedures, personnel and so on remained stable. This, of course, is the perspective from which the Nazi era can be viewed primarily as a collision between these survivals and the dissolving processes of the new regime. However, another thread of continuity which tends to be less emphasised in the administrative context is the persistence of attempts to solve the fundamental structural problems of the German state, especially the central problem of federalism and administrative decentralisation.

(pp. 238–9)

Caplan's thesis is that: 'The structure of government in the Third Reich was characterised as much by the dissolution of Germany's federal constitution as by the erection of a one-party state, and the two processes developed side by side' (p. 245). She arrived at this conclusion after closely studying the policies and decisions of those running the public service, in particular after 1933 those of the Interior Minister, Wilhelm Frick.

Evidence for such an interpretation rests in a close examination of the evolution of policy within the Interior Ministry, in the analysis of its connections with the other major arms of the civil administration (the judicial and financial systems), and in its relations with the other governmental agencies, including those thrown up from within the NSDAP [the Nazi Party].

(p. 245)

Caplan's discovery of the struggle to maintain a unified and effective federal bureaucracy as a major theme of German government was itself guided by a theoretical assumption, namely

that the reproduction of the state must be grasped as a process of the continual renegotiation of relations between its constituent institutions or apparatuses, a process which also comprehends the internal reproduction of the institutions themselves. . . . If the reproduction of the state is conceived in this way, then it is clear that a dualist model of the Nazi state will not be adequate to comprehend the process. Neither the chronological opposition between the pre-Nazi and the Nazi state, nor the structural opposition between stability and dynamism, takes account of the fact that the civil service, like other constituents of the state, was engaged in a permanent round of adaptive reproduction.

(p. 251)

Thus Caplan's theoretical preconception of the nature of a vital political process led to her discovery of a new major theme in German political history in this period.

Sometimes historians tailor the period of social history they choose to write about to suit the interpretation they prefer. Thus W.L. Burn, when considering how to structure a history of mid-Victorian Britain, decided to confine himself to a relatively short period, 1852–1867, because he judged it to have an identifiable character of its own. This he set out in *The Age of Equipoise*, 'in which the old and the new, the elements of growth, survival and decay, achieved a balance which most contemporaries regarded as satisfactory' (Burn, 1968, p. 17). There were railways, but horses were still a major form of transport. There were gas lights, but the oil-lamp and candle were widely used. There was also a balance, 'fortuitously rather than deliberately achieved, between the State and the sub-ordinate centres of authority, between centralization and localism, between compulsion and free choice' (p. 330). The idea of a balance enabled Burn to describe all kinds of contrasts in Victorian society, the poor and the affluent, the pious and the sceptical, and so on. In effect, Burn found many different things in a state of equipoise, a state of balance. It is a metaphor which helped to sum up many characteristics of the age.

It is interesting to notice that Burn rejected other characterizations of that period, such as 'The Railway Age' and 'The Age of the Inspector', because they were 'insufficiently comprehensive' (p. 17). Even Walter Bagehot's title 'The Age of Discussion' he considered inadequate because it cannot accommodate the decisive actions taken in this period, for instance those concerning the Indian Mutiny, divorce, limited liability and medical practice (p. 18). Burn clearly thought it very important to present an interpretation which would synthesize as much information about the period as possible.

It is important to add that not all generalizations and classificatory statements are interpretations of an historical subject. In his book *The Making of Victorian England*, for example, G. Kitson Clark explicitly denies any intention 'to draw a comprehensive composite picture of the Victorian period' (Clark, 1962, p. 1). Instead, he picks out several trends in the period which relate to a large number of facts about Victorian England. He calls them 'forces', and they include the growth of population, the growth of industry, the increasing role of the government administration, the movement from oligarchy to democracy, and the revival of religion. 'Like different currents in a fast-moving river,' he said, 'they rush forward together in the same bed' (p. 289).

LITERARY INTERPRETATIONS OF HISTORY

Hayden White has said that historians who write narrative accounts of the past interpret their information in accordance with literary models, adopting one or another kind of plot, comedy, tragedy, romance or satire. Before explaining his theory more fully, let me remark what an extraordinary theory it is. As I have shown in this chapter and the last, historians arrange their narratives, either to provide a descriptive explanation of an historical subject, or to illustrate an interpretation of an historical subject. It is significant that White's examples are drawn from nineteenth-century historiography, when literary forms might have had a greater influence on historical writing than they do today. Nevertheless it is astounding that White did not investigate modern historical interpretations to see what they were like, before writing so extensively on the subject. It is little wonder that although historians are rightly impressed by his scholarship, they do not find his theories very useful. It is certainly possible to narrate past events according to the structure of a literary plot, but historians do not find such interpretations particularly interesting.

White has confined his discussion of historical interpretations to a consideration of several classical forms of narrative. He believes that although descriptions of particular events in the past are determined by the evidence we have of them, they do not require any particular form of narrative emplotment. He relates the different kinds of plot rather vaguely to historians' moral and political concerns, suggesting that the choice of plot is influenced by these rather than by any particular features of the story. This explains why different historians have emplotted the same events in different ways. For example, whereas Michelet portrayed the French Revolution as a romance, highlighting the liberty, equality and fraternity achieved briefly during 1790, Tocqueville described it as a tragedy, in which the noble aspirations of the revolutionaries became transformed into a reign of terror. White explained that the different interpretations reflected the different values of the historians, and concluded that none of them should be regarded as true: 'Historical situations are not *inherently* tragic, comic, or romantic' (White, 1974, p. 282).

White's argument is unconvincing. He is correct if he means that there is more than one interpretation which can be given of complex events like the French Revolution. The Revolution certainly had both its glorious and its terrible moments. But he is wrong if he means that no characterization can be true of it.

White considered four kinds of plot: comedy, tragedy, romance and satire. Drawing upon the writing of Northrop Frye, White described the distinctive characteristics of each. For example, he described comedies thus:

> In Comedy, hope is held out for the temporary triumph of man over his world by the prospect of occasional *reconciliations* of the forces at play in the social and natural worlds. Such reconciliations are symbolized in the festive occasions which the Comic writer traditionally uses to terminate his dramatic accounts of change and transformation.
>
> (White, 1975, p. 9.)

The life of a subject cannot be portrayed as a comedy if there is no reconciliation of competing forces in its life at the end. The triumph of such reconciliation, we might say, constitutes the truth condition of comic plots. It is easy to see, then, why White wrote: 'I do not suppose that anyone would accept the emplotment of the life of President Kennedy as comedy' (White, 1974, p. 281). There was certainly no reconciliation of competing forces in his assassination. The plots which historians use have to fit the facts, have to be true to what is known of the history of the subject, and give an idea of it which is not misleading. If this were not the case, historians could presumably ignore the way Kennedy died, and emplot his death any way at all.

It is now possible to see why one might disagree with White when he wrote: 'Historical situations are not *inherently* tragic, comic, or romantic. . . . All the historian needs to do to transform a tragic into a comic situation is to shift his point of view or change the scope of his perceptions' (pp. 282–3). White presented a tragedy as a story in which the forces opposing a person's attempts at transcendence of a situation are revealed to be so great as to effect his or her destruction (White, 1975, pp. 9–10). A story of which this statement is true seems to be inherently tragic. The death of Kennedy, and even more the death of Martin Luther King (for he was a greater man who unleashed greater hostility), was truly tragic.

Notice, by the way, how natural it is to say that their *deaths* were tragic. Their *lives* could, perhaps, be regarded as romances, which White described as dramas 'of the triumph of good over evil, of virtue over vice, of light over darkness, and of the ultimate transcendence of man over the world in which he was imprisoned by the Fall' (p. 9). For both Kennedy and King inspired their generation to live nobly, and succeeded in some measure in limiting greed and injustice in the United States. Though their deaths were tragic, their lives were not. That is perhaps why White could write of President Kennedy's life: 'whether it ought to be emplotted romantically, tragically, or satirically is an open question' (1974, p. 282). To plot his life as a romance, one would have to play down the significance of his death, and highlight instead his effect upon his generation (supposing it to have been as good as I have described it).

On reflection, one is reluctant to agree that any life or event can be emplotted in various different ways. The reason for this reluctance is that we generally assume that these plots must characterize the lives and events as a whole, and not just draw attention to aspects of them. As a whole, the French Revolution and the life of J.F. Kennedy is neither clearly a romance nor clearly a tragedy. Because an interpretation of these events is meant to characterize them as a whole, neither plot is appropriate. It is my opinion that professional historians, for this reason, would not be happy with either interpretation. Neither does justice to the facts. Kennedy's life was a tragedy in that it provoked his assassination, and it was a romance because it succeeded in inspiring a generation of Americans to take pride in, and work for, their country.

I think that an important reason for Hayden White's reluctance to admit that certain events or lives are inherently tragic stems from his assumption that adjectives like 'tragic' and 'comic' apply to narratives, and that in reality there are no narratives of which they could be true or false. Like Ankersmit, he seems to assume that there were particular events in the past, but no such abstract things as revolutions and lives, which have what might be called an essentially narrative structure. However, as I argued in Chapter 2, it is quite reasonable and natural to say that these things have existed, and that they were sometimes tragic. It is interesting to note in a recent discussion of historical representation of Nazism and the 'Final Solution' White toys with the possibility of 'the events themselves' possessing 'a "story" kind of form', though he does not explain how this could be the case. Given this assumption, White admits: 'In the case of an emplotment of the events of the Third Reich in a "comic" or "pastoral" mode, we would be eminently justified in appealing to "the facts" in order to dismiss it from the list of "competing narratives" in the Third Reich.' The only way such plots could be used in narrating these events, he said, would be in an ironic representation of them (White, 1992, pp. 39–40).

For the sake of accuracy, one must distinguish statements which characterize something as tragic or romantic, and narratives which simply bring out the tragic or romantic features of the subject. The former can be true or false of the subject, whereas the latter can be only fair or misleading.

Hayden White, F.R. Ankersmit and H. Kellner have all argued that historical interpretations are inspired by metaphors, and for that reason cannot be true. The first point to be made in reply to this argument is that by no means all historical interpretations are metaphorical. To interpret the constitutional reforms in nineteenth-century Britain as extending democracy by extending the franchise is to provide a literal and accurate general description of them. But some interpretations do employ metaphors. Consider the following: 'During the decade 1870–80 one feature above all others shaped the surface of British politics – the personal duel, continuous save for a period following 1874, between two figures of tremendous stature, Gladstone and Disraeli' (Ensor, 1936, p. 1). Of course there was no literal duel between these two statesmen, but their relations resembled those of two men duelling, each trying to survive in office by 'mortally wounding' the other.

The second point is that metaphorical statements can be true or false. They are seldom literally true, indeed they are usually literally false. There was, literally, no duel between Gladstone and Disraeli. Rather, a metaphorical statement is metaphorically true, I suggest, if the subject of the statement has most of the relevant salient properties of the metaphorical object. The relevant salient properties are those relevant to the context of the statement. Here, for example, Ensor is writing of the political history of Britain, and so the relevant properties are those relevant to the political relations between Gladstone and Disraeli, their behaviour towards one another in the House of Commons and in their offices. If these relations exhibited some of the salient characteristics of a duel, salient that is in the public mind, then the metaphorical statement about them is metaphorically true. (For a fuller discussion of these points, see the last section of ch. 2, above.)

The conclusion to be drawn is that even if historians do adopt a literary framework of interpretation, and even if they employ a metaphor in their interpretation of past events, it remains the case that their interpretation can be true or false, fair or unfair.

THE OBJECTIVITY OF HISTORICAL INTERPRETATIONS

In 1935, Charles A. Beard published a paper entitled 'That Noble Dream', in which he attacked the possibility of writing objective history. Beard is well known for his economic interpretation of historical subjects, and in the essay he refers to the economic interpretation of the American Constitution that he had presented in *An Economic Interpretation of the Constitution of the United States* (1913). In it he argued that the Constitution was arranged to protect the interests of the property owners and traders. This was a signal departure from the usual account, which was that the Constitutional Convention was most concerned to establish institutions whose powers would be so balanced as to ensure the liberty of the people.

Beard says that he asked a colleague, H.L. Osgood, what he thought of his economic interpretation, and received this reply: 'Men of my generation grew up in the midst of great constitutional and institutional debates and our interest turned to institutional history. Profound economic questions have now arisen and students of the younger generation, true to their age, will occupy themselves with economic aspects of history.' (Beard, 1935, p. 322). Any interpretation, Beard went on to say, is 'simply the writer's version, construction, or conception of his subjects . . . not the absolute truth, of history' (p. 325).

There is no doubt that the interpretations which historians provide often reflect the interests and values held by themselves, their social group, or their nation. Beard assumed that interpretations cannot, therefore, be true or objective. That conclusion is, however, open to dispute. The fact that a summary description of an event, person or period is general and interesting does not imply that it cannot be both true and fair.

Early this century Heinrich Rickert argued strenuously that history can be objective so long as it is about universal values. Historians, said Rickert, should select events related to 'the general values embodied in religion, the state, law, customs, art, science, etc.' He went on:

> The fact that *cultural values are universal* in this sense is what keeps concept-formation in the historical sciences from being altogether *arbitrary* and thus constitutes the primary basis of its 'objectivity'. What is historically essential must be *important* not only for this or that particular historian, but for *all*.
>
> (Rickert, 1962, pp. 97–8)

Thus, for example, all historians would acknowledge the values for which state governments are instituted, namely the maintenance of peace and justice among their citizens, and so history which selected events relevant to this set of values would, he thought, be relative to a universally accepted value, and so be objective.

However, even if one acknowledged the existence of universal values embodied in the institutions to which Rickert referred, using these as a guide to historical interpretation would not entirely eliminate the influence of personal values. Suppose one decided to produce a political interpretation of a period, following Rickert's suggestion. One is still left with the choice of what political interpretation to provide. As David Thomas has said, one could describe modern Britain as 'a liberal democracy' or as 'a capitalist state'. The decision would very much reflect one's values and interests (Thomas, 1979, p. 134). It seems an undeniable fact that interpretive histories are at least to some degree subjective with respect to values.

Once this is recognized, it comes as no surprise to see that popular interpretations of historical subjects reflect the prevailing interests of a community. David Cannadine has shown how the interests of historians' societies have been reflected in their accounts of the Industrial Revolution in Britain. In the period 1880–1920, historians studied the social consequences of the revolution. Between the 1930s and the 1950s, interest focused on the cyclical fluctuations in the economy. From the 1950s to the 1970s the conditions of economic growth were studied. And since about 1974, Cannadine says, attention has been paid to the conditions which limited economic growth (Cannadine, 1984, pp. 131–72). Commenting upon one of these partial accounts of the Industrial Revolution, Cannadine writes: 'In that it draws attention to some important aspect of the subject, it is never going to be wholly "wrong"; but in that it gives disproportionate emphasis to a limited number of considerations, it is not likely to be wholly "right," either' (p. 171). Here we have evidence of a tension between a desire to focus upon interesting aspects of an historical subject, and a desire to provide a fair representation of it as a whole; between giving a partial interpretation of the subject which reflects particular interests, and a more comprehensive interpretation of it.

Although I admit that there is usually room for the choice of historical interpretations to be influenced by the personal interests of the historian, it seems that historians expect interpretations to meet certain objective criteria as well. For a new interpretation to be acceptable, it must synthesize more facts about the subject than those which preceded it, make more facts about the subject intelligible, as well as be so well supported by available evidence as to be rationally accepted as true. An interpretation is objectively good if it satisfies these conditions.

When Beard said that historical interpretations were not objective or true, he meant three things. First, he meant that the patterns historians describe in a subject are not really there, objectively. He wrote: 'Any overarching hypothesis or conception employed to give coherence and structure to past events in written history is an interpretation of some kind, something transcendent' (Beard, 1935, p. 324). Second, since an interpretation does not refer to anything that was really there, it cannot be true or false. Third, in Beard's opinion the source of an interpretation is the historian herself: 'Into the selection of topics, the choice and arrangement of materials, the specific historian's "me" will enter' (p. 324). The historian's choice, Beard said, will reflect her 'time, place, circumstance, interests, predilections, culture' (p. 324). So rather than being objective, according to Beard it seems more appropriate to think of historical interpretations as subjective.

Precisely these views seem to have been adopted by Peter Novick in his large book *That Noble Dream: The 'Objectivity Question' and the American Historical Profession* (1988). The 'myth' of objectivity, he says, is that there are patterns to be found in history, if only historians can rid themselves of preconceptions and personal commitments, to be free to discover them. The truth as Beard and Novick see it is that historical interpretations are not to be found in history, but are imposed upon it using concepts generated by the historian in the interests of the historian (pp. 1–2).

The truth is neither that historians discover patterns without drawing upon preconceptions, nor that the patterns do not exist in past events. Certainly historians bring concepts to bear when interpreting the past, just as we bring concepts to bear when perceiving the world. This does not imply that the general descriptions, or interpretations, which historians make using those concepts cannot be true. General descriptions have truth conditions, and if they are satisfied by the subject, then they are true. Moreover, if they are not misleading, they are also fair.

That leaves the question of how much an historian's personal commitments distort her judgement. There may be truth conditions for general descriptions, but biased historians may be casual about checking them, and certainly not worry much about the fairness of their descriptions. Furthermore, they might not bother considering other interpretations very carefully, to see whether they are of greater scope and explanatory power. So biased historians may not make sound judgements about the truth, fairness or goodness of their interpretations.

There is no denying that people cannot achieve a state of utter neutrality, committed to no values or principles, without projects or interests. Beard and Novick think that consequently the choice of interpretation is determined by the historian's interest in the subject. Since they believe that the patterns which historians describe are never suggested by the particular facts about the subject, there is no other explanation for them. Even if the patterns can be found in the subject, they would probably say that the historian's interests will determine which patterns they notice and choose to describe.

There is a lot of evidence that historians do pick out patterns which interest them. The same subject is often capable of several different, equally well supported interpretations. The important question is, does an historian's interest inevitably result in biased judgements, so that they cannot rationally consider whether the interpretation is true, fair or good?

Thomas L. Haskell has written a persuasive essay defending the possibility of sufficient detachment among historians to make accurate judgements. He said that detachment 'is the expression in intellectual affairs of the ascetic dimension of life' (Haskell, 1990, pp. 131–2). It involves temporarily setting aside what we wish to be the case, in order to discover what is really there, something people do in all walks of life. Haskell makes the important point that we can be intensely interested in the outcome of our investigations, and still manage to be sufficiently detached to conduct them rationally. He admits that some communities discourage independent thought, and provide such strong incentives for conformity that detachment becomes very difficult (p. 135). Nevertheless western historians do display considerable detachment very often, manifest in their willlingness to consider alternative views rationally in print (p. 135).

For example, when Christopher Hill first looked at the English Civil War, he did so with Marxist assumptions. In 1955 he wrote: 'the English Revolution of 1640, like the French Revolution of 1789, was a struggle for political, economic and religious power, waged by the middle class, the bourgeoisie, which grew in wealth and strength as capitalism developed' (Hill, 1955, p. 9). But later he expressed dissatisfaction with this interpretation, as not of sufficient scope nor of sufficient explanatory power:

> The importance of economic issues has been established; but we still have to find a synthesis which will take cognizance of this and yet give some explanation of why in 1640 not only M.P.s but a large number of other people thought bishops the main enemy; why there were so many conflicts before 1640 over the appointment of lecturers in town corporations; why, when the troops got drunk of a Saturday night in 1640, their animal spirits were worked off in the destruction of altar rails; why Cromwell's Army marched into battle singing psalms. . . . We also need far more understanding of ideas, especially at the point where they interact with economics. . . . Finally, questions of religion and church government should not be 'left behind the door'. We must have a better explanation of their importance for contemporaries than the theory that Puritanism helps landowners to balance their income and expenditure, or encourages the bourgeoisie to grind the faces of the poor.
>
> (Hill, 1958, pp. 24–5, 28)

Hill clearly had both a personal and a professional interest in maintaining a Marxist interpretation of the war, but he was sufficiently detached to acknowledge that such an interpretation was not a good one, that 'we still have to find a synthesis' to take account of many other important features of the war, and explain many more aspects of it.

I am not claiming that historians are always detached, only that they are often capable of being so, and of making rational judgements about the truth, fairness and worth of their interpretations. When historians are blind to their prejudices, then their colleagues, sometimes from other cultures, generally point them out.

Lawrence Stone, for example, has maintained that 1640 saw the start of a political and constitutional revolution in England, though the evidence does not support this interpretation of events that year. It took Paul Christianson to point this out. On Stone's own admission, he said, in the parliament of 1640 'no one dreamed of abolishing the monarchy or the House of Lords'; the members 'were reformers not revolutionaries'. Christianson goes on:

> Stone's picture of the members of the Long Parliament fits the known evidence supplied by detailed studies, but – since it clashes with the traditional assumptions [that the parliament was revolutionary] – he logically must either reject the assumptions or virtually explain away the picture. . . . By attempting to contain a prodigious amount of new wine in a modification of the old bottle at this stage, however, even Stone's sophisticated, subtle version explodes from the pressures of self-contradiction. Any similar attempt would suffer the same

fate, for ... detailed research has turned up too many anomalies for the old framework to handle.

(Christianson, 1976, p. 55)

The examples of historical practice in this chapter illustrate (1) that historians judge higher interpretations by objective criteria: of scope, intelligibility and truth; and (2) that they assiduously criticize existing interpretations in these regards, and seek better ones to replace them. It is possible at a certain stage in historical research for two or more different interpretations of the same subject to have equal merit, but after long and careful scrutiny, one usually proves superior.

5   The meaning of texts

Just as historians have interpreted events in a variety of ways, so too have they interpreted texts in many different ways. The variety of interpretations provides an immediate reason for doubting their objectivity. Once again, however, a study of historical practice reveals that historians have criteria for deciding which interpretations are superior, so that often a rational choice can be made between them.

The texts being considered in this chapter are mostly drawn from political theory, but the issues raised apply to texts in other fields as well, for example to texts in literature, religion, and history itself. What one finds immediately upon investigating the interpretation of such texts is a clear distinction between what might be called the basic meaning of a text, and a subsequent interpretation of it. Naturally texts only have meaning for people. The basic meaning of a text is the meaning which is agreed by most educated users of the language who are equally well informed on the subject of the text, and which, being basic, does not depend upon any other meaning of the text for its validity. Once the basic meaning of a text is known, then historians can sum up what it says in an interpretation of the text. The interpretation presents the significance of many parts of the text to which it relates. There are many fewer disputes about the basic meaning of a text than about its overall significance.

It is very difficult to formulate a satisfactory theory of meaning, and I shall not attempt to do so. The meaning of a descriptive sentence has been related to its truth conditions, to the intentions of the person who uttered it, and to social conventions, to name but three well-known approaches. Whatever meanings may be, it is usually possible to report the meaning of one sentence by means of another. Historians do this when the meaning of a text is obscure for some reason, perhaps because the language and/or the context is unfamiliar, and they want to state its meaning in words which the reader will easily understand.

It is my opinion that historians adopt uniform criteria for establishing the basic meaning of a text, which fix it largely beyond dispute. When they set about producing the basic meaning of a text, I suggest, they have these criteria in mind. For this reason, I would say that they can be said to be explaining what the text means, rather than interpreting it, at this stage. Once the basic meaning of a text is established, then it is interpreted, usually in one of two ways. One way is to formulate a general summary of the text, stating its main themes and arguments. This is a form of interpretation by generalization. The other way of interpreting a text is to identify its illocutionary force, which usually means stating the function of the text in the discussion of which it is a part. Often a text can be seen to perform several different functions, and it can be difficult to decide which makes most sense of it.

Occasionally an interpretation of a text influences an historian's decision as to its basic meaning. This happens at points when the basic meaning is uncertain, and an historian chooses that which fits her preferred interpretation of the whole text. Historians who know little about the author or the context of a text act on the assumption that the correct reading is that which best fits the overall tendency of the text itself. Unfortunately interpretations of the overall tendency of a text can vary a lot, so that this is not a reliable method of fixing the basic meaning of a text. The basic meaning of a text can usually be fixed without any reference to its overall interpretation. Scholars commonly agree about the basic meaning of a text, yet disagree about its overall significance.

There are several reasons for doubting the objectivity of both explanations of the basic meaning of a text, and the subsequent interpretations of it. The main objections to the possibility of reaching an objective understanding of the basic meaning of a text are as follows:

1 Most texts include phrases whose meaning is ambiguous and words whose reference is uncertain. So a precise statement of their meaning is impossible.
2 To say that these can be resolved by studying the context in which the text was produced assumes that the context can be fixed, which is not possible.
3 The interpreter brings many preconceptions about the meaning of the text to the task of interpreting it, as well as interests in the text, and the meaning given to it will reflect these.

There is only one important reason for doubting the objectivity of interpretations of texts, namely the huge variety of interpretations which is usually available, a variety reflected to some degree in the interpretations which historians actually give. Any choice between possible interpretations of a text, it seems, must be determined by the historian's interests.

First I shall consider the objectivity of explanations of the basic meaning of texts, and then, in the following section, look at the objectivity of interpretations. I shall argue that the explanation of the basic meaning of texts, and even the interpretation of those texts, is normally much more objective than critics have supposed.

THE BASIC MEANING OF A TEXT

Stanley Fish has declared that texts do not have a literal meaning:

> there is no such thing as literal meaning, if by literal meaning one means a meaning that is perspicuous no matter what the context and no matter what is

in the speaker's or hearer's mind, a meaning that because it is prior to interpretation can serve as a constraint on interpretation.

(Fish, 1989, p. 4)

It is important to contrast the literal meaning of a text with its basic meaning. The literal meaning is that which is entailed by the rules of the language of the text, both semantic and syntactic, but does not depend upon knowledge of the context in which the text was produced. Knowledge of the context can be vital in resolving ambiguities of meaning and uncertainties of reference, though such ambiguities and uncertainties do not always arise. Where they do, I suggest that the literal meaning of the text is indeterminate. The basic meaning of a text, as I shall use the term, is one in which any indeterminacies in the literal meaning of the text have been resolved.

The basic meaning of a text will include its metaphorical meaning, which is often quite different from its literal meaning. If someone says that his daughter is the apple of his eye, he does not mean it literally. Rather he means that she is the object of his attention and delight. It is commonly remarked that most metaphors are literally false. Similarly the basic meaning of a proverb usually differs from its literal meaning. If someone tells me not to count my chickens before they are hatched, they are literally referring to my chickens, of which I have none, but they intend me to understand the sentence metaphorically, as saying that I should not rely upon future uncertainties.

Generally speaking, the basic meaning of a text is that meaning which (1) does not violate any of the semantic and syntactic rules of the language in which it is written; (2) which resolves any obscurities of reference and ambiguities of meaning arising from these rules; (3) which provides a coherent body of information, or, if the text is no more than a sentence or two, which fits its context intelligibly; (4) which performs the first three functions to a much greater degree than any other reading which the text warrants; and perhaps (5) which convincingly explains away any failures to perform the first three functions (i.e. any inconsistencies between the reading and the rules of the language, any remaining obscurities and ambiguities, and any inconsistencies within the information it provides). If a reader cannot meet these requirements from a study of the text alone, then he or she may examine the context in which the text was produced. This will often locate the text in a wider frame of discourse and in an historical context which will clear up uncertainties of reference and meaning. If an adequate reading is still not available, the reader may then try to reconstruct the author's intention in order to resolve remaining uncertainties. Sometimes even recourse to the author's intentions will not remove all uncertainties, ambiguities and inconsistencies from one's reading of a text. These may in fact have been intended, as in the case of some diplomatic letters, and in some poems. Or they may not have been noticed by the author. In cases such as these, the reader appreciates an explanation of remaining inadequacies in the reading which accounts for their presence there. The reading of a text which is arrived at in this way, and which satisfies the five criteria listed above, is generally deemed to be the correct reading of the text.

Stanley Fish has argued that there is no correct literal reading of a text, and provides an example of a sentence whose meaning is ambiguous, and can only be settled by reference to the speaker's intention in uttering it (Fish, 1989, p. 185). Certainly there are sentences whose literal meaning cannot be determined simply by the rules of meaning and grammar. But there are many sentences which can be fully understood on the basis of linguistic rules alone, without any need to refer to their context. For instance, you can readily understand the sentence 'Dogs generally have two ears, four legs and one tail', and so decide whether it is true or false, simply from the rules of English. Not all sentences are ambiguous or indeterminate.

Fish has another reason for querying the literal meaning of texts. He argues that sometimes sentences which have been assumed to be meant literally are found to have been meant ironically. The reading depends upon assumptions about the intention of the author. Fish concludes: 'therefore, when that literal meaning has been set aside for an ironic one, what has happened is that one interpretive construct has been replaced by another. That is to say, *if irony is a way of reading, so is literalness*; neither way is prior to the other, in the sense of being a mode of calculation rather than interpretation' (pp. 194–5).

Fish misunderstands the situation. First, a literal reading of a text does not depend upon any assumptions concerning the author's intention at all. It depends simply upon the rules of the language. Second, as Fish admits, what leads scholars to suspect that an ironic reading of a text was intended, is a certain inconsistency within it. Fish considers Jonathan Swift's 'Verses on the Death of Dr. Swift', where the lines in which Swift praises himself fit awkwardly with the rest. Such an inconsistency is only apparent on a literal, or basic reading of the text. Indeed reading those lines as ironic is intended to remove that inconsistency. Third, to read a text ironically is to read it as having a certain illocutionary force, as will be explained in the next section. (Quentin Skinner has made the same point, at 1988, p. 270.) Such a reading requires an understanding of its literal or basic meaning to be effective. So, although it is reasonable to say that an ironic reading of a text is an interpretation of it, there is no good reason for saying that a statement of its literal or basic meaning is also an interpretation, resting on assumptions about the author's overall intention in writing it.

It is only by identifying the meaning of a text with its intended meaning, that Fish's argument can be sustained. Then you could say that the literal meaning involves an interpretation of the author's intention, that it be read literally rather than ironically. But as we all know, sometimes the literal meaning of a text differs from what the author sincerely meant by it. For instance, people sometimes use the wrong word, though from the context it is easy to see what they intend. Comedians trade on this fact sometimes, getting laughs from the dissonance. 'Captain Matthew Flinders circumcised Australia in a twenty-foot cutter', and so on.

In short, there are many sentences whose literal meaning is quite clear, and is not at all a matter of interpretation. Even so, there are also sentences whose literal meaning is indeterminate. For example, the meaning of 'That man is eyeing me' cannot be known until we know who is being referred to by 'that man' and 'me', and precisely what is intended by 'eyeing'. To discover these things, you would have to discover a lot about the context of its utterance.

That is why the difference between basic meaning and literal meaning is so important. The basic meaning of a sentence is one whose ambiguities and uncertainties have been resolved by reference to the context of its production, that is, to its verbal and historical context, and to the intentions of its author. In practice these almost always fix its meaning in a way which all would agree upon. A statement of the basic meaning of a text is correct if it is agreed upon by all educated, equally well informed, users of the language. Sometimes, as was admitted above, ambiguities and uncertainties remain even after the context has been investigated, in which case all will agree that the basic meaning of the text is uncertain, and no particular reading can be deemed correct.

It might be objected that any conventions, such as the five listed above, cannot be justified as yielding a correct understanding of a text without vicious circularity. If we were to say that these conventions are appropriate because in conforming to them we always arrive at a correct understanding of texts, that would indeed be circular, assuming that there is no independent check of their correctness. But if we say that in our community conformity to these conventions is what we mean by calling an interpretation of a text correct, then circularity has been avoided. The claim that a correct understanding of a text is one which satisfies certain conventional criteria does not necessarily entail any vicious circularity of reasoning.

Does it invite a charge of arbitrariness instead? This question is more difficult to answer. Perhaps it is enough to say that, as Saussure has taught us, many linguistic conventions are arbitrary. Saussure noted that the relations between signifiers (words) and signifieds (concepts), though fairly regular, are usually arbitrary. It would be no great surprise, then, if the relations between texts and their meanings are somewhat arbitrary too. They involve, at a minimum, rules of semantics and syntax which seem largely arbitrary, varying as they do from language to language. Whether they are arbitrary or not, the rules for interpreting texts generally enable quite effective communication of precise ideas, and that is what justifies them.

If the language of the text is not very well known by the reader, and the text provides a significantly large part of the evidence of that language, then the criteria are a bit different. The reader still wants to find a reading of the text which is as unambiguous and coherent as possible. But it must also be consistent with the rules of language which he or she judges to make best sense of all the evidence of that language available. Thus, for example, if a scholar were unfamiliar with Plato's Greek, he or she would look for readings of the Platonic dialogues consistent with the best theories of Plato's general semantics and syntax, as well as readings which are as unambiguous and coherent as possible.

An historically correct reading of an old text is one which rests upon a correct understanding of the language in which it is written. (A correct understanding of a language is one which would be generally accepted as correct by educated users of that language.) Knowing this, historians do not simply rely upon their own personal prejudices to suggest readings of old texts. Because they are searching for a reading which would have been generally accepted at the time of the text's composition, the historian becomes familiar with the language of the time and with the prevailing world-view in order to have a better chance of thinking of a reading which would generally have been adopted. If there is abundant evidence of that language, an historian can become so familiar with it as to be fully justified in saying that he or she correctly understands it. If the text is in a language which is, to some extent, unfamiliar and of which there is only a moderate amount of evidence, then the historian has to find a reading which fits what is known of the language as well as possible, and the probability of the reading being correct will vary depending upon the quantity of data and the degree to which the reading fits it.

Historians who study texts from cultures other than their own are only too well aware of the importance of mastering the language of those texts. This involves learning the concepts it employs, and how its literature portrays the society, indeed the world, of its day. To develop such mastery they immerse themselves in its literature and in the world-view of the times. J.G.A. Pocock has stressed the importance of this practice.

> only after we have understood what means [an author] had of saying anything can we understand what he meant to say, what he succeeded in saying, what he was taken to have said. . . .
> The historian's first problem, then, is to identify the 'language' or 'vocabulary' with and within which the author operated.
>
> (Pocock, 1972, p. 25)

> If . . . we are asked how we know the languages adumbrated [e.g. theological, legal and humanist] really existed, or how we recognize them when we see them, we should be able to reply empirically: that the languages in question are simply there, that they form individually recognizable patterns and styles, and that we get to know them by learning to speak them, to think in their patterns and styles until we know that we are speaking them and can predict in what directions speaking them is carrying us. From this point we may proceed to study them in depth, detecting both their cultural and social origins and the modes, linguistic and political, of assumption, implication, and ambiguity which they contained and helped to convey.
>
> (ibid., p. 26)

Historians frequently try to fix the meaning of a text by defining the key words it employs in terms of the author's personal world-view. This can be a very difficult task. When Peter Laslett presented his account of what Locke meant by 'property', he referred to no less than thirteen previous attempts to explain the term (Laslett, 1970, pp. 100–106; see footnote on p. 103). When John Dunn discussed Locke's notion of 'consent', he contrasted his view with those of J. Plamenatz and C.B. Macpherson (Dunn, 1980, pp. 29–52). To decide what was meant by the pamphlets which contributed to the American Revolution, Bernard

Bailyn made a special study of their use of the words 'power' (Bailyn, 1967, pp. 55ff.), 'constitution' (pp. 67ff.), 'liberty' (pp. 79ff.), 'sovereignty' (pp. 198ff.) and 'slavery' (pp. 233ff.).

What linguistic context should historians examine before they can be reasonably confident that they have mastered a language? There are two ways of answering this, one statistical and the other historical. First, they should examine as many examples of a discourse as are necessary for them to read such examples and experience no difficulty in understanding them. At that point there is little to be gained by studying more: a law of diminishing returns applies. Second, if they are interested in the meaning of a text for a particular individual or group, they can read much of the literature which that individual or group would have read, to become familiar with their particular understanding of the relevant discourse. It is reasonable to suppose that an understanding of a language which makes sense of large quantities of it is an accurate understanding. The chances of two different interpretations of a language working equally well are negligible, except in the case of individual words and phrases. While these remain ambiguous, historians must study as many instances of them as they can, until they discover one meaning which fits all contexts, or until they confirm the ambiguity of the word or phrase in that language. Of course it is always logically possible that a language can be understood in more than one way, so that it is possible that an historian's understanding of a language is mistaken. But if their understanding fits a large and varied sample of that language, together with the contexts in which it has been used, then we are justified in regarding that understanding of the language as correct, since in practice the chance of any other interpretation of the language being so successful is negligible.

And what historical context should historians study in order to understand an old text correctly? They should study the objects and events to which the text seems to refer, and try to imagine how these were conceptualized by their contemporaries by reading what they wrote about them. Information about these things is often useful in clearing up uncertainties of reference and ambiguities of meaning in a text. There is often a lot of independent evidence about the things to which a text refers, enough to warrant an historian saying that he or she has accurate knowledge of them. I have described the nature of that justification elsewhere (McCullagh, 1984, pp. 105–11).

Finally, an historian's knowledge of an author's intentions can also be well justified. To understand an author's intentions one must find an interpretation of the text which fits well with what is known of the author's beliefs, values and concerns. I consider intentions to be states of mind which cause authors to write as they do. For that reason, descriptions of an author's intention can be regarded as true or false, and not merely correct. Such descriptions are normally justified by means of an argument to the best explanation. (See for example my discussion of the interpretations of Hitler's intention in writing the Hossbach Memorandum: ibid., p. 121.) The important fact to notice here is that arguments to the best explanation are very commonly accepted as yielding conclusions which may be accepted as true. They may be false, but if one explanatory hypothesis is well supported, and is far superior to the others that can be thought of, it is reasonable to accept it as true (ibid., Chapter 2).

Historians look for accounts of the basic meaning of the text which fit well with what they know about its language, and if necessary with the circumstances of its composition and the intention of its author. These accounts are not simply a function of the historian's prejudices or preconceptions, but are hypotheses which, in many cases, are supported by quite a large amount of historical data. Gadamer portrays hermeneutics as like an aesthetic activity, ignoring the fact that it is an act of historical cognition. He likens the discovery of the meaning of a text to the recognition of the universal truth expressed in a work of art (Gadamer, 1975, pp. 145–6). Both are depicted as the product of a sort of game or conversation with the text, or with the work of art, in which one keeps correcting initial readings in the light of further observations. What he does not notice is that the hermeneutic exercise of finding a reading of a text which fits it well is part of the process of discovering the correct basic understanding of that text. If the understanding accords with the rules of the language of the text, and usually with the context of its creation, and with the author's intention, then it is the correct understanding of the text.

In discussions of the meaning of texts, it is common to distinguish the meaning of the sentences, according to the rules of language, the meaning of the utterance, taking into account the context in which the text was produced, and the meaning of the utterer, that is the meaning which the author intended to convey in writing the text. How does the basic meaning of a text relate to these alternatives? From what I have observed, our practice is to decide the basic meaning of a text by following the procedure described before. First we consider the meaning of the sentences, drawing solely upon our knowledge of the language, and if this is unambiguous, we go no further. If it is ambiguous, however, we refer to the context in the hope of clearing up the ambiguity. The sentence 'There are bats in the belfry' means one thing if addressed to the local pest controller, and another if spoken to the church cricket team looking for their equipment. If a careful study of the context fails to resolve the ambiguity, we then turn our attention to the speaker, and try to discover what he or she probably intended in saying what they did. Thus the meaning of a text may depend upon the meaning of the corresponding utterance, and even the meaning of the utterer, but it need not do so. Indeed, if the meaning of a text is unambiguous according to the rules of the language, it may differ from the meaning which the utterer intended to convey. Interestingly enough, precisely the same procedure is followed to determine the secondary meaning of a text as well.

I have suggested that one can sometimes justify one's understanding of the basic meaning of a text by reference to rules of semantics and syntax alone. In practice, however, providing a complete justification of an explanation of the basic meaning of a text in terms of these rules is virtually impossible, as the rules involved defy complete formulation. Competent language users know how to apply these rules, but not how to state them. In practice, therefore, we regard a statement of the meaning of a sentence as justified if most educated users of the language judge it to be correct.

Let me turn now to the objections listed at the beginning of this chapter, which argued that objective knowledge of the meaning of a text is not possible. The first was that many texts are ambiguous or very vague, so that any statement of their meaning must be a personal reading of them. This has already been addressed, by pointing out how we all consider the context of the creation of the text, and perhaps the intentions of the author, to resolve its ambiguities and uncertainties.

The second objection was that the context of an utterance cannot really be fixed, so that no reading which depends upon context can be fixed either. There are two quite different reasons for saying that the context of an utterance cannot be fixed. One is that the limits of the context cannot be fixed without making some arbitrary decision as to what is relevant and what is not. The second is that an historian's knowledge of the relevant contexts itself involves interpretation of 'texts', in a broad sense, and so cannot be known objectively.

What are the relevant contexts for determining the basic meaning of a text? The author's physical and social world, the author's language and culture, the texts the author has read, especially in the field or discourse of which the text is a part, should all these contexts be included? The scope seems enormous, but in practice it is much more restricted. In practice the context relevant to a text certainly includes all these things, but more particularly those close to the text and the occasion of its creation. Indeed the context can be circumscribed even more narrowly: it is primarily those things which are likely to have been a matter of concern to the author at the time, the people, events and issues which were likely to have been the focus of her attention.

Derrida denies that knowledge of the author's intentions and concerns is relevant to the meaning of a text. He points out that writing can communicate in the absence of its author, without knowledge of the author's intentions in writing it, or the context in which the author wrote (Derrida, 1982, pp. 316–17). Following Saussure, Derrida insists that the meaning of words is to be found in their role in a language, in their implications, associations and contrasts (Derrida, 1982). He goes beyond Saussure in allowing that the meanings which words have for any reader are also to be found in whatever literary and logical significance they may have for that reader. So Derrida finds a profusion of meanings for the texts he analyses, a profusion which he says is without limits. For him, a text

> is henceforth no longer a finished corpus of writing, some content enclosed in a book or its margins, but a differential network, a fabric of traces referring endlessly to something other than itself, to other differential traces. Thus the text overruns all the limits assigned to it so far.
>
> (Derrida, 1979, p. 84)

Derrida's theory of meaning is of some value, but it is far from adequate. He rightly describes the meaning of words as a function of their relation to other words associated with them in one way or another, though he should also have recognized the importance of their association with other things, such as objects in the world, experiences people have, and changes people want to bring about. The fact that many texts can be understood without knowledge of the circumstances of their composition does not mean that the words they use have no association with the world. Many words are commonly and regularly associated with things in the world, things which they refer to or bring about. We understand texts very often by knowing what they refer to or what they are intended to achieve, and that knowledge is not always purely textual, but often includes elements of experience.

However, even if Derrida's theory were augmented to include associations such as these, it still would not be adequate. For surely a theory of meaning should explain how we know the meaning of texts. Derrida's theory fails to explain how we use language to communicate as clearly and precisely as we do. It simply ignores the conventions by which we decide which, among the various possible meanings words can have, we should understand them to have in the case of a given text or utterance. To explain our success in understanding apparently ambiguous texts, Derrida would have to admit that we often refer to the context of their creation, and the intention of their author.

Suppose, to clarify the meaning of the statement, someone said that when the vicar said there were bats in the belfry, he was talking to the captain of a church cricket team who had been inquiring about equipment for the game. Derrida might say that in that case, one text is being read in relation to another, namely in relation to a report of what the vicar was doing at the time. It would seem, then, that the original text is being understood simply by being related to another text, not to the conditions of its creation at all. To say this, however, is to misunderstand the situation. For why is this additional text selected as relevant to the meaning of what the vicar said, and not any other statement? It is relevant just because it informs us of the conditions under which the vicar uttered the sentence in question. Those conditions are vital in determining the correct reading to the vicar's words, and the report of what the vicar was doing provides us with knowledge of those conditions.

This brings us to the second reason for denying that the context is determinate. Dominick LaCapra has expressed some concern about the practice of referring to the context of an utterance in order to understand it (see LaCapra, 1985, p. 105). He remarked: 'The difficulties in the process of inferentially reconstructing contexts on the basis of texts (in the large sense) are often obscured or repressed, especially when one is convinced that a context or a set of contexts must be a determinative force with full explanatory power' (p. 128). LaCapra does not go so far as to say these difficulties cannot be overcome, because historians have been strikingly successful in recovering the contexts of documents and using them to establish a convincing reading of them. Rather, he fears that preoccupation with context can blinker an historian from seeing the present significance of the text she is studying: 'over-contextualization is not only possible; it is frequently a clear and present danger in the writing of history. It occurs when one so immerses a text in the particularities of its own time and place that one impedes responsive understanding and excessively restricts the interaction between past and present' (p. 132).

The only serious worry about fixing the context of a text is when the available evidence is insufficient for an historian to be certain what the context was. In that case it is tempting for an historian just to assume a context which supports a preferred reading of the text, rather than admit uncertainty. A careful historian, however, will honestly admit the impossibility of knowing precisely what is meant.

The third reason for doubting that historians can possibly arrive at a correct reading of an old text is that historians cannot avoid being influenced by the traditional interpretations of a text in trying to discover what they mean, and also by their personal interest in the outcome of their inquiries, which will bias their thinking. Gadamer has drawn attention to the way in which we read texts according to received traditions about their meaning, and with an eye to their relevance to our present interests. LaCapra writes of yet another danger, the danger of 'uncritical transference', which involves 'imputing to the "other" traits one refuses to recognize in oneself' (p. 124).

All these sources of bias can be overcome by careful, critical procedures. Gadamer himself was at pains to explain how historians extend their understanding to include other cultures, and how they test any reading of a text for its coherence, both its internal consistency and its coherence with what is known of the world in which it was produced. My account of the basic meaning of a text is more specific. When an historian investigates the basic meaning of a text, she wants a statement she can understand which satisfies the five criteria listed above. When bias distorts the reading of a text, failure to satisfy one or more of those criteria will usually reveal that this has happened.

INTERPRETING THE SECONDARY MEANING OF A TEXT

Once the basic meaning of a text has been understood, historians then reflect upon its significance. Texts are historically significant in several different ways. They provide evidence of the beliefs and attitudes of their author, and evidence of the society in which the author lived. They may have stimulated responses in those who read them, responses of interest to the historian. But such causes and effects of a text are not what I refer to as its secondary meaning. The secondary meanings of a text are statements of its conventional significance, of what educated and well informed readers of the text would be conventionally justified in saying was its significance.

There are two kinds of conventional significance of a text which appear to be of particular interest to historians. They frequently try to summarize the main theses and arguments of a text, summing up in their own words the points made by the text at greater length. The result could be called a summary interpretation of the text. Second, historians are often fascinated to discover the illocutionary force of a text, how it could be understood in the context of its production. To state the illocutionary force of a text is to state what a text may be taken as doing in stating what it states: whether it is answering a question, defending an intellectual position, mocking a way of life, reporting a discovery, and so on. I will consider each of these kinds of interpretation in turn.

In each case, as I will show, there is a problem of deciding whether the historian should provide the secondary meaning of a text as this would have been understood by the community of the author, drawing upon its beliefs and conventions; or whether the historian should judge the meaning of a text for people like herself, reading it today. Both the historical and the current meaning of a text can be of interest, and both I think are equally legitimate, so long as they are clearly distinguished.

Interpretations of the secondary meaning of a text can vary a lot, as will be seen, and this might be taken to imply that there are no commonly agreed criteria for judging between them. However, in practice historians do criticize each other's interpretations, appealing to criteria similar to those used for judging interpretations of historical events and periods, discussed in the last chapter. The key criterion is scope: historians generally prefer interpretations which relate the greatest number of facts about the text. But intelligibility is also very important: the interpretation should enable the reader to see the point of much of what the text says. In addition, interpretations should not be very complex, and if possible should be coherent. Evidence of these standards is provided by the examples which follow.

The summary meanings of a text

A very common form of higher understanding of the meaning of a text is that achieved by producing an adequate summary of what it says, that is, of its basic meaning.

A common reason for summarizing an author's views is to compare them with those of others. J.G.A. Pocock has made a special study of the writing of James Harrington. In an essay entitled 'Machiavelli, Harrington and English Eighteenth Century Ideologies', he produced a summary of Harrington's political thought, quoting him only for the sake of illustration. His summary is often quite terse:

> Harrington's entire theory of monarchy can be reduced to two propositions: first, that the King's agents and servants must be supported either upon the land, as a feudal aristocracy, or about his person as praetorians or janissaries; second, that which ever of these methods is adopted, relations between the military class and the King will be so prone to tensions that monarchy can never be a stable form of government.
>
> (Pocock, 1972, pp. 116–17)

Pocock provided this summary of Harrington's theory in order to compare it with that of the first Earl of Shaftesbury. This practice is repeated throughout the essay. For example he used summaries to compare what he called 'the "County" vision of English politics' with Harrington's view: 'If we now summarize the main outlines of the "County" vision of English politics as it appears in a multitude of writings in the century that follows 1675, we may attempt to see what is Harrington, or rather neo-Harrrington, about it' (p. 124).

Historians aim to produce summaries which are accurate, informative and comprehensive. A summary is accurate if the statements in the text instantiate it and are not inconsistent with it. Informativeness decreases as generality increases, as a very general summary could be instantiated by a large number of diverse texts. So historians prefer a summary which is no more general than they require. The level of generality is that at which comparisons of interest can be made most clearly. A summary should be comprehensive in that it covers the various aspects of the basic meaning of the text in question, so that each significant part of the basic text instantiates part of the summary. Let me illustrate.

C.B. Macpherson's Marxist interpretation of Locke in *The Political Theory of Possessive Individualism* has earned much respect but also some criticism. Alan Ryan has argued that it is not accurate. For example, Macpherson said that Locke denied that labourers without property could be full citizens, as citizenship was reserved for those with property. Ryan objects that 'some plainly unambiguous statements by Locke . . . flatly contradict' this summary of Locke's views. Locke in fact maintained that all rational adults could be citizens, and denied citizenship only to 'Lunaticks and Idiots' (Ryan, 1965, p. 223). Macpherson was also mistaken in thinking that Locke restricted 'property' to goods, for Locke described property as that which others have no right to take without the person's consent, and specifically included such personal things as life, liberty and health. Ryan concludes that 'the force of Macpherson's account challenges one to produce some alternative picture that fits the text better than this' (pp. 227–8).

Dunn's criticism of John Plamenatz's interpretation of Locke reveals the importance of summaries being comprehensive if they are to be acceptable. Plamenatz, seeing Locke as a great liberal philosopher, assumed that Locke based political obligation upon the consent of the governed. But, Dunn points out, this interpretation ignores the theological dimension of Locke's thought. Referring to a large range of Locke's writings, Dunn shows that Locke grounded political obligation in man's duty to God of self-preservation. Since people cannot subsist without society, God, who wills them to subsist, also wills them to use their reason to discover the rules by which a society can be maintained, and to follow them. People consent to others having authority over them, so that consent is a necessary condition of political obligation. But what is also necessary, to drive them to obey, is duty to God (Dunn, 1980, pp. 29–33). By ignoring the theological dimension of Locke's thought, Plamenatz and others had produced a summary which said nothing about large and important parts of Locke's writings on political obligation. (Mark Bevir has also used discussions of Locke's writing as evidence of objectivity in judging the interpretations of texts (Bevir, 1994, pp. 337–9), though I did so first in McCullagh, 1991b, p. 315.)

When an important relevant part of any author's work is ignored by a summary description, the summary is prone to give a misleading impression of the whole. Pocock has explained how the habit of commentators in ignoring books III and IV of Hobbes' *Leviathan*, which discuss religious history, has led people to believe that Hobbes' thought was 'unhistorical' to a degree which it was not (Pocock, 1972, pp. 149–50). Indeed the practice has even fuelled the belief that Hobbes lacked religious convictions and was, perhaps, an atheist (p. 161). Pocock condemns such interpretations of Hobbes' writing and of his convictions as seriously misleading.

The most summary of all summary interpretations of a text are those which refer to the 'key idea' of an author's work. A key idea, it seems, is one upon which the other principle ideas to some extent depend. Once a work has been summarized, it is then sometimes possible to identify its key idea. For this reason, an interpretation of the key idea of a text could be regarded as a tertiary interpretation of the meaning of the text, depending as it does upon a secondary summary reading of the text.

In a thoughtful discussion of the fundamental idea in Harrington's political philosophy Pocock discusses C.B. Macpherson's belief 'that Harrington's system will not work unless entrepreneurial behaviour in land owners is presumed to be at its basis' (ibid., p. 111). Macpherson argued that changes in the social distribution of power in seventeenth-century England were seen by Harrington to be the result of changes in patterns of wealth, particularly land ownership. Pocock thinks Harrington saw it as the result of changes in the legal obligations which went with land tenure. Feudal obligations to serve an overlord gave place to the independent tenure of freeholders. Pocock argues that Macpherson's understanding of the key idea in Harrington's system is wrong because certain important features of his system do not depend upon it.

> Harrington's notion of the power which the man who has property exerts over the man who has none does not entail any particular description of the economic relations between the two men, or of the economic process in which the two are engaged. All that is necessary to know is that the one is independent and the other dependent on him.
>
> (p. 111)

In another essay, on 'Burke and the Ancient Constitution', Pocock explains how Burke's conservative political theory is an expression of a theory about the nature of English law developed by Sir Edward Coke and Sir Matthew Hale in the seventeenth century, a theory which maintained that English common law was based upon custom, interpreted and applied in courts, from time immemorial, and that it enshrined the practical wisdom of ages and so deserved the utmost respect. This theory was applied to the English constitution in what was called 'the doctrine of the ancient constitution', to defend the constitution against reform. That doctrine was respected by many in Burke's time, and was used by him in 1782 to oppose moves to reform it. Instead of talking about a 'key idea' Pocock here refers to a 'root idea': Burke 'roots his argument in the idea that the law is immemorial and customary' (1972, p. 229).

There has been some debate among historians about the appropriateness of summarizing texts in modern terms which the author would never have used. Quentin Skinner has shown that this practice, by historians who have not carefully understood the basic meaning of the texts first, can lead them to misrepresent them. For example, those who have interpreted the political views of the Levellers in seventeenth-century Britain as a 'philosophy of liberal democracy', simply because the Levellers were concerned with an extension of the right to vote, have completely mistaken their views.

> First the paradigm makes it unnecessarily difficult to account for some of the most characteristic features of Leveller ideology. For if we are programmed to think in terms of the 'republican secularism' of the movement, it is not surprising that their agonizings over the Monarchy and their appeals to religious sentiment begin to look somewhat baffling. And second, the paradigm of 'democracy' will tend to lead the historical investigation in rather inappropriate directions. Some anachronistic concept of 'the welfare state' has to be found in Leveller thought, as well as a belief in 'manhood suffrage', which they never in fact held.
>
> (Skinner, 1969, p. 27)

To describe the Levellers as presenting a theory of liberal democracy is thus not only unfair, in that it fails to accommodate many of their important concerns about the crown and religion, but it is also misleading in that it implies concerns for a welfare state and manhood suffrage which were not theirs at all. Such mistakes can be avoided, however, if the historian carefully checks whether the basic meaning of a text warrants the modern description of it.

To avoid misrepresenting people's ideas, Skinner believes historians should 'so far as possible ... think as they thought and ... see things in their way' (Skinner, 1988, p. 252). There is often no precise equivalent in our language for a word used in another culture, and he says that historians should study the use of such words in different contexts to capture their sense exactly (pp. 250–5). Skinner adds: 'the fact that we cannot be sure of translating it satisfactorily does not mean that we cannot hope to describe its range of references by means of something approaching an adequate English periphrasis' (p. 252). For example, there is no exact counterpart in English for Machiavelli's use of the word *virtù*: 'he used it if and only if he wished to refer to just those qualities, whether moral or otherwise, that he took to be most conducive to military and political success' (p. 253).

One problem with this careful attention to terms used by past writers is that it seems difficult to relate their ideas to modern concerns. Each writer used words in slightly different ways, with consequently different meanings, and so they cannot be said to have been discussing the same issue (p. 283). For example, Skinner notes:

> Historians have regularly discussed Machiavelli's theory in terms of its account of the relationship between the rights and interests of individual citizens and the powers of the state. But Machiavelli himself never employs the terminology of rights (*diritti*) or interests (*interessi*) at any point. The effect of revising his vocabulary in this way has been to supply him with a range of alleged beliefs about a number of topics on which he never pronounced.
>
> (p. 255)

Skinner concludes that 'there can be no histories of concepts as such; there can only be histories of their uses in argument' (p. 283).

In a thoughtful essay on this problem, John Dunn (1980, pp. 13–28) agrees that historians must take care not to misrepresent past thinkers, but argues that they should be willing to judge their texts nevertheless. Political thinkers, he says, were wrestling with problems very similar to those faced by people down the ages. Their assumptions about the nature of the problem might be different from ours, but Dunn thinks we can judge the adequacy of their solutions nevertheless. Despite the dangers of summarizing old texts in modern terms, John Dunn suggests that such summaries are useful in showing the modern relevance of the texts. He therefore applauds the practice, while remaining concerned about their accuracy.

> To present a complex argument from the past in terms of its significance for us may often seem mendacious and to present it with the greatest concern for historical specificity but without exploring its 'significance' is likely to seem trivial.
>
> (Dunn, 1969, p. 208)

> The history of philosophy, like the history of science, must needs be Whig as to subject-matter . . . [and] . . . Tory as to truth.
>
> (Dunn, 1980, p. 26)

Dunn thinks that historians should present past ideas in their own terms first, being very careful to conserve the truth, but then reflect upon them from a modern point of view.

The process of carefully judging the justification of a modern summary of an old text is well illustrated by J.W. Gough's discussion of Willmore Kendall's thesis that Locke's theory was not 'individualist', as has been commonly thought, but that it gives an 'authoritarian and collectivist' account of political power (Gough, 1956, ch. 2). To judge the adequacy of these descriptions, Gough interprets them and then looks for evidence relevant to them in Locke's writing. An 'individualist' theory, it seems, is one which presents government as severely limited by the rights of individuals. An 'authoritarian' theory insists upon the government's authority over individuals, unless the government is so bad that the people are entitled to revolt. There are passages in Locke which support both views, so how does Gough decide the issue? First, he carefully examines the crucial passages in context to see whether they do support the interpretation suggested for them. He finds that some which appear to support the individualist interpretation do not really do so, when studied in their context (pp. 29–30). Second, he points out that there is evidence for and against both readings, and that each can only be defended by ignoring as insignificant those passages which tell against it. As Gough puts it:

> Many critics have noticed features of Locke's theory which seem inconsistent with the usual individualist interpretation of him. The critics have varied, however, in the degree of emphasis they have laid on such discrepancies, and have generally tended to treat the individualism as fundamental, and to

minimize what is inconsistent with this, either ignoring it in their final verdict or dismissing it as ill-considered and unrepresentative of Locke's real view. Mr. Kendall, in effect, reverses this tendency. It is the individualist passages which are inconsistencies for him, and he emphasizes instead the points – and they certainly amount to a considerable array – on the other side.

(p. 28)

Finally, Gough concludes that the truth about Locke lies somewhere between the two extremes. His theory does not neatly fit either modern model, though it contains important elements of both.

> Was Locke then, after all, an individualist? I think we can say he was, but he was not a thorough-going, extreme individualist. . . . He stands mid-way between two extreme positions in politics. . . . We may conclude, then, that Locke was an individualist in a qualified sense. He did not imagine the state to be an artificially fabricated combination of naturally separate individuals; he did not champion the individual against the community, and barely considered the possibility of conflict between them. But the government he recommended was in effect the parliamentary limited monarchy approved of by his Whig contemporaries, and this meant that it would be constitutional and not absolute, and that it would not invade the liberties of the subject.

(p. 51)

Old theories seldom fit modern paradigms neatly, but they sometimes have important ideas and values in common. These are highlighted by modern summaries of them. The extreme interpretations of Locke were neither accurate, comprehensive nor fair. They implied positions contrary to those Locke adopted, and they ignored important parts of his theory, thus giving a misleading impression of the whole. That is why they were finally rejected by Gough.

The illocutionary force of a text

Another form of secondary meaning which interests historians is what is called the illocutionary force of a text. There has been much discussion of this concept since J.L. Austin introduced it in *How To Do Things With Words* (1962). Nevertheless Austin's own way of identifying the illocutionary force of a text remains quite good. The illocutionary force of a text is the kind of act which the person who produced the text can, according to convention, be said to be performing in uttering it in the context. It may be, for example, that the author is describing an event, answering a question, or criticizing a decision. This account effectively distinguishes the illocutionary force from the perlocutionary force of an utterance, where the latter corresponds to what the speaker intends to bring about by uttering it, such as educating the reader or impressing her with one's erudition. Intended outcomes such as these are not equivalent to the conventional significance of the utterance in context. As Austin said: 'Illocutionary acts are conventional acts: perlocutionary acts are *not* conventional' (p. 120).

It will not do to suggest that the illocutionary force of a text corresponds to the author's intention in producing it, though in fact it usually does. First, a text can have an illocutionary force which the author did not intend, and of which she was even unaware. For example an utterance might be presumptuous or defamatory when it was intended to be neither. These might be correct conventional descriptions of the force of the text in the context, even though they were not intended. Second, reference to the author's intentions does not suffice to distinguish illocutionary from perlocutionary force, since both are usually intended by the author by uttering the text. For instance, the author may intend both to describe an event and to inform the reader of it.

Quentin Skinner has argued for a distinction between the illocutionary *force* of an utterance, and the illocutionary *act* of uttering it with the intention that it have that force. He says: 'The illocutionary acts we perform are identified, like all voluntary acts, by our intentions; but the illocutionary forces carried by our utterances are mainly determined by their meaning and context' (1988, p. 266). He denies that there can be unintentional illocutionary acts, assuming, it seems, that acts must be intentional under every description (p. 265). I think that although actions are normally intentional under at least one description, there may be other descriptions of them under which they are unintentional. Thus I may be betraying a confidence in passing on what you told me, without intending to do so. All I intended was to communicate what you had confided in me, but in the context it would be appropriate to say that in doing so I was betraying your confidence in my discretion. That was the unintentional illocutionary act I performed in speaking as I did.

Because the illocutionary force of a text can be identified by noting the conventions of a discourse and the context of the utterance, historians can frequently discover it without knowing anything about the personal intentions of the author. Quentin Skinner, for example, has shown that John Locke, in his *Two Treatises of Government*, 'was rejecting and repudiating one of the most widespread and prestigious forms of political argument at the time'. Skinner did this simply by noting 'the prevailing conventions of debate about political obligation', the role of 'the ancient English constitution' in those, and Locke's failure to mention it (Skinner, 1974, p. 286). Similarly he has shown that Machiavelli in places 'challenges the prevailing assumptions of the mirror-for-princes writers', by comparing what those writers said with certain passages in *The Prince* (Skinner, 1978, p. 131). Skinner assumes that these implications of the texts were intended by their authors, which is probably true, though nothing need be known about their intentions to identify them. These are conventional secondary meanings of the texts justified by the context of the writing together with the rules of language which warrant the statements reporting them.

The only occasion on which the illocutionary force of a text cannot be inferred from the context, and can only be known by discovering the author's intentions, is when a description is meant to be ironic. For example, to decide whether Thomas Hobbes and Pierre Bayle meant their pious utterances to be taken ironically, historians have had to judge their intentions, as there is no hint of irony in their texts (Skinner, 1969, pp. 33–5). (See also 1988, pp. 270–1.)

Occasionally an historian detects an illocutionary force of a past text which would not have been recognized by the author or her contemporaries. In some cases historians have seen the relevance of one author's work to issues raised by another, a relevance which no one perceived when the first work was written. There are doubtless cases in which the evidence of one scientific experiment has refuted the theory of another scientist, without the experimenter or his contemporaries being aware of it. Similarly, at some time the argument of one philosopher must have refuted the position of another, without anyone noticing the fact when it happened.

These are cases of an accidental kind. Even more interesting are ascriptions of illocutionary force which could not possibly have been recognized by the author because they employ terms which were unknown to her. Skinner, for example, has said that: 'During the eighteenth century, the enemies of the ruling oligarchy in England sought to legitimate their attacks on the government by insisting that they were motivated entirely by reverence for the constitution, and thus that their actions deserved to be commended as patriotic rather than condemned as factious' (Skinner, 1979, p. 216). It is very doubtful that eighteenth-century British politicians would have recognized their explanations as 'legitimations'. Legitimation, as Skinner himself has acknowledged (Skinner, 1974, p. 292), is a Weberian term, and derives its modern meaning from Weber's theory of legitimation. Eighteenth-century politicians would have said they were justifying their attacks on the government, not legitimating them.

Sometimes the illocutionary force of a text is quite difficult to establish. In such cases, when it is difficult to decide the point of a text, disagreements about its secondary meaning are common. A good example is to be found in discussions of Plato's dialogues *Lysis* and *Phaedo*. The *Lysis* is an inquiry into the nature of friendship, and it seems to be entirely inconclusive, the discussion jumping from point to point, with each suggested analysis of friendship being shown to be quite unsatisfactory. The *Phaedo* presents arguments about the immortality of the soul, but all of them are plainly inadequate so that it is hard to see any point to the dialogue.

Hans-Georg Gadamer has considered the force of these dialogues. The basic meaning of Plato's text is never in doubt, so well is his Greek understood. Any ambiguities are seen to have been deliberately introduced as a play on words (Gadamer, 1980, pp. 9, 11). To help fix the intent of these dialogues, Gadamer considers their genre. He concludes that the *Lysis* is not a systematic inquiry but 'a discussion', a form of conversation in which 'we move within the live play of risking assertions, of taking back what we have said, of assuming and rejecting, all the while proceeding on our way to reaching an understanding' (Gadamer, 1980, p. 5). Since Socrates' discussion in the *Lysis* is with two boys, Lysis and Menexenos, Gadamer suggests that it is appropriate to find it inconclusive, 'for children do not yet know what friendship is and how complex a relationship an enduring friendship creates between the friends' (p. 6). The inconclusive arguments have a point though. When Menexenos cannot tell whether a lover becomes a friend of the beloved or vice versa, Gadamer says that Plato 'certainly wants us to sense that in actual friendship it is impossible to distinguish the lover from the beloved in this way and to say who is the lover and who the beloved' (p. 10). This, in Gadamer's eyes, is characteristic of the force of the discussion, and he goes on to find similar significance in other apparently inconclusive arguments.

Gadamer also detects implicit significance in the *Phaedo*. For example:

> When Plato has Socrates, in the hour of death, enter into conversation with 'Pythagorean' representatives of contemporary science, that is obviously meant to show that Plato saw it as his own task to unite the moral introspection for which Socrates stood with the scientific knowledge represented by the Pythagoreans.
>
> (p. 32)

Gadamer's central thesis is that 'the *Phaedo*'s poetic power to convince is stronger than its arguments' logical power to prove' (p. 22). He sums up his discussion with these words:

> Plato certainly does not want to say that he has proved the same immortality of the soul which is basic to the religious tradition. But what he does want to say is that the spreading skepticism resulting from the scientific enlightenment does not at all affect the sphere of our human life and our understanding of it. The growing scientific insight into the causes of coming-into-being and passing-away, into the course of natural processes, does not obviate the need for thinking beyond the reality of this world, and it has no authority to contest religious convictions. Thus the point of the demonstrations, it seems to me, is that they refute doubts and not that they justify belief.
>
> (p. 37)

For proof of the uncertainty of secondary interpretations of the *Lysis* and the *Phaedo* one need only glance at other books about them. David Bolotin has given a detailed account of the long dispute between Max Pohlenz and Hans von Arnim about the significance of the *Lysis* (Bolotin, 1979). Pohlenz argued that it was meant to show that friendship is related to erotic love in that it always includes an element of desire; whereas Arnim produced reasons for thinking Plato regarded 'true' friendship as existing only between good people who are quite self-sufficient, possessing the good already and so not desiring it. It is interesting to see how texts can be found to support both interpretations. As for the *Phaedo*, compare the following fairly recent interpretations:

> The subject of the discussion is the desirability of death.
>
> (Bluck, 1955, p. 1)

It will be well to ask what is the fundamental purpose of the dialogue. It is not, of course, to prove that the human soul is immortal, though much of it is devoted to arguments for that thesis; it is not to pay a tribute of admiration to a beloved friend and master, though that tribute is undoubtedly paid; it is not to expound or propagate a metaphysical doctrine, though the doctrine of Forms (Ideas) bulks large; it is, I would say, to extend and deepen through the mouth of a consciously Platonised Socrates, the essential teaching of Socrates himself, namely that man's supreme concern is the 'tendance of his soul', or (in more modern language) the furthering of his insight into moral and spiritual values and the application of that insight in all his conduct.

(Hackforth, 1955, p. 3)

The Pythagoreans, Aristotle argues, differ from Plato only in denying any separation between first principles – which they identify with numbers rather than 'ideas' – and the things said to be their imitations; the Pythagorean teaching on reincarnation, on the other hand, presupposes the separability of the psyche from the body. The attempt to reinterpret the meaning of 'separation', and in so doing to reverse the Pythagorean position, is, one might say, the fundamental intention of the *Phaedo*.

(Burger, 1984, p. 7)

With such a variety of secondary interpretations it is tempting to suppose that each represents a subjective viewpoint and that none can be judged to be superior to any other. But that is not what the commentators believe, as the quotation from Hackforth indicates. Certainly Gadamer defends his interpretations by suggesting that they account for more features of the dialogues than previous interpretations did. In particular he believes they account for the inconclusiveness of the *Lysis*, and the obvious inadequacy of the arguments in the *Phaedo*.

Occasionally the illocutionary force of a work is so clear that no one disputes it. This is the case in the commonly accepted reading of *Gulliver's Travels* as a political satire. This is an excellent example of a secondary interpretation of a text, one which states its additional illocutionary force and its secondary field of reference. *Gulliver's Travels* can be understood at a basic level as a story about the adventures of Gulliver. That, indeed, is how most people understand it today. To Swift's contemporaries, however, familiar with the details of political life in Britain, its force and its references appeared quite different. They took it to be, not just a story, but also a satire; it referred not just to Gulliver and the imaginary lands he visited, but also to political figures of his day with the intention of ridiculing them. A.E. Case has pointed out, for example, that when contemporaries read that the Emperor whom Gulliver encountered in his first voyage was 'strong and masculine, with an *Austrian* Lip and arched Nose, his Complexion olive, his Countenance erect, his Body and Limbs well proportioned. . . . His Dress was very plain and simple. . . . His Voice was shrill, but very clear and articulate', then they thought of George I's 'thick and ungainly form, his bad taste in dress, and his guttural and unintelligible pronunciation of the little English he knew' (Case, 1958, p. 71).

The interpretation of *Gulliver's Travels* as a political satire has the strongest possible support. It accounts for a very large number of the details of the story. (The third essay in Case's book explains the political allegories in detail.) It is an example of a genre familiar to Swift's contemporaries, and so readily identified by them. Similar justification can be provided for the interpretation of Cervantes' *Don Quixote* as a parody of both the aims and means of knightly chivalry. A.J. Close, in defending this reading of the story, wrote: 'The aims, like the acts, are a madly literal mimicry of the stereotype behaviour of the heroes of chivalric romance', and would have been immediately recognized as such by contemporary readers (Close, 1972, p. 13).

Of course the illocutionary force of a text is not always to be identified with a genre such as satire or parody. Often it is simply the conventional implication of the text in its particular context. For example, when a piano teacher tells a pupil that she played a piece beautifully, she is not only describing the playing, but by doing so she is praising the student, and by doing that she is encouraging her. These further descriptions are warranted by the rules of language and the context.

In what sense, if any, can an interpretation of the secondary meaning of a text be called 'objective'? Both general summaries and statements of the illocutionary force of a text can be true and fair. They are true if one set of their possible truth conditions is satisfied; and they are fair if they are comprehensive and not misleading. Under these conditions, they are also rationally defensible. Even so, they are not necessarily objective in the sense of being unaffected by the historian's values and interests. When several different interpretations are equally effective in making sense of a text, the one chosen by an historian often reflects his values and interests. This does not mean, however, that the various interpretations cannot all be true. Just as several different descriptions of a person can all be true, so too several different interpretations of a text, drawing attention to different features, can all be true. Plato's *Phaedo* might do all the things that scholars have suggested.

6 The truth of cultural history

In this chapter we turn from a study of the meaning of texts to examine the meaning of actions and artefacts, as it is pursued by historians of culture. I am particularly interested in the anthropological turn in cultural history, inspired by the theory and practice of Clifford Geertz. The criticisms which the work of Geertz and his colleague Robert Darnton has received for not paying enough attention to probable beliefs of the people whose actions they interpret, reflect their casual attitude towards truth. They have neither defined the objects of their inquiry precisely enough, nor recognized the forms of inference needed to arrive at the truth about past people's beliefs. The method of hermeneutic inquiry which they both preach and practise is one which yields coherence, and the coherence of their interpretations gives them an initial plausibility. It does not privilege evidence about the people's actual beliefs, however, so that often it produces descriptions of the meaning of activities which are unlikely to have been the meaning ascribed to them by the people involved.

Another issue related to the truth of cultural history concerns the views which some cultural historians hold about the nature of society. Some think that, because society is not something which can be perceived the way that trees and people can, it is simply a set of ideas about the duties, powers and relations of individuals who live together. Consequently they suppose that the best way, indeed the only way to investigate a past society, is by discovering what people at the time thought about it. Thus, for these people, social history becomes a branch of cultural history. Indeed, some go further and suppose that even the natural world can only be known through people's perceptions of it and beliefs about it. We seem to have no other access to the world around us than our perceptions of it, so it seems natural to think the whole world of past societies can only be revealed in the ideas of it held by those who inhabited it. Then all history becomes cultural history.

These assumptions start to falter when historians, in accordance with the New Historicism, begin to explain why people held the beliefs they did. This requires historians to learn what they can of the context in which the people lived, for example the events of their upbringing and education, the needs and interests which directed their behaviour and beliefs, the conventions of the society not always explicitly formulated by those who followed them. In short, to explain people's beliefs it is sometimes necessary to refer to facts about their environment of which neither they nor their contemporaries had any beliefs. In practice, historians do not always assume that the world of the past is simply the world as imagined by those who lived in it.

THE OBJECTS OF CULTURAL HISTORY

It has become difficult to specify a reasonable object of cultural history. Historians' preconceptions of what is an appropriate object of study have changed in recent decades. Once historians supposed that a community shared a common world-view, so that by studying highly articulate statements of it they could discover what everyone thought. Then it was supposed that different social groups probably view the world and particularly society differently. For instance episodes which capitalists would describe as free negotiations over workers' pay, workers would probably describe as immoral acts of exploitation. Just to check whether the beliefs of the various social groups were homogeneous, some cultural historians would undertake surveys of evidence, to justify a generalization about what the members of that group believed. Finally, as people studied the reception and interpretation of texts, it was thought that the meaning of an artefact or episode for any individual depends upon all the connotations it has for that person, how they see it as related to other things in their world and what they feel about it, as well as on their interests in it given their particular predicament. Consequently, cultural historians started to confine themselves to the meaning things had for particular individuals. (For a brilliant description of these developments, see Chartier, 1988, ch. 1.)

Some cultural historians have been remarkably vague as to whose beliefs they are studying, giving the impression that the beliefs of the individuals they describe are typical of those of a group, class or society, for otherwise they are of little historical significance. If the truth of an historical description is important, then it is vital that one knows precisely what is being described, for otherwise the truth of the description cannot be ascertained. If the beliefs of an individual are presented as typical of those of a group, then more evidence is required to establish that they were indeed typical. Suppose an historian wanted to discover a community's religious beliefs, say the beliefs of those in the Roman Catholic Church at a certain time and place. It is probable that lay people, priests, local theologians, and books in the theological library would all give different accounts of those beliefs. It would clearly be wrong to assume uniformity of beliefs, though all might hold some beliefs, such as a belief in Jesus' divinity, in common. One suspects that failure to specify precisely whose beliefs are being studied reflects a lack of interest in the truth of the description.

Dominick LaCapra has observed a tendency of cultural historians to generalize from a small sample in his essay 'Is Everyone a *Mentalité* Case? Transference and the "Culture" Concept' (1985, pp. 71–94). Carl Schorske, in his history of Vienna at the end of the last century (*Fin-de-Siècle Vienna: Politics and Culture*. New York, 1980) found evidence of 'a crisis of liberalism', 'a guilt-ridden escape from politics into the psyche and art,' which he then assumed true of the whole city. LaCapra remarks:

> The 'crisis' of liberalism was at best a part of a much larger and more complex crisis – dynastic, national, international, ethnic, sexual, class – that can be centered on it only through a dubious tropological movement [seeing the part as the whole]. To see that larger crisis in the primary, unified light of a crisis of a liberal polity may result in a largely fanta-sied [sic] Vienna.
>
> (LaCapra, 1985, p. 84)

LaCapra's other example is a work by Robert Darnton (*The Literary Underground of the Old Regime*, Cambridge, Mass., 1982) in which the author assumes that a whole class of French society saw the world the same way as those who wrote the grubby books he studied. As LaCapra says: 'Darnton never proves that his best-sellers reflect more than the somewhat philistine and resentful mentality of their Grub Street writers. He can tell us relatively little about the way what sold well was actually read and used' (p. 88). Clearly the problems of verification were not taken very seriously by these historians.

The tendency to extrapolate from a small sample, to say that the beliefs of one group represent those of a whole population or class of which they were a small part, is one consequence of being casual about the truth. Another is the reverse, a tendency to imagine uniformity in a community, and to ascribe general beliefs to a small group which might not have held them, or at least not all of them, at all. An example which Roger Chartier has discussed is the essay by Robert Darnton (1984) entitled 'Workers revolt: the great cat massacre of the rue Saint-Séverin', which describes how some apprentices and journeymen, who worked in a printing shop in Paris in the 1730s, with much hilarity condemned and executed a large number of cats on gallows in a courtyard. To make sense of this, to us bizarre event, Darnton began by pointing out that the torture and killing of cats was very common in Europe at the time. Indeed he called it a ritual, and listed many examples of it in Spain, France and England (pp. 90–2). To Europeans of that time, he said, cats were thought of as agents of the devil, or of witches, possessing occult power to do harm; and they also had sexual significance, suggesting female sexuality ('pussy'), and cuckolding of men (pp. 92–6). On the basis of this account of the general symbolic significance of cats at the time, Darnton developed a hypothesis about the intentions of the apprentices and journeymen in this particular case. Their master, in ordering the massacre of the cats, seriously believed that, as they howled at night, they were hatching some harm for him. Even the apprentices thought them 'bedevilled', so were quite happy to kill them. The main target, however, seems to have been the mistress of the house, who was having an affair with her confessor. In killing her favourite cat, they assaulted her, as punishment for her behaviour; and also attacked her house, for treating the workmen very meanly. They also, by symbolically 'ravishing' their mistress, mocked and insulted their master, both for his meanness, and as a cuckold. Finally, by killing off the vagrant toms, they punished the wife's lover (pp. 96–100).

Reviewing this essay, Roger Chartier remarks that it is a mistake to assume the meaning of symbols is constant among a large population for a long time. Rather, in a society as fragmented as French society in the eighteenth century, different groups probably read the same symbols differently.

> Therefore it seems difficult to postulate that at a given moment and in a given place, a particular culture (for example, that of Parisian printing workers in the beginning of the eighteenth century) is organized in accordance with a symbolic repertory the elements of which are documented at various dates between the sixteenth and the nineteenth centuries and in multiple sites. . . .
>
> [I]t is . . . doubtful that [urban artisan] culture was really playing with the full repertory of diabolical and carnival motifs that Darnton attributes to it. This would suppose that the collective action that takes place on the rue Saint-Séverin carries with it an entire set of beliefs, rites and behavior difficult to imagine as simultaneously inhabiting the mind of urban printshop workers of the eighteenth century.
>
> (Chartier, 1988, pp. 104, 109)

There is one distinction which cultural historians are very conscious of, however, namely the distinction between the concepts they would use to describe the world and the concepts used by the people they are studying. Clifford Geertz, for example, in his paper '"From the native's point of view": On the nature of anthropological understanding' (1976), says it is impossible to experience the world as others do, but it is nevertheless possible to learn of the concepts others use in describing it (p. 228). Geertz makes a distinction between the concepts which the 'natives' use, and those which specialist commentators might make about them. Following Heinz Kohut, he calls the former 'experience-near' and the latter 'experience-distant' (pp. 226–7). It seems that the 'natives' may know of the latter, but also may not. An interesting ethnographer will use both kinds of concepts without confusion, but doing this is not easy, as Geertz remarks:

> To grasp concepts which, for another people, are experience-near, and to do so well enough to place them in illuminating connection with those experience-distant concepts that theorists have fashioned to capture the general features of social life, is clearly a task at least as delicate, if a bit less magical, as putting oneself into someone else's skin.
>
> (p. 227)

It seems to me that Geertz is right in saying that to get a correct understanding of another culture one must first of all reach an adequate understanding of their discourses, for they provide information about the concepts in terms of which people in that culture see the world. Unfortunately, when interpreting people's behaviour Geertz sometimes forgets the distinction he had so carefully enunciated, and introduces concepts from modern theories without making it clear that these were not in the natives' minds.

For this practice Geertz has been roundly criticized. Vincent Crapanzano, for instance, has commented upon his famous interpretation of the practices of Balinese cockfighting (see Geertz, 1972):

Without any evidence he attributes to the Balinese all sorts of experiences, meanings, intentions, motivations, dispositions, and understandings. He writes, for example:

> In the cockfight man and beast, good and evil, ego and id, the creative power of aroused masculinity and the destructive power of loosened animality fuse in a blood drama of hatred, cruelty, violence, and death. It is little wonder that when, as is the invariable rule, the owner of the winning cock takes the carcass of the loser – often torn limb from limb by its enraged owner – home to eat, he does so with a mixture of social embarrassment, moral satisfaction, aesthetic disgust, and cannibal joy.
>
> (Crapanzano, 1986, p. 72)

Crapanzano goes on to give more examples of Geertz's personal reading of the significance of Balinese cockfights, commenting: 'Cockfights are surely cockfights for the Balinese – and not images, fictions, models, and metaphors' (ibid., p. 73). At the very least, Crapanzano challenges Geertz to provide evidence of the Balinese viewing their cockfights as he does.

Clearly it is important to make some fairly obvious distinctions here. We should distinguish: concepts the natives would have used; concepts which correctly describe their attitudes and feelings, though they are not concepts familiar to them; and concepts which describe the social significance of a ritual in terms of a social theory. The Balinese might have been vaguely aware that cockfighting is enjoyed by them partly as a contest of sexual power, since the word 'cock' is ambiguous in their language as well as ours. But it is unlikely that they would have recognized it as 'a formal simulation of status tensions' (Geertz, 1972, p. 214), 'a simulation of the social matrix, the involved system of cross-cutting, overlapping, highly corporate groups – villages, kin-groups, irrigation societies, temple congregations, "castes" – in which its devotees live' (ibid., p. 205), as these are terms taken from western social theory.

The importance of understanding a people's discourse first, and their behaviour only in terms of it, can also be illustrated from the work of Rhys Isaac. At the conclusion of his prize-winning book *The Transformation of Virginia 1740–1790* (1982), Isaac offers 'A discourse on the method'. Referring to Geertz's essay, Isaac notes 'the importance of the distinction between observers' categories (that is, our own as twentieth-century social scientists) and participants' categories (that is, those of the past peoples we study)' (p. 325). He declares: 'Ethnographers cannot understand and translate action-statements unless they have some comprehension of the culture; but such grasp can only be effectively acquired by close attention to particular action-statements' (ibid.). Action-statements, the context makes clear, include not just the utterance of words, but also 'gesture, demeanour, dress, architecture' and the like. In the text of this fascinating book, Isaac repeatedly uses contemporary writing to interpret the artefacts and events of the period. In the examples given in the last section on method, however, he draws much more upon his imagination, and so is more likely to project his own understanding onto those he studies. A sense of the difficulty of interpreting remote cultures can perhaps be conveyed by some detailed examples.

The method which Isaac advocates is the analysis of historical episodes. One is an episode recorded in the diary of a gentleman planter, Colonel Landon Carter, in 1766. Here is an extract which Isaac considers:

> My man Bart came in this day, he has been gone ever since New year's day. His reason is only that I had ordered him a whipping for saying he then brought in two load of wood when he was coming with his first load only. This he still insists on was truth Although the whole plantation asserts the contrary, and the boy with him. He is the most incorrigible villain I believe alive, and has deserved hanging; which I will get done if his mate in roguery can be tempted to turn evidence against him.
>
> (ibid., p. 331)

Isaac points out first of all that Bart can be seen here 'assigning to his master the estimable role of fair judge in appeal', and that Carter accepted this role and reacted accordingly (p. 342). Was Carter conscious of the role he was adopting? Isaac thinks he was: 'the forms of judicial action were present in his own consciousness – present not merely as metaphor but as institutionalized social constraint' (p. 348). In fact it is very difficult to know how conscious people are of the roles they adopt, but Carter would probably have agreed that this was his role, if asked. Then Isaac detects some other roles being played by Carter: 'In the end Carter, a righteous father and angry patriarch, was chastising a rebellious dependent' (p. 347). Now it is possible that contemporaries could have seen Carter's behaviour as fitting either of these models. But could Carter have consciously adopted all these roles at once? Isaac thinks he could: 'the two *metaphors* of authority – the judge and the patriarch – were in marked degree *interchangeable*. They stood as two sides of the same coin: either can be presented uppermost – the other is known to be simultaneously present' (pp. 347–8). No evidence is offered of Carter's reflection upon his role as judge and patriarch, and although contemporaries may have interpreted his behaviour in terms of them, one wonders if Carter was really aware of them either during the episode itself or when he recorded it in his diary. There is no doubt that people often adopt roles suggested by their society, but they are seldom conscious of doing so. At least the roles in this case were both familiar to members of Carter's society.

That is not so clearly the case in another episode. The details of this are also recorded in Carter's journal. An oxcarter called Simon had run away, and another of Carter's slaves, Willy, found and captured him. In the process Willy incurred the hostility of Simon, and the jealousy of some other slaves. Isaac interprets Willy's action in reporting his capture of Simon to Carter in terms of Peter Blau's theory of social exchange, to which he refers explicitly.

> Willy's actions have to be understood as part of a proposed *exchange*. He was offering information and collaboration to the master in expectation of goodwill. He calculated that the benevolence of the master would offset the malevolence

of those whom he had offended. Although this example is obvious enough, it serves to draw our attention to a constant *accounting process* – most of it far more subtle and elusive than this – that runs through nearly all significant interaction. The gratifications in social transactions are not, of course, exclusively or even primarily material. Respect, approval, thanks, kindness, and companionship are some of the most valuable considerations sought; while scorn, deferential self-effacement, malice, and hostility are among the prices dearly paid.

(ibid., pp. 338–9)

He goes on to describe Willy's behaviour as 'social trading', in which Willy sought 'feedback' from a 'significant other'.

Perhaps Isaac is right in supposing that Willy 'calculated that the benevolence of the master would offset the malevolence of those whom he had offended', though one doubts that the calculation was consciously made. It would have been reassuring to find evidence of the theory applying in this situation at all. There can be little doubt that Willy wanted his master's approval, and perhaps some reward, but there is no evidence that he was particularly worried about the attitudes of Simon and the others. This is clearly a modern interpretation of the incident, in terms which the agents were unlikely to have used.

Even when an historian is scrupulous in describing the beliefs of another culture, modern ideas can creep in. An example can be found in the impressive reconstruction of the culture of the Marquesa Islands in the Pacific by Greg Dening (1980). Once again, Dening is conscious of the problem of distinguishing their world-view from his own:

Understanding others . . . can have two meanings. It can mean entry into the experience of others in such a way that we share the metaphors that enlarge their experience. Or it can mean that we translate that experience into a model that has no actuality in the consciousness of those being observed but becomes the currency of communication amongst the observers.

(ibid., p. 86)

The problem is that in explaining what the key metaphors meant to the natives, the anthropologist can scarcely avoid using concepts from her own culture which would have been unknown to the natives concerned. Some of these concepts probably represent native concepts fairly accurately. For example, Dening thinks the concept of *tapu* (taboo) very important to the Enata people, and he explains numerous everyday objects and activities which were forbidden and honoured among them. For instance, it was forbidden for men to eat with women; and men's heads were honoured in various ways (pp. 51–8). Then Dening says: '*Tapu* was an organizing principle of Enata's social and physical environment. It defined their personal space and gave order and focus to their larger environment' (p. 58). This is a statement about the function of the concept in their society which they would not have made. It is clearly part of Dening's model, not their metaphor. (Compare: '*Tapu* was their metaphor. Our proposition that it was a metaphor is the model of this work' (p. 88). Dening would probably agree that this statement about the function of *tapu* in their society is a modern reflection, and does not represent the thinking of the Enata people, though he does not say so. Notice how easy it is, though, to move from saying what the concept meant to those who used it, to saying what it signifies to the historian.

Earlier mention was made of the tendency of some cultural historians to extrapolate from a small sample, to say that the beliefs of a group represented those of a large population of which the group was a small part.

To judge the truth of ethnographic descriptions, it is important to know precisely what they are describing: the people's beliefs, their attitudes, or the significance of their behaviour in terms of a modern theory. It is also vital to know which individuals or groups of people are being described, to avoid careless generalization without justification.

THE INADEQUACY OF HERMENEUTICAL CIRCLES

The failure of so many distinguished anthropologists and cultural historians to establish the truth of their accounts of people's beliefs might be linked to the method of verification which they have adopted. Geertz and others have described the process of achieving understanding of a foreign culture in terms of the familiar hermeneutical circle (Geertz, 1976, pp. 239–40), in which the meaning of a sentence is grasped from a knowledge of the meaning of the words which compose it, and ambiguities in the meaning of those words are resolved by reference to the meaning of the whole. In the case of ethnographic understanding, the alternation is between what individuals say about the object or episode under consideration, together with their behaviour concerning it, and a hypothesis about their beliefs and attitudes being constructed by the historian. The hypothesis about their beliefs and attitudes has to fit or cohere neatly with the people's words and actions. A vivid example of the process of justifying an ethnographic explanation is provided by the debate between Marshall Sahlins (1981 and 1995) and Gananath Obeyesekere (1992) over whether or not the people of Hawaii once regarded Captain Cook as an embodiment of their god Lono. Sahlins, who says that they did, and Obeyesekere, who denies it, both try to show that their explanation of the behaviour of the Hawaiians towards Captain Cook fits the known facts best.

One worry about this account is that it leaves the origin of the hypothesis unaccounted for, and permits sceptics to say that it could be entirely fanciful. Consider the behaviour of Willy in finding the runaway slave Simon, capturing him and returning him to his master. Isaac very plausibly attributes this to Willy's hope of favours in return, referring to Blau's theory of social exchange. But there could have been other reasons which fit the available evidence equally well. Perhaps he nurtured a secret hatred of Simon; perhaps he thought capturing Simon would be fun. Why does Isaac not explore these alternative possibilities? Perhaps because once a hypothesis has been found which neatly fits the known facts, no further justification of it is thought necessary.

The point is that if a hypothesis fits the facts, that shows it is coherent with what is known, but does not show that it deserves to be believed true. It might cohere well with what we know of Balinese language, of Freud's theory of symbolism, and of male vanity to suggest that Balinese cock fights were symbols of a competition in masculinity, but it is doubtful that the men involved really saw them that way. Coherence is not enough to establish truth. One wants evidence which unequivocally implies what they thought of the matter, statements and behaviour which could be explained no other way. Hypotheses about what such activities meant to those involved have to be justified by arguments, such as statistical inferences or arguments to the best explanation (see McCullagh, 1984, chs 2, 3). If one of those involved in the cock fighting generally told the truth, and said that most men thought the success of their cocks reflected upon their manhood, and nothing implied the contrary, then it would be reasonable to believe the report to be true. In the absence of such direct evidence, however, the hypothesis remains a matter of speculation.

Even when there is no evidence which directly implies one hypothesis, historians still look for evidence which will support one hypothesis over others. When I examined some cases of ethnographic history, I discovered that hypotheses were not simply spun from the imagination, but were inferred from other facts known about the case, or about similar cases. I found, for example, that Michael Ventris drew upon general knowledge of the nature of languages in formulating hypotheses about the meaning of the Minoan script known as Linear B (McCullagh, 1984, pp. 111–12). To interpret the Mayan glyphs, J. Eric S. Thompson assumed they would be related to the languages of their descendants in Middle America and Mexico (ibid., pp. 114–15). In judging explanatory hypotheses, I noted that historians take into consideration their plausibility, that is the degree to which they are implied by other known facts, and the degree to which their negation is implied by other known facts (pp. 19–24).

Even in cases which seem utterly remote from anything we know, there are several assumptions which limit the range of possible explanatory hypotheses. I suggest that in explaining what the people say and do, we are guided by the following assumptions:

1 We expect others to have similar beliefs to us about the perceptible properties of medium-sized objects which can be perceived in the world, but are prepared for them to have different classificatory schemes and beliefs about their nature.
2 We assume they, like us, recognize causal connections in nature and see relations between beliefs, reasons and actions, but allow that they may believe in other processes of change as well, especially change brought about by spiritual forces, and change resulting from symbolic enactment.
3 We do not assume that others share our values in any detailed sense, but expect that all people are moved by the same human needs: for example, a need of food, protection, procreation, and society. We can therefore expect to understand much of their behaviour as relating to needs such as these.
4 It is very difficult to say what standards of rationality we should assume in other cultures. Ethnographers begin, it seems, by expecting quite a high degree of

coherence, but are willing to allow inconsistencies among people's beliefs and values if this is necessary to account for all that they do and say.

We accept as probably true any account of a group's attitude towards something or reasons for doing something which satisfies the quite minimum requirements of the first three conditions just mentioned, and which provides a good explanation of that group's words and deeds in relation to the object or action. (The conditions to be satisfied by a good explanation have been set out in McCullagh, 1984, ch. 2.)

A fascinating example of ethnographic history which satisfies these require- ments is provided in Inga Clendinnen's book *Ambivalent Conquests. Maya and Spaniard in Yucatan, 1517–1570* (1987), where she explains why the ancient Mayas sacrificed youths by cutting out their living hearts. She begins by warning that we must set aside certain western presuppositions, namely that sacrifice is the offering up of something of value 'as a token of submission or propitiation before a notably jealous and watchful personal god'. And she said 'we must reconsider the clear distinction we ... draw between human, and animal and vegetable life' (p. 177). The bodies of the Maya were nourished on plants, and they saw human blood as akin to the sap of plants (p. 180). At times of crisis, particularly of likely crop failure, Clendinnen sees them as trying to restore the regular patterns of nature by somehow stimulating the relevant god to action through the offering of blood (see pp. 146–7). Sometimes it seems that blood was a symbol of rain, as in a ritual in which burning wood was quenched in blood (p. 175); and sometimes it seems to have been a symbol of fertility, as when genital blood was shed (pp. 180–1). A pulsing, bleeding heart must have been a very vivid symbol of life. Clendinnen includes a Mayan drawing of a tree of life springing from the open chest of a sacrificial victim (p. 185).

> The gods were aloof and (were it not so anachronistic a word) mechanical in their functions. Men's ritual actions could do no more than invoke those functions through mimicry, and do something to regularise them when the movement faltered. Thus the drawing forth of blood, from oneself or, in times of crisis, from a human victim, could well have been understood as the introduction of a potent fuel to aid the workings of the great cycles of the universe.
>
> (p. 181)

What makes this account plausible is that it fits the criteria just mentioned, as well as those for being a good explanation of the ritual. It presents a universe in which medium-sized objects are as we perceive them, though the cycles of nature and history are thought to be in the control of gods. It employs a fairly familiar idea of symbolic enactment as a means of bringing about change, be it rain, fertility or just renewed life. And it relates the ritual to basic human needs.

Not all rituals have instrumental value, as the Mayan sacrifices were intended to have. Some, like the giving of presents or parties in our culture, are often just expressions of attitudes to others. Some ritual acts are both expressive and instrumental. In partaking of Holy Communion, Christians consume broken bread and wine which they regard as at least symbols of Christ's broken body and his blood, thereby affirming what they take to be their relationship with Christ, a relationship of identification. The ritual is clearly expressive. It might also be instrumental, being intended to strengthen the faith of the believer. Both secular and religious rituals often express social and political relationships. J.H.M. Beattie sums up the findings of several anthropologists in these words:

> Among the various qualities and values which social anthropologists have shown to be symbolised in ritual are difference in social status, the need to keep separate things which there is a danger of confusing, such as different lineages, generations and sexes, or different roles where these are not clearly distinguished in secular terms, lineage and tribal values, political power and authority, as well as the social order itself.
>
> (Beattie, 1966, p. 66)

Anthropologists have discovered that many rituals which seem pointless to outsiders have definite symbolic, expressive value within their own culture. They are made intelligible when their significance is explained. Rituals may have a social function of reinforcing the relationships which they express, but as before, this is an almost secondary attribute of them, and seldom consciously intended.

One way in which reverence for coherence limits historical inquiry is by inhibiting the consideration of alternative hypotheses, and the search for a reasonable way of choosing between them. Another bad influence of respect for coherence is that it discourages recognition of complexity and inconsistency in people's beliefs. Robert Muchembled, for example, pointed out (in *Popular Culture and Elite Culture in France, 1400–1750*, Baton Rouge, 1978) that in the eighteenth century, authorities in France disciplined people's bodies, at home, in school, in the army and the factory, 'in the name of the panoptic, therapeutic state and the dictates of capitalism' (Porter, 1991, p. 91). Roy Porter, commenting upon this account, points out the presence of contrary attitudes to the body, widely held at the same time: 'in other important respects the eighteenth century was an epoch notable for its respect, both theoretical and practical, for the individual autonomy and proprietorship of the body.' He cites 'the philosophical critique of slavery, based upon self-proprietorship of one's body', and the practice of doctors in letting sick people decide whether or not to accept the treatment they recommended (Porter, 1991, p. 91). Porter concludes: 'It would thus be a mistake to regard the trends of eighteenth-century thinking as unidirectional; cross-currents and counter-movements were powerful' (p. 92). An assumption that the true description of an historical subject will cohere neatly with all the evidence about it is incompatible with the fact that sometimes the truth about an historical subject, such as eighteenth- and nineteenth-century French attitudes to the body, is contradictory. It is possible that the very same individuals saw their bodies as instruments which should be devoted to the service of an employer or the state, and as property over which they had complete rights.

My conclusion is that the ideal of hermeneutic harmony has proved inadequate, and has lulled some historians into thinking they have arrived at the truth about the past when they have not.

INTERPRETATION WITHOUT MISREPRESENTATION

Traditionally cultural historians have tried to make the ideas of a past culture intelligible to readers in their own culture without radically misrepresenting them. The possibility of doing this has become problematic, according to current theory, for two reasons. First, the historian's account, based upon his reading of the evidence, will inevitably be filtered through the lens of his own concepts, language and interests, with some inevitable distortion; and second, the reader will interpret what the historian says through the lens of her own concepts and interests, to produce a second distortion. It is unlikely that the historian's idea of a past person's idea will be accurate; and unlikely that the reader's idea of the historian's idea will be accurate. On top of this, of course, is the fallibility of historical inferences, which are sometimes based upon scant evidence.

To try to minimize the distortion introduced by the historian's interpretation of evidence, some historians prefer to give the reader the evidence and let her interpret it for herself. Artefacts are photographed and documents are quoted at length, to bring the reader closer to the past. These certainly make the past more vivid, but as a strategy for removing the distortions introduced by the historian's reading of the data it is generally disastrous. First, the material has been selected by the historian from the mass of stuff which is usually available, so that it presents only a partial picture of the past. The uninformed reader has no way of knowing how typical it is. Second, the average reader lacks the expertise to know the significance of what is presented, to know how the language of the text worked in the society which produced it, and how objects pictured, the events described and the attitudes expressed related to other things going on at the time. Expert historians, thoroughly immersed in the culture and society of the period they are describing, are much better equipped to interpret its artefacts than is the average reader.

The gap between the historian and the reader is seldom very great if the historian is from the same culture as the reader, sharing the same language and concepts. The interests of the historian and reader sometimes diverge, but the accuracy of an historical account is to some extent ensured by the professional requirement to provide justified and fair descriptions of the past. When interests produce unjustified or misleading accounts, then colleagues with different interests often correct the mistakes, so long as they are free to do so. The problem of misrepresentation is often much less severe than philosophers imagine.

The major problem for cultural historians who are trying to impart an accurate account of past people's ideas is that of providing an accurate translation. The concepts of one culture do not always translate readily into those of the historian's culture. In that case the historian has to describe them as carefully as she can. In an essay on this problem, Talal Asad (1986) points to an example in which an anthropologist has used phrases in his own language which have quite different connotations to translate some key concepts in another culture, and indeed in which he appears to go so far as to correct the native beliefs from a western point of view (ibid., pp. 153–6). These are temptations which a sensitive ethnographer would be careful to avoid. Of more interest is Asad's account of the way in which anthropologists must sometimes bend and extend their language to represent foreign concepts. He admits that 'this pushing beyond the limits of one's habitual usages, this breaking down and reshaping of one's own language through the process of translation, is never an easy business' (p. 157), but argues that it is necessary if the beliefs of others are to be translated and not transformed. He cites as an example the development of Arabic to express a number of European ideas (p. 158).

A second aspect of the problem of intelligibility is the need which historians feel to make sense of statements and rituals which seem quite bizarre to modern readers. This problem received very detailed consideration in what were called problems of rationality in anthropology. We judge beliefs to be irrational when they appear to be false, unjustified or self-contradictory. Should we apply the same standards of rationality to other communities? What appears false to us may appear certainly true to them, for instance that gods send the rain. Authorities which we doubt, such as witchdoctors, might be commonly respected in those communities. In fact anthropologists seem to allow that a number of basic beliefs of other communities might be different from our own, but they generally adopt the same standards of rationality as we do, relative to those basic beliefs. If, relative to their basic beliefs, a statement seems to be irrational, they will look for some way to make it intelligible. It is often possible to make sense of strange statements by explaining the ideas which lay behind them. A well-known example is Evans-Pritchard's explanation of the saying of the Nuer people that twins are birds. This is strictly nonsense, of course, and the Nuer people do not treat twins as birds, or get the two confused. But both are believed by them to be special expressions of Spirit, 'people of the above', 'children of God', so that 'a bird is a suitable symbol in which to express the special relationship in which a twin stands to God' (quoted in Lukes, 1970, p. 206). This is quite straightforward and acceptable, but consider the Catholic belief that consecrated wine really is the blood of Christ. They say that, though they would be appalled if it really did become blood. If educated members of our own community can believe such contradictions, why should we expect members of other communities to hold rational beliefs? It seems that we begin by assuming people's beliefs to be rational (the 'principle of charity'), and if we finally cannot make sense of some of them, judge those to be irrational. The criteria for rationality have to be expanded, however, to allow that mythical and symbolic statements can be both meaningful and rational, even though they are strictly false. One can agree that the story of Adam and Eve is false, yet hold that it is an important myth, expressing a universal tendency to sin and to suffer as a consequence. One can agree that wine is not blood, but agree that it can be a powerful symbol of Christ's blood, which is in turn a symbol of his life-giving Spirit.

Some ethnographers have decided that any attempt on their part to interpret and translate the views of other cultures is so likely to mislead that readers should be left to interpret the data for themselves. George E. Marcus and Michael M.J. Fischer (1986) have described this as a modernist response to the problems of representation (pp. 67–73). The modernists they cite are less convinced of the coherence of people's beliefs than traditional ethnographers, and make little attempt to relate their observations to any possible comprehensive world-view. Indeed they are wary of drawing any particular implications from what they observe, preferring just to record their observations and leave readers to draw their own conclusions. Of course some interpretation and translation is involved merely in reporting their observations, but it is much less than has been traditionally offered. This reticence to draw firm conclusions from their observations would be justified if many different interpretations of the data were possible. But in practice this is seldom the case. As James Clifford has said:

> whereas the free play of readings may in theory be infinite, there are, at any historical moment, a limited range of canonical and emergent allegories available to the competent reader (the reader whose interpretation will be deemed plausible by a specific community). These structures of meaning are historically bounded and coercive. There is, in practice, no 'free play'.
>
> (Clifford, 1986, p. 110)

Ethnographers should not assume certainty when it is not justified, and should honestly explain the basis of their more tentative conclusions. And they should translate and explain their conclusions as sensitively and fully as they can. But there is no good reason for their refusing to attempt to reconstruct the views of people in other cultures.

THE NEW HISTORICISM AND ITS PROBLEMS

Historicism is the doctrine that the meaning of events is given by their historical context. At the turn of the century Europeans still felt optimistic about human progress, and commonly interpreted events as contributing one way or another to that. The catastrophes of war and economic depression suffered earlier this century put an end to that optimism, and historians have become less inclined to think in terms of progress. The New Historicism is a doctrine that sees events as the product of several specific local social and cultural forces influencing the people involved, inclining them to act as they did. In particular, New Historicists believe that the meaning of texts which people have produced in the past must be understood in relation to their social setting. The content of these texts is assumed to be just a function of the context in which they were produced. To fully appreciate their meaning, therefore, one must understand that context.

Along with this theory of meaning, some New Historicists have an ontological theory which reduces the past to texts. They argue that (1) social powers and relations are not real, but are ideas which people have about the social world in which they live; and (2) that people's ideas about the world are really texts which they utter or would consent to, and like all texts are framed in concepts that the people have acquired from their culture, and reflecting the beliefs and attitudes of their culture as well. As Hayden White expressed it: 'New Historicism is reductionist in a double sense: it reduces the social to the status of a function of the cultural, and then further reduces the cultural to the status of a text' (Veeser, 1989, p. 294).

There are many elements of the New Historicism which can be contested. Its theory of meaning seems to overlook the possibility of originality in the production of texts. If the ideas, values and attitudes expressed in a text are determined by the culture of the author, how can they be developed and changed? This problem has worried Frank Lentricchia, who wants to restore the subject as a source of invention, though hardly knows how to do so (in Veeser, 1989, pp. 241–2). New Historicists' social theory involves them in a massive contradiction. If society is but an idea, a text that people would produce, and either does not exist or cannot be known independently, how can New Historicists refer to the social context of past texts to discover their meaning? They can only refer to the author's beliefs about society, not to society itself. Furthermore, if society is just people's idea about it, it cannot influence them in ways of which they are unaware, for instance by inculcating class, race or gender bias, which historicists are often anxious to expose. It seems better to allow that social powers and relations are real, and that people sometimes know about them and sometimes do not.

The problem the New Historicists have about truth, which is the subject of this chapter, is as follows. According to historicists, texts are products of local influences and so cannot be supposed to provide an accurate account of any subject they may be describing, whatever an accurate account might be. They will inevitably be couched in concepts preferred by the writer, include elements valued by the writer, and be designed to further the professional, social and financial interests of the writer. That is why it is so important to understand the context of a text if one is to appreciate the significance of what it says. The problem is that all this inevitably applies to the text of the historian as well: it cannot be regarded as providing a true and fair description of past subjects for the reasons given. In that case, it seems that the aim of the New Historicists is unattainable, for they cannot reach the truth about the historical influences which shaped past texts. (Brook Thomas has noted this problem in Veeser, 1989, pp. 184–8.)

When Stanley Fish discussed this problem, he noted that some historians such as Elizabeth Fox-Genovese had resolved it by simply declaring that historians can discover the truth about the past. His reply is that historians cannot know the past because in describing the past they use a language, 'and that language must itself proceed from some ideological vision' (Veeser, 1989, p. 305). This vision, he explains, provides the perspective for their account of the past, and a criterion for deciding what to include in the history. Note how ineffective this argument is. The fact that historians use a language and ideas when describing the world does not imply that their descriptions of the world must be false. The language and concepts used by an historian might be perfectly appropriate to the subject, and could provide a true description of it. I suspect that Fish meant something more sweeping: that our concepts can never capture the world, or can never be known to do so. That is a big claim which was discussed before, in Chapter 1.

Rather than admit that historians can know the truth about the past, Fish tries to resolve the epistemic problem another way. He declares that 'the practice of giving historical accounts' and 'the practice of theorizing their possibility' are quite different and 'have nothing to do with one another', so that the outcome of one has no bearing upon the outcome of the other (pp. 307–13). He argues: 'a conviction that all facts rest finally on shifting or provisional grounds will not produce shifting and provisional facts because the grounds on which facts rest are themselves particular, having to do with traditions of inquiry, divisions of labor among the disciplines, acknowledged and unacknowledged assumptions (about what is valuable, pertinent, weighty)' (p. 308). What Fish quite fails to notice is that among an historian's assumptions is the conviction that the influences upon her are not sufficient to prevent her from observing evidence accurately and assessing its historical significance correctly, in short the conviction that she is capable of reaching the truth. If an historian believed otherwise, as Fish does, she would not proceed. Far from being independent, the conclusions of philosophical scepticism about history have immediate implications for historical research. Fish says you cannot 'simultaneously stand within a practice and reflectively survey the supports you stand on' (p. 314), but this is either trite or nonsense. It is trite if it means that while investigating the past, an historian is not, at that moment, reflecting upon the foundations of her discipline. It is nonsense if it means that a practising historian can never do so, and never be affected by the conclusions she draws as a result. Some practising historians such as Jane Tomkins have indeed reflected upon this issue, and have chosen to ignore the implications of that reflection, carrying on regardless (p. 304). It is more rational, however, to try to resolve it.

Historicists focus so completely upon the cultural influences upon our thinking that they overlook the grounds of our confidence in the truth of our descriptions of the world. These are our capacity to perceive and describe the world accurately, and our ability to draw justified inferences from those perceptions. The fact that people have certain preferences does not mean they cannot reach true, justified conclusions about the past. Their descriptions might be biased, unfair in some way, but they could still be true as far as they go. As I explained at some length in Chapter 1, cultural relativism is compatible with historical truth.

7 Causal, contrastive and functional explanations

Historians not only describe past events but often explain why they occurred. They frequently note causes of important events, and sometimes give quite detailed explanations of how an event came about, or of why one event happened rather than another which might well have been expected in the circumstances.

To judge the truth of their assertions that one thing was a cause of another, and to judge whether their causal explanations could be objective, it is necessary to analyse the nature of causes and causal explanations quite carefully. For instance to decide whether it is true that the bad harvest in France in 1788 and the consequent steep rise in the price of bread was a cause of the French Revolution, it is important to know what the phrase 'was a cause' means. If it means 'was sufficient to produce' the revolution, then the statement is probably false. The high price of bread certainly contributed to revolt against the government in 1789, but the actions it sparked were by themselves not enough to overthrow the monarchy. If it means 'was necessary in the circumstances' to bring about the revolution, then it probably was, because revolts in response to the high bread prices helped to destroy royal administration, especially in the provinces. The revolution would have been different, and probably less successful without those revolts. So to judge the truth of causal statements, one must know precisely what they mean.

In my last book I presented an analysis of causes as contingently necessary for their effects (McCullagh, 1984, ch. 7). That analysis needs to be corrected in two ways. First, if the relations between historical events are probabilistic rather than deterministic – that is, if causes do not necessitate their effects but just make them more probable – one cannot strictly say that an historical cause was ever necessary for its effect. All one can say is that in the absence of the cause, the probability of the effect's occurrence was less than it was given the presence of the cause. For instance, one cannot say that in the absence of the high bread prices the French Revolution would not have occurred, for it might have. One can say, however, that the probability of its occurring would have been less than it was.

The second change that needs to be made to that earlier analysis of causation is that it needs to be augmented, to do justice to an important aspect of what we mean when we say one event caused another. To say that one event caused another also means that it brought its effect about, and on pp. 177–88 of this chapter I offer a further analysis of causes which explains precisely what this means. I will show that a cause is an event which triggers a disposition in something to produce a certain kind of effect, and thus sets in train a tendency for such an effect to occur. This is how causes bring about their effects.

The analysis of causal explanations has passed through several stages in the last few decades, and I give a brief résumé of that process in the next section. At one extreme has been the covering-law model, which describes causal explanations as deductive or inductive arguments. At the other has been a pragmatic analysis which says that a causal explanation is simply a description of any causes of an event which interest the person providing it.

From a careful analysis of historical practice I discern two dominant models of causal explanation, which I call 'causal' and 'contrastive'. Causal explanations are essentially a kind of genetic explanation. They tell a story of how an event came about, beginning with the cause which first increased the probability of the effect significantly, and proceeding to describe subsequent causes which altered the probability of the outcome, right until its final occurrence. Contrastive explanations have a quite different purpose, which is to point to some event(s) or condition(s) which made the occurrence of an event more probable than that of another which might well have been expected in the circumstances. Sometimes the events which made the difference were indeed causes of what happened, but often the contrast is explained by referring to conditions favouring one outcome rather than another which were not causes at all. Once the purpose and structure of these two kinds of explanation is understood, it is possible to judge the adequacy of particular explanations offered by historians along these lines.

The third section of this chapter on pp. 194–204 discusses functional statements and functional explanations. Historians sometimes point out the social functions of certain institutions and rituals, hinting that they exist because of their useful functions in society. It seems that functional explanations constitute a unique kind of explanation, explaining the existence of something as a consequence of its effect, but after careful analysis of them I show that this is not so.

THE COVERING-LAW MODEL AND ITS CRITICS

C.G. Hempel's analysis of explanations about fifty years ago received a lot of attention, not only from philosophers of science but from philosophers of history as well. He said that events in history as well as in science are explained by finding circumstances which made their occurrence necessary, or very probable, according to some covering law (Hempel, 1965, ch. 9). Some counter-intuitive implications of this theory can be avoided by requiring that the explanations refer to conditions which were not only sufficient for the outcome, but also necessary for its occurrence in the circumstances.

Why is this theory no longer thought adequate as an account of explanations in history? One of the most influential critics of a scientific model of historical explanation was R.G. Collingwood. Whereas scientists look for the external causes of events, according to covering laws, historians, he said, study human actions and artefacts and explain them by stating the reasons people had for performing them. Historical explanation, therefore, is quite different from scientific explanation. To discover the thoughts expressed in human actions, he said, the historian is not guided by laws, but draws upon his imaginative understanding of what thoughts would have given rise to that behaviour in the circumstances. He even said we are capable of re-thinking the thoughts of past people, because their thoughts continue to live today ('Human Nature and Human History', in Collingwood, 1946).

William H. Dray built upon Collingwood's ideas, and after an extensive critique of Hempel's theory, set out a theory of rational explanation, which he contrasted with causal explanation of the sort Hempel had promoted. Rational explanations, he said, do not show that an action was likely to occur in the circumstances, but rather show the point of what was done. They do not depend on covering laws, but on an appreciation of what would have been a reasonable response to the circumstances. Indeed, if people have free will, then their actions are the result of freely made choices and are not determined by causes at all (Dray, 1957, ch. 5).

There is no doubt that history is largely about human actions, and actions are generally explained in terms of the reasons for which they were done. There is some doubt that the reasons have to be as good as Dray supposed. Dray said that in explaining the reasons for a person's acting, 'the perception of appropriateness is the historian's usual criterion of understanding'; and that 'when we do employ this criterion, we cannot help certifying the agent's reasons as good ones, from his point of view, for doing what he did' (Dray, 1963, pp. 72, 73). Now when is an action reasonable from the agent's point of view? Clearly if it follows from his beliefs and values as the most appropriate in the circumstances. But how many of our actions are as rational as that? We often act a bit impulsively to achieve goals which grab our attention, when we should perhaps have been doing something else, had we been rational. Dray has set a very high standard of rationality, even allowing as he does that the agent's beliefs and values themselves may not be rational. Not many actions could be shown to be rational according to this standard, so not many could be understood on this model.

In fact rational explanations do not show that an action was reasonable from the agent's point of view, but rather they set out the reasons – desires, beliefs, principles and values – which moved the agent to perform it. The reasons for which an agent performed an action might not make it appear 'the thing to have done', given the agent's beliefs and values. The standard of rationality involved in rational explanations is lower than that. It is enough if they provide some reasons, some premises from which one can see that the action was a rational thing to have done, relative to those premises alone.

This brings me to the second important objection to Dray's theory, which was first raised by John Passmore in his review of Dray's book. Dray did not, in his book, distinguish reasons which an agent may have had which justified an action from the reasons for which the agent did it. These are not always the same, and historians who want to understand a person's behaviour surely are interested only in the latter. In reply Dray acknowledged the distinction, and agreed that the reasons for which an agent acted are the only reasons which provide an understanding of why an action was done (Dray, 1963, pp. 71–2). But he did not say how the two sets of reasons could be distinguished; nor did he appreciate the significance of the objection to his theory.

Donald Davidson explained the difference between these two kinds of reasons by saying that the reasons which explain an action, rather than merely justify it, are those reasons which caused the agent to do it (Davidson, 1963, p. 9). Allowing that causes may be necessary but not sufficient for their effects, which means that reasons need not determine actions, this account of the difference seems entirely plausible. Then the interesting question to ask is, why are these reasons of more interest to an historian than the reasons which justify the action? If the purpose of rational explanation were merely to establish the rationality of the action from the agent's point of view, would not either set be acceptable? Indeed the rational justification might be preferred, because it is usually more impressive, from a rational point of view, than the actual reasons for acting, when these differ. It usually refers to deeply held values, whereas the actual reasons for acting have often more to do with shallow self-interest. The point is that historians are interested in the reasons which actually moved the agent. If they want to know why an action occurred, they evidently do not want to see that the action was rational, but to know what brought it about, the causes which led to its occurrence.

Dray's analysis of historical explanations was of great importance, because it forced philosophers to turn from scientific models and consider rational explanations. But it is misleading in suggesting that historians want to understand individual actions by seeing that they were rational from the agent's point of view. In practice, most actions are not rational in this sense, though they are normally done for reasons of some sort. But the reasons are sometimes ones of which the agent, on reflection, would be somewhat ashamed.

It is also wrong to suppose that reasons cannot be causes. Dray is correct in saying that rational explanations display a rational connection between reasons and action. But for the explanation to be satisfactory, there must be a causal connection as well, the reasons must not only make the action appear at least to some extent reasonable, they must also be what moved the agent to perform it.

That is not to say that Hempel's model of explanation is acceptable after all. The main objection to it as a model of historical explanation is that the causes which historians describe to explain an event seldom make its occurrence very probable. Consider, for instance, people's reasons for acting. Suppose you wanted a cup of coffee, and so left your desk and walked to a cafeteria to get a coffee. Your action can be explained by saying you wanted some coffee, and believed the best way to get some in the circumstances was to go to the cafeteria and buy some. Do those reasons make the action very probable? All sorts of things could have arisen, both in your mind and in your office, to prevent you. You might have decided to put off the coffee till you had finished a letter; the telephone might have rung and prevented you from getting it. The reasons for getting the coffee do not make the action very probable. They make it more probable than it would have been had you not had those thoughts, but by no means very probable.

When I considered the nature of causes in history in 1984, I suggested that although they seldom make their effects very probable, they can always be said to have been necessary for the occurrence of those effects in the circumstances. If the causes had not occurred as and when they did, then neither would the effects (McCullagh, 1984, ch. 7). This analysis of causation has been developed in a sophisticated way by David Lewis (1973). He extended it to apply to systems which are not deterministic but probabilistic, as most psychological and social systems are. One can say of causes in such systems that if they had not occurred, then the probability of their effects occurring would have been less than it was (Lewis, 1986a). Causes of both kinds, Lewis said, can go back in time to the beginning of the universe, forming chains of counterfactual dependency. Lewis went on to give a very simple account of causal explanation: 'to explain an event is to provide some information about its causal history' (Lewis, 1986b, p. 217). The information provided in a causal explanation, he said, should be of the kind required by the person for whom it is designed. In other words, to explain an event just pick out from its great chain of causes those which interest you.

Lewis' theory is reminiscent of one which Michael Scriven had put forward in 1966, in an essay entitled 'Causes, Connections and Conditions in History'. Scriven wrote: 'The search for causes proceeds in a context which indicates two connected features: (a) the *type* of factor which is of interest, and (b) what may be called a "contrast state"'(1966, p. 254). His theory was that to explain an event the historian picks out those causes of a kind which interests him, and which suffice to make the event being explained more probable than a contrast state. Thus one might ask for proximate rather than remote causes of the outbreak of the First World War, and ask why it broke out in 1914 rather than at another date.

Notice how far we have come from Hempel. For Scriven and Lewis, causal explanations are not designed to show that an effect was very probable, in accordance with a covering law. Rather, they simply describe some of the causes, the contingently necessary conditions, of the effect which are of interest. These will certainly be events or conditions which increased the probability of the effect, but not necessarily by very much. The important point is that the probability of the effect would have been less without them.

Notice also how subjective causal explanations are, if Scriven and Lewis are right. There is some evidence to support their theory. In everyday contexts people are often interested in causes of a particular kind, for practical purposes. If a husband murders his wife, the doctor looks for the medical causes of death, the policeman for the person who brought death about, the psychologist for their state of mind at the time, and the social worker for the domestic situation which led to the act. Historians seldom have an immediate practical interest in the causes of past events. They are usually interested in all the causes, the whole causal process, that brought them about. For example, usually they ask for both proximate and remote causes of a war if they are trying to explain its occurrence. There are, however, exceptions to this generalization which support Scriven and Lewis' theory. Historians do sometimes describe only those causes which interest them. Some historians are interested in the very detailed processes of political and diplomatic decision-making which led to war. And others, often using comparative methods, inquire into the general preconditions of conflict. Frequently these preferences are linked to political interests: liberals focusing upon the importance of diplomacy, and socialists on the structural basis of war. (See Stretton, 1969, pp. 56–60.)

After studying historical causes and causal explanations for some time, I have developed an analysis of these which differs from Scriven and Lewis', and which implies that causal explanations are not as unrestricted as they have said.

CAUSES AND CAUSAL EXPLANATIONS

I assume that the aim of a theory of causes is to find those features of causes which explain why we call some things causes but not others, in other words to find the distinguishing characteristics of causes. It should also capture some of our essential intuitions about the nature of causes. Lewis' analysis fails on both counts. I am not referring to some problems with overdetermination and pre-emption, which seem to provide exceptions to his theory. Even if we agree that causes are all contingently necessary for their effects, or increase the probability of their effects, there are still reasons for denying its adequacy.

One objection to Lewis' theory is that it allows too many things to be causes. According to Lewis, causal relations are transitive, so the causes of any event include every contingently necessary event and state of affairs for it going right back to the beginning of time. That means very remote events are causes of what happens today. It means that the Big Bang at the beginning of the universe caused a leaf to fall, or a person to smile today, and my great great grandparents' decision to have children was a cause of my writing this sentence. I suggest that we do not normally regard very remote events, such as these, as causes of what happens today.

The second objection is related to the last. One reason why we do not count remote events as causes is that our concept of a cause includes the idea of something bringing about its effect. My greeting a colleague in the corridor caused her to smile, not the explosion which started the universe. The reason we are unwilling to admit remote events as causes is that they do not seem to have been active in bringing about their effects.

It is tempting to draw the conclusion that causes are not only contingently necessary for their effects, but must make them very probable as well. There are two difficulties with this proposal. The first is that many causes do not make their effects very probable, just more probable than if the cause had not happened. Sometimes people have reasons for doing something, like clean out their cupboards or write a personal letter, but put off doing so for a long time. When they do act on those reasons, we know the reasons caused their action, but we could not have predicted when or even whether they would have acted on those reasons with any confidence. The probability that they would do so at any time was very small. So causes do not always make their effects very probable. The most one can say is that they make them much more probable than they would have been in the absence of the causes.

The second problem with saying that causes make their effects very probable is that quite often an effect is the outcome of a number of interacting causes, and the regular consequence of none of them. It is better to say, therefore, that causes tend to produce effects of a certain kind, but that that tendency can be offset by other tendencies at work in the situation. This way of talking about causes is common among those who think of causes as exercising 'causal power'.

A theory of causes as events which have tendencies to produce effects of certain kinds can be derived from a theory of causal power presented by R. Harré and E.H. Madden. They said that causes bring about their effects through the exercise of the causal power of something. They analyse causal power in this way: "'X has the power to A" means "X will or can do A, in the appropriate conditions, in virtue of its intrinsic nature"' (Harré and Madden, 1975, p. 86). Thus sunlight has the power to start a fire if it is focused by a piece of glass upon some leaves. For a fire to start you need both the sunlight and the glass and leaves. It is the conjunction of these things which produces the fire. Any event which produces that conjunction, I say, can be regarded as the cause of the fire. It might be the smashing of a glass bottle thrown from a passing car into the countryside on a sunny day which produces that conjunction. It might be the rising of the sun flooding light onto a verge where glass and leaves are already in place which produces the conjunction. The cause of an event is a conjunction of things which together have a tendency to produce a certain kind of outcome.

Examples from history are easy to find. Notice how the assassination of the Austrian Archduke Ferdinand sparked off the First World War. Apparently the foreign minister of Austria-Hungary in 1914, Count Leopold von Berchtold, urged on by his chief of staff, Conrad von Hoetzendorf, wanted to make a bold move in the Balkans, and was looking for an excuse to declare war on Serbia. The assassination of the Archduke on 28 June was attributed to the Serbs, and was generally reckoned to provide an adequate reason for war. Even so, given Russia's support of Serbia, Berchtold was not willing to risk war without German support, and the consent of Hungary. He sought and received this support and consent, so on 23 July he declared war on Serbia (Taylor, 1954, pp. 520–3). Prior to the assassination, one could say that Berchtold wanted to declare war on Serbia whenever he could find an excuse which would assure German support and Hungarian consent. The assassination provided those conditions, so he declared war. The conjunction of his desire and the conditions necessary for it to find expression caused him to declare war.

Harré and Madden did not notice that in certain circumstances causes have a more or less predictable chain of effects. For example, if you put your hand in a fire, then your hand will be burned, you will feel pain, and you will probably cry out. All these effects are natural consequences of the first event. You could even say that fire has the power to burn a hand which is put into it, to cause a person pain who puts their hand into it, and to cause a person to cry out who puts their hand into it. Fire is liable to bring about these effects when part of a human body is put into it. The person might be brave, and not cry out when hurt by the burn, despite a tendency to do so. In that case their desire to suppress expressions of pain set in train a tendency which was greater than their tendency to cry out. You might say, wasn't it the burn which caused the pain and the pain which caused the cry? How can one say that putting one's hand in the fire caused the cry? I think we can say this because it is a regular consequence of putting one's hand in a fire. It might be mediated by a series of sub-events, but that is quite compatible with a macro story.

I have said that a cause is an event which produces a conjunction of something that has a tendency to produce an effect of the kind which occurred in certain circumstances, and the presence of those triggering circumstances. Harré and Madden said that things have the causal powers they do 'in virtue of their intrinsic nature'. Consequently they say the causal powers of a thing exist as a matter of natural necessity: 'they must behave in the specified way in the given circumstances, or not be things that they are' (ibid., p. 91). A thing does not always manifest its causal power, of course, even in the relevant circumstances, because other powers at work might prevent it. The power of sunlight to start a fire in certain circumstances might be offset by the power of rain to put one out. But the existence if not the manifestation of a causal power is a natural necessity.

One can see how this applies in history. The tendency of an historical agent, be it a person or a corporate body, to work for a certain outcome in certain circumstances is usually, perhaps always, the result of certain intrinsic beliefs, values and attitudes which they hold. I take it that these are not just dispositions to behave in certain ways, but are states of the brain or mind which necessitate such dispositions. Alternatively, the effect of a change in a social system can be understood as a function of the rules and habits governing the people involved in that system. If you drive over the limit and a police person spots you, then you are normally fined, because the law is that speeding motorists will be fined. The law is intrinsic to the legal system. It would be going too far to say that people's responses to a law are a matter of natural necessity because human behaviour is not as predictable as that. But given the nature of a law or convention, their response is often made very probable given the circumstances which triggered it. The responses of individual agents are sometimes unique, because their desires and beliefs are unique.

In April 1861, the Confederates opened fire on Fort Sumter in Charleston, South Carolina. Lincoln immediately mobilized against the south. Why? Because he believed that the authority of the Federal government should be respected throughout America to preserve the Union, and had demonstrated this belief by vowing to supply the Fort whose garrison was close to starvation in the face of southern hostility. That belief was part of Lincoln's intrinsic nature at the time, and it motivated his determination to defend the Union's federal authority by arms if necessary.

In this example, one would not say that Confederate firing upon Fort Sumter had the power to move Lincoln because of the intrinsic nature of that firing. The disposition is Lincoln's alone. Sometimes, however, it seems that an effect depends upon the intrinsic nature of both the elements of the conjunction. Thus a bushfire depends upon both the heat of the sunlight, focused through a glass, and the nature of the leaves, which have to be dry to burn easily. Focused sunlight has the power to burn dry leaves, and dry leaves are liable to burn under focused sunlight. Similarly, fire has the power to burn human hands, and cause pain and cries of distress because of the intrinsic nature of the fire, namely its great heat, and the intrinsic nature of human anatomy, which determines its response to fire. A human body is liable to burn, feel pain and cry out when put in fire; and fire has the power to burn a human body, cause it pain and cause it to cry out. The effects are all consequences of the nature of the things involved in the causal conjunction.

This analysis of causation applies to causal relations between theoretical entities as well. Theories posit theoretical entities and relationships between them. These relationships are often causal. In an economic theory which relates the supply, price and demand for goods in a freely competitive system, for example, the demand for a good will tend to vary inversely with its price: as the price goes up the demand goes down, and vice versa. The demand could be said to have a disposition to change in this way in the given circumstances, and the disposition refers to just a tendency, which could be offset by other forces operating in the economy. For instance if the supply of a good is known to be very limited, then the demand for it might stay strong even when the price increases, because demand for a good has a tendency to remain high when it is in short supply. Why does demand have these tendencies? One could explain it as a function of the intrinsically rational and selfish nature of consumers, who on average try to maximise gain for themselves in the circumstances. If the price of a good goes up, they will naturally prefer the cheaper good, other things being equal. Similarly, if they know the supply of a good is short, they will stock up with it even though the price is quite high. The generalizations which express the causal tendencies can be discovered simply by noting customer behaviour, without any reference to their rational selfish nature. But the theory about their nature helps to explain the generalizations discovered by observation.

Harré and Madden said that sometimes we know the regular disposition of something to cause certain effects in certain circumstances but do not know what it is about the nature of the conjuncts which produces that tendency (ibid., p. 87). Indeed at a fundamental level of physics, fundamental forces are identified just by their dispositions to produce certain effects in certain circumstances. There is nothing more to their nature than that (p. 11, 177–9). The disposition of something to produce a certain effect can be called its power or potential, and the tendency which is produced when that power is triggered, the authors call a force (pp. 167–8). The word 'tendency' is rather ambiguous between potential and force, though I use it to refer to an active force. The ultimate constituents of matter, they say, have their powers identified with their natures. They call these 'Parmenidean individuals' (pp. 162–3).

Causal tendencies do not always find expression, even when activated, because other forces in the field sometimes inhibit them, so causes do not regularly produce certain events as their outcomes. Rather causes regularly produce tendencies to produce certain kinds of events; and if there are no other forces affecting the outcome, then they will indeed produce events of the kind described. Statements of causal regularities are therefore more like theoretical than empirical statements, describing what generally happens under certain ideal conditions.

There are three ways in which one can justify generalizations relating causes to the tendencies they produce. One is by explaining how they are implied by the intrinsic nature of one or both of the conjuncts which make up the causal event. Consider the generalization: if I scold conscientious students who lack self-confidence, then they will tend to become distressed. One might, for example, argue that a conscientious student strongly wants to do well, but one who lacks self-confidence is readily convinced that they are of little positive value, and that in these circumstances a scolding is experienced as both a severe disappointment and confirmation of the inferiority the person feared. People who experience something as confirmation of something else which they really fear generally tend to be distressed. So it is predictable that the generalization is always true that if anyone scolds a conscientious student who lacks self-confidence then they will tend to be distressed.

The second way in which one can justify a generalization like this is just by observing a large number and variety of cases. It is difficult to say how many cases are needed. One needs enough to be confident that there are no exceptions (see McCullagh, 1984, ch. 6). The third way of justifying a causal generalization is by inferring it from a higher-level generalization. People who lack self-confidence are distressed by any humiliation, so conscientious students who lack self-confidence will certainly be distressed by a respected teacher who scolds them for bad work.

The effects of a causal conjunction can themselves trigger further events. Suppose your shout of pain wakened your baby brother who happened to be sleeping near by, and made him cry in fright. That effect is the consequence of the conjunction of the shout and the sleeping baby, who is liable to wake up and cry when he hears a loud noise. The cause of an event is the conjunction which produced it in virtue of the disposition of one or both of the conjuncts. I do not think that causal relations are transitive. Although your shout caused the baby to cry, your putting your hand into the fire did not cause the baby to cry. We might explain why the baby cried in the circumstances by telling a story which begins with your putting your hand in the fire, but that is another matter which will be discussed soon. We can explain events by describing chains of causes, but causes themselves produce only those effects which can be explained as consequences of the dispositions they trigger.

To illustrate this point, let me return to the example of the outbreak of the First World War. Strictly speaking, the murder of the Archduke caused Austria to declare war on Serbia. Russia, a strong supporter of Serbia, immediately mobilized troops to frighten Austria against proceeding further. In response to Russian mobilization, the German generals declared war on Russia, arguing that this was necessary for German defence. The French had an alliance with Russia and refused to remain neutral, so the Germans declared war on France as well. Only after Germany invaded Belgium in order to attack France did Britain decide to enter the war against her. Given the structure of European alliances and the attitudes of the individual leaders of European powers, the murder of the Archduke can be seen to have made a general European war to some degree probable, and so helps to explain it. Nevertheless it would be wrong to say that, for example, the Germans declared war on France because a Serb murdered the Austrian Archduke. The Germans declared war on France because they wanted to protect Germany, and they believed that in the case of danger the best method of defence was attack. When they declared war on Russia, they were in danger of a French attack, as France was an ally of Russia. It was this conjunction of their dispositions and the circumstances which made them act as they did.

The causes I have described so far have all been immediate causes of their effects. Is it reasonable to talk of 'underlying causes' of an historical event? I suggest that the 'underlying causes' of an event are very often events which produced the disposition which finally caused the event. Thus the underlying causes of the First World War were the events which increased rivalry between the great powers to the point where they were willing to fight each other over any slight pretext. Raymond Aron, for example, wrote:

> The historian, concerned to show the causes of an event, puts two questions, both legitimate, but which must be carefully distinguished. First of all, why did war come at that particular time; and, given the situation, who were the men, or what were the circumstances, that precipitated war? Secondly, how was the situation which led to the war created? The first question refers to what are generally called the immediate causes, the second to what are called the remote origins.
>
> (Aron, 1958, pp. 67–8)

Aron went on to explain the growing tensions between the great powers, and the alliances they formed. He summed up thus:

> The growing tension centered about three principal difficulties: the rivalry between Austria and Russia in the Balkans, the Franco-German conflict over Morocco, and the arms race – on sea between Britain and Germany, and on land between all the powers. The two last causes produced the situation, the first one kindled the spark.
>
> There are doubtless those who contend that the immediate cause matters little, and that war might have broken out just as easily in 1911 as in 1914. The contention readily suggests itself and is not easily disproven.
>
> (ibid., p. 71.)

Once the rivalry between the powers had become intense, the disposition to fight on any pretext had been established. The events which strengthened that rivalry certainly help to explain why the war occurred. Strictly speaking, however, events which strengthened international rivalry were causes of that rivalry, but not causes of the war. It was the rivalry which brought about the war, not the events which produced the rivalry.

Often a causal conjunction does not produce its effect immediately because the tendency it sets in train is retarded by other causal forces present in the situation. In fact contingencies may occur which either retard or hasten the original tendency. For example, suppose sunlight has started a small fire among some leaves, a shower of rain might dampen them and retard the fire; and then a strong hot wind might dry the leaves and spread it quickly. Because both events influenced the outcome, I would regard both as causes of what finally occurred. The first cause of an event is the conjunction of things which tended to produce it, and then all the subsequent events which affected the outcome are causes as well. The outcome is always a product of all the relevant forces at work in the situation.

A simple example of an initial force being retarded by another is provided by A.J.P. Taylor's explanation of why Sir Edward Grey, the British Foreign Secretary, did not recommend a declaration of war on Germany immediately after she had declared war on France. Taylor writes: 'it was impossible for Grey to make any clear declaration; public opinion would not have allowed it' (Taylor, 1954, p. 525). Taylor's argument goes like this. Suppose Grey had felt a strong moral obligation to support France against Germany, so that, when Germany declared war on France, Grey was strongly inclined to recommend that Britain declare war on Germany. His Prime Minister Lloyd George, the Liberal Party and the country at large had little interest in European affairs and certainly did not want to be embroiled in a war. So Grey's inclination to support France would have been checked by his stronger wish to recommend only those policies which would be generally supported by the government and country.

Here is another example of a causal force being affected by circumstances which alter its power to produce the effect. Once the American Civil War had started, and Union armies moved south to re-establish federal control, then a force was in operation which would, if unchecked, have succeeded in restoring federal authority in the south. In fact, of course, the Union armies were resisted by Confederacy armies, and the outcome was a function of the relative strength of those conflicting forces. The strength of the Union advance, however, was reduced in 1862 by the incompetence of several Union generals, namely George B. McClellan, John Pope and Ambrose E. Burnside; and it was strengthened in 1863 and 1864 by copious supplies of men and materials. This example concerns the causal forces impinging upon the tendency of a large group of people rather than an individual.

As was said before, once a conjunction of events has activated a force, the outcome depends upon the other forces impinging upon it or affecting the outcome independently. Suppose Grey wanted to declare war on Germany out of loyalty to France, but was prevented from doing so by the reluctance of the British people. When it became clear that Germany was going to invade Belgium *en route* to France, the British were appalled at this violation of national sovereignty, and backed war against Germany for that reason. This was an independent reason for declaring war on Germany, which strongly reinforced any weak initial inclination to do so from loyalty to France. All the forces which produce an outcome are causes of it.

It is sometimes useful to distinguish the initiation of a force in history from its final outcome. This is certainly the case when many events intervene between the two. For instance, Lincoln's decision to reclaim the south set in motion a military drive to reassert his authority over it, but the outcome of that drive was not settled for several years. Historians quite properly distinguish explanations of the outbreak of the Civil War, which focus upon events that increased hostility between the two sections, and explanations of the outcome of the war, in terms of the contingencies which affected the relative strength and effectiveness of both sides. Similarly explanations of the outbreak of the First World War are quite different from explanations of the ultimate defeat of the Axis powers. In explaining the outcome of a force, historians have to describe the other forces at work in the situation, and often explain these by describing events which account for their relative strength and weakness. For instance the strength of the southern Confederate army was increased in 1862 by a law conscripting soldiers, passed by the Confederate Congress; and their resources were increased by the printing of treasury notes (McPherson, 1989, pp. 430, 439).

In identifying the causes of an event and explaining its occurrence, an historian has to pay attention to the description of the event, for that indicates what aspect of the event is of interest. Consider, for example, the death of Eichmann. From a judicial point of view that death was an execution, and as such was the result of a judicial process, and the criminal acts which set that process in train. From a medical point of view his death was a cessation of bodily functions caused by hanging and asphyxiation. Historians are usually interested in only a few aspects of the events they study, and want to know the causes and explanation of the event having those characteristics.

Some philosophers have thought that causes are abnormal events which account for their effects. H.L.A. Hart and A.M. Honoré, for example, offered a striking example to illustrate this theory. Suppose a man had stomach pains. The doctor, they said, would assume that it is normal for people to eat parsnips, and would identify the man's gastric ulcers as the cause of his pain. His wife, on the other hand, would take his ulcers as normal, and attribute the pain to his having eaten parsnips, which he seldom did. Their theory was that causes are abnormal events, and that what counts as normal varies with one's point of view (Hart and Honoré, 1959, p. 22). In fact in these cases the doctor and the wife are giving contrastive, not causal explanations. The doctor is explaining why the man has a pain when he eats parsnips, whereas most people do not; his wife is explaining why, with his ulcers, he has a pain when normally he does not. Contrastive explanations are quite different from causal explanations, as I shall show in the next section. The cause of the man's pain was, of course, his eating parsnips when, because of his ulcers, he was disposed to experience pain whenever he ate parsnips. It was the conjunction of eating parsnips when he was in that fragile state that caused the pain.

Causal explanations of events usually begin with the first event whose occurrence made the final event significantly more probable than it previously had been, and then describe the sequence of causes which brought about the event being explained, together with the contingent events which had an influence along the way on the outcome. From this practice it seems that such explanations are designed to meet an interest in prediction and control. When the events being explained are historical events, then prediction and control cannot be the immediate interest. I think, rather, the interest is in detecting who and what were responsible for the outcome, with an eye to praise and blame. If a European war could have been seen as a probable outcome of Austria's declaring war on Serbia with German support, then that action may have been partly to blame for what happened. Evidence of a connection between explanation and responsibility is easy to find in relation to the First World War.

It is not always easy to decide where an explanation should begin. For example, how should one explain the occurrence of the First World War? The assassination of Archduke Ferdinand made the war very likely in the circumstances. The competition for colonies between the great powers, Britain, France, Germany and Italy, made war to some extent likely, given their habits of backing colonization with military power. In the end, of course, although this competition increased tensions between the great powers, the war was not triggered by a colonial dispute. The development of nationalism and capitalist imperialism could possibly be cited, as it was likely to produce some tension between the great powers, and thus slightly increase the probability of war. But that outcome is uncertain, so it is not clear that these movements really do explain the war.

There are two ways in which a causal conjunction can be said to have made a remote event more probable than it otherwise was. The first is when that conjunction has a regular tendency to produce events of that kind. Thus putting one's hand in a fire regularly produces a cry of pain. The second is when in the particular circumstances one can predict the outcome, even though it is not a regular effect of the cause. Thus one could have predicted the baby sleeping near by would waken and cry, and so could explain this event by referring to that painful accident. The murder of the Archduke explains the outbreak of the European war, not because such an event given the dispositions of European statesmen had a tendency to produce such a war, for it only had a tendency to move the Austrian government to declare war; rather it was because the consequent involvement of other European powers could have been predicted in the circumstances.

Quite often historians begin an explanation with what were referred to before as underlying causes. These are causes of the disposition or dispositions which were finally triggered to set in train the chain of events which produced the outcome. Thus explanations of the First World War begin with descriptions of events which increased national rivalry among the European powers. The American Civil War is commonly explained by describing events which made the north and the south increasingly hostile towards one another. The assumption seems to be that given the strong dispositions, it was quite probable that something would trigger the tendency towards mutual hostility which had been built up. In other words, events which established these dispositions made the final outcome, in these cases a war, more probable than it would otherwise have been.

There are many different ways in which dispositions can be produced among a group of people. E.A. Pollard, for example, said that northerners developed a hatred of the south out of jealousy for their superior way of life.

> There is a singularly bitter hate which is inseparable from a sense of inferiority; and every close observer of Northern society has discovered how there lurked in every form of hostility to the South the conviction that the Northern man, however disguised with ostentation, was coarse and inferior in comparison with the aristocracy and chivalry of the South.
>
> (Quoted in Rozwenc, 1972, pp. 8–9.)

Once again the by now familiar causal pattern emerges. People who develop a sense of inferiority tend to hate that which causes it; the southern way of life made the northerners jealous, triggering that innate disposition; so they tended to hate the southerners.

Rational explanations take a similar basic form. Here is an extract from J.F. Rhodes:

> when events are reduced to their last elements, it plainly appears that the doctrine of States' rights and secession was invoked by the South to save slavery, and by a natural antagonism, the North upheld the Union because the fight for its preservation was the first step toward the abolition of negro servitude.
>
> (ibid., p. 51)

The south was disposed to defend slavery, on which their economy and way of life depended, which meant that if they thought something was threatening their right to own slaves, they would try to eliminate that threat by the most effective means they could think of in the circumstances. As northerners tried to curtail the spread of slavery through Congress, and criticized it in literature like *Uncle Tom's Cabin*, and even attacked it in the case of John Brown's insurrection at Harper's Ferry in 1859, the south became increasingly concerned about the danger which the north presented to their institution of slavery. These events triggered southern attempts to prevent the north from interfering with slavery, first by defending states' rights to decide upon slavery irrespective of the views of the federal congress; and after the election of the northern Republican Abraham Lincoln to the presidency, by finally seceding from the Union, and the sphere of federal authority altogether. These were the most effective ways of protecting slavery they could think of in the circumstances. A similar kind of analysis can be given of northern attitudes and behaviour. Assuming the northerners wanted to abolish slavery, which in fact a minority did before the war, then that means they were disposed to bring about that effect in the most efficient way they could in the circumstances. In this case, according to Rhodes, that was by using Union power, in Congress and on the field, to eradicate it.

The general schema for such explanations is as follows: if someone wants a goal G, and believes that the best way to achieve G in situation S is by performing action A, then if S occurs to trigger their dispositions, they will tend to do A. Most rational explanations in history assume a knowledge of the triggering situation, and just describe the desires and beliefs which made the agent respond as he or she did. The strength of a person's tendency to act according to their desires and beliefs when the situation is appropriate varies with several things: with the strength of their desire and belief, and with their general disposition to act rationally. The manifestation of the tendency, which is different from its strength, depends also upon other forces which influence the agent at the time, other desires, for example, or just lethargy.

C.A. Beard's explanation of the American Civil War refers to a conflict of economic interests between the two sections. The industrial north wanted to protect and promote its growing industries, and the agricultural south wanted to enjoy the profits of unimpeded exports. Each side was disposed to further its economic interests any way it could, and both used Congress, when they could, for this purpose. Between 1852 and 1860 the south dominated Congress, and passed measures damaging to the north. This increased northern hostility, for people naturally tend to oppose those who thwart their economic interests. When Lincoln came to power, southerners, disposed to defend their economic interests in this new situation, did what they thought best, and seceded from the Union. When they resisted Lincoln's attempt to maintain federal authority in the south by firing on Fort Sumter, the northerners sent troops against them.

These examples have been given largely to show how the present analysis of causation invariably applies. They raise the issue of objectivity which is central to this book. The objectivity of historical explanations will be discussed at greater length in the last section of this chapter, but already a few points can be made. There are two places where personal interests can influence the causal explanations which historians produce. First, there is often a choice of several different ways of conceptualizing an effect, and that choice determines which causal process they will describe. Historians, for instance, will generally be more interested in the judicial processes which led to Eichmann's death than in its physical causes. Second, in some cases there are quite a large number of possible causal processes for an effect from which historians can choose to explain it. The American Civil War between the slave owning states of the south and the Unionists of the north was the result of a growing hostility between the two sections which has been explained in several different ways. In complex situations like this, when several different issues are involved, historians often disagree as to which causal process was the most important.

It is common to think that the historian's personal interests also determine how far back along the causal chain they go in explaining an event. In practice, as Hugh Stretton has pointed out, historians sometimes do focus upon just those causes which interest them, and ignore others which were influential (Stretton, 1969, chs 2–4). On my analysis, however, to do this is to produce an incomplete causal explanation, for a complete explanation begins with the first event which made a significant difference to the probability of the effect's occurrence. Indeed I would go further and say that such truncated explanations are positively misleading, for they give the impression that earlier causes played no significant part in bringing about the effect.

Causal and contrastive explanations

Michael Scriven said that historians frequently look for causes which made the occurrence of an event more probable than the occurrence of some assumed or specified contrast state. Contrastive explanations of individual events are quite common, though they are by no means the only form of explanation – as Scriven and others, such as Bas C. van Fraassen (1980, ch. 5) and Alan Garfinkel (1981, ch. 1), have supposed. Contrastive explanations need to provide only enough information to show that one outcome was more probable than another, whereas causal explanations give an account of the whole causal process which brought about a certain outcome.

Previous writers have paid little attention to a very important feature of requests for a contrastive explanation. When one asks why did X happen instead of Y, one does so on the assumption of a certain state of affairs from which either of the contrasted outcomes could have resulted, or from which what did not happen seemed more probable than what did. Suppose two men were fighting and I ask why one won and not the other, believing that each had as good a chance of winning as the other. The question could be stated more accurately thus: given that both men were fighting as hard as they could, why did one win rather than the other? What is required then is to explain why the force of one fighter was more effective than that of the other. The answer could have been that he was stronger, fitter, more skilful or more experienced than the other, or any combination of these. Alternatively suppose it was well known that one fighter was stronger than the other, and so could have been expected to win, then in explaining why the other won against this background assumption one must provide information about what affected that superior strength: perhaps he was ill that day, or had received a gash over his eye early in the fight; or perhaps the strength of one was more than matched by the skill and ferocity of the other. The adequacy of a contrastive explanation depends not only upon the contrast to be explained but also upon the causes which have been assumed in asking the question.

Contrastive explanations are essentially predictive. Once an historian has provided reason for thinking one outcome was more probable than another in the circumstances, his job is done. There is no need to describe the sequence of events by which the outcome finally came about. For instance, once it is known that the strength of one fighter was more than matched by the skill and ferocity of the other, no more need be said to explain why the latter won. Such explanations depend upon general knowledge: if two people are fighting, and though one is stronger the other is more skilful and ferocious, then the latter will probably win. There is no need to describe, round by round, how the victory was achieved.

On the other hand, in providing a full causal explanation, historians often provide contrastive explanations as well. Take for example Alan Bullock's explanation of Hitler's policy towards Czechoslovakia at the Munich Conference on 29 September, 1938. Bullock quite rightly began his account with Hitler's early hatred of the Czechs during 'his Vienna days', when he resented the way they challenged the supremacy of the Hapsburgs. Later their strong army and defences threatened his plans to extend the Reich to the east. In November 1937 he spoke of his plans to annex the country (Bullock, 1952, p. 402). Bullock then describes Hitler's preparations for invasion, his marshalling of troops and his rousing of the Germans in the border Sudetenlands to find an excuse to attack the Czech government. There was a setback in May 1938 when the Czechs mobilized and the British and French governments warned Hitler of the danger of war. This belligerence was short-lived, however, and Hitler's plans proceeded unchecked. Another distraction were the visits of the British Prime Minister Mr Chamberlain, who attempted to broker a peaceful resolution of the growing tension. Then on 28 September, when war seemed inevitable, Mussolini, fearing a European con- flagration for which he was ill prepared, asked Hitler to delay. Mussolini suggested a conference, and produced a draft of what became the final agreement, in which France and Britain, Czechoslovakia's allies, agreed to make the Czech govern- ment accept German occupation of the Sudetenland, destroying her defence system and driving her President into exile. Prior to the conference, and after it, Hitler wanted to take the whole of Czechoslovakia by force. Why did he agree to this peaceful means of limited occupation? Bullock answers this question by saying that Hitler had noted the German people's lack of enthusiasm for war, the warning of the heads of the Army and Navy of the chance of defeat were a European war to develop, and the reluctance of Mussolini to mobilize. These facts explain both why he agreed to hold the conference and accept its peaceful recommendations, and why he did not launch a military attack on Czechoslovakia on 1 October as he had planned (ibid., p. 432).

In this case the conditions which explain why Hitler did not invade Czecho- slovakia did not make that negative decision a covering law. It is not the case that every dictator aware of the chance of ultimate defeat is more likely to refuse to attack than to attack. Indeed given his hatred of the Czechs, Bullock makes it clear that Hitler might well have gone ahead regardless of the risk. These just happened to be the circumstances in recognition of which he paused, and because he did so we assume that his concern about ultimate defeat overcame his desire to proceed. Certainly such considerations tend to make ambitious dictators pause, but the strength of their concern cannot be predicted.

Contrastive explanations commonly show that the force tending to produce one outcome was less than the force which produced another. When two forces are in opposition, then events which weaken one automatically make the other relatively stronger. In this way the same events sometimes explain what did happen, and why a likely alternative did not. To return to the causes of the American Civil War, conflict between the north and the south over slavery prior to 1854 had not divided them for several reasons. Two important causes of unity had been a spirit of compromise between the sections, which resulted in notable agreements about slavery in 1820 and 1850, and the existence of national political parties which put national interest before sectional interest most of the time. After 1850 that spirit of compromise became increasingly strained, until with the Kansas-Nebraska Act of 1854, allowing slavery above the 36 30' parallel which had been agreed as the limit in 1820, sectional rivalry broke out unchecked. As a result the Whig party was destroyed, and a new northern party, the Republican, was born. Forces making for political unity had been severely weakened, and those for sectional rivalry had been strengthened. The same events help to explain both why the war finally broke out, and why war became more probable than peace.

Causal explanations as genetic

It is interesting to compare the account of causal explanation which I have given above with John Herman Randall jr.'s analysis of a genetic explanation in *Nature and Historical Experience* (Randall, 1962, ch. 3). There have been other analyses of genetic explanations, as will be seen, but his is closest to historical practice. Randall, most appropriately, illustrates this kind of explanation by describing the way we explain the growth of a plant. The chemical constitution of a seed, he says, determines what the seed can become: 'it operates as a set of limits, boundaries beyond which the operations of the seed's processes of growth cannot go' (p. 73). We would probably speak of the genetic, rather than the 'chemical', constitution of the seed as having this function. For the seed to grow, however, it must interact with other things, with soil, moisture and sunlight. 'They are selective of the powers of that constitution, determining which of them shall be realized within the limits set' (p. 73).

Randall believes that historical explanations take the same form.

> Just as the material cause of the seed's career is its chemical powers and constitution, so the material cause of any human history is the institutionalized, socially organized behavior of men, and in just the sense in which that career can be understood in chemical terms, as the chemical interaction of various factors in the environment with the chemical constitution of the seed, so human histories can be understood in *psychological* terms, as the interaction of the various factors in the human environment with the behavior-patterns of human groups.
>
> (p. 83)

He explains that the behaviour patterns of the various organizations in society limit what any given group can do (p. 81). The history of any institution is the history of its interaction with others in the pursuit of its goals.

You can see how useful this model can be. Just as a seed has the potential to grow a certain way if suitably nurtured, so individuals, groups and institutions with definite aims will act in certain ways if given suitable circumstances. One important difference is that whereas the weather cannot change a seed's genetic structure, circumstances can cause people to modify their aims over time. Another difference is that genetic processes in nature are of a common general kind, whereas many genetic processes in history are unique, depending upon the particular aspirations of people, and the circumstances in which they act. Historians have discovered some general processes of change, and these are discussed in Chapter 9 below. But frequently the processes they describe, like the example to be given shortly about the origins of the British Labour Party, are unique.

Genetic explanations are teleological explanations, explaining a certain outcome, such as a plant blooming, as the result of a process of development. In history these outcomes can be either intended from the beginning or unintended consequences of certain events. The achievement of an ambition is typically intended; whereas events like environmental pollution are generally unintended consequences of earlier events.

The concept of genetic explanation could possibly be extended to include cases in which a group of people aim, not to achieve one single final outcome, but to provide a continuing service to the community as best they can. Most institutions do this, and their history can be understood as the interaction between that basic intent and the circumstances which dictate, to a large extent, how it can be fulfilled.

Ernest Nagel (1961, pp. 564–8) and C.G. Hempel (1965, pp. 447–53) have analysed the logical structure of what they call genetic explanations very closely. In fact the models they produced are of a sequence of changes, each providing a necessary but not sufficient condition for the next. Each stage is explained as the probable outcome of the previous stage, together with other circumstances. There is no mention, in all this, of any continuity of purpose or even continuity of direction. Thus they ignore a very important feature of genetic explanation, notably its teleological characteristic. Indeed their models are of a narrative explanation of change. Nagel uses the example of the change in the Earl of Buckingham's attitude towards a marriage between Prince Charles, later Charles I of Great Britain, and the Spanish Infanta Maria in 1623. At first Buckingham approved it and went to Spain to arrange it, but after unpleasant experiences with the Prince in Spain, he came to oppose it. Hempel's example is of 'the origin and development' of the practice of selling papal indulgences, which began in the ninth century, when absolution was promised to crusaders killed in battle. In 1199 indulgences were given in exchange for money, and then subsequently at increasingly frequent intervals. Finally not only the pope but his agents were empowered to sell them throughout Europe. In this case we have, not a reversal of policy but an extension of it. In both cases the historian aims to explain each stage of the change, and is not particularly focused upon the final outcome. This pattern of explanation has already been discussed in Chapter 3, as it is commonly used to explain major events.

Once the teleological nature of genetic accounts is recognized, one can understand why they begin where they do. Genetic explanations naturally begin with something which makes the occurrence of an outcome probable from the start to an extent which is not negligible. Thus the existence of a thriving plant is explained by a story which begins with the planting of a seed. The mere existence of the seed does not make the existence of the plant very probable: most seeds perish. But the planting of the seed greatly increases the probability of a flourishing plant coming into being. There are other, perhaps equally probable outcomes, such as the failure of the seed to germinate because it was not watered, or the failure of the seedling to survive because the sun scorched it. But from the beginning of the process there is some probability of the final outcome, and this is nowhere indicated in Nagel and Hempel's model. What successive contingencies do is alter the probability of the different outcomes. If the seed is watered, and the seedling is shaded from scorching heat, then the chances of its becoming a flourishing plant are increased. The story comes to an end with the last event which alters the probability of the final outcome.

The advantage of this analysis is that it explains why historians choose the information they do in constructing teleological genetic accounts. The facts they report are all events which have some effect on the probability of the occurrence of the outcome. In the course of a teleological history it is normal to find that some events occur which actually reduce the probability of the outcome, though their influence is usually offset by subsequent events.

A good example of teleological history is Henry Pelling's *The Origins of the Labour Party, 1880–1900* (1965). The story which he tells is too complex to report in detail, but it is easy to highlight its more important stages. Pelling identifies the birth of the Labour Party in Britain with the formation of the Labour Representation Committee in February 1900, on which several socialist groups and trade unions were represented, which grew in strength until in 1906 it succeeded in returning 29 members to Parliament. Why, then, does Pelling begin his account of the origins of the party in 1880? Because that year saw the first feeble attempts by socialist groups to co-operate in order to get representatives in Parliament, with the formation of the Democratic Federation (later the Social Democratic Federation) under the presidency of H.M. Hyndman. Here, then, the process of forming a labour party began.

The story of the growth and ultimate failure of the SDF is an important stage in Pelling's history. By 1884, he notes, 'the S.D.F. seemed to have every hope of rapid progress. It had secured the services of a number of able men, many of them both well-off and generous. The best-known of these was William Morris' (p. 27). It had affiliations with several other societies, and the support of both weekly and monthly journals. The potential for growth and success seemed great. But although it continued to exist into the twentieth century, it did not attract mass support from the working class, and eventually failed. The conditions of its failure are of interest, if only because they remind us of what was needed for success. The demise of the SDF was largely the result of two circumstances. The first was the establishment of the Fabian Society in 1884, which defended socialist policies but hoped that they could be achieved by converting the existing parties to adopt them, arguing against the more revolutionary methods advocated by the SDF. The second condition was the willingness of one branch of the Liberal Party to make some reforms in the interests of workers, and the widespread belief that this was the most realistic way of achieving them. The TUC set up a Labour Electoral Committee (later Labour Electoral Association) in 1886 to encourage this process. In this climate of opinion, then, how was the Labour Party born?

In 1892 a new organization was formed, thanks largely to the work of a newspaper editor, J. Burgess, who produced the *Workman's Times*. It was called the Independent Labour Party, and he organized branches of it around Britain, especially in the industrial north. It promoted the idea of achieving socialist aims by parliamentary means. Some of its ideas were popularized by Robert Blatchford, notably in a series of essays published under the title *Merrie England*. But the aims of the ILP did not receive substantial working-class support until they were endorsed by the British Trade Union Congress in 1899, which voted for the formation of the Labour Representation Committee. What brought the unions around? Pelling mentions several contingencies which influenced their thinking. First there was the realization, following Kier Hardie's experience in 1888, that the middle-class local caucuses of the Liberal Party would not accept Liberal-Labour candidates (pp. 65–9). Then towards the end of the 1890s, employers and their representatives increased their attacks upon trade unions as impediments to industrial progress, and threatened to cripple them, as trusts and combines had done in the United States (p. 196). The unions saw that they needed stronger representation in Parliament to defend their interests. What finally swung them firmly behind the Labour Representation Committee was the Taff Vale Case, in which the courts fined officers of the Railways Union over strike action (p. 213). They saw an urgent need for legislation to protect their right to strike.

Thus Pelling charts the failure of one organization to organize a labour party, and the success of another, once it joined with the TUC. Their fortunes depended upon circumstances, almost all of which were outside their control. It was not until the trade unions felt very threatened, and saw no other way of influencing Parliament, that they lent their weight to the Independent Labour Party's programme of establishing and supporting a parliamentary labour party.

It is clear that the eventual formation of the parliamentary Labour Party constantly directs Pelling's selection and arrangement of material. For example, the reason he mentions the McKinley tariff imposed by the USA in 1890 was that it reduced the market for textiles produced in Bradford, which caused the mill managers to try to reduce wages, which in turn led to a strike by the workers and their formation of the Bradford Labour Union, which became an important supporter of the Independent Labour Party. The first national conference of the ILP was held in the Bradford Labour Union's hall in January 1893 (pp. 94–112).

An interesting question raised by the Nagel–Hempel analysis of genetic explanations is that of whether they should show each stage of the story to have been very probable. Nagel and Hempel, wedded to a covering-law model of explanation, declared that they should. In fact historians seldom supply enough information for this purpose. The Bradford Labour Union provided strong support for the Independent Labour Party, but there is no generalization by which this could have been predicted. It was the result of a member of the Bradford Union, W.H. Drew, taking a leading role at the meeting of ILP representatives, held during the TUC in Glasgow in September 1892, when the Bradford conference of the ILP was arranged (Pelling, 1965, p. 112). The role of Drew at this meeting was one of those contingent facts which play such an important part in genetic explanations. But Pelling does not explain precisely why Drew was willing and able to play such a role, or why his prominence led to the decision to hold the conference in Bradford. Given that a Bradford representative played a leading role at that meeting there is quite a strong probability that it would decide to hold the conference at Bradford, but by no means a very strong probability.

The aim of genetic explanations is not to make each stage of a story seem probable, but to indicate events, often unexpected contingencies, which influenced the probability of the final outcome. On this point it is perhaps worth noting how W.B. Gallie modified his views about the relation between the events described in a genetic explanation and the final outcome. In his first essay on genetic explanations, Gallie argued that the causes mentioned in such explanations were necessary but not sufficient for their effects (Gallie, 1955). In the book which he wrote later, however, he said that 'following a story must be a kind of inductive exercise ... aimed at eliciting from successively presented bits of evidence, better and better or progressively more exact forecasts of what is to come' (1964, p. 32).

I conclude, then, that causal explanations are teleological, and fit Randall's model of genetic explanations.

FUNCTIONAL EXPLANATIONS

Why do firms continually try to reduce the costs of production? To remain competitive and increase profits. Why do we breathe? To keep alive. Do some events occur because of their effects? Functional explanations seem to say that they do. In that case, functional explanations are a very strange sort of causal explanation indeed. In this section I will examine functional explanations, and finally conclude that there is no good reason for thinking events are caused by their effects.

To begin with it is important to distinguish functional descriptions and functional explanations. The former just describe the functions which something has; the latter suggest that something exists because of its functions.

Historians do not always distinguish these two different kinds of functional understanding, and consequently it is sometimes difficult to interpret their statements. Consider, for example, Natalie Davis' discussion of the charivaris in France in the late Middle Ages. First she discusses 'Abbeys of Misrule' who mocked various authorities in riotous parades and carnivals: magistrates and other authorities were mocked, and husbands were beaten by their wives. She considers several functional accounts of these events. Keith Thomas viewed the carnival as 'a prepolitical safety valve for the members of a structured, hierarchical society' (Davis, 1975, p. 103), pointing to their social function. Mikhail Bakhtin thought 'the carnival is always a primary source of liberation, destruction, and renewal' of the social order (p. 103). Davis, noting in particular that these carnivals were run by male adolescents and that they often focused upon marriage relations, concluded that they had the following functions:

They gave the youth rituals to help control their sexual instincts and also to allow themselves some limited sphere of jurisdiction or 'autonomy' in the interval before they were married. They socialized them to the conscience of the community by making them the raucous voice of that conscience.

(p. 108)

What is unclear in all of these cases is whether the historian is simply noting certain functions served by the charivaris, or making the further suggestion that the charivaris occurred because they served these functions.

The same applies to Davis' discussion of 'sexual inversion, that is, switches in sex roles, . . . in literature, in art, and in festivity' in pre-industrial European society (p. 129). She notes that 'anthropologists generally agree that they, like other rites and ceremonies of reversals, are ultimately sources of order and stability of a hierarchical society. They can clarify the structure by the process of reversing it' (p. 130). But Davis challenges this account of the function of sexual inversion.

I want to argue that the image of the disorderly woman did not always function to keep women in their place. On the contrary, it was a multivalent image that could operate, first, to widen behavioral options for women within and even outside marriage, and, second, to sanction riot and political disobedience for both men and women in a society that allowed the lower orders few formal means of protest.

(p. 131)

There is a hint in the text that Davis thinks the participants acted as they did from a desire to achieve the functions she has noted. She writes that 'the stimulus to inversion play was a double one – traditional hierarchical structures *and* disputed changes in the distribution of power in family and political life' (p. 150).

It is quite difficult to distinguish functions from common effects. When Peter Achinstein analysed functions, he noted three kinds: 'design-functions', 'use-functions', and 'service-functions' (Achinstein, 1983, pp. 272–8). Design-functions of a thing refer to the effects it was designed to have; the use-functions are the effects which something is used to achieve, whether it was designed to achieve them or not; and the service-functions are the effects which something actually has, whether these were intended or not. But in the latter case, how can one distinguish the functions a thing serves from its other effects? Achinstein attempted to make this distinction by saying that functions are effects which 'confer a good' (p. 276). If he is right, then judgements of service-functions at least must be subjective, relative to the values of the person making the judgement as to what good a thing serves.

To avoid this subjective element, philosophers usually describe functions as being of just two kinds: those effects which a thing is regularly intended to have; and those effects which a thing regularly has in a system. Ernest Nagel defines the function of a thing as the effect it has in enabling a system to work in a certain environment (Nagel, 1961, p. 403; cp. Nagel, 1977, pp. 271–9). In Nagel's view, every system has a goal, 'in virtue of the organization of its parts' (p. 273), and to identify a system one must discover whether a process has indeed got a goal. He says one can tell this by noting the 'plasticity' of a process, that is the degree to which there are alternative ways of achieving the goal, and its 'persistence', that is the degree to which changes in the process are compensated for to ensure that the goal is achieved (p. 272).

The clearest examples of functional statements are those relevant to biological systems. These systems, in plants and animals, have the goal of maintaining the health of each individual so that they can flourish and reproduce in their environment. The various organs and their dispositions can be understood as having special roles within the biological systems with this as their goal. What is less clear is whether there are social systems as well as biological ones. Social organizations do seem to provide straightforward examples of social systems, dedicated to their various purposes: factories, schools, hospitals and so on. In each of these there are various offices and practices which have readily identifiable functions, some intended and others unintended, some commonly recognized ('manifest') and others not ('latent'; see Merton, 1967). But what about society as a whole? Talcott-Parsons saw it as a self-regulating entity, with various institutions whose function is to maintain harmonious relations between its parts and enable it to flourish in its environment (see Berkhofer, 1969, pp. 183–4). However, conflict theorists such as Ralf Dahrendorf deny that society is normally a harmonious entity, and instead view it as a battleground for different interest groups (Berkhofer, 1969, pp. 206–7). The social and the biological have been related by Bronislaw Malinowski, who suggested that social institutions function to meet people's natural needs, for food, shelter, sexual satisfaction, protection and so on (see Cohen, Percy S., 1968, pp. 40–1).

One could perhaps resolve the disagreement between Parsons and Dahrendorf as follows. It has been observed that groups of people whose members not only have interests in common but are aware of constituting an interest group, are naturally disposed to act both in their own interests as a group (to maintain their power, size, cohesion, etc.) and to further the purposes for which the group exists. When a society constitutes such an interest group, with its members aware of their common interests in co-operating for mutual security and well-being, then it generally acts to maintain its ability to maintain itself and to serve those interests as well. Societies are most conspicuously aware of their common interests when under attack in a war. The larger a society, the more difficult it is to achieve a sense of common interest. Small societies in a somewhat hostile environment, such as the Australian aboriginal tribes which Emile Durkheim studied, achieve a sense of community more readily. They are most likely to achieve the 'collective consciousness' of which he wrote, a point which is supported by what Durkheim wrote about it in *The Division of Labour in Society* (1964). However, if in a large society the dominant group is acting, not in the interests of all but in the interests of just themselves, then there will be fewer social changes which can be correctly related to the well-being of society as a whole. Marxists believe that governments in the past have always represented the interests of the dominant class.

If the practices of a social group contribute regularly to the maintenance of that group, or further the purposes for which the group exists, then those regular effects of the practices are their social functions. This account can obviously be adapted to natural organisms, whose parts function to maintain the viability of the organism as a whole, and contribute to its function, which is usually that of survival and reproduction. Social systems have a huge variety of purposes, from organizing tennis to organizing war. The practices of members of a group can serve functions which are intended or unintended, manifest or latent, and they can contribute either to the strength of the group or to the purposes which it is meant to serve. Regular effects which do not contribute to the strength or purposes of the group should not be regarded as 'functions' of its activities.

In the light of these remarks, what can be said about Davis' statements concerning the functions of charivaris and sexual inversion? Charivaris, she said, met some of the personal needs of the young men who engaged in them, an idea of which Malinowski would have approved. They also contributed to social cohesion, by relieving young men's frustrations at being powerless, and by 'socializing' the men to adopt the important social values they defended. These were important social functions of the charivaris. When it comes to sexual inversion, however, Davis argues that it not only reinforced normal social relations by clarifying them, but it also was a vehicle for criticism and change of social relations both within society and within the family. Should the changes which the practice of sexual inversion brought about be regarded as functions of the practice, or just as common effects? The answer depends upon whether such changes were merely regular consequences of the practice, or whether they helped to maintain the social system or further its purposes. Davis clearly believes the latter, that the practice did serve a useful social function.

It is important to acknowledge that there are regular social effects of some practices, though one would not call them functions. The example which Michael Lessnoff gives, taken from Gunnar Myrdal's book *An American Dilemma*, is a good one. Myrdal suggested that discrimination by Whites against Negroes in America had the function of lowering the Negro standards of living and conduct. Such discrimination 'made the Negroes relatively poorer, less educated, more prone to crime, etc.; and these facts in turn made Whites discriminate against them' (Lessnoff, 1974, p. 113). As Lessnoff says, these effects did not further the survival and well-being of the society; but they did serve to perpetuate disrespectful relations between Whites and Negroes within that society.

Sometimes historians not only describe the function which something served, but explain it by saying that it occurred because it had that function. If the function was an intended function, then such explanations can readily be understood as referring to the agent's purpose in acting. But if the function was not intended, then it is difficult to make sense of the claim that something occurred because of the function it served. Such a statement seems to be saying that an effect was the cause of its cause, which is nonsense. What are functional explanations like, and can they ever be justified?

According to G.A. Cohen, Marx offered a functional explanation of some important historical facts. Cohen quotes passages from Marx which show that in his opinion 'the class which rules through a period, or emerges triumphant from epochal conflict does so because it is best suited, most able and disposed, to preside over the development of the productive forces at the given time' (Cohen, 1988, p. 15; and see 1982, pp. 160–6). Marx also said that the cultural institutions and prevailing ideology of a society are those which best serve to stabilize the economic structure (the 'relations of production') (Cohen, 1988, pp. 8–10, 12–13). So, for example, although the manifest function of Calvinism was to achieve salvation through sobriety, industry, and frugality, Marxists would consider that it was widely accepted because of its latent functions of maintaining a diligent workforce and facilitating the accumulation of capital which supported the capitalist economic structure (see Cohen, 1982, p. 279).

The logical structure of functional explanations has proved a bit difficult to state. Cohen has shown that they depend upon a generalization of the following form: 'IF it is the case that if an event of type E were to occur at $t1$, then it would bring about an event of type F at $t2$, THEN an event of type E occurs at $t3$', where neither $t2$ nor $t3$ precedes $t1$ (Cohen, 1982, p. 260). On the basis of a generalization like this, one can assert that an event of type E occurred because it had the consequence of type F. An example which Cohen discusses is: 'Whenever an expansion of scale would lead to economies, an expansion of scale occurs' (Cohen, 1982, p. 265). He points out that such a statement says nothing about the process whereby the consequence brings about the antecedent event. Sometimes expansion might occur because managers see that it would lead to economies. On the other hand a principle of natural selection might apply, so that those industries and organizations which do not expand are extinguished by the competition (Cohen, 1982, pp. 287–9).

The importance of the generalization underlying good functional explanations can be appreciated when one considers what Jon Elster calls 'the general functionalist fallacy' (Elster, 1983, p. 60). This is the fallacy of supposing that any event which contributes to the well-being of a system must have occurred because of its effect. 'It is true, for instance, that internal cleavages in the working class serve the interest of the capitalist class, but from this we should not conclude that they occur because they have this effect' (p. 60). Elster does not relate such cases to the generalization, but a moment's reflection shows that they are excluded by it. For it is not true to say that, within a capitalist system, whenever a division in the working class would be in the interests of the capitalist class, that such a division occurs.

C.G. Hempel has objected that explanations based upon generalizations such as Cohen's do not adequately account for things if only because they fail to show why the outcome was produced by the thing being explained and not by anything else (Hempel, 1965, p. 310). The generalization required for an adequate functional explanation in Hempel's opinion is one which states that *only* E-type events could produce F-type events, but such generalizations, he said, are seldom warranted (p. 311). For example, to explain the expansion of industries (E) by saying that it led to economies (F), one would have to show that nothing else besides such expansion could have achieved economies. Otherwise economies might have been achieved in other ways, say by reducing wages, and so the expansion of industry has not really been explained. In reply to Hempel, Cohen says that in many cases there is no practical alternative means of achieving the specified outcome (Nagel makes a similar point about natural systems in 1977, p. 292); and where there are, one could alter the generalization to indicate the range of possible means which could be chosen (Cohen, 1978, pp. 275–6). In the latter case the explanation provided would not be very strong, as it could not specify precisely how the outcome would be achieved, but it would be of some value just the same.

Jon Elster's objection to functional explanations is that they might well fail to identify the correct cause of an event. The advantage an event provides to a system could be just an epiphenomenon of that event, whose cause lies elsewhere. For example, the submission of subjects to rulers in classical antiquity was no doubt beneficial to the rulers, but was caused by their fear of the consequences of resistance. So the generalization 'whenever general submission to rulers would be useful to those rulers, then such submission occurred', would be true, but it would be false to say that the submission was caused by its effect on the political system (Elster, 1983, p. 67).

How can mistakes like this be avoided? Elster says that functional explanations are only credible when a 'feedback loop' has been shown to exist between the kind of effect and the kind of cause (p. 61). That is to say, the reader requires details of the mechanism whereby the needs of a system bring about events which will meet them. This information explains why the generalization upon which a functional explanation depends is true.

What worries people most about functional explanations is why the generalizations upon which they rest should be true. Why should a system which needs a certain adjustment if it is to operate efficiently regularly generate the condition which it needs? In nature, and in some machinery, the regular adjustment can often be explained as the effect of a feed-back mechanism. Food deprivation in animals causes hunger pains which drive them to seek food. Air heaters have thermostats which adjust the heat so that the air does not get too hot or too cold. But do such mechanisms exist to regulate the life of social groups? Cohen admits that he does not know what they are: 'I do not have a good answer to the question how productive forces select economic structures which promote their development' (1988, p. 17). He adds: 'This seems to me an important area of future research for historical materialists, since the functional construal of their doctrine is hard to avoid' (p. 12). Alan Ryan denies that feedback mechanisms operate in society, arguing that functional explanations in the social sciences can be 'unpicked . . . into intentionally based ones' (Ryan, 1970, p. 194). That is, he thinks all functional generalizations about society can be explained as the outcome of a process of human deliberation, decision and action.

Several philosophers have supposed that functional generalizations can be explained by reference to laws of natural selection. Both Jon Elster and Russell Hardin, for example, have argued that, just as the process of natural selection can explain why species which are poorly adapted to their environment die out, and why those which are well adapted prosper, so too natural selection operates in the market-place in freely competitive economies, so that those whose practices make them profitable survive and those whose practices do not, fail. This explains why, among firms in a competitive market, if certain practices make a firm profitable, then those practices are generally adopted, even though this function of the practices is not recognized (Elster, 1983, pp. 57–8; Hardin, 1980, p. 756). Similarly it has been noticed that members of Congress in the USA who frequently assist their constituents by intervening in government bureaus, are more successful at the polls than those who do not. This explains why, among US members of Congress, if a member can help a constituent by intervening in government bureaus, then that member will do so, even if he or she is unaware of the electoral implications of doing so. Members of Congress who did not adopt this practice, did not get re-elected. Incidentally, this practice has had the unintended effects of increasing the size of the bureaus, and consequently of increasing the need for help with the bureaucracy. (I disagree with Hardin's analysis of this case. See Hardin, 1980, pp. 757–8.)

But such appeals, to generalizations of the kind 'if a certain characteristic gives an institution a distinct advantage over its rivals, then institutions having that characteristic will come to predominate', do not provide the kind of justification which Elster himself showed to be necessary. They may help to explain the prevalence of such institutions in a competitive environment, but they do not display any mechanism whereby the outcome brings about the characteristic in question. Indeed the causes of the characteristic sometimes have nothing to do with the outcome, which is, in Elster's words, a mere epiphenomenon. In the example just given, firms which adopted efficient business practices were said to do so unaware of the competitive advantage which those practices produced. They were just following traditional 'rules of thumb' (Elster, 1983, p. 58).

Philippe Van Parijs has provided a very clear exposition of the ways in which some functionalist generalizations of Marxists can be justified (1981, ch. 6). In particular he considers why it is that government policies in capitalist economies are normally to the advantage of the capitalist class. Sometimes this can be explained as an effect consciously intended by the members of the government. Sometimes it may be an unintended consequence of their policies of which government members are aware, and of which they approve, so that it provides an important reason for their continuing with the policy. But, finally, it can be an entirely unintended consequence of the government's need to provide policies which will enhance its own chances of survival. To provide finance to implement its programme as well as to fill the coffers of the party, every government will try to maximize economic activity in whatever way seems appropriate in the circumstances, so as to maximize revenue from taxation and from donations. In a capitalist society, the level of economic activity is largely a function of business confidence, and this in turn is a product of the expected, indeed of the actual, size of profits on investment. Consequently, governments which survive, or which want to survive, must adopt policies which will benefit the capitalists. Such policies constitute what Van Parijs calls 'an attractor', a state of equilibrium to which all government policies in capitalist societies tend to gravitate. If governments have a long term in office, their policies will be to the long-term advantage of the capitalists; if they have just a short term, then they will be to their short-term advantage, to make them immediately attractive to the electorate. If working-class resistance to some of these policies constitutes a threat to the smooth functioning of the capitalist economy, then in the interests of capitalists it would have to be reduced by the adoption of some socialist policies, even though the taxes needed to pay for these would reduce the amount of money which can be retained by the capitalists from their profits. Van Parijs allows that the outcome of tussles between the government and aggressive workers' bodies can be difficult to predict: 'Evolutionary attractors must here give way to saddle points, and the tools of game theory must be brought in' (p. 198).

What conclusions should be drawn from this example? The points I would make are as follows. If, as is suggested in the discussion, a government's reasons for supporting the capitalists are that it may collect large amounts of taxation, and attract generous support to party funds, then once again, the fact that this policy also helps to serve the interests of the capitalist class is an unintended effect, an epiphenomenon, of the policy. That effect does not explain the existence of the government's policy, and so the explanation offered is irrelevant to Marxist theory. Of course it is possible that a government wished to further the interests of the capitalist class, in which case the justification for saying that those interests were responsible for government policy is the familiar kind of explanation in terms of the agent's purposes.

Although this is a plausible explanation of the generalization that in a capitalist society, if a piece of legislation will be in the interests of the capitalists, then it will be enacted by the government of the day, it is not the sort of explanation we associate with the Marxist theory of historical materialism. This rests, rather, on the assumption that a society's superstructure of laws, institutions and ideology will always tend to 'correspond' to the most productive relations and forces of production (Parijs, 1981, p. 199). But why should this be? Parijs suggests that it is unlikely to be true that people generally want to increase production, though I think this is precisely what Marxists assume. Instead, he suggests it is true because if the superstructure of a society does not 'correspond' to the relations and forces of production, then there are likely to be severe crises in that society, conflicts for example between the industrialists and the government. It is to avoid such conflicts that societies normally adopt, or at least maintain, laws and institutions which correspond to the relations and forces of production in the society (pp. 202, 210). Once again, the cause of the policy is not equated with the function it serves, so that the function could be called an epiphenomenon of that policy. The correspondence between the superstructure and the relations and forces of production is designed to avoid severe crises, not to further the forces of production as Marxist theory suggests. The service done to those forces is just an unintended consequence of the policy. At times Van Parijs seems aware of the inadequacy of these explanations (they 'fail to *make sense* of historical materialism by suggesting the operation of a plausible mechanism' (p. 208)), but he elaborates them just the same.

We suspect that when natural organisms produce what is needed for their reproductive success, they have feedback mechanisms built into them which ensure the supply of what they need. The presence of these mechanisms justifies the functional generalizations used to describe the lawlike relation between the organism's needs and the events which meet those needs. But why do social groups act to ensure their survival? Evolutionary theories do not supply the sort of explanation we require to show that there is a functional relation between the needs of a group and the policies it adopts. There are two well-known kinds of explanation which would be adequate, in those cases in which they apply. And I would like to suggest two more kinds of explanation as well.

The first familiar form of explanation is the purposive one: groups adopt policies which promote their survival because that is one of their deliberate goals. The second familiar kind of explanation is the one which Van Parijs calls a 'reinforcement evolutionary' kind. In this context it would explain the adoption of advantageous policies by groups by saying that, when a group experienced the advantages which a certain policy gave it, then it would be prone to adopt that policy in future. This kind of explanation relies upon the generalization that people, and animals, adopt patterns of behaviour whose consequences they have experienced as beneficial, and they avoid patterns of behaviour which they have found to be harmful. Elster calls these 'filter-explanations' (1983, p. 58), though he fails to understand their relation to functional explanations.

There are two other mechanisms by which we might explain why groups adopt policies which promote their survival. The first is straightforward: they could have established institutions – rules, subcommittees, computer programs – which alert the group to its needs as they arise and perhaps propose ways of meeting them. Institutions of this sort would be closely analogous to the thermostats and other regulatory mechanisms in machines. The existence, and efficient functioning, of such mechanisms would explain the lawlike connection between a group's needs and its behaviour.

My second suggestion may be more contentious, but I think it is much more important than has generally been realized. I think people, and animals, are naturally disposed to identify their physical, personal and social needs, and to try to meet them in a way which seems appropriate to them in the circumstances. (See below pp. 226–31, 250–8 on how objective interests explain actions.) It is this natural disposition which I think Marx assumed to be the driving force of history. G.A. Cohen explicates this tendency as a result of people's rationality, saying that people see what they need and then try to supply it (1982, pp. 150–60; 1988, pp. 85–7). But why should people respond thus to their perceived needs, if they were not already inclined to do so? I think the theory that people are naturally inclined to pursue their objective interests is better. Another point at which I might disagree with Cohen is that, to defend Marx's theory, he suggests that people generally want to increase their production, which makes it difficult to explain long periods of economic stability without growth. I would rather say that people try to meet their needs as best they can, not that they constantly strive to acquire more than they need. That might be hard to believe in the twentieth century, but animals display our natural tendencies more accurately than those of us brought up to worship material possessions. They seldom seek more than they need. (E.L. Jones (1988) believes that people do normally seek economic growth, and explains periods of stability by referring to forces which inhibit growth at those times. It is hard to prove which theory is superior.)

The main trouble with this fourth attempt to explain why groups act to protect their own interests is that it is very hard to state the precise conditions under which people pursue their objective interests. Even if it is admitted that people all have the natural disposition to do so, it must also be insisted that people often act for other reasons instead, for instance in the pursuit of truth, beauty or goodness. When will a group put its own interests ahead, for example, of its principles? Rather than compromise, it might choose extinction. In this respect, functional explanations in the social sciences differ from those in biological sciences. The feedback mechanisms in nature work more or less invariably: we always perspire when we are hot, in order to get cool, and we always shiver when we are cold in order to get warm. But our natural disposition to act in our own objective interests is often set aside by other concerns. Similarly, we do not always act in ways which have been positively reinforced by our past experiences; nor do we always adopt the policies for group preservation which our subcommittees recommend to us. In short, groups do not always act in their own interests.

The implication is that functional explanations are not predictive. To explain a group's behaviour in terms of its interests, or in terms of its experiences, even when no other purposeful explanation of its behaviour is available, is not to refer to facts which make that behaviour very probable. Rather it is to refer to facts without which the group would probably not have behaved as it did, and which made their behaviour more probable than it would otherwise have been. In that sense such explanations refer to circumstances which caused the group's behaviour.

But if groups do not regularly act in their own interests, are there any true generalizations of the form needed to warrant functional explanations of their behaviour? The truth of the matter is that these generalizations are much less true of the behaviour of social groups than they are of the behaviour of biological and mechanical systems. There is a strong tendency for groups to act so as to preserve their strength, especially while they are felt to be performing a useful function, if only the latent function of providing a friendly meeting place. So generally, if a policy must be adopted to meet a present or anticipated need of the group for its survival, then that policy will be adopted. But this is not invariably the case; other concerns can override this natural tendency.

To conclude: events never occur because of their effects. They sometimes occur because their effects serve a function, meet a personal or social need which people have identified and decided to satisfy, or which people are naturally inclined to satisfy whenever it arises. The awareness of a need causes the action, which produces an effect to meet it. Functional explanations are only special cases of rational explanations or explanations in terms of objective interests.

To point out the individual and social functions of certain events and practices, like the charivaris, is of interest. But to show that they occurred because of those functions provides greater understanding. However, it is not always possible to be sure whether the functions were recognized and intended. Perhaps that is why historians who provide a functional account of such practices remain vague as to whether they are offering an explanation, or merely a description of the behaviour they are considering.

THE OBJECTIVITY OF CAUSAL EXPLANATIONS

Causal explanations of physical events are often indisputable. Why did that piece of copper expand? Because being copper it was disposed to expand when heated, and it was heated. If (1) the facts are correct, namely the copper was disposed to expand when heated, it was heated and it did expand, and (2) no other events occurred which would affect the size of the copper, then the causal explanation is correct.

Causal explanations of historical events are seldom so neat and uncontentious. Even if the relevant facts are well established, there are often quite a lot of events which affected the outcome, and there is sometimes disagreement as to their causal significance. Historians choose those causes which they judge to have been very influential in bringing about the effect.

The most intransigent disagreement is between historians who believe that people act according to their socio-economic interests, and those who think people act only, or at least very largely, according to their principles, values and beliefs. This disagreement was vividly manifest in Herbert Butterfield's criticisms of explanations offered by L. Namier and his school of the behaviour of MPs in eighteenth-century Britain. Namier was inclined to think that people entered Parliament, joined factions and voted on bills according to their socio-economic interests. He considered that the reasons they gave were lightweight legitimations, offered *ex post facto*, to justify decisions made from self-interest (Butterfield, 1957, p. 213). Butterfield, on the other hand, placed much more weight upon people's reasons for acting. 'For the sake of historical explanation itself,' he wrote, 'we must watch human beings deliberating and choosing their conduct; and ... we must examine the considerations upon which men make their decisions' (p. 206).

For example, on 6 April 1780, John Dunning moved 'that the influence of the Crown has increased, is increasing, and ought to be diminished'. The motion was carried 233 to 215. Butterfield said that we should see such an action as deliberately designed to reduce the power of the Crown in government (pp. 204–5; and see pp. 270–4). Namier's followers would say the motion was supported by MPs keen to please their country electorates, which were disgusted with the failure of Lord North to retain the American Colonies and with the high taxes he levied. Butterfield thinks they were seriously concerned about the influence of the sovereign in government, and wanted to reduce it. He said: 'we hear too much about structure and vested interests, and too little about those higher political considerations which clearly enter the case at these important points in the story, and which help to turn the study of history into a political education' (p. 205).

Butterfield finally conceded that perhaps 'the ideal kind of history' is one in which 'both structure and narrative combined' (p. 207). Certainly explanations in terms of interests alone are not enough, he said. 'Men do not support the government merely because they enjoy profits and places. . . . Human beings are the carriers of ideas as well as the repositories of vested interests' (pp. 210, 211).

The historiography of the causes of the outbreak of the American Civil War in 1861 is a rich field for causal interpretations. To mention just three, some historians have favoured a rational explanation, some an explanation in terms of economic interests, and some have explained the war as driven by irrational emotions. For example, James Ford Rhodes attributed the war to the conviction of northern Republicans that slavery was wrong. When Lincoln, a Republican, was elected President in 1860, the southern states seceded to protect their rights. In other words, the war was fought in the rational defence of moral and constitutional principles. Charles A. Beard is famous for his economic interpretation of its causes. During the period 1850–1860, he said, the southern plantation interests dominated the American government, through the Democratic party. But their interests were directly opposed to those of the industrial north, so that when Lincoln and the Republicans came to power in 1860, the south seceded.

The so-called 'revisionist' historians, J.G. Randall and Avery Craven, denied that economic and cultural differences between the north and south were enough to cause the war, and instead blamed the leaders of the country. With an eye on the European dictators of the 1930s, Randall believed that wars are caused by strong leaders behaving irrationally. 'When nations stumble into war,' he said, 'or when peoples rub their eyes and find they have been dragged into war, there is at some point a psychopathic case. Omit the element of abnormality, or of bogus leadership, or inordinate ambition for conquest, and diagnosis fails.' (J.G. Randall, quoted in Rozwenc, 1972, p. 172.)

Craven also appealed to a theory which gave prominence to psychological causes of conflict. He said that differences between the north and the south came to be seen as matters of principle, to be defended at all costs, so that rational discussion and compromise were not possible (quoted in Rozwenc, 1972, p. 177). He summed up his interpretation of the coming of the Civil War in these words:

the three great strands of development, in the life span of a generation of Americans, were tangled together in such ways as to push reason aside and to give emotion full sway. Unparalleled expansion only served to magnify and intensify sectional differences and raise the question of Constitutional rights in the spread of institutions and peoples to new territory. Growth shifted the old balances of power and posed anew the insoluble problem of minority and majority rights. Intense humanitarian impulses and awakened religious feelings supplied the emotions with which sectional positions and sectional interests could be glorified. All contests became part of the eternal struggle between right and wrong. This caused the break-up of national political parties which had constituted the main element in American nationalism.

(Craven, 1957, p. 15)

While prominence is given to irrational emotional responses as a cause of the conflict, notice how sophisticated this interpretation is, how broad its scope and how rich its explanatory power. Craven defended it by showing how, again and again, it is supported by the facts. For example, he noted that following Chief Justice Taney's ruling in the Dred Scott case:

> Once more facts yielded to passions. Republican newspapers, led by the New York *Tribune*, turned on Taney and the Court with distortion and abuse. . . . Republican politicians, even Seward and Lincoln, went on repeating the false charges of a slave-power conspiracy and arousing the fears of common men against insidious foes.
>
> (1957, pp. 385–6)

Craven was able to show repeatedly, and in detail, how the voices of reason and compromise were drowned by passionate avowals of principle, section against section.

When there is more than one respectable theory about the causes of an event, and there is no way of conclusively proving one theory superior to the rest, then if historians follow just one of those theories, their causal explanation should be called an interpretation of the causes of that event. An interpretation, as I have explained before (1984, pp. 231–3), is one of several equally warranted accounts which can be given of some subject. A plausible case can be made for the rational, economic and emotional explanations of the secession and war.

W.H. Dray thought that the choice among various causes of the Civil War was based on 'moral considerations' (Dray, 1964, p. 55). This is plausible when historians were clearly looking for someone to blame, as some early historians were, blaming either the north (E.A. Pollard) or the south (H. Wilson); and as were the revisionist historians just quoted. It is less plausible in other cases, such as Rhodes' and Beard's histories, where differences rather reflect different presuppositions about the causal power of principles and interests. The search for causes might be motivated by an interest in moral responsibility, but the selection of causes need not be dictated by moral prejudices.

Given the variety of causal judgements, it might seem that a decision as to the causes of the Civil War is nothing but a matter of personal opinion. An examination of historical writing reveals, however, that this is not the case. Historians normally argue for their explanation by showing that alternative possible causes either did not exist, or were not significant in bringing about the war. Their explanations are an expression, not only of their general beliefs about the relative importance of causes, but also of their reading of the particular events leading up to the war. Explanations not well supported by the basic facts have to be modified or set aside. Let me illustrate the kinds of argument that take place.

Some of the early historians of the war looked for single causes to explain it. For instance Rhodes wrote: 'of the American Civil War it may safely be asserted that there was a single cause, slavery' (quoted in Rozwenc, 1972, pp. 49–50). Beard considered Rhodes' thesis, that the war was ultimately fought because of the northerners' desire to abolish slavery, and argued at length that such a desire was not present in the Republican programme before the war. Beard concluded:

> Since, therefore, the abolition of slavery never appeared in the platform of any great political party, since the only appeal ever made to the electorate on that issue [in 1844] was scornfully repulsed, since the spokesman of the Republicans emphatically declared that his party never intended to interfere with slavery in the states in any shape or form, it seems reasonable to assume that the institution of slavery was not the fundamental issue during the epoch preceding the bombardment of Fort Sumter.
>
> (Quoted in Rozwenc, p. 87)

He went on to argue that southern commitment to states' rights was not as deep as A.H. Stephens had assumed, as southerners ignored them when it suited them, as in supporting the Fugitive Slaves Bill. In his judgement: 'major premises respecting the nature of the Constitution and deductions made logically from them with masterly eloquence were minor factors in the grand dispute as compared with the interests, desires, and passions that lay deep in the hearts and minds of the contestants' (quoted in Rozwenc, 1972, pp. 89–90). Beard saw economic interests as fundamental. When the north won control of the presidency with the election of Lincoln, the south feared he would use his power to exploit them for the benefit of the north, and so seceded. The north wanted a large pool of money and free labour, he said, to develop its industrial and farming economies, and was eager to use the resources of the south, so it fought to retain the Union (pp. 68–74).

Beard finds this general view of the motives at work prior to the war reflected in particular events which preceded it. While the Democrats ruled Congress, they passed a number of bills aimed at extending the right to own slaves to new territories, and reducing protective tariffs and shipping subsidies to foster free trade, which was in their interests as exporters of tobacco and cotton. These and other economic measures, Beard said, infuriated northern industrialists. When Lincoln was elected, southerners feared a reversal of their fortune (pp. 74–84). Beard's narrative of events leading to the war illustrates his general thesis that economic concerns were the basic motive for the war.

Subsequent historians, as might be expected, have been critical of Beard's explanation. Randall said that few of those involved in the war had strong economic interests, and anyway economic interests were scarcely promoted by division and war:

> As for the Civil War the stretch and span of conscious economic motive was much smaller than the areas or classes of war involvement. Economic diversity offered as much motive for union, in order to have a well rounded nation, as for the kind of economic conflict suggested by secession.
>
> (Randall, quoted in Rozwenc, p. 170)

Randall's preference for his explanation, in terms of irrational motives, was not arbitrary, but a result of careful examination of what happened prior to the war.

Explanations which focus upon just one kind of cause for an event as large as the American Civil War are prima facie suspect. A satisfactory explanation, I think, to be fair should acknowledge all the major motives at work, and all the circumstances which affected the nature and probability of the outcome. It might not be possible to find one motive which moved everyone equally. Instead historians should acknowledge the complexity, allowing that people were motivated in varying degrees by moral, political, economic, cultural and emotional factors. Even so, they will probably disagree about the relative importance of these causes in motivating people because they hold different views of human nature. For that reason their explanations can be called interpretations, and are to some extent subjective.

In the interests of truth, some have said that explanations should be as detailed, as 'fine grained', as possible (see below, Chapter 11, pp. 290–7). As has been said before, this suggestion confuses accuracy with precision. Quite general descriptions of causal processes can be true, just as true as very detailed ones, though they are not as precise as the latter. Very general explanations are only unsatisfactory when they are grossly misleading. To explain the American Civil War in terms of just one or two motives would be grossly misleading, for that would give a false impression of the variety of motives which drove the sections to war.

8 Explaining individual actions

In this and subsequent chapters I examine certain common kinds of causal explanation in history more closely, to identify their structures and presuppositions as clearly as I can. Explanations of individual actions are discussed in this chapter, explanations of collective actions in the next, and explanations of social change in Chapter 10. It is interesting to compare the logical structure of the explanations which historians give in practice with the model of genetic causal explanation given in the last chapter. To do that I have to uncover the logical structure of the explanations commonly found in history books. It is also interesting to notice the way in which historians' general presuppositions about the causes of events in the world influence their choice of explanation. Some of these assumptions are contested, as will be seen.

To explain human actions, be they individual or collective, historians generally look for reasons (beliefs, desires, principles and values) which the people had for what they did, and if these seem to explain their actions adequately, the historians often stop their explanations at that point. If the reasons seem inconsistent with the agent's other beliefs, or if no reasons can be found at all, historians are then driven to look for other causes of the behaviour, such as emotions, habits, interests, or cultural and social influences.

This way of explaining actions can be criticized. If causal explanations normally take the genetic form outlined in the last chapter, I suggest that historians should always go behind the agent's reasons if they can, to the first event which significantly increased the probability of the action occurring. To pick out only one or two causes from the whole causal story, I suggest, gives a misleading impression of how the world works. In particular, to stop with rational explanations when one can find them is to ignore the influence of human nature and of society on human behaviour. I think that historical explanations in practice reflect historians' personal interests more than they should.

There are reasons why historians do not always provide full explanations of actions besides a lack of interest in them. Suppose a scientist performed some experiments which confirmed his daring theory, so he decided to publish it. His reasons for publishing were that he had confirmation of his theory, and both desired and believed he should publish interesting well-confirmed theories whenever he could. Should an historian also mention that conducting the experiments and publishing his findings was conventional behaviour for a scientist, and was in his professional interests, for if he did not do so he would miss promotion, or even lose his job? An historian might well complain that these points are so obvious they do not need to be stated. Furthermore, they do not explain why he decided to publish when he did, which was what interested the historian.

In response I would say that if we did not know the scientist was acting in a conventional manner and in his own interests, then we would have a severely truncated understanding of his behaviour. If this information is already known to the reader, or has been adequately conveyed in calling the man a scientist, then it need not be further spelt out. But sometimes the background to an action is not known, and then I think it should be supplied, however briefly.

The main purpose of this chapter is to describe the common practice of historians looking for a rational explanation of individual actions, and describing further causes of the actions only when the rational explanation seems unsatisfactory. It also provides a list of nine different ways of explaining actions, eight of which historians have resorted to when a simple rational explanation seems inadequate.

In the process of doing these things, I respond to some alternative views about the nature of explanations of individual actions. Some philosophers have thought that the purpose of explanations of actions is to show the actions to have been very probable, or very rational, or both. I shall argue that in fact acceptable explanations seldom show either of these things. The reasons for which people act, for example, seldom make their actions very probable, as there are usually several things a person could easily have decided to do instead; nor do they make them appear very rational, as people seldom judge the rationality of their decision to act, being content with a decision which appears to further their goals without obviously contravening their principles.

Furthermore, some people are inclined to confine the explanation of actions to reasons which the agent would have given for them. There are a couple of reasons for doing so. One is the belief that people normally act freely on the basis of reasons, so that it is wrong to suggest they are influenced by other factors. Since Marx, Freud and Nietzsche, it seems very hard to believe this any more, for they have shown how often people act quite unawares in pursuit of their socio-economic interests, their unconscious desires, and a satisfying life style. Another reason for confining explanations to the agent's reasons is the thought that to do otherwise, and explain an action in terms of some modern theory, be it psychological, cultural or social, would be anachronistic, imposing categories of the present upon the past. I think that to deny the influence of the unconscious, of culture and of society upon human behaviour is to give a quite false impression of human autonomy. We simply are not as free to choose what to do as some suppose. So long as the historian does not suggest that the agent was aware of influences of which he or she was not aware, then anachronism can be avoided. In explaining an action, the historian should describe all the influences which moved the agent to act. To select only those which interest the historian would result in a partial and thus misleading explanation of the action.

In the second, concluding section of the chapter I address a major objection to a causal theory of historical explanation, namely the claim that reasons are not causes. The argument that reasons are logically related to actions and so cannot be causes of them is not persuasive. People often have reasons for doing something, but fail to act on them. More worrying is the fact that reasons cannot be perceived, but seem to be part of an interpretation of behaviour in its context. But reasons really do seem to have causal power, and in that case must exist.

IDENTIFYING THE CAUSES OF ACTIONS

The analysis of causal explanations given in the last chapter implies that an adequate explanation of an action will go back to the first event which made an action of the kind described significantly more probable in the circumstances than it had previously been, and then describe all the contingently necessary events which altered the probability of such an action up until it occurred. This may mean going behind the agent's reasons for acting to cultural influences or social facts which inclined the agent to perform such an action in the first place. The selection of causes will be based upon assumptions about what kinds of event cause actions, and these general assumptions should be well supported by evidence. Moreover, a good causal explanation will also provide enough information for the reader to be able to see why each cause altered the probability of the action in the way claimed by the historian. This usually requires information about the situation to which the agent was responding, and possibly relevant desires, beliefs, principles and values.

Historical practice, it must be admitted, is not always guided by this prescription. Historians sometimes mention just the causes of an action which interest them, and do not look for all the causes which produced it. If the chosen reason or other cause is judged to have made the action very probable, then many historians will not look for more causes. If it is hard to see why that cause made the action more probable, more of the setting will be described until the connection can be understood. If there is reason to think that the agent was more likely to do something else, then a contrastive explanation will be sought, to show why the expected action was not performed in place of the actual action. The need to provide an explanation which is credible also drives historians to produce more information at times. If the cause cited by an historian is inconsistent with other facts known or assumed about the agent or the situation, then a further explanation of how the cause came to exist will be provided. These practices reflect the need for explanations to be intelligible and credible. I suggest that they should also be comprehensive if they are not to be misleading.

In the past, there have been philosophers who have said that explanations of actions should refer to conditions which made their occurrence very probable; or which made the actions entirely reasonable from the agent's point of view in the circumstances. C.G. Hempel thought that to explain an action, historians should discover a person's reasons for acting, and also establish that the agent was by nature rational in their behaviour, that is that they usually did what they judged to be reasonable. By providing this information, he said, the historians would have shown that the person's actions were very probable (Hempel, 1963, pp. 100–1). Hempel argued that merely 'to show that an action was the appropriate or rational thing to have done under the circumstances is not to explain why in fact it was done' (p. 102). People can have reasons for an action, but not act on those reasons. To explain why an action was done, therefore, one must know 'that the agent was at the time disposed to act in accordance with the standards [of rationality] invoked, and that the external circumstances did not prevent him from doing so' (p. 103). Indeed, Hempel said, when historians explain an action by giving reasons for it, they generally assume that these conditions existed (p. 103).

Hempel was right to draw attention to the difference between having reasons for an action and acting upon them. To explain an action, historians look for the reasons which influenced the person to act as they did, not just for reasons by which they could have justified the action, but which did not move them at the time. This is because historians want to know what brought the action about, what caused it. Hempel was mistaken, however, in supposing that if people are rational it is always very probable they will act on the reasons they have for acting. We all avoid doing what we know we should at times, or desire to do one thing but desire to do another more, and so do not do what we have reason to do. So when historians explain an action by describing the agent's reasons for doing it, they do not imply that the action was very probable in the circumstances.

W.H. Dray, in reaction to Hempel, wrote that when historians explain actions, they are not trying to show that their occurrence was probable, but rather they give the agent's reasons for performing them (Dray, 1957, ch. 5). The aim of such explanations, Dray said, is to show that the action was a reasonable thing to have done in the circumstances, from the agent's point of view.

There are two difficulties with Dray's theory which have been raised by critics and discussed by Dray, but have not been resolved. The first has to do with the degree of rationality which Dray believes to be required of rational explanations. Dray allows that people's beliefs about a situation might be mistaken. All that he requires is that the 'reasons, if they are to be explanatory in the rational way, must be *good* reasons at least in the sense that *if* the situation had been as the agent envisaged it . . . then what was done would have been the thing to have done' (p. 126). Dray went on to say that to judge a rational explanation the historian will appeal to 'a principle of action' of the form 'When in a situation of type C_1 . . . C_n the thing to do is x' (p. 132). He makes it clear that such a principle should reflect the views of most people, of what most people would think an appropriate response in certain believed circumstances.

Why does Dray insist that the reasons which explain an action must be judged by the historian to have been good reasons, from the agent's point of view? One fact which would incline a philosopher to this view is that to interpret a person's behaviour we normally look for reasons she had which we can see would have made it an entirely reasonable thing to have done in the circumstances. I have given an example of this procedure elsewhere, in a discussion of ways in which historians discover people's mental states (McCullagh, 1984, pp. 118–28). The example is of R.G. Collingwood's inference as to Julius Caesar's intentions in invading Britain in 54 BC. Collingwood argued that the most reasonable plan for Caesar to have adopted, given that he wanted to subdue Britain and stop British forces from joining his enemies in attacking Gaul, was to conquer and secure the whole of Britain, so he concluded that that had been his intention (pp. 122–3). This principle of interpretation of human action is part of what is meant by 'the principle of charity'. What Dray has overlooked is the way in which we proceed once we find no perfectly rational explanation for an action. We then search for any reasons the person may have had for acting, allowing that these might not be very rational. For instance, they might include poorly justified beliefs, or desires contrary to the agent's deeply held principles. An example of action based on poorly justified beliefs will be given shortly, of historians trying to understand why Neville Chamberlain adopted a policy of appeasement towards Hitler. Historians agree that such a policy was not the most rational to adopt in the circumstances, yet Chamberlain had reasons for pursuing it. A 'rational ex-planation' aims simply to discover the reasons for which an action was done, whether or not in our judgement they were perfectly rational from the agent's point of view.

To establish even a weak standard of rationality, however, requires the historian to recognize the relation between certain reasons and the action performed in response to them as rationally intelligible. This judgement does not require imaginative re-enactment of the agent's situation, as Rex Martin, following R.G. Collingwood, has suggested (Martin, 1977, ch. 3). Nor does it require knowledge of a principle of action about the most reasonable way of responding to certain circumstances, as Dray proposed. Rather, it requires no more than an ability to follow a modified version of the well-known practical syllogism, to see that the conclusion of such a syllogism follows from its premises. The most common such syllogism is as follows: If a person wants to achieve goals $G_1 \ldots G_n$, and believes that in the circumstances quite a satisfactory way of achieving such goals is by doing action A, then that person will be inclined to do action A. The 'goals' mentioned here should be taken to include various moral and social standards of behaviour which the agent wants to respect, and various interests which the agent wants to protect, as well as certain changes which the agent wants to bring about. A 'quite satisfactory' way of acting is one which does not contravene the agent's standards, nor damage her interests, and is likely to achieve the changes she wants. Neither the goals nor the means chosen for achieving them need be the most rational which the agent could have thought of. The important thing is that they were the reasons which actually moved the agent to act.

There are many things besides reasons which incline people to act, and historians who wish to give a full and accurate explanation of an action will report all that were influential. Here is a list of the most common kinds of cause which historians refer to when explaining individual actions:

1 Habits, often producing a conventional response to a situation.
2 Events which produce new beliefs or desires, which in turn provide reasons for an action.
3 Events which produce certain emotions, which find expression in action.
4 Traits of character, convictions or dispositions which produce certain kinds of response to a situation.
5 Biological needs, which seek satisfaction through certain kinds of action.
6 Personal needs or interests which people try to meet by certain kinds of action.
7 Events which produced unconscious psychological dispositions, which find expression in action.
8 Events which cause someone to adopt cultural norms new to them, which find expression in action.
9 Social sanctions, which move people through fear of punishment or hope of reward to act in certain ways.

A fair explanation is one which describes all the causes which influenced a person to perform an action. Historians, however, are seldom aware of the whole list, and might not agree with it all were it presented to them; nor are they generally aware of the need to give the whole causal story to avoid misrepresenting it. They are aware, however, of another convention, namely: if an explanation seems to be inadequate for some reason, then they should look for more causes to strengthen it. There are two common ways in which explanations are found to fall short: (1) there is reason to doubt that the cause really existed; and (2) if it did exist, it does not make it more likely that the agent will act in response to that cause rather than in response to some other cause we know about (this is a problem about the vector of forces acting on the agent). Let me illustrate how perception of these failures leads historians to uncover more of the causal story.

First, here is a well-known example of an explanation of an action which refers to beliefs that people felt to be incredible, which therefore required further explanation. It concerns an explanation by G.M. Gathorne-Hardy of why the British Prime Minister, Neville Chamberlain, attempted to settle the differences between Britain and Germany over German claims in Czechoslovakia by negotiating with Hitler in Munich in September 1938. The explanation is essentially quite simple. Chamberlain was convinced that international differences should be settled by 'the machinery of conference', and he believed 'that both Hitler's and Mussolini's aspirations were confined to the redressal of certain limited grievances, and that, if these were satisfied, they could be brought to sit round a conference table in the traditional way, and that a general and peaceful European settlement might thus be achieved' (Gathorne-Hardy, 1950, p. 477). He therefore, quite consistently, thought it reasonable to attempt to settle differences which had arisen over Czechoslovakia by negotiating with Hitler, and was keen to do so.

The reason why this explanation is generally thought to be unsatisfactory as it stands is that the beliefs attributed to Chamberlain are scarcely credible. Knowing what we do of Hitler, it is hard to believe that Chamberlain thought his aspirations were limited, and that European peace could be secured by discussion. Gathorne-Hardy is aware of how difficult it is to accept that Chamberlain had these beliefs, and therefore strengthens his explanation by extending it. He points out that Chamberlain's beliefs 'had numerous and distinguished supporters in England' (p. 477), suggesting a degree of cultural determinism: Chamberlain's beliefs were espoused by others he was likely to respect. Gathorne-Hardy also explains that Chamberlain held these beliefs because he wanted them to be true. If they were not true, then peaceful resolution of Europe's problems would be impossible, and 'Mr Chamberlain's mind revolted from what he called "this bleak and barren policy of the inevitability of war"' (p. 477). Here Chamberlain's irrational beliefs are explained by reference to his deep fear of war, an emotion which prevented him from carefully considering the likelihood of their truth. Given this additional information, the original explanation appears credible.

The next example, of an explanation which seemed inadequate given other forces at work in the situation, is much less familiar, but it is neat, and illustrates several points very well. In particular it shows how the search for the true cause drives an historian to reject several simple explanations, and devise a suitably subtle one. In June 1139, in Oxford, King Stephen arrested Roger, Bishop of Salisbury, his son Roger the Chancellor of England, and his nephew Alexander, Bishop of Lincoln, and had them give up the keys of their castles to supporters of the King before releasing them again. Why did he do so?

The first explanation, the public account so to speak, is straightforward enough, showing it to have been a conventional response in accordance with the laws of the day. The arrests were in response to a fight at the King's court between the Bishop's men and those of Alan of Brittany, who was a strong supporter of the Crown. The historian Isobel Megaw explains that 'Stephen, like his royal predecessors, as upholder of the Anglo-Saxon tradition, and as feudal overlord, had to take prompt measures to deal with this flagrant breach of the king's peace' (Megaw, 1949, p. 33). He therefore arrested those who were feudally responsible for the men involved in the fight, and ordered them 'to make satisfaction to the king as feudal transgressors by giving up the keys of their castles as pledge of faith' (p. 33). The punishment was in accordance with the law and tradition, which the King was bound to uphold.

Although this explanation of events is entirely justified, it is not satisfactory as an account of the King's personal reasons for the action, because in this one move the King lost the support of the Church in England which he had previously been eager to ensure. Given an impending invasion by Matilda, who claimed to be the rightful heir to the throne, the loss of church support was a very serious loss indeed. Prima facie it was not reasonable for the King to lose so much just to uphold feudal law.

Megaw reports that both contemporary and modern historians have thought the King's action to have been irrational, and have attributed it to 'his own or his friends' personal spite and jealousy, and a desire to demonstrate his personal power' (p. 34). This is to offer an emotional explanation of it: the King was jealous of the power of the Church, which was formidable, and wanted to seize any pretext to show that his power was superior. His emotion blinded him to the political implications of his action.

This explanation is rejected by Megaw, however, as 'consistent neither with his character nor with his former skilful policy' (p. 34). That is to say, these are good reasons for thinking the emotional explanation to be false. Megaw offers a rational explanation for Stephen's action instead. The bishops had accumulated considerable wealth and had built many castles. Roger of Salisbury had been a supporter of Matilda's, and quite irregular in his attendance at court. Stephen could not afford to let him and his family switch their allegiance to Matilda, and so seized their assets for himself. He probably hoped to retain or regain the support of the Church through his brother, who was Bishop of Winchester. Consequently, Megaw says, his action was 'not in the least surprising' (p. 35). Notice that the explanation does not make the action appear highly rational or highly likely – the alienation of the Church was a high cost, and in the outcome Henry of Winchester turned against the King. But it perhaps succeeds in making the action appear reasonable from the agent's point of view, and there is no good reason for denying its truth. It explains why the King was willing to implement feudal law in the way he did.

When Megaw explained King Stephen's reasons for arresting the bishops, to prevent their supporting Matilda, she did not discuss any alternative. The explanation she gives is a causal, not a contrastive explanation. The only alternative possibly envisaged was that of not seizing their castles and so of preserving a nominal alliance with the Church. To show that the action taken by the King was either more rational or more probable than continuing the alliance, Megaw would have had to discuss the possibility of the King's ensuring that, should Matilda invade England, the bishops would remain loyal. King Stephen had succeeded in winning their support for his claim for the throne, against Matilda's, so he could possibly have wished to preserve their loyalty. But no alternative was discussed. Megaw was content to find reasons for the action, and to leave it at that.

It is often easy to explain away an unusual action as an emotional response, rather than discover the reasons for it. Here is another example of this being done. In 1879, Henry Parkes, Premier of New South Wales, proposed a bill, the Public Instruction Bill, which terminated state aid to religious schools, but offered clergy an hour each day to teach religion in state schools instead. Why did he do so? Contemporaries saw his action as an emotional response to an attack on state schools by the Roman Catholic archbishop, R.B. Vaughan, and his suffragan bishops, spread through a pastoral address on Catholic education. It described state schools as 'seedplots of future immorality, infidelity, and lawlessness' (Martin, 1980, p. 309). Contemporaries viewed Parkes' bill as 'repression of the arrogance of four bishops', 'as a reprisal upon the pastorals' (p. 310). The suggestion was that the bishops' attack on state schools so angered Parkes that he determined to make the Catholic Church suffer by withdrawing state aid to its schools. Note how the public explanation focuses upon the immediate circumstances in which the action occurred.

When historian A.W. Martin turned to consider Parkes' own reasons for the bill, he found good evidence in support of a rational explanation for it. Parkes had previously, in 1876, expressed his agreement with a reduction in state aid to church schools, so that more funds would be available for building new state schools, so urgently needed in the rapidly expanding community. Martin concludes: 'The bishops affected the timing, heated the atmosphere and – ironically enough – smoothed the passage of the government's legislation, but they did not in any fundamental sense cause it' (Martin, 1980, p. 310).

In explaining the occurrence of individual actions, historians want to present the causes which really led the agent to act as he or she did, but they are not, like scientists, interested in prediction. They are not trying to show that the action was very probable. Even in cases of contrastive explanation, the historian is trying to show merely that one action was more likely than another, not that it was *very* probable in the circumstances. Nor are the historians, like decision theorists, interested in discovering the most rational action the agent could have performed. Rather, they are interested simply in the causal process by which the action in question came about. If they wanted to maximize the predictive power of their explanation, they would have to pile up information about the agent's state of mind until, if possible, they had shown the action to have been much more probable than any likely alternative. If they wanted to demonstrate the rationality of the action, once again they would have to consider a wide range of the agent's beliefs, values and goals, to demonstrate that the action was more reasonable than any alternative. But historians do not normally explain actions in either of these ways. Rather they are content to look for causal processes, like those I have described, which the evidence suggests brought about the action being explained.

Before proceeding to describe each of the nine kinds of explanation listed above, let me note another matter which these examples raise. Explanations of a person's action can be given from at least three quite different points of view: that of the on-looker, that of the agent, and that of the historian. The examples just given show how unreliable the explanations of on-lookers can be. They are generally shallow, because on-lookers do not know much about the agent's beliefs and character. They look for a conventional explanation, for example seeing King Stephen's action as simply carrying out the requirements of the law; or they look for an emotional explanation, like those who attributed Parkes' termination of state aid to religious schools as an emotional response to criticism by the Catholic Church. The explanations given by contemporaries are suggestive, but not reliable.

How reliable is the agent's own explanation? Many would think it definitive. When it comes to knowing what moved a person to act, who is in a better position to know than the agent herself? In fact people are generally very good at knowing the reasons for which they acted, the beliefs which influenced them, and sometimes they are aware of emotions which moved them as well. But they are not very much better than the historian in identifying the other kinds of cause: conventions, traits of character, biological drives and personal needs, unconscious psychological dispositions, or the influence of their culture and society.

There are three reasons why people might want to privilege the agent's point of view. One is that they might believe people only act on reasons, and are never influenced by the other causes I have listed. This belief is so implausible, you might doubt anyone would hold it. But in defending a view of people as rational and responsible for their actions, many philosophers are at least sympathetic towards it. Philip Pettit, for example, has recently written: 'I hold that socially resourced though we are, our ordinary psychological self-image is fundamentally sound: the agency recognised in that image is not compromised by the existence of social regularities' (Pettit, 1993, p. xiii). Pettit allows that people are sometimes moved by forces other than the reasons of which they are aware, but he denies that this happens often (p. 273). In fact, however, it has been established that there are many influences upon people's behaviour, not all of which they are conscious of, and historians generally accept this fact, and look for evidence of them.

The second reason for wanting to confine explanations of actions to the reasons given by the agent is a desire to avoid anachronism. Indeed this desire often goes with an idea that historians should simply describe the past as the people at the time saw it, and not intrude their own explanatory theories at all. Problems of anachronism are important, and I discussed them in the chapter on ethnographic history (see pp. 156–69). Historians must maintain a clear distinction between the concepts they bring to a description of the past, and the concepts people in the past had of the events going on around them. However, that distinction can easily be maintained. Should one not explain the progress of the Great Plague because the people at the time lacked scientific knowledge of how it was spread? Modern understanding of the past can be just as fascinating as the ideas people in the past had of the world. Historians who explain an action by referring to a person's character trait, of which they were oblivious, just add to our understanding of that person's behaviour. The more causal relations we can uncover, the better we understand the past.

For example, a stark contrast exists between the views of the people of Salem village, Massachusetts, in 1692, and those of historians explaining their behaviour. The inhabitants of Salem in 1692 believed that strange, unconventional behaviour of girls and women in their village was caused by the devil, who had been encouraged to operate in this way by other members of the community, whom they called witches. Over a score of those accused of witchcraft were hung, and more than a hundred imprisoned. Knowledge of the beliefs of the village people about the cause of women's erratic behaviour is essential in explaining their extremely hostile responses to these fairly innocent folk. At the same time, historians have also employed their own beliefs about the nature of normal causal processes to critique the beliefs of those involved, and to offer explanations of their own. Paul Boyer and Stephen Nissenbaum (1974), for instance, explained the accusations of witchcraft in Salem as cases of 'psychological projection', in which some attributed great evil to people they hated (pp. 143–52). This hatred they explained, in turn, as the result of economic and social differences (pp. 161–7; 180), and the anxieties these aroused (p. 209). In particular they thought it rooted in a complex and ambivalent attitude from a traditional Puritan perspective to the 'emergent mercantile capitalism' associated with many of those accused (p. 209).

It is unlikely that any of the accusers would have acknowledged this attitude as the cause of their behaviour.

A final worry concerns the appropriateness of the various causal explanations which might be given of an action. Explanations are always related to just one or two aspects of an effect, indicated by the description given of it. The worry is that different causes explain an action under different descriptions. Thus feudal convention required that those who started a fight at King Stephen's court be punished, but it does not explain the particular form which the punishment took. That is explained by an account of the King's reasons for gaining control of the bishops' castles, to prevent their being used against him in favour of Matilda. If an historian wants to explain the King's action in detail, it seems irrelevant to explain it in more general terms, as 'a punishment' for instance.

Notice how natural it is to begin an explanation of King Stephen's action with the fight which required a punishment, and then to explain why Stephen decided the punishment should take the particular form it did. With more information the historian could then explain precisely what the King said and did to carry out his decision. From a logical point of view it seems that historians decide upon a description of the event which they want to explain, and then look for causes of the event under that description or under any other description which that description entails. Having decided that she wanted to explain why King Stephen took the keys of the bishops' castles, Megaw could also explain why he wanted to punish them at all, since that action was viewed in that context as a punishment. Similarly historians explained why people in Salem levelled the particular charges they did against individuals, but also explained why they made any accusations of witchcraft in the circumstances.

When there are two or more views of the genesis of the same action, one might wonder which if any is true. The answer is clear enough. The understanding of the agent(s) is important, because agents often know the reasons which moved them to act. But they can remain ignorant of what the historian detects as their true motives. The opinions of contemporaries are of interest in helping to explain their responses, but unless they are very close to the agent, they are frequently misinformed and biased. The most reliable explanation of an action is the historian's, if there is adequate evidence, for it is based upon the best current theories and careful research. Of course an historian's explanation is fallible, capable of being changed in response to new theories and/or new evidence. But if it is based on well-established theories, and good evidence, it is worthy of the most respect.

Here, now, is a summary of the nine kinds of causal explanation which historians give of individual actions. There may be more, but these are fairly common.

(1) Conventions and habits

A very large proportion of human actions are conventional and habitual. Historians are not always aware of this, as they often focus upon unique or novel behaviour.

There are standard procedures for many of the things that we do at home, at work, in shops and restaurants, when travelling and so on. There is no need to investigate a person's personal reasons for acting, when what they have done is respond in a perfectly regular, conventional way. Indeed if an action is truly habitual, the agent will have given no thought to it, but have performed it automatically. It is important to realize, though, that what appears to be a conventional response is sometimes made for special reasons, in which case to explain the action as just conventional is to misrepresent its causes. For example, when King Stephen arrested the peers in 1139, although he was following a convention in punishing those feudally responsible for a fight, he did so for particular reasons, as was explained in the last section. Some philosophers are reluctant to admit that we are creatures of habit, and look for reasons for action every time.

Conventional responses to situations can involve the adoption of either a rule, a role, a routine or a ritual. *Rules* generally stipulate the precise form of the response which is required, like stopping a car at a red traffic light, whereas roles define a strategy and manner of response. One's role as a customer in a shop is to act so as to purchase what one wants for an agreed price in as pleasant a manner as possible. This normally involves asking questions, examining products and discussing price.

Erving Goffman (1971) and fellow ethnomethodologists have studied the way in which *roles* are determined, partly by the setting and partly by the roles attributed to one by others in that setting. As has been said, a role usually involves standard ways of acting towards others in the setting, often for the purpose of bringing about some social change. They need not require the performance of precise rituals, but there are usually familiar patterns of response associated with a role. Consider, for example, the roles of people in a shop, a school, a hospital, and a prison. In acting out a role, a person expresses attitudes of deference or authority, co-operation or hostility, to others in the scene; and they use their prerogatives to achieve an outcome of a certain kind, if they can. Those outcomes are often means of fulfilling the responsibilities which go with the role.

One interesting fact about social roles is that people can adopt a social role without realizing it. People are usually aware of their official roles, the roles to which they have been appointed. But one can adopt other roles, like that of the rebellious teenager, or the disappointed wife, almost unconsciously. In a very thoughtful discussion of the conflict between Archbishop Thomas Becket and King Henry II in 1170, Victor Turner (1974) suggested that towards the end Becket, almost unconsciously, adopted the role of a martyr. 'It was the root paradigm of martyrdom – with its rich symbolism of blood and paradise – which gave him a frame and fortification for the final trial of will with Henry whom he had loved and whom he could never really hate' (p. 87). This suggestion helps to make sense of Becket's final acts of provocation, almost threatening the king with a huge cross (pp. 90–1), and finally appealing to Rome (p. 93). Turner explains these aspects of Becket's behaviour by suggesting that he was unconsciously following the pattern he knew of other martyrs, who had sought heaven by dying for their faith.

Routines are just sequences of acts which are laid down by rules as the way of achieving a certain outcome. Sometimes the routines are very strictly defined, like the routines on a production line, or in servicing aeroplanes. Sometimes they are more loosely defined, like routines in an operating theatre, or those involved in cleaning a house. They are, nevertheless, fairly precise, unlike roles. To understand a routine, one must see the point of each step of the procedure.

People often follow rules, roles and routines automatically on the appropriate occasion, and if such behaviour is habitual, it needs no further explanation to be intelligible. On the other hand, people often follow conventions deliberately, usually because they believe it is appropriate to do so. This is particularly true of rituals.

A *ritual* normally expresses values which are important to society, or to that segment of society involved in the ritual. Sometimes a ritual is nothing more than an affirmation of those values, like the ritual of applauding a good concert performance, saluting a senior officer in the armed forces, or standing for a judge in court. But often it also marks a change in social status, such as admission of a new member to a guild or society, the passage from childhood to adulthood, and the granting of authority to a king. To enhance the expression of values, a ritual normally involves symbols. To understand a ritual, to understand why it is performed, one must understand both its symbolism and its purpose. In addition, rituals usually have social functions besides those primarily intended, and by understanding those unintended functions one understands more of its significance. (Functional understanding was discussed in the last chapter.)

To understand the events which constituted the coronation of Queen Elizabeth II, one must recognize them as an ancient ritual, full of symbolism, which bestowed royal authority upon the then Princess Elizabeth. Only when the proceedings are seen as a ritual in this way is the point of the various activities and regalia which make up the ceremony clear, and their at times quaint form understood. The presentation of the Bible, for example, is to remind the monarch to keep God's holy law. When the archbishop 'makes the cross on both her hands, her breast and the crown of her head, he places her in the tradition of the Kings of Israel and of all the rulers of England' (Shils and Young, 1953, p. 69). This is part of the anointing of the monarch, which consecrates and sanctifies her for her royal office. The drawn sword presented to her is a symbol of her power, and the orb a symbol of the sphere of her responsibility. The crown and sceptre symbolize her authority.

When a conventional response to a situation is performed knowingly and deliberately, then it deserves a kind of rational explanation, roughly of the form: the agent A believed the situation to be of kind S, and believed the appropriate way to behave in S was by performing action X, so A did X. Those who believe in our capacity to choose and act freely and rationally might regard an explanation of this form as satisfactory, as stating all the reasons which moved the agent to act. Determinists would probably add to the list of reasons: A wanted to act in an appropriate way in S. Determinists assume that all actions are caused by desires.

When a conventional response is automatic, made from habits socially acquired, then it is not made for reasons, and does not deserve a rational explanation. A habit is a disposition to act in a certain way on recognizing a certain situation. The action is explained by noting that the agent had the relevant habit, and that the agent perceived the triggering situation. The whole process can be quite unconscious, as when we pick up a fork to eat with, or when we adopt a habitual role, for instance of a soldier showing respect to a superior officer by saluting and calling him 'sir'.

(2) Rational explanations

Historians assume that actions which were not habitual were done for reasons, and they explain them if they can by describing those reasons. The cause of a rational action is usually an event which produced a new belief or desire in the agent which, in the context of her other beliefs, desires, principles and values, led her to decide that the thing for her to do in the circumstances was what she in fact did. The explanation usually includes a description both of the event which led to her deliberation and action, and of the other thoughts which contributed to the decision she made as to what to do. The explanation does not pretend to be a description of the agent's actual processes of thought, because those processes are usually somewhat disorganized, repetitive and often irrelevant. The historian simply sums up the reasoning which is thought to have moved the agent to decide to perform the action in question. Traditionally all the beliefs, desires, principles and values involved in a person's deciding what to do have been called causes of the consequent action. Strictly speaking many are existing dispositions, and the cause of the action is the event that introduced a new belief or desire which, in the context of the others, inclined the agent to act.

It is difficult to state accurately the various patterns of reasoning which lead people to decide to act. Roughly speaking historians describe the agent as considering the salient circumstances and, in response to these, wanting to do one or more of several things: to pursue a certain goal; or apply a certain principle of action, a norm of some kind; or adopt a certain role; or carry out a certain routine; or enact a certain ritual; or just express a certain feeling, attitude or opinion. In each case the historian reports what the agent wanted to do, and perhaps believed that he or she should do. Then there is usually a statement explaining that, or why, the agent believed that the action in question was an appropriate way of fulfilling his or her desire.

Philosophers who study rational decision-making procedures have considerably enriched our appreciation of the complexities of deliberation. In particular they have reminded us that people value possible courses of action not only for their utility, but according to a variety of other criteria, for instance according to personal interests, moral and aesthetic principles, and various standards of excellence, each of which contains a whole range of ideals which are only roughly ordered, if at all, so that calculating and comparing the desirability of possible actions is a very difficult task. A further complicating factor is uncertainty, at times, about the probable outcomes of alternative possible actions. For these reasons it is often difficult to infer what a person will decide to do. Historians can do little more than describe the values and beliefs which were, as far as they can judge, influential in arriving at a decision. Sometimes there is more than one reason sufficient to move a person to act, and in those cases all the reasons should be given, to keep the account fair and not misleading. (In cases of overdetermination, one cannot say that each reason was necessary in the circumstances for the decision to act; but one can say that if none of those reasons had occurred to the agent, they would not have acted as they did. So they were jointly, if not singly, necessary for the action in the circumstances.)

Historians' main concern in explaining individual actions is to identify the reasons for which the agent acted. They have a preconception of the kinds of reasons for which people act, like those just listed above. They look for instances of such normal patterns of reasoning which would not only make the action appear to be a fairly reasonable thing to have done, but which also fit other facts known about the agent. The truth of the explanation is of paramount importance.

Rational explanations, as these may be called, are designed to make the action appear reasonable from the agent's point of view, but only in a very limited sense. Historians are seldom interested in judging whether it was the *most* rational thing the agent could have done in the circumstances. It is commonly impossible to judge what would have been the most rational thing for an agent to have done. Historians just explain an action by drawing attention to a normal causal process which seems to have brought it about. It is usually enough to show that, given just the beliefs and desires, principles or interests which are mentioned, the action was reasonable, that it was an appropriate way of trying to achieve what was wanted.

Sometimes people act irrationally, so that a rational explanation of their action is not available. John Elster has made a special study of irrational behaviour, and the various typical causes of it. He has noted, for example, cases of indeterminacy, in which a person has no reason for preferring one response to a situation over others, so that the action they chose to do is somewhat arbitrary; cases of weakness of will, where people have good reason for doing one thing, but opt for another which they find more congenial; and cases of wishful thinking, in which people hold beliefs which they have reason for thinking false, simply because they want them to be true, and then act on them. (All these are described in Elster, 1989, ch. 4.) These are three common causal processes, which Elster calls 'mechanisms', that can be investigated by historians when the attempt to find a rational explanation fails. They are not included in the nine on my list, because historians do not often refer to such processes. Elster has also noted that people sometimes act irrationally from a desire to conform to social norms; and from emotion (chs 12 and 7 respectively). I have already said something about conventional behaviour. Let me add a word about emotions.

(3) Emotional responses

Philosophers of history have paid no attention to emotions, but they are frequently described in historical writing as explanations of individual actions. An emotional response is one in which an agent's interpretation of a situation causes feelings which restrict the agent's capacity for a rational response. The feeling can cause the agent to focus upon one desire, usually concerning the object of the emotion, without considering others; and/or to seize upon one way of achieving a goal, usually a way which is immediately available, rather than consider others; and/or the feeling can impair the agent's ability to perform the action precisely as intended. Responses which are affected by emotion in any of these ways are emotional. Rational responses which are accompanied by emotion but are not in any way limited by it, are not considered as emotional in the present context. (These issues are discussed at length in McCullagh, 1990.)

Emotions are commonly caused, it seems, by desires or aversions together with certain evaluative judgements about the object of the emotion. For instance, if Parkes, as Premier of New South Wales, wanted his state schools to have a good reputation, and believed the Catholic bishops had maligned them unjustly, he might then become angry at their behaviour. The judgements involved are not always rational. For instance, the people of Salem judged neighbours for whom they felt some antipathy to be witches on quite inadequate pretexts, and then cried for their execution.

Abnormal emotions may be caused by abnormal desires. A terrifying experience with a dog might leave someone abnormally afraid of them, and this might cause that person to experience an abnormal emotional response to any dog they happen to meet. People also have emotional responses to things which have been related in their experience to other objects of emotion. Thus a person may be distressed at losing a piece of cheap jewellery, because it was her mother's, whom she loved. Then again, emotional attitudes can be acquired unconsciously from others around us, with whom we identify to some extent. For example, it is hard to remain calm when your friends are panicking. Finally some emotions are caused by displacement. Freud observed that, particularly in dreams, people who feel a strong emotion about one thing will displace that emotion onto another, especially if the original emotion is one they are ashamed of. These are some of the ways in which historians can account for unusual emotions.

As was mentioned at the end of the last chapter, Avery Craven blamed the growing hostility between the North and the South in America before the Civil War on emotion. In Chapter 6 of *The Coming of the Civil War*, for example, he examines the northern attack on slavery. A rational explanation would attribute that attack to perceived ills in the plantation system of the south. But Craven doubts such an explanation is adequate, for there were cases of injustice and inequality in their own environment which the northerners ignored (Craven, 1957, p. 128). Craven ascribes passionate anti-slavery rather to the jealousy of poor, hardworking northerners towards the idle rich life style of the southern planters. In fact, Craven says, 'the aristocracy which was threatening American freedom and equality had been produced largely by the new economic shifts in the North-east itself. The cotton planter was much more a symbol than a reality to most of them.' Their 'envy and even hatred' was turned upon the aristocrats of the south (p. 131). As one who oppressed and exploited his fellow men, the slaveholder was an enemy of democracy. In his self-indulgent life style, his passion for war and his licentious conduct with Negro women, he was a flagrant sinner. 'Thus it was that the slaveholder began to do scapegoat service for all aristocrats and all sinners. To him were transferred resentments and fears born out of local conditions' (p. 150). These attitudes to southern plantation owners were fostered, said Craven, by massive propaganda in the north. 'Where argument and appeal to reason failed, the abolitionists tried entertainment and appeal to emotion.' *Uncle Tom's Cabin* was the most successful of a deluge of publications (p. 145).

The structure of the argument is easy to see. The reasons given for attacking the planters were not convincing, for had the northerners been truly concerned about equality and purity they would have attacked the inequality and sinfulness around them. Instead, the planters became a symbol for the aristocrats of the north, who were prospering when so many were not. The envy and anger felt towards them was displaced upon the planters of the south, and particularly upon the institution of slavery which manifested most vividly their anti-democratic and wicked ways. This displacement was reinforced by a huge propaganda campaign, highlighting the bad features of the southern aristocrats. Here is a causal story which explains the origins of some of the emotions, namely those of the northerners, which eventually led to war. Craven explicitly acknowledges his indebtedness to the psychological theory of 'inferiority complexes, and repressed desires' in developing it (p. 117).

(4) Traits of character

Sometimes actions are the expression of deep-seated individual attitudes and dispositions, often allied to strongly-held principles. These can be mentioned to explain reasons people had for acting, as for example Chamberlain's conviction that the horrors of war should be avoided at almost all costs helps to explain the reasons he gave for a policy of appeasement. Character traits can also help to explain actions, by showing that they were the sort of thing one could expect a person with such convictions or attitudes to do in such circumstances.

The line dividing those dispositions which form part of a person's individual character from their other natural dispositions is very hazy indeed. Sometimes the contrast is clear enough. For instance, almost all people are disposed to seek food when hungry, so that is not a disposition which forms part of a person's individual character, but not all are disposed to treat people of another race with respect. The latter clearly is a trait of individual character. But is the disposition to acquire goods as cheaply as conveniently possible, to drive a hard bargain as they say, a natural or a personal disposition? Such problems of classification do not matter for present purposes, as I only want to display the logical structure of the understanding which information about such dispositions supplies, no matter how they are classified.

A nice example of explanation by reference to a personal disposition is provided by Oliver MacDonagh in his biography of Sir Jeremiah Fitzpatrick (1981), a Catholic doctor in eighteenth-century Ireland. Fitzpatrick undertook a large number of campaigns to ameliorate conditions which caused unnecessary suffering, such as the revolting state of Irish prisons, the inhuman exploitation of children in charter schools, the grossly inadequate medical services provided by the army, and the unhygienic living conditions of soldiers in barracks and sailors in ships.

Such activity was unusual, and at the beginning of his biography of Fitzpatrick, Oliver MacDonagh considers why such a man would adopt such policies. There is no evidence that he did so from religious conviction, or even from any specific principle, though he did applaud Economy, Policy, Humanity and Common Sense. These provided standards by reference to which his policies could be rationally justified. MacDonagh believes, however, that he acted as he did from a profound dislike of 'suffering, of blood and death', and a disposition to prevent it by bureaucratic means wherever he detected it (pp. 32–7).

This explanation of many of Fitzpatrick's actions is one which explains their uncommon humanitarian and bureaucratic tendencies in terms of a disposition which the historian has detected in his character, and which he has judged as the most likely cause of his adopting the policies he did. It is possible that Fitzpatrick was scarcely aware of his own attitudes. He provided reasons for his policies which appealed to publicly approved values. His support of Irish prison reform in 1763, for example, was a consequence of his conviction that in their present state the prisons fostered disease, which was undesirable, and that they crowded debtors and the insane together with convicted criminals, which was unjust. Neither he nor his contemporaries were likely to refer to his basic humanitarian and bureaucratic tendencies to explain his behaviour. MacDonagh did so because although many people applauded policies which were humane and just, few pursued them with the vigour of Fitzpatrick.

Precisely how do dispositions such as these relate to the policies they explain? They frequently entail a lawlike generalization concerning the person who has them. Thus, as MacDonagh said of Fitzpatrick: 'anything was liable to be taken on as his concern when the prospect of pain or popular degradation met his inconstant eye' (p. 3). Given that he had humanitarian and bureaucratic tendencies, it was probable that, if he identified an institution which was causing suffering, then he would seek some bureaucratic means of improving it.

(5) Biological needs

Although much of our everyday behaviour is motivated by biological needs, historians are seldom interested in actions as banal as eating and sleeping, and so do not often have to refer to biological needs to explain people's reasons for action.

A biological need is the lack of some kind of thing which a person needs, or must have, to maintain the healthy state of their body, to reproduce, and perhaps to ensure the healthy nurture of their family. Needs can be recurrent, such as the need for food, rest and shelter, or they can be occasional, such as needing medicine when one is sick. People naturally try to ensure that their recurrent needs are provided for, and that they are able to meet occasional needs should they arise.

Malinowski was fond of explaining social institutions in terms of their biological functions, but at present very few individual historical actions are explained this way. The actions by which people satisfy their biological needs are commonly thought to be of a private, domestic nature, of no particular interest to historians.

One can imagine social scientists of the future paying more attention to the influence of these needs on public life however. We are already aware that hunger will drive people to revolution. Is it a basic desire for security which drives them to condone huge armament programmes? Does the desire for security also explain our inhumane attitude towards criminals, and our excessive defence of property? It seems likely that traditional male attitudes towards women, seeing them as sex objects and wanting them to stay at home, stem from a basic drive for sexual satisfaction. In despotic regimes, humiliating acts of compliance are often driven by a natural desire for survival. Thus several individual and communal attitudes may be driven by biological needs.

One example of explanation in terms of biological needs concerns W.E. Gladstone's practice of saving the prostitutes of London. Not only did he found and support refuges for them, but for years he used to seek them out at night, and encourage them to give up their profession. Some historians have interpreted this simply as an expression of Christian concern. Thus Philip Magnus wrote: 'In his rescue work he found a priestly office which he could fulfil as a layman, and in which his duty to God and man could be discharged together' (Magnus, 1954, p. 107). But the time Gladstone spent with prostitutes seemed to some more than Christian charity required. His diaries reveal that it was also motivated by sexual desire. H.C.G. Matthew has noted this, and his explanation of Gladstone's behaviour makes due allowance for the biological motive: 'for Gladstone rescue work became not merely a duty but a craving; it was an exposure to sexual stimulation which Gladstone felt he must both undergo and overcome' (Matthew, 1986, p. 91). After particularly exciting encounters, Gladstone would chastize himself by flagellation.

(6) Personal needs

Our personal needs are those things we need to maintain and perhaps enhance our personal, as distinct from our bodily, well-being. It seems that they include the following:

1 For the maintenance of a sense of identity we need people to recognize us as having feelings and desires, knowledge and will.
2 For the maintenance of and perhaps increase in our self-esteem we need respectable social status and power, and the opportunity to do things which are generally regarded as of value.
3 For a sense of self-fulfilment we need opportunities to acquire knowledge, to develop and use some of our talents, to express our convictions and to carry out our plan of life.

We may say that it is in people's interest to obtain whatever they need for their biological and personal well-being. The objects of such needs are also the objects of their interests. Recognizing this fact helps to make sense of talk about objective interests, which quite often feature in historical explanations.

The list of personal needs just provided reflects our culture's understanding of human nature, and will doubtless be further refined as our understanding improves. Because we believe these needs to be universal, we can call them objective needs which everybody has whether they are aware of them or not.

When David Miller considered the nature of human needs, he clearly thought that one could not claim any set of personal needs to be universal, because people have quite different beliefs about the purpose of life. We might value self-fulfilment, but many ascetics, both eastern and western, do not. He therefore related needs to 'the aspirations and ideals of the person concerned' (Miller, 1976, p. 131). As another author, David Braybrooke, remarked, it can seem 'arbitrary and officious' to suggest that all people share the needs which we identify from our corner of our culture (Braybrooke, 1987, p. 12). The reason for believing them to be universal, however, is not that we are excessively paternalistic, but that we believe all people do in fact pursue them, whether they can identify them or not. Ascetics are clearly acting to preserve self-esteem and to carry out a plan of life which they value, which is a mode of self-fulfilment. They deny the importance of a sense of personal identity, but because we all have a natural inclination to seek confirmation of our identity in society, they have to discipline themselves severely, often by withdrawing from society, to resist that natural tendency. People can act contrary to their human needs, but only with considerable difficulty.

The needs which have been mentioned, both personal and biological, are basic human needs, conditions necessary for our physical and personal well-being. The ways in which these needs can be met will differ from one situation to another. We may say that people have an *objective* interest in whatever will help to meet their needs in their particular situation (see McCullagh, 1991a).

People's *subjective* interests are those things which they believe are necessary for their well-being, and although these usually correspond to their objective interests, they are sometimes different. We can be mistaken about what is for our own good. There is some disagreement at present about the causal priority of people's consciously held desires and values *vis-à-vis* their unconscious interests. Some think the former generally direct actions, and some the latter. Historians generally assume that people will further their subjective and objective interests as efficiently as they can, and if free to do so will generally defend them with a determination that corresponds to the degree to which they seem threatened.

Barry Hindess has recently argued that interests only explain actions when the agent has identified them, and has deliberately decided to further them (Hindess, 1986). He denies that they can unconsciously influence people's thinking and behaviour. Hindess has written most illuminatingly about the process of identifying interests, showing how it can involve quite difficult judgements as to what course of action will promote a person or a group's well-being in the circumstances. Given the complexities involved, it seems almost self-evident to him that they must be consciously arrived at. In that case, once an interest has been decided upon, it could become a goal of action pursued in the normal, more or less rational, way.

What Hindess has overlooked is the evidence that people do identify and pursue their interests unconsciously at times. Marx, Nietzsche and Freud have taught us that people often serve interests which they will not admit, and indeed may well deny. Marx showed how commonly people pursue their class's socio-economic interests, often with 'false-consciousness', quite unaware that they are doing so. Nietzsche remarked how well-suited middle-class morality is for the protection of the weak people who espouse it, even though they declare it is in the interests of the community. And Freud has argued that many actions could best be understood as caused by a drive for sexual satisfaction, even though this motive is repressed and denied by those who perform the actions. The unconscious influence of self-interest can scarcely be denied. (For a fuller discussion of this issue, see pp. 250–8 below.)

We come across such cases in our everyday experience. Consider a Member of Parliament who ignores his or her electorate for years, and then, just a few months before an election, professes a sincere concern for its well-being and promises improvements in schools, roads, hospitals etc. after the next election. Most electors doubt the truth of the professed concern for the electorate, and ascribe the promises to self-interest, quite correctly I suggest. One can multiply such cases. Consider the executive who is curt and uncaring to those under him, but very friendly to his superiors. It seems right to doubt the genuineness of that friendship, and to ascribe the behaviour to self-interest.

In the light of this evidence we are compelled to allow that people are often able to identify and to pursue their interests unconsciously. Explanations of actions in terms of unconsciously held interests will show that the action was indeed in the agent's interest, and assuming that the agent was able to identify it unconsciously, it will explain the action as an expression of the agent's disposition to pursue that interest.

Probably the historian best known for explaining individual actions in terms of personal interests was Sir Lewis Namier, whose work I have mentioned before. The first chapter of his book *The Structure of Politics at the Accession of George III* (1963) is entitled 'Why Men Went Into Politics', and the only explanations he considered are those which refer to self-interest: a desire for honour, wealth, influence, professional advancement, business advantage, and even immunity from prosecution. Such interests, he said, are 'almost universal and usually unavowed', and last a long time (p. 7). He was happy to admit that the pursuit of self-interest was sometimes unconscious: 'the idea that the politically active part of the nation had a claim to maintenance on the State was generally accepted, even if it remained subconscious' (p. 16). Numerous individual instances of advancement are cited, for example that of Charles Jenkinson, who rose through the ranks of government and died the first Earl of Liverpool (p. 11). MPs might profess a concern for the welfare of the country and of their constituents, but their actions were frequently motivated by self-interest.

Probably Namier's explanation of why people entered politics and voted in parliament is unbalanced. Many doubtless did so from noble ambitions, to serve their country and their friends. But much of the behaviour which Namier explains has no such explanation. Members of Parliament may not generally have planned to exploit the state to the benefit of themselves and their acquaintances, but that is in fact what they did. It is hard to see how one could account for the extent of this behaviour without referring to the self-interest of those involved.

Marvin Harris has said that all actions should be explained as furthering the agent's interests, if possible. Only if interests cannot explain them, he said, should we look for an explanation in terms of ideas (Harris, 1979, p. 299; cp. p. 56). Generally, he thinks, the reasons people give for their actions are designed, whether consciously or not, to further their own biological needs and personal interests (though he does not use these terms). Consequently he would explain the Aztec practice of eating their prisoners by pointing out that they had no other ready source of the proteins they needed to keep well, rather than explain the practice in terms of their religious beliefs (see Harris, 1979, pp. 334–40). Harris allows that people sometimes act in accordance with their beliefs and values and not their interests, but then it is still the case that their system of beliefs and values is one which is generally directed to furthering their interests (pp. 302–3).

Few agree with Harris that all human actions are driven by self-interest. People sometimes act according to convention, or out of charity or on principle, contrary to their own interests.

Another objection to explanations in terms of self-interest alone is that they can seldom account for details of human behaviour which are of interest to the historian. Marshall Sahlins has complained that Marxist explanations of social behaviour, in terms of material interests, could not account for that behaviour in anything like the detail which a cultural anthropologist could. He said:

> The nature of the effects cannot be read from the nature of the forces, for the material effects depend on their cultural encompassment. . . . Nothing in the way of their capacity to satisfy a material (biological) requirement can explain why pants are produced for men and skirts for women, or why dogs are inedible but the hindquarters of the steer are supremely satisfying to eat.
>
> (Sahlins, 1976, pp. 206–7)

Similarly, he argued, the ways in which people pursue their economic interests are culturally determined. 'An industrial technology in itself does not dictate whether it will be run by men or by women, in the day or at night, by wage labourers or by collective owners, on Tuesday or on Sunday, for a profit or for a livelihood' (p. 308).

I would add that even cultural explanations are often not detailed enough for historians. To explain why someone chooses to have their beef rare with horseradish sauce one may be compelled to consider that person's individual preferences, for cultural norms may not dictate their choice. Sahlin was writing about conventional behaviour within a society. But historians often explain individual actions, and to do that in detail they must refer to the individual desires and beliefs of the agent.

Notice, however, that to elicit the whole causal story, an historian must be willing to consider an action at several different levels of generalization. To explain why someone is eating beef with horseradish sauce one might have to refer to personal preferences. To explain why he is eating beef, one might refer to cultural preferences. To explain why he is eating, one would refer to his biological needs, or possibly to social conventions (if he was not in need of food).

(7) Unconscious psychological dispositions

The scientific respectability of psychological theories is much debated, but they are occasionally used by historians to explain unusual actions. The most popular theories are those which suggest that the kind of action in question was motivated by a disposition which itself was the outcome of a previous pattern of experience. There are also theories which explain behaviour as a response to a situation facing the agent at a particular stage in his or her personal development. Erik H. Erikson, for instance, explained Martin Luther's crisis of faith as part of an 'identity crisis', one of a series of crises people go through as they mature (Erikson, 1972).

A well-known example referring to a previous experience is the explanation offered by A.L. and J. George (1956) of Woodrow Wilson's hostility to criticism, both when he was President of Princeton University and later when President of the United States. They explained his angry reactions as stemming from a need to compensate for humiliations he had suffered from his father when young, humiliations which had generated an anger which he had had to suppress at the time. The anger he had felt towards his father, of which he was ashamed, was displaced onto those who criticized him.

Almost all psychological explanations of actions are disputed, because there is often more than one plausible psychological explanation available. Saul Fried-länder has usefully summarized a number of explanations of Hitler's hatred of the Jews (Friedländer, 1978, pp. 45–8), and W.M. Runyan has listed thirteen explanations of why Van Gogh cut off his ear (Runyan, 1982). It can be difficult to prove that one psychological explanation is clearly superior to others. Even the Georges' carefully researched theory about Woodrow Wilson has been criticized (see Cocks and Crosby, 1987, chs 11–13).

The logical form of these psychoanalytic explanations is usually the same. Some early pattern of experience is said to have given rise to a certain disposition to react in a certain way in certain circumstances, and the action being explained is identified as an expression of that disposition. The generalizations tacitly appealed to by such explanations, either saying that such causes produce such effects, or that such effects have such causes, have proved very difficult to justify. If the event being explained, such as Van Gogh's self-mutilation, is interpreted symbolically, that adds yet another element of uncertainty to the explanation.

Given these uncertainties, some psychoanalytic accounts of people's behaviour should be regarded as interpretations of the unconscious causes of actions. This is the case whenever there is more than one more or less equally justified causal account available. There must also be considerable doubt concerning their truth, as the various theories lack adequate justification.

There has been an effort to justify the claim that some psychological accounts are true, that they correctly identify the causes of a person's remarkable behaviour (e.g. Ricoeur, 1977, pp. 270–3). There is a particular worry that psychoanalysts are so guided by their preconceptions that they are blind to alternative patterns of explanation. To prevent such bias D.P. Spence has advocated 'a Know-Nothing hermeneutics':

> Only a Know-Nothing hermeneutics is capable of taking the position that we have no idea what patterns, if any, are present and that their discovery can only result from a series of small decisions that are always checked against other parts of the material and with the patient himself. The patient, of course, is not always right; but then neither is he always wrong.
>
> (Spence, 1988, pp. 62–84)

Adolf Grünbaum (1985) insists that general causal claims in psychology, as in any science, must be verified by J.S. Mill's methods of agreement and difference (*passim*), though he does not assess the possibility of doing this successfully. I suspect that because people's actions can have so many different possible psychological causes and effects, it will be very hard to use Mill's methods productively. Richard J. Bernstein wrote in 1988: 'Despite many claims and counter claims there is (as of now) no widespread rational agreement about what parts of psychoanalytic theory have been confirmed or disconfirmed by empirical tests. Even more important and more fundamental, there is still a great deal of disagreement (and confusion) about the very meaning and criteria for the empirical testing of psychoanalysis' (Bernstein, 1988, p. 114).

At present, it seems that explanations which rely upon complex psychoanalytic theories, such as Freud's, cannot be proven true. There remain many low-level psychological generalizations, however, which are quite well attested, and can be used to explain behaviour. B.A. Farrell has argued this point in his book *The Standing of Psychoanalysis* (1981, esp. ch. 7). His examples of low-level generalizations include: 'All young boys are sexually attracted to the mother and sexually jealous of the father'; 'When a person suffers frustration, he is liable to regress to an earlier stage of development' (p. 37). It seems to me that generalizations like these are best understood to be statements of a tendency or disposition which is common, but perhaps not universal, and is not always manifest on appropriate occasions because it can be overridden by other tendencies. Still, they do describe common causal processes, and so they may help historians and others to identify the cause of certain patterns of behaviour, and even of certain events, under the appropriate description, when no other explanation is available.

Even relatively low-level generalizations such as these, however, are not so well confirmed as to warrant confident inferences about a person's childhood experiences, simply on the basis of their adult behaviour. There are too many different possible explanations of adult behaviour to be sure of any inferred cause for which one has no independent evidence. Erik H. Erikson, for example, confidently inferred Martin Luther's relations with his father and mother on the basis of Freudian theory. He avowed that Luther secretly hated his father. 'Do we have any proof of this? Only the proof which lies in action delayed, and delayed so long that the final explosion hits non-participants. In later life Luther displayed an extraordinary ability to hate quickly and persistently, justifiably and un-justifiably, with pungent dignity and with utter vulgarity' (Erikson, 1972, p. 62). Similarly he infers his relations with his mother from his later behaviour.

> A big gap exists here, which only conjecture could fill. But instead of conjecturing half-heartedly, I will state, as a clinician's judgment, that nobody could speak and sing as Luther later did if his mother's voice had not sung to him of some heaven; that nobody could be as torn between his masculine and his feminine sides, nor have such a range of both, who did not at one time feel that he was like his mother; but also, that nobody would discuss women and marriage in the way he often did who had not been deeply disappointed by his mother – and had become loath to succumb the way she did to the father, to fate.
>
> (ibid., p. 69)

It is unlikely that these generalizations are true. Could not someone else have inspired Luther's songs of heaven? Could he not have valued both masculine and feminine traits in his character without having felt like his mother? Could he not have been disturbed by other cases of the humiliation of wives, besides his mother's? Erikson seems blinded by his theory.

Even when there is independent evidence of the kind of cause indicated by these low-level generalizations, one can only rely upon them for an explanation if no other possible cause seems likely. One is often tempted to suppose that there may be quite plausible physical or rational explanations for patterns of behaviour, such as Woodrow Wilson's outbreaks of anger, which at least deserve careful consideration. And even if the cause is psychological, one suspects that there may have been several different childhood experiences which could have produced it.

Given the profound uncertainties about psychological theories of the origins of human behaviour, it is understandable that historians are generally wary of using them.

(8) The influence of culture

Historians sometimes explain a change in a person's attitudes or beliefs as reflecting those of the people with whom that person had associated. In 1851 Henry Parkes published an article critical of the radical Republican views of J.D. Lang, views which he had supported only the year before. Why did he do so? The explanation which A.W. Martin prefers is 'that new political and business associations were ... modifying Parkes' radicalism'. They included well-to-do businessmen, professional men, and landed proprietors. 'None of them was republican and most were already known as "liberals"' (Martin, 1980, p. 101). It was the influence of their views, Martin suggests, that led Parkes to act as he did. Of course their influence does not explain the details of Parkes' attack on Lang, but it does account for its anti-Republican, liberal tone.

The explanation depends upon a lawlike generalization of universal scope, namely: people frequently adopt the beliefs and responses of those classes or groups whose friendship they value. The first item in this list of causes of individual actions was about conventional responses to situations, which are often habitual. This is one kind of cultural determinism. The kind being considered now is slightly different, referring not to responses but to attitudes. Historians sometimes explain actions as reflecting an attitude which the agent has acquired from the culture of her friends.

Most of our attitudes are derived from our culture. Some of these we are deliberately taught at school and at home; some we acquire unwittingly from the media and from social encounters. It is not surprising that the ideas we acquire in these ways are often inconsistent. Different groups have different beliefs and ideals. From our business friends we may learn to exploit others; and from our Christian friends we may learn to love them. Our sports coach will encourage us to be tough and determined to win; and our humanist friends will insist we treat all people fairly. No wonder historians do not expect people to be entirely rational.

Some social scientists have been so impressed by the influence of culture on human behaviour that they assume all our responses are culturally determined. They believe that we always follow the rules and adopt the roles which our society teaches us are appropriate to whatever situation we are in. Indeed they think that our culture directs our interpretation of every situation that confronts us as well. Thus among symbolic interactionists, M.H. Kuhn and his school at the State University of Iowa adopted a deterministic model. Kuhn said that 'the individual . . . derives his plans of action from the roles he plays and the statuses he occupies in the groups with which he feels identified – his reference groups' (quoted in Meltzer and Petras, 1972, p. 52). Most, however, believe that although the people with whom one relates may suggest ways of responding to situations, one is still free either to adopt that suggestion or to reject it, as one thinks best.

Erving Goffman, for example, has drawn attention to the way in which people can choose what role to adopt in a situation, defining it as they wish. Interaction, according to him, involves negotiating an agreed definition of a situation and of the respective roles to be adopted within it. (See Wilson, 1983, ch. 8 for his and other non-deterministic views.) But some object to even that amount of individual freedom. John Wilson has written:

> Symbolic interactionists probably grant too much autonomy to the individual. Roles are said to shape individual behaviour only in the sense of being options or tools for optional use.
>
> This [regrettably] rules out the possibility that an individual's actions are grounded in norms which have been thoroughly internalized, so that what he *wants* to do is also what he *ought* to do.
>
> (Wilson, 1983, p. 140)

One problem for theories of either cultural or social determinism is the difficulty they have in accounting for radical innovation. Foucault, although impressed with the way in which people's roles and status are imposed by the words others use in talking about them, and with the way in which their freedom to act is limited by the structures of power in their society, nevertheless believed that we can and should resist these constraints, to achieve our autonomy (Schürmann, 1985). Certainly some degree of autonomy seems a precondition of originality.

At the very least historians are aware that although people often adopt the attitudes of their friends, they sometimes have sufficient independence of mind not to do so, or only to adopt those attitudes of which they approve. When it seems unlikely that a person would adopt a role or a norm unthinkingly, then any adequate explanation of their action must explain why they decided to adopt it. In that case a cultural explanation alone would be unsatisfactory (Ryan, 1978).

(9) The influence of society

The facts about a person's society are commonly thought to influence their behaviour in three ways. First, people take them into consideration in planning their actions. They note both the distribution of power in society, the wealth and authority of individuals, groups and institutions, and the relationships and processes which characterize the society, particularly people's habits, attitudes and obligations towards one another. All these can affect the outcome of any action that might be decided upon. Second, people's perception of society, of its relationships and processes, on occasion stimulates them to action, either to try to change the structure in some way, or, more commonly, to alter their place within it. And finally, facts about social rewards and penalties for certain kinds of behaviour often influence people to act to their own advantage. Historians can sometimes explain an action by referring to one of these ways in which society influenced the agent.

The influence of social sanctions is not the same as the influence of the attitudes of one's friends. In the case of cultural explanations, the assumption is that the agent had acquired, 'internalized' as they say, the norms of the social group to which she belonged. There is no reference to sanctions, just to the appropriation of ways of interpreting situations and of ways of responding to them. The kind of social explanation being considered here differs from cultural ones in that the reason for which agents are said to have acted as they did is not that they had internalized a norm, but that they followed it out of a fear of the penalties for not doing so and hope for the rewards for compliance – whether these hopes and fears were conscious or not. Frequently, of course, actions admit of both explanations: they are done in conformity to internalized norms, and because they are socially sanctioned.

The generalization invoked in explanations which refer to social sanctions is that people will generally respond to a situation as their society requires if the sanctions for compliance are strong. The frequency of compliance is largely in proportion to the actual strength of the sanctions, and a subject's ability to tolerate them. Wealthy people are not deterred by parking fines, but poor people are. A secure boss is not deterred by unpopularity, whereas an elected union representative may be.

A vivid example of such a social explanation is Marcel Mauss' account of the conventions governing potlach among north-west American Indians, in his classic book *The Gift* (1966). The chiefs of these Indian tribes regularly held festivals at which they gave large numbers of extravagant gifts to all who could attend, sometimes going so far as to just destroy valuable items in an amazing exhibition of their wealth. The conventions governing potlach were complicated, as Mauss explains. But one fact he gives special emphasis: these apparently voluntary acts were actually impelled by very severe social sanctions.

> A chief must give a potlach for himself, his son, his son-in-law or daughter and for the dead. He can keep his authority in his tribe, village and family, and maintain his position with the chiefs inside and outside his nation, only if he can prove that he is favourably regarded by the spirits, that he possesses fortune and that he is possessed by it. The only way to demonstrate his fortune is by expending it to the humiliation of others.
>
> (p. 37)

The gifts received at one potlach must be repaid with interest at another. 'The obligation of worthy return is imperative. Face is lost for ever if it is not made or if equivalent value is not destroyed. The sanction for the obligation to repay is enslavement for debt' (p. 41).

This is an excellent example of the way in which social sanctions can drive people to act in a way which is otherwise quite irrational. Often the Indian chiefs could scarcely afford to destroy or give away all that they did, so that such behaviour seemed contrary to their natural interests. One cannot understand it until one discovers the penalties that the chiefs would suffer for not doing so.

Explanations which refer to people's needs and interests, to their psychological history, or to the influence of a person's culture or society, are often in terms which are meaningful to the historian, but which would have been completely alien to the people whose actions are being explained. Some think that historical explanations should always be written from the agent's point of view, believing that history written from the historian's perspective is somehow anachronistic. It would only be anachronistic if the historian suggested that the agent acted with these causes consciously in mind. Careful historians do not do that. Sometimes an explanation of an action in terms of the agent's reasons for acting is quite unsatisfactory, perhaps because it seems to be inconsistent with what is already known about the agent or the situation. Then there is an urgent need to describe the causal process further, so as to remove the apparent inconsistencies. The wish to find psychological explanations for cases like Hitler's attitude towards the Jews is driven, not by a dilettante interest in psychology, but by the need to explain something which is so bizarre as to demand an explanation, and having nowhere else to turn. When it seemed surprising that Parkes should express liberal rather than his normal radical views, Martin drew attention to the liberal opinions of his new friends. Then again, that Indian chiefs should offer gifts to their friends is no surprise, but that they should offer so much at such expense to themselves appears to be irrational, until one learns what social penalties they would suffer if they failed to do so. Then their desire becomes quite intelligible. Explanations which refer to these causes of human behaviour are not anachronistic, and are indispensable in rendering strange behaviour intelligible.

CAN REASONS BE CAUSES?

Probably the most detailed consideration of this question is that given by Rex Martin in *Historical Explanation. Re-enactment and Practical Inference* (1977). Martin finally denies that reasons can be causes, but I will argue that this conclusion is not necessary, and that it is at least reasonable to consider them as causes.

Martin summarizes and refutes two well-known lines of argument for the view that reasons and the actions they explain are related analytically, that is that reasons logically entail their corresponding actions, and therefore cannot possibly be causes of them. First there are arguments from the meaning of the words 'intention' and 'goal'. Alan Donagan said that to have an intention means acting in accordance with it if you can. If you do not act appropriately, then it can be rightfully said that you did not have the intention so to act. F. Stoutland said the same about the word 'goal'. One cannot be said to truly have a goal if one does not pursue it under suitable conditions (pp. 164–5). It seems to me that we often say people have a certain intention, even when they fail to act on it when the appropriate occasion arises. They can tell us of their intention, and even make plans for acting on it, yet ultimately fail to do so. Weakness of will is a well-known phenomenon. So Martin denies that words like 'intention', 'goal', and 'purpose' logically imply the performance of a corresponding action. We can certainly imagine people not acting on their intentions (pp. 168–9).

The second line of argument is one which refers to the way we verify intentions. Von Wright has pointed out that we always verify intentions by referring to what people have said or done, which provides evidence of them. But to do this, he says, requires that intentions be logically related to their actions: to have an intention is to act accordingly, report it, acknowledge it, and pursue it (pp. 172–4). Martin replies that Von Wright has not proved an analytic connection between intentions and actions, but merely reported how we assume such a connection to exist (p. 175).

Despite these criticisms of the claim that intentions and actions are related analytically, Martin does not allow that the relation is causal. This is because he thinks that if one has an intention, and all the conditions are propitious for fulfilling it, then one will act accordingly. The relation is not analytic, he says, but we regard the connection as true without exception. Suppose someone had an intention to do one thing, such as assassinate the President, but at the last moment did something else, such as eat an apple, then Martin argues there must have been another intention at work at that moment, namely the intention to eat an apple (ch. 10). Martin interprets the generalization that people always act on their intentions when conditions are appropriate as a basic way we have of thinking about actions, 'a conceptual representation of our understanding of how actions happen' (p. 198). When someone does not act on their intention, he says, we find their behaviour quite unintelligible (p. 201). He says the generalization provides the foundation of a language game, a way we have of talking about actions, as Wittgenstein put it (p. 203). He also likens it to one of R.G. Collingwood's 'absolute presuppositions' of our discourse (pp. 209–10). (More recently Martin seems to endorse Collingwood's idea that reasons can be causes (Martin, 1994, p. 155), though his reasons for such a change of mind are as yet uncertain.)

The best reason for adopting a Wittgensteinean interpretation of mental terms, however, is one which can be built upon the following remark by Wittgenstein himself: 'What is the natural expression of an intention? – Look at a cat when it stalks a bird; or a beast when it wants to escape' (*Philosophical Investigations* I.647, see Wittgenstein, 1968, p. 165e). According to Wittgenstein an intention is not a physical thing or a mental event to be examined. Rather it is a way of interpreting the behaviour of an animal, or a person, in a certain context. It is a way of talking about them, a kind of language game. This theory of mental terms and rational explanations has been developed by Brian Fay in *Social Theory and Political Practice* (1975). There he writes:

> Intentional explanations, for example, make sense of a person's actions by fitting them into a purposeful pattern which reveals how the act was warranted, given the actor, his social and physical situation and his beliefs and wants. An intention is no more 'behind' the action than the meaning of the word is 'behind' the letters of which it is composed, and is no more an 'invisible mental cause' of an act than is a melody the invisible cause of the pattern of notes that we hear at a concert.
>
> (ibid., pp. 73–4)

Fay means to say that intentions are not things that really exist and direct human behaviour. Talk of intentions is merely talk of reasons for action, which is warranted by the situation according to the rules of our language and culture.

Why, then, should reasons be regarded as causes? The answer is, because they can exist independently of actions, and they seem to have the power to incline people to act in certain ways. We sometimes know them by interpreting behaviour in its context. But their explanatory power is undeniable, and if they are to explain why people have acted in certain ways, they must be said to have causal power.

It might be replied that they cannot be observed, so surely they do not really exist. The answer is that the forces of nature cannot be observed either, but no one doubts their existence. We say gravitational force really exists to explain why things fall to earth; we say magnetic forces exist to explain why metal objects are attracted to magnets. These are theoretical entities, whose existence is posited to make sense of observed regularities. Similarly, mental states are theoretical entities which are posited to make sense of regularities in human experience and behaviour. Functional theories of the mind, like those of Hilary Putman and Jerry A. Fodor (see Fodor, 1981), are based on this assumption.

People's intentions incline people to act a certain way, but other forces can operate upon them to prevent them acting that way. Tiredness or lethargy can be enough to stop some people from acting on their intentions. Other reasons, such as desires and beliefs, also operate to incline people to change their minds, to form new intentions. There is no need to assume a deterministic theory of the mind, but experience tells us that reasons do influence people, sometimes powerfully. Much human behaviour can be explained by supposing that reasons can be causes.

Martin is right in saying that the concept of having an intention to do X in circumstances C conceptually entails doing X in C, assuming nothing will prevent one from doing so. In this respect it is the same as all causal dispositions, for they all mean certain effects will occur in certain circumstances. It also entails that one will normally report such an intention when asked about it, and seek various different ways of implementing it if impeded. Martin thinks such dispositions cannot be causes because they conceptually entail certain patterns of response. But we commonly allow that certain events can be both conceptually and causally related to their effects. If you swallow a bottle of strong poison you will die. If you do not die, it was not a strong poison. However, one would surely not deny that swallowing the poison caused your death. So long as the two events can exist independently, one can be the cause of the other. Similarly, intentions can be causes of actions.

9   Explaining collective actions

Historians frequently try to understand why groups of people acted together as they did in the past. It is convenient to regard social groups as being of roughly three kinds. First there are aggregates, groups of people who act in a similar way largely on their own initiative, such as voters at an election. Second, there are social groups which are formed when several people commit themselves to a joint action for some purpose. The third kind of social group is the organization, which is an institution whose members have more or less clearly defined roles, designed to achieve a common purpose. People who join such institutions commit themselves to acting in the ways defined by the institution, fulfilling whatever role they have assumed in accordance with its rules. Our present concern is with the actions of groups of the first two kinds, that is with the actions of aggregates of individuals, and with the behaviour of more or less co-ordinated social groups. The behaviour of organizations is certainly of interest to historians, but beyond the scope of this work.

It is often possible to explain a collective action by means of a lawlike generalization relating it to some other event. For example, many people migrated to Australia from Ireland during the 1840s to escape debt and degradation during the dreadful famine. One could probably explain their behaviour in terms of a generalization: in times of extreme hardship, people will often migrate to better lands, if they can. There is some concern about the truth of such generalizations, for human behaviour is seldom as regular as they suggest. This problem will be discussed in the next chapter, which is about such structural explanations. There I will discuss two ways of coping with exceptions to social generalizations. One is to qualify the generalization so as to exclude all the exceptional conditions that one can think of. Another, more useful solution, is to interpret the generalization as a statement of a tendency, which can be counteracted by other tendencies at times. The important point to note at this stage is that collective actions can often be explained in terms of social generalizations, as part of some theory of social change.

This chapter, however, is devoted to explanations of collective actions which adopt what is often called 'an action approach'. That is, it is about explanations which focus upon the ways in which individuals were moved to behave as they did.

Some consider that the only way in which actions should be explained is in terms of the reasons which people took into account in deciding to perform them. Philip Pettit calls this 'an inference theory' of human action, as opposed to a 'decision theory' and 'rational choice theory' (Pettit, 1993, pp. 239–45, 272–6). An important feature of his inference theory is the claim that 'desires are rationally grounded' in evaluations (p. 240). All actions, in his opinion, are products of thought and judgement. This supports Pettit's conviction of the autonomy of humans, their freedom to act according to their beliefs. A major part of his recent book *The Common Mind* (1993) defends his belief in human autonomy against those who have suggested that it can be overridden or 'outflanked' by social facts (ch. 3). Decision theory suggests that people are moved by their desires, sometimes without basing them upon any evaluative judgement; and rational choice theory assumes that people are motivated by self-interest. Pettit resists both, to preserve his faith in autonomy. But it is widely known that people do not always act in an entirely rational, autonomous way, as even Pettit admits occasionally. People often act from habit and unreflective desire; and they are victims of unconscious motives. To ignore these fundamental causes of much human behaviour is to overlook important forces at work in society.

Those who favour an action approach to the explanation of collective actions face a particular difficulty. They have to explain, not only why the individuals acted as they did, but also why so many of them acted in the same way. Methodological individualists have been loath to discuss this question, and I suspect that is because it points to some sort of social determinism. They would probably ascribe a common response to common rationality. But rationality alone will not explain it. People only respond to a situation the same way if they have similar beliefs about it, and similar values and desires. So to explain a collective response from the perspective of individuals, one must draw attention to the source of those common beliefs and desires.

Historians and social philosophers have located the source of common responses in social conventions, cultural ideology and objective interests. In discussing each of these I shall consider how they influence human behaviour, and in particular whether they ever override human rationality and autonomy. I shall argue that in each case people can respond rationally to the forces which are at work influencing them, but that quite often people follow the social force without reflection. These social forces do not deprive people of their autonomy, but often people do not exercise the autonomy they possess.

If there are three different ways of explaining collective actions, does that mean that particular historical explanations involve a choice, made according to the historian's preferences? In that case historical explanations would be quite subjective. In practice there certainly can be multiple causes of collective actions. People stop at red lights partly from habit or convention, partly because they want to avoid a possible accident and a fine, and also because it is in their own interests to do so. Historians do often mention only those causes which interest them, so that their explanations are rather subjective. However, I would urge that a fair explanation would set out all the major causes, so as not to misrepresent the causal story. Where this convention is adopted, the only room for choice is in deciding the relative importance of the various causes at work, as this depends upon the historian's view of human nature.

COLLECTIVE ACTIONS AS EXPRESSIONS OF COMMON DISPOSITIONS

The theory that many of our actions are conventional responses to conventional interpretations of situations has been thoroughly studied by social scientists. Perhaps the most famous is Pierre Bourdieu, whose influential but difficult book *Outline of a Theory of Practice* (1977) has drawn attention to the important role of dispositions in determining human behaviour. During their upbringing, he said, people acquire dispositions to interpret situations in certain ways, to envisage certain possible outcomes and to respond with certain patterns of behaviour. Each person's set of dispositions, or habitual practices, Bourdieu calls a 'habitus'. 'If agents are possessed by their habitus more than they possess it, this is because it acts within them as the organizing principle of their actions' (p. 18). The practices which people adopt, he says, are those which serve their interests.

Bourdieu believes that both individual and group behaviour is best understood as an expression of dispositions.

> In short, the habitus, the product of history, produces individual and collective practices, and hence history, in accordance with the schemes engendered by history. The system of dispositions . . . is the principle of the continuity and regularity which objectivism discerns in the social world without being able to give them a rational basis. And it is at the same time the principle of the transformations and regulated revolutions which neither the extrinsic and instantaneous determinism of a mechanistic sociologism nor the purely internal but equally punctual determination of voluntarist or spontaneist subjectivism are capable of accounting for.
>
> (p. 82)

Many collective expressions of protest in eighteenth-century Europe have been explained as conventional responses to perceived injustices. Historians such as George Rudé (1964) and E.P. Thompson (1968) have discovered that, for example, numerous bread riots in England were a conventional response to what the people judged to be an unjust increase in the price of bread when bread was in short supply. In these riots, the people seized grain and sold it at what they deemed to be a fair price, often returning the money to the grain merchant. Rudé pointed out other conventional forms of protest: the peasant Jacquerie, for example, and the modern industrial strike (p. 5). Charles Tilly has also written an interesting account of the variety and nature of traditional 'repertoires of collective action' (1978, ch. 5). He remarks that 'collective action usually takes well-defined forms already familiar to the participants, in the same sense that most of an era's art takes on a small number of established forms' (p. 143).

> Hijacking, mutiny, machine breaking, charivaris, village fights, tax rebellions, food riots, collective self-immolation, lynching, vendetta have all belonged to

the standard collective-action repertoire of some group at some time. People have at sometime recognized every one of them as a legitimate, feasible way of acting on an unsatisfied grievance or aspiration.

(ibid., p. 153) (See also Rudé, 1981, ch. 15.)

So convincing has this view of riots as conventional responses to perceived injustices become that recent historians have warned of the dangers of applying it uncritically. John Stevenson says that 'one of the subtler forms of condescension in historical writing is to see all violence as "protest" and all the participants in riots as sobersided and self-conscious proletarians' (Stevenson, 1979, p. 4). He goes on to remind us how unlikely it is that all members of a crowd had the same intentions (p. 11). Nevertheless, in many cases the great majority of people involved in the bread riots did seem to know what they were about: increases in the price of bread affected all.

It would be quite wrong, however, to suggest that all collective actions are caused by people following conventions. Quite often people act together in response to a leader who talks them into it. For example, E.P. Thompson identified another kind of riot, namely 'the deliberate use of the crowd as an instrument of pressure, by persons "above" or apart from the crowd' (Thompson, 1968, p. 67). He wrote of the London crowd led by Wilkes in the 1760s and 1770s as a good example (p. 76). They rioted for the sake of 'liberty', but many had only a confused and hazy idea of what that involved. They simply acted as their leaders ordered.

When leaders persuade their followers to behave in an unconventional way, others are often taken by surprise. The unconventional behaviour of the English archers at the Battle of Crécy (26 August 1346) is a case in point. Let Edouard Perroy tell the story.

> Why did Edward [Edward III, King of England] come out victorious in this unequal battle, in which in normal circumstances he should have been crushed? Chroniclers have blamed the rashness of the French knights, who dashed forward to attack with foundered horses, and charged blindly without waiting to regroup. In fact, Edward owed his triumph, strange as it may seem, to his numerical inferiority. To have awaited the enemy in the open, to have sought a hand-to-hand fight between the knights, that is, to have waged war according to the rules which he himself respected and his vassals certainly wanted to observe, would have been unpardonable folly. He had to resort to improvised ruses, of which, in his heart of hearts, he was somewhat ashamed. He had chosen favourable ground, which enabled him to follow the enemy's move-ments. His cavalry, impatient to join battle, were held back by his orders. Fences and hedges concealed the despised infantry. First the Welsh archers were ordered, by very rapid fire, to decimate the horses and unhorse the knights. Even a few cannon, still reserved solely for siege warfare, were perhaps used to create panic at the right moment. When the mêlée began, it was a frightful butchery. All the flower of the French nobility . . . strewed the battlefield with their bodies.

(Perroy, 1962, p. 119)

There is a large literature examining the variety of types of social response. Erving Goffman (1971) and H. Garfinkel (1967) were founders of the work, showing how people learn not just rules but more importantly roles and even what might loosely be called 'characters' which others expect them to play. R. Harré and P.F. Secord have extended the analysis to include routines and rituals as well (1972, ch. 9).

Is an explanation of collective action in terms of social conventions compatible with a view of humans as rational, autonomous agents? Or does it imply a degree of social determinism?

As the quotation above revealed, Bourdieu wants to find a position between these two extremes. He portrays people as only partially aware of the dispositions which drive them.

> Because his actions and works are the product of a *modus operandi* of which he is not the producer and has no conscious mastery, they contain an 'objective intention', as the Scholastics put it, which always outruns his conscious intentions. . . . It is because subjects do not, strictly speaking, know what they are doing that what they do has more meaning than they know.
>
> (Bourdieu, 1977, p. 79)

An example of social conventions at work is given by Bourdieu in a paper entitled 'Marriage Strategies as Strategies of Social Reproduction' (1976). His basic thesis is that you can make more sense of common marriage and inheritance practices of the peasants of Béarn in the Pyrenees if you see them as conserving certain socially transmitted values and principles, which are not always made explicit, than if you try to find a rule which the people followed deliberately. The marriages were designed to maintain the 'material patrimony', by keeping the land together, and to maintain the 'symbolic patrimony', by retaining the social status of the family, at the same time preserving if possible the principle of primogeniture, allowing the eldest son to inherit the land. The main function of marriage remained 'to reproduce the lineage and thereby its work force' and 'to assure the safeguarding of the patrimony' (p. 122). Every marriage required the development of a particular strategy which would satisfy as many of these principles as possible. The principles underlying each decision are seldom made 'completely and systematically explicit', but explain the strategies adopted better than any rule. Apparent rules are sometimes broken, for example when there are no sons a daughter may inherit a patrimony, as the best strategy to adopt given the principles at work. The predisposition to act in accordance with all these principles is the 'habitus' which governs these aspects of the peasants' lives.

Anthony Giddens locates people's knowledge of social rules in their 'practical consciousness', as opposed to their theoretical understanding (Giddens, 1984, pp. 21–3; 90). Practical consciousness seems to be consciousness of how to proceed appropriately in a situation (Giddens draws upon Wittgenstein's analysis of understanding here). It is not propositional knowledge, but know-how. It is learned, but unreflectively. Many of our dispositions are just acquired by unconscious imitation of others, it seems. This process obviously involves some abstraction from observed practices, so that the appropriate rule can be applied in a new situation. We seem to learn social behaviour rather as we learn language, by learning how to apply the relevant rules without necessarily being able to state them. This is a form of social conditioning. One can, of course, formulate some of these rules and discuss them. But people usually follow them quite automatically, quite habitually.

If this account of much conventional behaviour is accurate, then the influence of custom upon an individual does involve mental processes of comparison, abstraction and application: comparison of similar situations, abstraction of the relevant principles at work which should be followed, and application of those principles to the particular circumstances at hand. The process of following conventions does not entirely bypass the person's mind. But conventional responses cannot be regarded as necessarily fully rational and autonomous, either, as people do not always reflect upon the rules they follow. We all have a natural inclination to conform to what others expect of us, at least to some extent, probably because we are unconsciously aware that it is generally to our advantage to do so.

It is often difficult to know whether people who act in a traditional way have done so because they know and approve of the tradition, or if they have acted without realizing that they were moved by a disposition which they had acquired from their society. Consider, for example, the seventeen rules governing Balinese cockfighting which Clifford Geertz lists in 'Deep Play' (Geertz, 1972, pp. 207–10). Geertz says that he extracted these rules both from a study of behaviour at cockfights and from statements provided by informers. He asserts that 'the Balinese peasants themselves are quite aware of all this and can and, at least to an ethnographer, do state most of it in approximately the same terms as I have' (p. 210). Nevertheless one can imagine many Balinese following these rules by just conforming to practice, having acquired the disposition to do so by following others, without ever formulating the rule behind the practice. How natural it would be to follow a rule such as this quite unreflectively: 'If an outsider cock is fighting any cock from your village, you will tend to support the local one.'

It seems that people are often unaware of why they respond to certain situations as they do, beyond thinking that such a response is appropriate. Few are aware of the influence of cultural conditioning. They are simply conscious of their predicament, and of what their community would agree is the appropriate response to it. They will naturally be inclined to do what their community expects, but remain free to defy that expectation if they want to, as every teenager knows!

RATIONAL EXPLANATIONS OF COLLECTIVE ACTIONS

Historians sometimes explain a collective action by saying the people were influenced by an ideology, which guided their thinking so that they all responded to a situation in the same way.

George Rudé has discussed reasons for collective actions in his book *Ideology and Popular Protest* (1980). He distinguished two kinds of ideology which direct group behaviour: 'inherent' traditional beliefs about people's rights, and 'derived' systems of thought, which are more carefully structured doctrines formulated by writers.

Examples of inherent beliefs in eighteenth-century Europe are the peasants' belief in their right to land, the townspeople's belief in their right to buy bread at a 'just' price, and widespread beliefs in certain traditional liberties. These formed part of the *mentalité* of the people, and help to explain the occurrence of many strikes, food riots and peasant rebellions. Rudé remarked that these were largely backward-looking, conservative motives, driving people to assert old rights in the face of change. Ideologies of this kind underlie many conventional interpretations of and responses to situations, such as were described in the last section.

The second kind of ideology, formulated by authors of political ideas, is generally forward-looking, justifying changes which increased the rights of one group or another. The writings of Rousseau, Taine and Marx have been popular in inspiring revolutionary movements. To be acceptable, such theories have to accord with people's traditional values, Rudé said, and they must also be judged likely to yield desirable improvements in the existing circumstances. The theories are sometimes modified by those who use them, in accordance with their particular desires (Rudé, 1980, ch. 2; see also Rudé, 1981, ch. 14). In the French Revolution, Rudé observed, both kinds of ideological motivation were at work: 'the insurgents of May 1795 wore on their caps and on their blouses the twin slogans "The Constitution of 1793" and "Bread"' (1981, p. 220).

It is interesting to see how well Rudé's analysis fits Bernard Bailyn's explanation of the American Revolution in *The Origins of American Politics* (1970). Bailyn begins with an account of the inherent traditional beliefs of eighteenth-century Americans: 'The starting point is the intellectual environment of eighteenth-century politics, the culture of which it was a part' (pp. 14–15). There was pride in the British Constitution, forged out of the struggles of the seventeenth century, which ensured individual liberty by balancing the rights of the Crown, the aristocracy and the Commons. The balance prevented the evils of tyranny, oligarchy and mob rule. Bailyn then describes the literature produced by opposition groups in Britain, especially during Walpole's regime, articles written by John Trenchard and Thomas Gordon ('Cato') on the left, and by Viscount Bolingbroke, in *The Craftsman*, on the right. Both sides attacked Walpole's government as using its power corruptly to undermine the liberties of the people in the pursuit of private interest. Bailyn says it is remarkable 'the speed with which the [American] colonists soaked up the protest literature of the opposition and incorporated its main propositions into their basic perceptions of public life' (p. 54). The reason this propaganda was attractive, he said, was that Americans resented what they regarded as the unwarranted power of royal governors to veto colonial legislation, to prorogue and dissolve provincial lower houses of Assembly, to appoint and dismiss judges and magistrates, indeed to create courts, and to exercise numerous other executive privileges. Thus an attack on the authority of the British government was justified as being in defence of a traditional liberty from tyranny.

Bailyn's book was designed to explain 'why there was a Revolution' in America (ibid., p. 13), especially to explain 'what the leaders of the Revolutionary movement themselves said lay behind the convulsion of the time – what they themselves said was the cause of it all' (p. 11). He makes it clear that he is accounting for the whole revolutionary movement, noting that the views concerning the British government which he described were expressed 'by John Adams, continuously, elaborately, year after year from 1765 to 1775', as well as by Samuel Adams and Thomas Jefferson (p. 12). The revolutionary movement is normally seen as beginning with resistance to the Stamp Act of 1765, culminating with the Declaration of Independence proclaimed on 4 July 1776, and concluding with the peace treaty of 1783. Bailyn explained why the Americans wanted to free themselves of British government. What he did not attempt to explain is why American resistance took the particular forms that it did. One could say that he explained the acts of rebellion under one description, but not under another. Rational explanations are designed, like all causal explanations, to be appropriate to those aspects of the action being explained which interest the historian.

To explain the particular form of a collective action, the historian usually has to provide details of the particular beliefs, desires and plans of the people involved, which directed their behaviour. These are usually worked out by the group at a meeting, often on the recommendation of a leader. One of the acts of rebellion during the American Revolution is popularly known as the Boston Tea Party. If an historian wanted to explain why some fifty Bostonians, dressed as Indians, boarded three British ships and dumped some three hundred chests of tea they were carrying into Boston Harbour on the evening of 16 December 1773, then Bailyn's explanation would scarcely be adequate. It does not explain why this form of rebellion was chosen. To find an explanation of why these Bostonians decided to dump the British tea, one might well turn to Robert Middlekauf's book *The Glorious Cause, The American Revolution, 1763–1784* (1982). His explanation vividly reconstructs what he believes was in the minds of those involved. They were, he says, reacting to the Tea Act of May 1773. This Act allowed the East India Company to sell tea direct to America, without going through British intermediaries or paying British tax, thus reducing its price below that of Dutch tea which was being consumed without the payment of duty. The Americans had stopped buying British tea while the British government had continued to impose a threepence-a-pound duty upon it, and this had cost the East India Company dearly. The new arrangement was clearly designed to make British tea attractive again to Americans, and thereby to help the Company regain its profits. But the Act still required the Americans to pay tax on the tea, which they bitterly resented. This is why the Bostonians and others resisted the importation of British tea. They saw it as a scheme to trick Americans into accepting the British government's right to tax them. At a meeting held in Boston on the evening in question, many refused to accept the tea and pay the tax. Middlekauf sums it up with these words:

> Why we may ask did this convulsive reaction [to the Tea Act] occur? . . . The answer has much to do with how the colonists understood the Tea Act. They believed that the Act left them no choice; it forced the issue; it expressed

still another claim by Parliament of the right to tax them. This claim meant, as far as they were concerned, that the English plot to enslave them had been revived. If they went on paying the duty now that the government's intentions were laid bare, they would be co-operating with the enslavers.

(ibid., p. 221)

In fact the precise composition of the group involved in the event is uncertain, because they were disguised. They are thought to have included some merchants who had not been allowed to sell the tea – the five merchants who were allowed to sell it were all relations or friends of the loyalist governor, Hutchinson. And it probably also included 'mechanics', tradesmen who wanted to shake off British restraints on local manufacture. These groups would have been motivated out of immediate self-interest to accept the reasons for defiance set out above. Those who benefited from the British administration were not. (See Ernst, 1976.)

Martin Seliger has contrasted 'fundamental ideology', which sets out funda-mental principles of political theory, and 'operative ideology', of principles, including prudential ones, which are used to justify particular policies (Thompson, 1984, p. 79). When groups of people band together to perform a collective action, they often accept the arguments of their leaders. Those arguments include statements of principle, as well as proposing practical ways of implementing them. Such arguments could be said to provide a sort of ideological justification for the collective action. It is an ideology of a limited kind, but it is usually embedded in a grand ideology familiar to those involved. Strictly speaking, an ideological description of ideal political principles and relations does not, by itself, entail any particular course of action. Moral and practical considerations are also important in deciding what to do to bring about an ideal state of affairs, as Michael Oakeshott reminded us in 'Rationalism in Politics' (Oakeshott, 1962; cp. Rayner, 1980). But an ideology can certainly set goals, and so guide and legitimate action.

I have said that an ideology can provide people with common reasons for action, in particular with common goals. These can be used as the basis of a rational explanation of a collective action, such as a revolution or a local rebellion, as well as for the continuation of a set of institutions. Does that mean that historians regard people who respond to an ideology as rational and autonomous?

To answer this question, one must take note of a distinction between two basic conceptions of ideology which John B. Thompson has identified. The first he calls a 'neutral conception', which sees ideology simply as a prevailing set of beliefs about certain institutions and practices. The second is a 'critical conception', according to which ideology 'is essentially linked to the process of sustaining asymmetrical relations of power – that is, to the process of maintaining domination' (Thompson, 1984, p. 4). Thompson prefers the second conception, which is derived largely from the work of Marx and Engels. According to this account, ideologies are theories about social obligations designed by a governing class to legitimate and strengthen its rule. Consequently, such an ideology does not represent the true state of affairs, which would expose injustices in the existing system, but rather produces a 'false consciousness' of the nature of society. The governing class uses its economic and social superiority to promulgate its own ideology by every means: in the law, in education, literature and the media. In effect, ideology of this kind is a form of propaganda, an instrument of political domination.

It is clear that those who act in accordance with an ideology like this are irrational in two ways. First, they are accepting a set of beliefs which is obviously false. And second, they are following those beliefs, not because they have appraised them rationally, but because they have been conned into accepting them by those whose authority they respect. (See Boudon, 1989, ch. 4 for a discussion of these points.)

Thompson, as I said, prefers the critical conception of ideology as a form of political domination (see for example p. 134). Ideologies are usually thought to be in the interests of those who promulgate them, but it is not the case that that is their only function, or even their main function. They are often designed to justify important social institutions, practices and policies. The word can be applied, not just to political theories, but also to economic theories, social theories, even to educational, legal and religious theories. Furthermore, it is not essential to an ideology as I am using the term that it be false or misleading. A set of beliefs about society could be true and still used to legitimate certain social programmes. Nor is an ideology always designed to perpetuate the power of an existing dominant group. It could be used to critique an existing government, even to justify a political revolution, as I have shown. In other words, I think the 'neutral conception' of ideology is the broader concept, and the 'critical conception' just a special case of the broader kind.

If an action is guided by an ideology which does not misrepresent the structure of society, but simply offers a justification of some of its institutions and practices, then such an action is not necessarily irrational. The people involved might have examined the ideology very critically, and have good reason for thinking it correct. Even if the historian thinks the reasons mistaken, that does not mean that people who followed them were acting irrationally from their point of view. The only residual point is that people who act according to an ideology are very often uncritical, and accept it out of respect for those who promote it and from a desire for the benefits it envisages. As Boudon has said, those who follow leaders in producing social change are often unable to assess the truth of the ideology presented to them as they simply lack the relevant information to do so (Boudon, 1989, pp. 95–9). Still, they act on the reasons available to them, and that is all that is required to declare them rational and autonomous.

It must be admitted, though, that those who actively promote an ideology often seek an emotional as well as a rational commitment to it from their followers. After seeing the effects of European dictators using modern propaganda techniques before and during the Second World War, the so-called 'revisionist' historians, James G. Randall and Avery Craven, found a similar misuse of political status to inflame public passions in the years preceding the American Civil War.

Let one take all the factors – the Sumter manoeuvre, the election of Lincoln, abolitionism, slavery in Kansas, cultural and economic differences – and it will be seen that only by a kind of false display could any of these issues, or all of them together, be said to have caused the war if one omits the elements of emotional unreason and overbold leadership. If one word or phrase were selected to account for the war, that word would not be slavery, or state-rights, or diverse civilizations. It would have to be such a word as fanaticism (on both sides), or misunderstanding, or perhaps politics. To Graham Wallas misunderstanding and politics are the same thing.

(Randall, quoted in Rozwenc, 1972, p. 175.)

Clearly Randall believed that American politicians often produced irrational beliefs as well as strong passions in their followers. Each side, the north and the south, created fears of the other side which were unjustified. By following their propaganda, the people did act irrationally, just as by following Nazi propaganda, Germans accepted irrational beliefs about the Jews and the superiority of the Aryan race (Goldhagen, 1996). There was information available to these people with which they could have criticized the false declarations of their leaders.

So, often ideologies are false, and those who accept them do so irrationally. Emotions often cause irrationality, in familiar ways. If people strongly desire or fear a certain state of affairs, they are prone to focus upon a statement about it quite uncritically, and to act in response to it without much reflection (see McCullagh, 1990). Emotion, therefore, often provides a good explanation of irrationality. Southerners so feared an attack on their right to own slaves that they would do anything to keep northerners, represented by Lincoln and the Republican party, at bay, even though the threat to their institutions before the Civil War was not really very great. Passionate people can act rationally, but often they do not. It is certainly wrong to suppose that those who act in accordance with ideology always act quite rationally and autonomously. They often act for reasons which they could have recognized as false.

EXPLANATIONS WHICH ASSUME COMMON INTERESTS

Another way in which historians frequently explain collective actions is by assuming they are performed out of self-interest. Indeed rational choice theory assumes that people will want to maximize their own interests, particularly their economic interests. (For a clear statement and interesting discussion of the theory, see Little, 1991, chs 3, 7.) Economic theories assume this too. As I pointed out in the last chapter, however, people's objective interests are not just economic. They include all that is important for their well-being, things such as health, sex and friendship, social status and power, and career opportunities (see above, pp. 226–31).

The assumption that people act for self-interest can produce very plausible explanations of collective behaviour. For example, some of the most interesting explanations of why groups of German people supported Hitler's National Socialist Party despite its dangerous and irrational ideology, have been those which point out how that Party's programme seemed likely to satisfy people's interests. Small businessmen and artisans, who suffered during the economic depression of the late 1920s, hoped that the Party would defend them from large-scale capitalists and from organized trade unions; by 1932 the large landowners and big industrialists saw the Party as a defence against communists; and the youth, depressed by the shortage of jobs and the failure of other parties to help them, responded to the nationalism and heroic idealism of the Nazi propaganda. Thus the Party met the economic and personal interests of large groups within the community (see Stachura, 1983, pp. 20–3; and Schoenbaum, 1967, p. 70). Even without adequate documentary evidence, these explanations are very plausible.

Raymond Boudon turned to explanation in terms of the agents' interests as an alternative to explanation by covering laws (which will be discussed in the next chapter). He said that actions should 'be seen as having an *adaptational* function for the actor' in the situation (Boudon, 1986, p. 30), and to be rational in that very broad sense (p. 51). He also prefers this to the simple action approach. In his earlier work, Boudon had explained collective actions by referring to agents' preferences and objectives (Boudon, 1982, pp. 9, 153–4). But as these are often difficult to discover, he now suggests that it is enough to see that the response to the situation was one which any person, similarly placed, would be likely to make.

To discover people's interests in acting, Boudon pays particular attention to the situation in which they were placed. This enables him to infer people's reasons for acting in much more detail. For example, Weber had suggested that capitalists adopted Calvinism because its doctrines supported their desire to work hard and accumulate wealth. But much more can be explained, Boudon remarked, if the historian examines the particular circumstances of sixteenth-century capitalists, as Trevor-Roper has done. For example, businessmen in the great old cities of trade, such as Milan and Antwerp, who adopted the new faith, found it was in their interests to move in the face of Counter-Reformation forces to freer cities like Amsterdam (pp. 147–9).

Social scientists have developed models of rational behaviour, especially rational economic behaviour, on the assumption that people always act in their own individual economic interests. This has proved a very useful assumption for predicting general economic behaviour, so much so that exceptions to the rule have become matters for investigation. For example, it has been remarked that it is often not in an individual's own best interest to act generously for the common good, notably when the same benefits will be enjoyed by contributing little. Thus it may not be in the interests of a worker to pay quite large union dues when he or she will benefit from union activity anyway if others contribute to it. Why, then, do so many people give generously for the benefit of a group, when it does not appear to be in their individual interests to do so? Why are there not more 'free riders'?

To preserve the assumption that people generally act out of economic self-interest, sociologists have searched diligently for self-interested motives for those who support group interests. Russell Hardin, for example, has shown that once a group activity is under way, people are moved to support it by various positive and negative incentives. A trade union may arrange certain benefits for its members, and may foster social disapproval of those who refuse to join it. Such social pressure is only effective in fairly close communities. It is more difficult to explain how co-operative ventures get going in the first place, if you assume that people act out of self-interest. Hardin suggests that when a relationship between people is ongoing, it is rational for them to co-operate for their common advantage, so long as they see that if one defects then others will withhold benefits from him or her (Hardin, 1982, pp. 13, 145ff., 193–4).

Michael Taylor has endorsed Hardin's views, stressing especially the importance of social sanctions in fairly tight-knit communities. In his opinion, if people are likely to benefit considerably from participation or will be harmed significantly by failing to participate in group behaviour, then they will probably participate out of self-interest. Taylor concludes that the poor are more likely to participate out of self-interest than the rich. So self-interest is likely to be the reason for revolutions and rebellions of the poorer classes (Taylor, 1988, pp. 90–2). But both Hardin (1982, ch. 7) and Taylor allow that participation in group behaviour is not always motivated by self-interest. Taylor remarks that sometimes people contribute as a matter of principle, sometimes from altruistic concern for others, and sometimes just for the fun of doing so (pp. 87–90). Self-interest is undoubtedly a very strong motive for human behaviour, but not a universal one. Nevertheless, especially in the absence of evidence of other plausible motives, it remains reasonable for historians to look for self-interested goals in trying to explain human behaviour.

Generally historians assume that people recognize the ways in which their well-being may be affected by the events which happen in their vicinity, and consciously formulate goals which they know to be in their own interests. But there is compelling evidence to suggest that people sometimes act in their own interests without being aware of the fact (see McCullagh, 1991a). It seems that people can be unconsciously influenced by their interests, and pursue their own well-being while believing that they are acting for other reasons. Marx and Engels were convinced that people pursue economic self-interest even when they argue that they are acting for legal, moral or religious reasons. The formulation of these legitimating ideologies, said Engels, is 'carried out consciously but with a false consciousness' (quoted by Eyerman, 1981, p. 75), implying that people who construct ideologies are sometimes unaware of the fact that they are doing so to further their own interests. On the other hand, Marx thought that the processes of historical change are hastened if people are made aware of their interests in a situation, and are encouraged to defend them deliberately. In the *Manifesto of the Communist Party*, for example, he wrote of the communists in Germany that

> they never cease, for a single instant, to instil into the working class the clearest possible recognition of the hostile antagonism [of interests] between bourgeoisie and proletariat, in order that . . . after the fall of the reactionary classes in Germany, the fight against the bourgeoisie itself may immediately begin.
>
> (Marx and Engels, 1888, p. 90)

Most sociologists favour explanations of collective action in terms of articulated group interests. For example, in response to 'breakdown theories', which see rebellion as a natural consequence of weakening of social restraints, the Tillys

> have slowly been shaping a counter-argument to them. This counter-argument emphasizes the importance of solidarity and articulated interests instead of disorganization and hardship. It treats collective violence as a by-product of collective action – a by-product, because the violence grows out of the *interaction* of organized groups which are carrying on sustained collective action. For the most part, the violence occurs when one group resists the claims being made by another.
>
> > (C., L. and R.Tilly, 1975, p. 243)

People's articulated interests do not always correspond to their real objective interests, as people often mistake what is important for their well-being. But articulated interests often explain people's behaviour very well. Charles Tilly therefore prefers to explain particular collective actions in terms of the agents' consciously formulated interests, whether they correspond to their objective interests or not. He does not entirely rule out the possibility that people will inevitably pursue their objective interests, as Marx had supposed, but he said that he would 'treat the relations of production as predictors of the interests people will pursue on the average and in the long run' (Tilly, 1978, p. 61). In other words, he believes people's objective interests generally influence their behaviour, but not on every occasion.

Charles Tilly also points out some difficulties in explaining actions by referring to objective interests. Short-term interests may differ from long-term interests, in which case, which is assumed to be operative? Jon Elster has noted some other contrasts: 'transitional or steady state, immediate or fundamental, economic or political' (Elster, 1983, p. 60). There is no denying that people's objective interests can be of all these kinds, and perhaps more, but that poses no difficulty to the present account. Knowing the range of possibilities, historians will simply look for one which provides an explanation of the action in the circumstances.

Karl Mannheim has illustrated the importance of objective interests in explaining group behaviour most impressively. He identified five political philosophies, or 'ideologies', in his day, and showed how each served the interests of the group which espoused it. The five theories were what he called bureaucratic conservatism, conservative historicism, liberal-democratic bourgeois thought, the socialist-communist conception, and fascism. For example, commenting upon the sort of historical conservatism expressed by Burke and by many German conservatives in the nineteenth century, which claimed that government was best left in the hands of those families that had long experience of political power, Mannheim wrote:

> The sociological roots of this thesis are immediately evident. It expressed the ideology of the dominant nobility in England and in Germany, and it served to

legitimatize their claims to leadership in the state. The *je ne sais quoi* element in politics, which can be acquired only through long experience, and which reveals itself as a rule only to those who for many generations have shared in political leadership, is intended to justify government by an aristocratic class. This makes clear the manner in which the social interests of a given group make the members of that group sensitive to certain aspects of social life to which those in another position do not respond.

(Mannheim, 1960, p. 107)

In Mannheim's opinion 'every form of historical and political thought is essentially conditioned by the life situation of the thinker and his groups' (p. 111).

The assumption that people sometimes act unconsciously out of self-interest is particularly plausible when the reasons given for an action suggest a selflessness which is at variance with those people's customary behaviour. Consider a politician who visits her electorate for the first time for years just prior to an election, and shows an uncharacteristic concern for the people there, promising all kinds of improvements once she is returned. It is just possible that the politician believes herself to be really concerned for the well-being of the voters, and fails to recognize the self-interest in her behaviour. Certainly the voters are likely to be sceptical of her professions of care. Indeed these days we suspect self-interest behind every political statement, sometimes perhaps mistakenly. It is particularly seldom that a large group of people acts altruistically. When the American people claim they are defending a natural right to liberty, no doubt quite sincerely, one suspects that economic and political advantage is lurking in the background. It is said that the planters in Virginia owed British merchants over two million pounds at the beginning of the Revolution, twenty or thirty times all the money in that State.

In the case of politicians who profess concern for their electors, the cynical amongst us are inclined to suspect that the objective interests are the only motivating factors, and that declarations of concern are simply made for effect. In that case, a causal explanation of the politician's behaviour must focus upon those objective interests, and not upon the statements of good will. In most cases, however, people's legitimation of their behaviour does have a causal part to play: if their actions could not be justified, they might well have not been performed. If the Americans could not justify rebellion, it is unlikely that it would have received such widespread support. However, historians must also be aware of the importance of self-interest as a motivation, and most of them are. Bailyn made a special study of the ideological basis of the Revolution, but other historians give full accounts of the economic and political advantages of which the people must have been more or less aware.

The theory that people are rational and autonomous is severely qualified by the fact that much human behaviour is motivated, often more or less unconsciously, by self-interest. For that reason, Pettit is loath to admit the power of self-interested motives in our lives. He is particularly opposed to.the suggestion that they can function unconsciously, allowing that this happens very rarely:

No doubt that story sometimes applies; no doubt the best of us are subject to occasional self-deception about the things that move us. But the idea that the story applies to most of us most of the time is extravagant and implausible. Under this mode of reconciliation [of rational choice theory with Pettit's 'inference theory' of rational human nature], the epistemic cost of coming to accept rational choice theory would surely be too high; it would require too deep a revision of the view we spontaneously take of most human beings.

(Pettit, 1993, pp. 273–4)

But what Marx, Freud, Nietzsche and others have taught us, is that people are not as rational as they commonly believe themselves to be. The enlightenment theory of rational human nature has to be severely qualified by the recognition of very strong natural motives which often drive us, whether we are aware of the fact or not.

Barry Hindess has argued trenchantly against the view that people's actions can be explained by their objective interests, interests of which they may even have remained unaware. He maintains

that interests have consequences only in so far as they provide some actor or actors with reasons for action; that they must be formulated or find expression in reasons for action that are formulated. . . . The notion of interests that are real or objective (unlike other interests that actors may believe themselves to have) has no explanatory significance with regard to the actions of those whose interests they are thought to be.

(Hindess, 1986, p. 128)

Hindess developed his ideas about the nature and function of interests out of a critique of those Marxist theories which suppose that the position of a class in a social structure alone determines the class' interests; and that those interests will inevitably direct the behaviour of members of that class. Hindess has three major reasons for denying that objective interests explain collective actions. The first is his denial of the existence of objective interests. 'Interests are not fixed or given properties of individuals or groups', but are 'products of assessment' (Hindess, 1987, pp. 112–13). Far from being determined simply by the position of a class in a social structure, Hindess said, interests are also relative to values, to goods which one wants to achieve; and the way in which people define their interests depends upon their beliefs about the most effective way of achieving those goals in the circumstances. Clearly, Hindess argues, class interests cannot just be read off from the class structure. Nor do people necessarily pursue their class interests. People have many different goals and values, and which they pursue depends upon their assessment of their importance. So, Hindess concluded, interests can explain actions only as conscious reasons for what was done.

His second objection is that we have absolutely no idea how objective interests, if they do exist, could move people. The theory which suggests that they do, he says, 'leaves us with no account of the mechanisms whereby parties, unions or state agencies can be said to act in terms of class interests, and it is unsatisfactory even in the case of human individuals' (Hindess, 1987, p. 112). And third, given that people have numerous interests at any one time, Hindess says that to mention one or two objective interests does not explain a person's actions, because it does not explain why they acted to further those interests rather than any others. As he wrote in a letter to me:

> The explanatory load that may be carried by interests that are objective . . . seems to me extremely limited. To the extent that I may be said to be acting in my interests, there remains the question of why those interests rather than other interests I might equally be said to have but not to pursue. Reference to my interests or their objectivity does not provide an answer to that question.
>
> (Letter dated 15 August 1988; quoted with permission)

Hindess' first objection is valid, but does not have the implications which I suspect he believes it to have. Certainly a person's interests are not simply a function of their place in a social structure, but are 'products of assessment' which involves reference to values. But the values which relate to objective interests are those which are objectively related to human well-being. To flourish, humans have certain biological and personal needs, which have been listed above (see pages 226–7). A person's position in a social structure determines their objective interests only in relation to these basic needs. The poor might have an interest in obtaining a greater income; the wealthy might have an interest in protecting their property. Hindess believes any assessment of a person's interests must be made consciously, so that interests can exist only as conscious ideas of possible goals. But evidence points to the fact that people pursue their interests unawares, at times; so I think that people can assess their interests unconsciously. Their assessment may not always be objectively accurate, for it may be based upon mistaken beliefs about their circumstances or about the best way of furthering their interests in the circumstances. Strictly speaking we should distinguish a person's objective interests, which are what they need to flourish in their circumstances, from their assessment of those interests, which may or may not be correct. The important point for this analysis of historical understanding is that people are often driven to identify and further their objective interests, as best they can, quite unconsciously. It seems that we have an innate drive to do so.

These remarks help to answer Hindess' second objection, that we have no idea how objective interests could affect human behaviour. People are uncannily aware of what they need to live well, and have a strong disposition to pursue it. Freud has shown that often our behaviour is unconsciously motivated by a desire for sexual pleasure. But that is only one of the motives which drive us, often unconsciously. Another is the desire for power, as Nietzsche showed. Sometimes we consciously recognize and endorse the interests we want to pursue; but sometimes we do not, focusing perhaps upon nobler reasons for our behaviour.

Hindess' third objection is that even if we allow that people are disposed to pursue their objective interests, identifying those interests does not explain their behaviour because it does not enable us to see why they followed just one of those interests rather than any other interests or goals they held at the time. But this objection assumes a function of explanation which is quite unrealistic. Historians almost never try to explain why people did what they did instead of doing anything else that they might have done. They are content to describe the reasons which led to the action, and leave it at that, unless there is a special reason for expecting the people to act differently. They almost never have enough information to explain why one action was preferred above all others. Indeed I doubt that choices between possible actions are always made for good reasons, that is, I doubt whether the kind of explanation Hindess wants could possibly be given.

A further objection, along the same lines, has been made by Christopher Lloyd. He said that even if we know people have been moved to follow their interests, we need to know more to explain their collective behaviour, because collective behaviour is a product of group planning and resources. He expressed the point thus:

> for history to be *explained* by the rational pursuit of class interests there has to be shown the existence of class solidarity, class consciousness, class power, and a clear concordance between class aims and actual historical outcomes. Otherwise the argument slips into an expedient and *post hoc* holistic reification.
>
> (Lloyd, 1986, p. 259).

What Hindess and Lloyd have failed to understand is that explanation in history is almost always *post hoc*. No individual or group action is the inevitable outcome of the conditions which preceded it. People could always have chosen to pursue different goals from those which they in fact adopted. The most historians can do is look for plausible reasons or causes of what did eventuate. Their task is to show what causes were operative, not to show that the action was highly probable. But objective interests are not merely inferred from the action they explain. They must also be plausible, given the social or physical predicament of the agent. As a need becomes greater, so it becomes increasingly likely that people will act to meet it. So sometimes group actions can be shown to have been very probable, namely when they are a common response to a common pressing need. But a group of people may choose, individually, to act in accordance with interests which are not very pressing. Reference to their common interest might accurately explain their behaviour, even though it could not show that it had to occur.

The Tillys were well aware of this fact, as the following extract shows.

> In a general way, there was a good deal of economic malaise in the industrial North [of Italy] and in Sicily after 1888. Yet this depression does not in any way predict or specify where and when violence will take place. What does? The coincidence of recent organization and activation of workers and peasants with disturbance fits again and again.
>
> (C., L. and R. Tilly, 1975, p. 162)

Charles Tilly argued that before people will rebel they must have, not only a strong common interest in doing so, but also be organized, have considerable resources, and have an opportunity to act effectively together (Tilly, 1978, chs. 2, 3). Under these conditions it seems very likely that rebellion will occur.

A final objection to explanation of collective action by reference to interests is to be found in George Rudé's review of the Tillys' book, *The Rebellious Century* (1975). Rudé objected to 'the Tillys' . . . neglect of popular ideology as an element in protest' (Rudé, 1976b, p. 451). This must be taken into account, Rudé argued, if you are to understand the form which a rebellion took. For example, 'the persistence of an older, traditional or "inherent", ideology may well help to explain the reluctance during [a] transitional period to abandon old forms of protest for new' (p. 450). The shift from 'predominantly reactive' defence of established rights to a 'proactive' claim to new rights can also be explained best as the result of a change of thinking about their situation (p. 451).

To be fair to Charles Tilly, he subsequently paid some attention to the agents' beliefs about appropriate forms of behaviour in his discussion of 'repertoires of collective action' (Tilly, 1978, pp. 151–9). He allowed, briefly, for the influence of 'new ideologies, new creeds, new theories of how the world works', but was uncertain what importance to accord them in accounting for revolutionary change: 'how great an independent weight to attribute to ideological innovation is another recurrent puzzle in the analysis of revolution' (p. 204).

As Tilly went on to remark, the publication of revolutionary ideologies usually does something to hasten a revolutionary process. But what ideologies explain most of all is the direction which a revolution takes. Tilly was more interested in accounting for the occurrence of rebellion than in the form of particular revolutions. As he wrote in the introduction to *From Mobilization to Revolution* (1978): 'I will often illustrate from specific historical circumstances . . . but the pages to follow will concentrate on the general analysis of collective action' (p. 5). Group interests in fact can to some extent explain both the occurrence and the direction of a revolution. But they seldom explain the direction taken in any detail. That does not matter, if it is of little concern to the historian.

To sum up: collective actions can be explained as simply a rational response to a common predicament by a number of people employing the same sets of beliefs and values. But often collective behaviour is not as rational and autonomous as this. It is frequently caused by common habits of conventional response; by a common irrational acceptance of an ideology; or by the influence of common objective interests. Historians generally have all these possibilities in mind, when they search for the causes of a collective action.

10 Explaining social changes

The social world is a world of social entities, having social properties and involved in social practices. Ordinary men and women inhabit the social world, but they do not constitute it. In Britain, for example, Parliament consists of the Crown, the House of Lords and the House of Commons. Different individuals hold the offices of King or Queen, Lord and Member of Parliament, but the offices survive them all. The social institutions of a community provide a framework for social life which fixes relations between people to a large extent, enabling people to get along quite well together for the achievement of their various purposes.

Social entities include the following: various things with social significance (such as money, contracts, prices, ballot papers, laws); individual social offices (e.g. the Crown) or social types (e.g. a student); social aggregates (e.g. doctors); social organizations which are planned (e.g. a university); unplanned social organizations (e.g. the economy of a country). These social entities have social properties, among which are the following: roles; duties, responsibilities and obligations; rights and privileges; status or prestige; property, power and authority. Individual social entities are often involved in socially defined practices on appropriate occasions: for example in following certain procedures, rituals and conventions; and following certain rules, be they linguistic, constitutional, military and so on. Social organizations sometimes follow conventional practices too. For present purposes, social structures include political, economic, legal, educational, military and so on, not just what are sometimes considered simply social.

A social change is a change in one or more social entities, and/or their properties, and/or their practices. For example, a change in the constitution of a country, as when America threw off British rule in the 1780s and adopted a Republican constitution, constitutes a great social change. It replaced one complex system of government with another. A social change might involve no more than a change of the people who fulfil social offices, a change of king or government, for example, though strictly speaking this is not a change in the social structure at all.

Whereas there are just a few common ways of explaining collective actions, there are numerous ways of explaining social changes. These various ways can be broadly classified, however, under two headings. Some explain social changes as the result of individual actions; and others explain social changes in terms of social causes, according to some appropriate general theory.

The search for general social explanations of social change was inspired by the covering-law model of explanation, and the story of that search will be described below. Pages 262–9 explain the difficulties encountered in trying to find predictive generalizations governing social change. Pages 270–80 look at the turn to comparative history, and the use of Mill's methods to discover the social causes of social changes. These methods were designed to discover natural, not social causes, and have been of very limited value to historians. They have enabled historians to discover some previously overlooked conditions necessary for a kind of historical change, which have been useful in giving contrastive explanations, explaining for example why a revolution was successful in one case but not another by identifying a cause necessary for success that was present in the first case but not the second. However, comparative methods are not able to establish generalizations listing all the conditions necessary and sufficient for a kind of social change.

A much more fruitful way of explaining social change has been to identify forces for change in a society, and then see how they interact in particular cases. By comparing many cases, social scientists and historians can certainly discover tendencies at work in certain kinds of society, which can be offset by other tendencies. They postulate these tendencies to explain observed patterns of social change, just as scientists postulate physical forces to account for patterns of physical change. Such tendencies are not observed regularities, and cannot even be reduced to statements of observed regularities, for they are frequently not realized. They are theoretical concepts, interpreted realistically to explain the social changes which have occurred. The pattern of explanation they provide is similar to the pattern of genetic causal explanations described earlier, in Chapter 7. Examples of this approach will be discussed on pp. 281–9.

Before examining these attempts to produce a social theory of social change, various kinds of explanation in terms of individual action will be described in the first section. These are the kinds of explanation which historians prefer, because they employ no special theory of social change, but rather rely upon knowledge of the sorts of processes with which we are all familiar. They identify what happened, at an individual level, to produce a change in a society. Historians who confine their explanations to such everyday accounts do not always notice, however, some of the conditions necessary for a movement for change to succeed, conditions which the general theories, making use of comparative studies, have identified. For example, the success of a political revolution depends not just upon the actions of the revolutionaries, which historians are quick to describe, but also upon their superior strength in comparison with the strength of the government they wish to overthrow.

One of the advantages of explanations of social change which refer to individual actions is that they can usually explain the change in much more detail than an appeal to general theory can. Thus, suppose a fall in income causes a business to dismiss staff. A story of how the manager considered her predicament and decided who had to go would explain why the individuals were selected who were finally fired. Economic theory would predict that some would have to go, but could not explain why certain individuals were chosen. On the other hand, economic theory can explain staff layoffs when no details are known, which is often the case in history.

Does this mean that when the details are available, historians should always explain social changes by referring to the individual actions which caused them? Certainly not. In these cases it depends upon the level of generality at which the historian has decided to write. Imagine trying to write the history of a general depression by telling the detailed history of every firm. It would be incredibly long and boring. However, the history of just one industry would probably require the detailed action approach.

EXPLANATIONS WHICH REFER TO INDIVIDUAL ACTIONS

Probably the first social structures were created by individuals with a strong personal following, who declared themselves leader of a tribe. Ever since, social structures have been created, modified and destroyed by leaders with the power to impose their will upon the people. Napoleon replaced the trappings of democratic government in France with an imperial government more autocratic than the monarchy which the Revolution had destroyed. Hitler transformed a fragile democracy in Germany into a personal dictatorship. Today, government ministers restructure public services, and chief executive officers restructure companies in an authoritarian, if not an autocratic way. Most sweeping and sudden social changes have been the work of individuals with the power to impose their will on the community. Changes produced by committees are usually piecemeal, involving compromises, and slower, as each stage is discussed and approved.

Historians often explain how the action of an individual produced a change in a social structure. This way of explaining structural change has been well described by Clayton Roberts (1996, ch. 7). Particular events, he said, can reinforce a social structure, or undermine it, or initiate a new structure. For example, here are some of the events which, he says, weakened the power of the English Crown in the sixteenth century.

> Henry VIII's decision to go to war against France in 1544 meant that monastic lands that would have made the Crown financially independent were sold off to pay for the war. An adverse decision by the common-law judges in 1568 deprived the Crown of a chance to profit from England's reserves of coal. Elizabeth's decision to put political goodwill before fiscal efficiency resulted in a failure to adjust revenues to meet the rising costs engendered by inflation. The government failed to alter the Book of Rates to reflect the steady rise in import prices.
>
> (p. 141)

In fact, of course, only the first of these diminished the resources of the Crown. The others represented lost opportunities to increase its wealth. The form of the explanation, however, is clear enough. A change in the power of the Crown is explained by describing individual actions which diminished it.

Even more striking is an explanation of the growth of the hostility of Parliament towards the Crown prior to the outbreak of Civil War in 1642. This too was the result of individual actions. According to Roberts, Lawrence Stone pointed out that older members of Parliament had been offended by 'the corruption of Buckingham in the 1620s and then . . . the tyranny of Charles, Laud and Strafford in the 1630s' (Roberts, 1996, p. 148). Finally, Roberts says, they were annoyed by 'the King's refusal to dissolve the Irish army, his plotting with the English army, his taking advice from gentlemen of the bedchamber, [and] his favoring Catholics' (p. 114). These events changed the Parliamentarians' attitude to the Crown from one of respect to one of defiance, as they sought 'to wrest military, executive, and ecclesiastical power from the king' (pp. 113–14). Thus historians can understand the particular reasons for the growing hostility of the Parliamentarians without having to invoke a general theory about the causes of political revolution.

Some social changes are produced by collective action. Sometimes they are logical functions of collective actions. A rise in the price of a commodity is the logical result of all those who sell it requiring more for it in exchange. A rise in the birth rate is the logical consequence of more individual babies being born than before. Some changes are not logical but conventional consequences of collective actions. Thus a change of government might be the consequence of a majority of the electorate voting for a new party to govern them. Finally, some are just the effect of collective action, as when people in the western world decided to accord women greater rights. Not all social changes are intended, of course. One unintended effect of the women's movement seems to have been to leave many men confused about their roles in society.

Enough has been said, I hope, to show that there is a great variety of ways in which individuals can bring about social change. Historians are aware of these, and can identify the causes operative in each particular case. Because there is such a variety of ways in which social changes are brought about, it has proved extremely difficult to find plausible general theories of social change. Nevertheless the attempt has been made, not without some successes, and to this attempt we shall now turn.

THE REGULARITY (POSITIVIST) THEORY OF EXPLANATION

This theory of social explanation is probably called 'positivist' because it was recommended by Auguste Comte in his *Cours de Philosophie Positive* (1830–42). Comte said that explanations of social change should be based upon laws of cause and effect which are testable by observation, like the laws of science. He opposed religious explanations, in terms of God's influence on events; and he opposed explanations in terms of other metaphysical forces, like Hegel's Spirit, which was said to be moving in history to make humankind more rational, self-conscious and free. These theories could not be tested. He also preferred scientific explanations because they were of practical use, unlike those teleological ones. Scientific explanations enable people to predict and control events by identifying conditions necessary and sufficient for their occurrence.

Some serious problems arose in trying to provide explanations on the positivist model, which I will discuss in this section. I will first describe attempts to discover general laws describing conditions *sufficient* to produce certain effects. It has proved difficult to find all the conditions which must be present for certain social effects to occur. The most we can show are conditions which make the outcome highly probable. Next I consider the problem of establishing *the counterfactual force* of such generalizations, which they must have for explanatory purposes. They must be able to state that if the conditions ever were present then the effect would occur. Finally I discuss the need for causal laws to state conditions which were *necessary* for the occurrence of the effect, or at least which were such that their absence would have made such an effect far less probable in the circumstances. We have general knowledge of the various possible causes of many events, and on the basis of this historians pick out the causes of particular events whose occurrence they want to explain.

Sufficient conditions

The causal generalizations which social scientists have discovered do not state sufficient social conditions for certain changes, but rather provide evidence of certain tendencies at work. A well-known example is to be found in Durkheim's study of suicide. Durkheim noticed that the rate of suicides varied between different social groups, though the individual reasons for suicide were remarkably similar. To explain why more people committed suicide in one group rather than another, he looked for relevant social differences between them. He noted, for example, that 'Suicide varies inversely with the degree of integration of the social groups of which the individual forms a part' (Durkheim, 1952, p. 209). Those who belong to the Catholic Church, who are married, and who live in a settled rural community are less likely to commit suicide than are Protestants who are single and live in towns where there is much social mobility. Using this generalization Durkheim could account for variations in the rate of suicide between different places, thus providing useful contrastive explanations. Clearly, however, social isolation does not suffice to produce suicide; it merely produces a tendency in that direction among some people.

Many lawlike generalizations are to be found in economics. Some are so familiar as to be commonplace. For example, we all know that if two or more products meet a need equally well, and one is significantly cheaper than the rest, then sales of the cheaper product will be higher than those of the more expensive. The comparison of prices helps to explain differences in the market share of two products, providing a useful contrastive explanation. But the comparative cheapness of a product is not the only factor which contributes to large sales, so by itself it does not provide an adequate causal explanation.

Social scientists and historians found that they could often identify social causes which made a certain kind of change quite likely, but frequently circumstances intervened to prevent the usual effect. To overcome this problem, historians looking for a statement that was universally true would qualify their generalization, to take account of all the possible intervening conditions they could think of. Even so it was probable that they had overlooked some, and so they would declare the generalizations were true only *ceteris paribus*, other things being equal, i.e. non-interfering.

Here is an example of a qualified generalization from economics. Raymond Boudon has set out the conditions under which it is true that if the price of a product goes up, then demand for it will fall.

> Let us suppose that product P meets a need, that on average each individual consumes p units of P per unit of time, and that on the market there is a product Q with exactly the same virtues as P. Let us also suppose that Q is as well known as P, that is, that everyone is just as well informed about not only its existence but also its qualities. Further, let us suppose that both products have the same 'image', in the sense that there is no difference between them as far as their secondary characteristics rather than their fitness for purpose are concerned, that is, that there are no non-essential differences (such as one being a home and one a foreign product) that might affect purchasing behaviour. If all these conditions ... are met ... an increase in the price of P will cause a fall in demand.

> (Boudon, 1986, p. 63)

Why is Boudon so confident that under these conditions the generalization is true? A positivist would say because the generalization, so qualified, can be verified by observation. Under these conditions it can be seen that an increase in the price of P will always be followed by a fall in demand for it. The positivist looks for lawlike generalizations which can be proved from observation. In fact, I suggest, what makes this generalization very plausible is the fact that it is implied by basic rational choice theory. Assuming that people want to maximize benefit to themselves, and that they have complete knowledge of the range of products and complete freedom of choice, then they will prefer the cheaper product. But the positivist does not appeal to theory, just to what can be observed.

What one observes in the real world, however, is that all sorts of unpredictable things can occur which falsify such generalizations. Even if all the conditions set out by Boudon are satisfied, it might happen that information about a future shortage of products like P and Q causes people to buy all they can, in which case demand for P would increase, even though its price increases relative to other equivalent products. One can never be sure of all the conditions under which generalizations like the one being considered are true. This inability to know that one has identified all the *ceteris paribus* conditions has led some authors to declare that such generalizations are untestable (Rosenberg, 1976, p. 134; Hausman, 1981, p. 26; Klein, 1982, p. 42).

Here is another example, this time of a social historian trying to arrive at a true causal generalization about the causes of food riots. In an interesting reflection upon the causes of popular disturbances in England between 1700 and 1870, John Stevenson admits that food riots commonly occurred when food prices were high and were judged to be unfair, so that these can be held to be common causes of the riots which did occur. But such circumstances did not always produce riots:

> There were many occasions when crowds assembled or milled about, rumours circulated, and a kind of 'pre-riot' situation developed. At this stage a great deal depended on relatively fortuitous factors: time and again disturbances were averted by the intervention of magistrates addressing angry crowds or by a judicious show of force, and leaders of agitations themselves often took decisive action to urge their followers to disperse when it appeared events might pass beyond their control. But inevitably in many of these situations, an inexperienced troop commander, an over-zealous policeman, a particularly determined section of a crowd, or some other event could tip the balance one way or another.
>
> (Stevenson, 1979, pp. 303–4)

Does it really matter if the causal generalizations used to explain social changes are not universally true? In practice we look for causal explanations which make the outcome as probable as possible. Sometimes this probability is very high. For example, I cannot think of any more circumstances under which Boudon's generalization would be false, assuming a free market. So it could be used, once all the qualifications had been added, to explain a fall in demand very effectively. On the other hand, food riots cannot be so readily predicted, so it seems we have to be content with a much weaker explanation.

Counterfactual force

So far I have been discussing the difficulty of finding universal generalizations for use in explanations, but another problem is deciding their counterfactual force. To explain the occurrence of social events we need generalizations which say what conditions would produce such changes, whether those conditions actually exist or not. Some universal generalizations are only accidentally true, and lack counterfactual force. The fact that everyone who has come into my room today has been wearing shoes does not imply that if someone else were to enter she would be wearing shoes. Generalizations of a counterfactual form are said to be lawlike, as opposed to accidental, indicative conditionals. The truth of lawlike generalizations is not just a matter of chance. (For a fuller discussion of this distinction, see McCullagh, 1984, pp. 132–9.)

The generalizations which historians discover frequently appear to be nothing more than general descriptions which are just accidentally true. Georg Simmel (1977) suggested that such generalizations are best seen as general descriptions of what happened in a certain period. He said that 'they constitute reality as if "from a distance"' (p. 138), like a work of art.

> The work of art may only represent the most general elements of reality in imaginary forms. Nevertheless, these forms have their own "truth" insofar as

they maintain a constant relationship – even though it may be pale and indistinct and only determined by the sense of this particular style – to the immediacy of existence.

(p. 139)

By calling these generalizations just general descriptions of how things usually happened, Simmel implied that the generalizations had no counterfactual force, and so could not justify any causal claims. If so, one could not use them to argue that a certain event was either necessary or sufficient for another, because from a distance one overlooks exceptions to the rule which nevertheless may exist.

It is certainly difficult to prove that the causal generalizations which might help to explain social changes are indeed lawlike, with counterfactual force. Charles Tilly is one who has examined as many instances of the generalizations he frames as he can find, in order to test their validity. He has recognized, as have most social scientists, that social generalizations are nearly all true only in certain restricted social and cultural conditions, that is, only in certain societies for certain periods of time. As sociologists study historical examples more closely, he said, 'the attempt to formulate general laws of revolution, of social movements, or of worker organization will give way to a quest for regularities in the collective action of particular historical eras' (Tilly, 1981, p. 44). In seventeenth-century France, for example, Tilly said that peasant rebellions were not designed to seize control of the land from landlords, as some 'widely held sociological models of peasant rebellion' (p. 139) suggest (he mentioned theories by Jeffrey Paige (on pp. 109–10), Gerrit Huizer (on pp. 110–11) and Henry Landsberger (on p. 11), as all stating this view). Rather he found that they were generally directed against government exactions in support of the armies. On the basis of his study of numerous such rebellions, Tilly put forward the following generalization about seventeenth-century France:

> Where peasant communities have a measure of solidarity and some means of collective defence, where new or increased claims clearly violate publicly known agreements or principles, where some visible person or group that is close at hand stands to gain by the new demands on the peasants, and where effective coalition partners are available to the peasants, collective resistance becomes likely. When that resistance is sustained and involves organized attacks on the enemy, we have peasant rebellion.
>
> (p. 139)

Tilly's generalization is based upon a virtually exhaustive study of peasant rebellions in seventeenth-century France. But even so, how can we be sure that it has counterfactual force, and that it is not just accidentally true of the cases he has studied?

There is no doubt that if this or any generalization is true of a wide variety of cases, then it is more convincing to explain this fact by declaring the generalization to be lawlike, than by saying that the similarities were all a coincidence, a matter of chance. The greater the number and variety of cases studied, the more reliable the generalization will be. I suspect that Tilly's data warrant us believing his generalization to have counterfactual force within the place and period he has studied, namely within France in the seventeenth century.

What helps to establish the counterfactual force of generalizations such as these, I think, is the social theory from which they can be derived. It is widely assumed that people will generally defend their own interests whenever they perceive them to be threatened and are able to do so. Indeed Tilly's generalization says little more than that! This generalization underlies such an immense range of observable cases as to be virtually uncontested. But as I said before, positivists try to justify their lawlike generalizations by observation, not by theory. A theory posits the causal influences at work, rather than describes an observable regularity.

Necessary conditions

For positivist explanations to be satisfactory, they cannot state just circumstances which would have made an event of the kind being explained very probable. They must also describe causes of such an event, events or states of affairs which were necessary in the circumstances for its occurrence. To use a familiar example, a fall in air pressure explains the occurrence of a storm whereas a fall in a barometer does not, for although each is sufficient to make a storm probable, only the fall in air pressure is necessary for its occurrence. In the social sciences we cannot prove that a cause was strictly necessary for its effect, that is that the effect could not possibly have occurred in its absence, but we can argue that had the cause not occurred the probability of such an effect would have been much less in the circumstances.

To identify the causes of an event, historians make use of what Michael Scriven called 'backward-looking generalizations' (Scriven, 1966, pp. 250–4). Most events in history can have a variety of causes. Backward-looking generalizations set out the variety of possible causes of an event. These generalizations have to be lawlike too, stating what would be the possible causes of a certain kind of event were it to occur. (For a discussion of judgements of contingent necessity, see McCullagh, 1984, pp. 185–93.)

Let me first illustrate this process of identifying causes with an example from physics. Nancy Cartwright says that, according to current physical theory, there are two or three possible states of affairs which could cause two bodies to be attracted to one another. They might be attracted by simple gravitational force, as stated by the law of gravitation; they might be attracted because of their electrical potentials, as specified by Coulomb's law; and it is possible that they are attracted because of certain nuclear forces (see Cartwright, 1983, pp. 57–73). Suppose that scientists have examined a very large number and variety of cases of attraction, and have found that all of them took place in one or other of the three kinds of conditions just mentioned. It would be reasonable for the scientists to believe that this list exhausts the possible causes of attraction, even though there is no way of proving this belief to be true, and even though it could be false. Consequently, it would be reasonable for a scientist to say, in any particular case of two bodies being attracted, that the event was caused by whichever of these three conditions happened to be present. It is possible that a fourth, unknown cause, was present and operative; but in the circumstances it is reasonable to believe otherwise.

Precisely the same can be said of social causation. The well-known very general theories of social change describe different common causes of social change. Functional theories point to a disturbance of the equilibrium of a social system threatening its viability; conflict theories refer to conflicts of interest which cause change when the power of the governing class is weakened; and there are other theories, such as what Percy S. Cohen calls 'the malintegration theory', which identifies incompatibilities between different parts of a social system as the cause of social changes (1968, pp. 186–91), and 'the cultural interaction theory', which explains social change as the result of the interaction of two different cultures (p. 203). When social scientists or social historians find one of these theories exemplified in a particular situation relating to a particular social change, then there is a good chance that the theory has correctly identified an important cause of that social change.

In all these cases, the scientist and the historian do not expect to find a universally necessary condition of the change they are investigating, for none exists. Rather they want to discover what conditions were necessary in the circumstances for the occurrence of that change and tended to produce it. If they have a more or less exhaustive list of the alternative possible causal processes, and can find only one of them present in a particular case, then they are justified in saying that it was very probably necessary for the occurrence of the change in question in those circumstances. They could be wrong, for there could have been another cause operative of which they were ignorant, which brought about the change instead.

Sometimes a social change is known generally to be the cumulative effect of several important causes. Thus when Phyllis Deane wanted to explain the economic development of Britain during the Industrial Revolution, she began by stating: 'If we ask ourselves what are the main determinants of economic growth ... we can classify them under four main heads: natural resources, technical progress, accumulation of capital and increase in the labour supply' (Deane, 1965, p. 134). These may not all have been necessary, but they generally are, so Deane looked for evidence of them all.

Positivists hope to produce explanations which refer to conditions which made the effect inevitable, that is, which were sufficient for its occurrence. Such an understanding is what is needed for perfect prediction and control. As Cartwright has argued, it is almost impossible to satisfy this requirement in the natural sciences, because in reality there is so often some extraneous force which could interfere with a common causal process. The possibility of such interference is much greater in society, where extraneous contingencies often intervene to disrupt normal social processes. Adequate explanations are not necessarily predictive. Explanations are retrodictive, explaining why something happened once we know that it has. The fact that it occurred implies that the process which produced it was not interrupted, or rather, was not totally disrupted. But that process, even in isolation, might not have made the occurrence of the event inevitable, nor even very probable. In nature many causal processes merely make their effects probable, and in society this is normally the case.

There is a further problem about positivist explanations which must be mentioned. Sometimes the generalization used in such explanations itself seems to cry out for explanation. We may not doubt that the regularity it describes truly exists, but we wonder why the causes have the tendency to produce the effects that they do. There are two kinds of further explanation which can be relevant at this point. One describes the intervening social process; and the other describes the intervening psychological processes as well. Let me illustrate. It is well known that in many societies, when banks raise interest rates on home loans, the housing industry tends to lay off tradesmen. Knowing this, you might wonder why, and the kind of information you want is about the social process which connects the two. As rates go up, the number of loans falls, so that demand for new housing is reduced, and builders, lacking money to pay all their employees, are compelled to lay some of them off. Here details of the intervening social process explains why the generalization is true. But each of these links in the chain could require explanation, and the processes by which they came about involve psychological facts, referring to people's desires, beliefs and de-liberations. As mortgage rates increase, many people decide they cannot afford to repay a loan, and so choose to put off the purchase of a new home. That is why as interest rates increase, the number of loans falls, and the demand for new housing is reduced.

On the other hand, some social regularities, like those relating the demand for a product to its cost, are so familiar and well understood in terms of existing theories that reference to them requires no further explanation at all. So if historians pick out regularities which conform to existing well-known theories, then they will not need further explanation. Until a generalization can be related to a well-established theory, it remains a bit tentative.

The generalizations of most use to historians are those which identify tendencies at work in history. Because tendencies are often offset by other forces in the field, generalizations describing them are not descriptions of an invariable sequence of events, or even of a sequence which occurs with a great frequency. Tendency statements are parts of a theory designed to account for observed patterns in nature. For instance the arc of a child's swing is a function of the force of the push and the force of gravity, working against one another.

Rather than look for highly qualified generalizations which describe what generally happens in a certain society during a certain period, historians prefer to know what tendencies were at work, and discover the different ways they interacted on each occasion. A person's tendency to buy an imported product because it is cheaper than its competitors can be offset by a tendency to buy a local product when it is available, even though it is more expensive than others.

THE USE OF COMPARATIVE METHODS TO PROVIDE CAUSAL EXPLANATIONS

As it is very difficult to discover the causes sufficient to produce social changes, many historians and others have turned to using Mill's methods of comparative analysis, which help to identify conditions necessary, if not sufficient, for certain kinds of outcome. Nancy Cartwright has even recommended this move in physics. She has pointed out that these methods are in fact the basis of experimental procedures, in which individual variables are altered to see whether there is a corresponding effect in the phenomenon to be explained (Cartwright, 1983, pp. 7, 58, 98). Cartwright observed: 'Although philosophers generally believe in laws and deny causes, explanatory practice in physics is just the reverse' (p. 86). This opinion is not widely held (see for example Redhead, 1990, pp. 145–7), but it represents one reaction to positivism.

John Stuart Mill's 'methods of experimental inquiry' are set out in his book *A System of Logic* (Bk 3, ch. 8). It is worth quoting these methods of discovering causes, as Mill stated them most succinctly.

> First Canon: If two or more instances of the phenomenon under investigation have only one circumstance in common, the circumstance in which alone all the instances agree is the cause (or effect) of the given phenomenon. (The Method of Agreement)
>
> Second Canon: If an instance in which the phenomenon under investigation occurs, and an instance in which it does not occur, have every circumstance in common save one, that one occurring only in the former; the circumstance in which alone the two instances differ is the effect, or the cause, or an indispensable part of the cause, of the phenomenon. (Method of Difference)
>
> (Mill, 1949, Bk 3, ch. 8; pp. 255, 256, 259)

Mill's Third Canon was the combination of these two. These methods are useful in identifying causes necessary for the occurrence of an effect. It might be thought that if one condition (C) is present whenever a certain effect (E) occurs, as in the First Canon, that it must be both necessary and sufficient for the effect. This is not so, for there might well be cases in which C produces another outcome. These cases would not have been examined by following the First Canon. Suppose you wanted to know what caused people to die, who coughed up blood. You might find that all cases had one thing in common, namely tuberculosis infection. It would be wrong to conclude that TB was sufficient as well as necessary for such deaths, because many who get TB recover from it. Mill's canons are of use only in helping people discover conditions necessary, but not sufficient, for a certain kind of effect. To test the sufficiency of a cause, one would have to follow a different canon: If a circumstance or group of circumstances established as necessary for the phenomenon under investigation is always followed or accompanied by that phenomenon, and no other condition accompanies every case, then that circumstance or group of circumstances is sufficient for the given phenomenon. We could call this the Method of Constant Conjunction.

Even in cases of natural science, Mill's methods are not sufficient to prove beyond all possibility of error that a circumstance is universally necessary for a certain kind of effect. They would establish a circumstance as universally necessary only if every relevant case had been examined. In practice there always remains the possibility that an unexamined case will show that something previously judged to have been universally necessary for an effect was not. Nevertheless, if quite a large number and variety of cases have been examined, and the conditions set out in these canons are met, that would make it reasonable to believe that a necessary condition for the phenomenon in question has been identified.

Although some have advocated the use of Mill's canons for discovering causes of social change, Mill himself declared them unusable in social contexts (Mill, 1949, Bk 6, ch. 7, pp. 573–8). Concerning the Method of Agreement, he said that social changes are usually produced by such a plurality of causes that there is no hope of isolating just one as significant in all cases, as required by the Method. And concerning the Method of Difference, he noted that social changes never occur in precisely similar situations, save one, as required by that Method. The methods were designed for the investigation of natural, not social, causes, ideally in experimental conditions in which the number of possible causes could be limited. Why, then, have they proved popular with some social scientists?

The answer, I suggest, is that although they cannot be used to prove causal relationships in the social sciences, they suggest ways of testing and improving general causal hypotheses. If some kind of event or state of affairs is necessary for the occurrence of another, then we will expect it to be present whenever such an effect occurs, and we will expect the effect to be absent in its absence.

A neat example of these methods of testing causal generalizations can be found in George Rudé's essay 'The Study of Revolutions' (1976a). Rudé admires Lenin's theory of the causes of revolution. It consists of four points, he said. A political revolution is likely to occur if there is a crisis within the ruling class; the suffering and resentments of the common people have become acute; political activity of dissident groups has increased; and there is revolutionary leadership, willing and able to mobilize popular resistance to the existing regime. To demonstrate the importance of the last factor, which sociologists have often overlooked, Rudé noted situations in which only the first three conditions existed, and no revolution occurred: Germany in 1848, the 1860s, 1923 and 1931; Russia in 1859–61, 1879 and 1880, 1904 and 1905; Italy in 1920; and Holland in 1787. On the other hand, he said, all four conditions were present prior to the American, French and Russian revolutions (pp. 75–6). These cases suggest that the fourth condition is necessary, and in the presence of the others sufficient, for the occurrence of a political revolution.

Hugh Trevor-Roper (1984) used historical comparisons to test causal hypotheses and also to seek the true causes of the persecution of witches in Europe in the sixteenth and seventeenth centuries. The persecution of witches became steadily worse in Europe between 1500 and 1650, and Trevor-Roper asked: 'How are we to explain this extraordinary episode in European history?' (p. 97). He considered two possible causal explanations which others had suggested. The first was that such persecution was a product of superstition. But Trevor-Roper observed that people were no more superstitious in these centuries than in the Dark and Early Middle Ages, when there had been no persecution. So superstition was not sufficient to produce persecution. The second explanation he tested was that which attributed the witch-craze to the miseries of the fourteenth century, particularly to the Black Death and to the Hundred Years War. But he noted that by the sixteenth and seventeenth centuries those miseries had passed, and Europe was enjoying a period of recovery and expansion. In this case misery was not a necessary condition of persecution. Finally, Trevor-Roper noted a similarity between the persecution of Jews by the Inquisition in Spain and that of the witches in the Alps and the Pyrenees, which he said 'suggests . . . that the pressure behind both was social. The witch and the Jew both represent social non-conformity' (p. 110). The persecution of Communists during the period of McCarthyism in the USA in the 1950s he saw as confirming this hypothesis. These, he said, were times when 'social fear, the fear of a different kind of society, was given intellectual form as a heretical ideology and suspect individuals were then persecuted by reference to the heresy' (p. 128).

Christina Larner, however, has pointed out that while fear of non-conformity may have motivated the élite, peasants often accused people of witchcraft to explain misfortunes in their personal lives. Furthermore, massive persecution of 'witches' was also a product of changes in the law, which made it possible to accuse people of witchcraft without fear of recrimination, and of the development of theories of witchcraft which were widely disseminated once printing began (Larner, 1984, pp. 48–60).

These remarks illustrate the limitations of the comparative method. They can be summed up by saying that the number and variety of cases which historians consider are almost never, on their own, sufficient to warrant causal claims. It is always possible that there are unexamined cases which show that something identified as a cause is not universally necessary or sufficient for a certain kind of event. The desire to suppress non-conformists did not explain peasant de-nunciations of witches, so it was not a universally necessary condition of their persecution. It was, however, necessary in many cases; that is to say, it was often contingently necessary. Nor was it sufficient, because large-scale persecution depended partly upon the other factors mentioned by Larner. And there is no way of being sure that she has noticed them all.

Theda Skocpol is well known for promoting Mill's canons as the best means of establishing hypotheses about the causes of collective behaviour and social change. She refers to Samuel Beer, Neil J. Smelser, and her teacher, Barrington Moore jr. as previous exponents of this method (Skocpol, 1984). Arthur L. Stinchcombe also deserves credit for employing it. Skocpol claims to have employed this method in her grand book *States and Social Revolutions. A Comparative Analysis of France, Russia, and China* (1979). Social revolutions, she says, 'centrally involve class struggles and result in basic social-structural transformations' (pp. 28–9). But such revolutions, as she understands them, also involve profound political changes. 'Social revolutions ... have changed state structures as much or more as they have changed class relations, societal values, and social institutions' (p. 29). Existing general theories about the causes of revolutions are unsatisfactory, Skocpol argues, partly because they use very vague terms whose scope is indefinite ('What society, for example, lacks widespread relative deprivation of one sort or another? And how do we tell a synchronized social system when we see one?' (p. 34)), and partly because they have not been adequately tested against historical cases. Marxists, for example, in highlighting class conflict and changes in class relations as causes of revolution, 'have not devised ways to test whether these factors really distinguish between revolutions and other kinds of transformations or between successful and abortive revolutionary outbreaks' (p. 34). She advocates the use of comparative methods 'to develop, test, and refine causal, explanatory hypotheses about events or structures integral to macro-units such as nation-states' (p. 36).

Skocpol believes that historical comparisons can be used to 'validate' causal claims:

> France, Russia, and China will serve as three positive cases of successful social revolution, and I shall argue that these cases reveal similar causal patterns despite their many other differences. In addition, I shall invoke negative cases for the purpose of validating various particular parts of the causal argument. In so doing, I shall always construct contrasts that maximize the similarities of the negative case(s) to the positive case(s) in every apparently relevant respect except the causal sequence that the contrast is supposed to validate. Thus, for example, the abortive Russian Revolution of 1905 will be contrasted to the successful Revolution of 1917 in order to validate arguments about the crucial contribution to social-revolutionary success in Russia of war-related processes that led to the breakdown of state repressive capacities.
>
> (p. 37)

Skocpol argues that the revolutions of France, China and Russia were very different in many respects, so the features they had in common may well have been of causal significance. To check whether they were, she contrasts them with situations in which a number of the suspected causes were present but a revolution did not occur, to see whether any of the causes she had identified were absent. For example, in each of the three countries she found that the monarch was unable to organize an adequate military force because 'agrarian structures impinged upon autocratic and proto-bureaucratic state organizations' (p. 99). In Japan, however, the crisis sparked by the arrival of Americans in 1853 did not lead to the fall of the Emperor, because there was not a strong landed class able to impede government reforms, as in France and China; nor did the Emperor have to rely so heavily upon foreign money to maintain his power, as did the Tsar of Russia (pp. 100–4).

Using such comparative methods, Skocpol locates three common causes of the successful social revolutions she has chosen: '(1) the incapacitation of the central state machineries of the Old Regimes; (2) wide-spread rebellions by the lower classes, most crucially peasants; (3) attempts by mass-mobilizing political leaderships to consolidate revolutionary state power' (p. 41). Her analysis is plausible, but the question to be asked is whether it is indeed 'validated', or proved correct, by the comparative methods she has used. There is good reason to doubt that it is.

Although Skocpol believes the comparative methods to be of value, she is nevertheless also aware of their shortcomings. She admits that they cannot yield universal causal generalizations. Revolutions can occur in a variety of different ways, depending upon the internal social and political structure of the country, and its external situation as well (pp. 288–92). Even in the cases of France, Russia and China, the comparative methods do not in themselves guarantee the accuracy of the analysis. History does not permit perfect control of all potentially relevant variables.

> Thus, strategic guesses have to be made about what causes are actually likely to be operative – that is, which ones could, or could not actually affect the object of study. The upshot is that there always are unexamined contextual features of the historical cases that interact with the causes being explicitly examined in ways the comparative historical analysis either does not reveal, or must simply assume to be irrelevant.
>
> (pp. 38)

So there may be important common causes which the historian has overlooked. And it is possible that the correlations which the historian has noted do not represent a causal relationship, but are between things which have a common cause. Skocpol remarks that Smelser has discussed ways of handling these difficulties (p. 303, note 96). Smelser rightly suggests that comparative methods become more reliable when a large number and variety of cases are studied (Smelser, 1976, pp. 200–2). But when, as in Skocpol's study, the number of cases is small, then 'the number of potentially operative variables ... far exceeds the number of cases studied' (p. 202), and they cannot be controlled. Similarly Ragin has written of studies such as Skocpol's: 'there is rarely a sufficient variety of cases to prove or disprove causal arguments' (Ragin, 1987, p. 31). They certainly do not validate her conclusions, as she claimed.

When the number of observed correlations between two variables is large, then they may provide significant support for the claim that the two are causally related. This will be so when either they are made from such a variety of circumstances that other possible causes of the effect are reduced if not eliminated; or when the observations are of very similar cases, and variations in the supposed cause are regularly accompanied by corresponding variations in the effect, and no other regular change can explain it (see Smelser, 1976, pp. 211–20). Even so, an investigator cannot be quite sure that the real cause has not been overlooked. Charles Tilly has summed up the difficulties in interpreting evidence of concomitant variations quite vividly.

> Let us suppose, for example, that the positive association [in developing countries] between levels of schooling at the beginning of a period and the

extent of economic growth during the period held up through a wide variety of samples, measures, and specifications of the model. That association would still be compatible with any of the following interpretations:

1 Increases in schooling do, indeed, promote economic growth.
2 Economic growth promotes increases in schooling.
3 Increases in schooling are unrelated to economic growth, but level of schooling and current rate of economic growth both depend on the extent of previous contact with rich countries.
4 Increases in schooling are unrelated to economic growth, but economic growth is now in the early stages of a long-term diffusion from countries with high levels of schooling to countries with lower levels of schooling.
5 A temporary wave of economic growth is in the late stages of propagation from countries with low levels of schooling to countries with high levels of schooling.

If the dependent variable had been static (as it often is in such analyses), even a wider range of interpretations would have been consistent with the evidence.

(Tilly, 1984, pp. 36–7)

If the comparative methods do not validate Skocpol's analysis, then why is it so plausible? I suggest that the analysis is plausible because it is based upon theories which are already accepted as probably true, and because the cases which Skocpol has examined support and do not invalidate those theories. Skocpol is aware that a priori generalizations play a part in forming her hypotheses: 'some theoretical ideas always need to be used to set up the terms of a comparative investigation' (1984, p. 384). But she has not appreciated the degree to which these generalizations support the hypotheses based upon them. Skocpol begins by assuming a conflict theory of society. Skocpol, like Marx, Dahrendorf and others, believes that societies are always divided into groups with conflicting interests, and that order is maintained by the power of a dominant group. Once the power of an inferior group is thought equal or superior to that of a dominant group, then social struggle is likely. And if the dominant group is in fact weaker, then it will be displaced. (For a useful comparison of consensus and conflict theories, see Percy S. Cohen, 1968, pp. 166–72.) On the basis of this theory, Skocpol looks for evidence of powerful interest groups which are so dissatisfied with the government of a country that they would like to take control; and evidence of government weakness sufficient to allow it to be displaced. She is particularly proud of having discovered two causes of government weakness or strength which have been overlooked in traditional Marxist accounts. One is a country's international relations. The French government in the eighteenth century was unable to carry out its tax reforms, against the resistance of the *parlements* and people, and after the War for American Independence it was financially exhausted. The calling of the Estates General was meant to solve the crisis, but it precipitated the attack on the Crown and a political revolution. The Tsarist government of Russia was crippled by the First World War, leaving it vulnerable to a Bolshevik revolution.

The second is the observation that the power of a state is not always a function of its social support, as has been supposed, but can be quite independent of class backing, residing in a bureaucracy, police and army directly under government control (1979, p. 29).

Skocpol's analysis gains its plausibility from the plausibility of the basic theory on which it is built: if a powerful interest group in society wants to displace the government, and the government becomes sufficiently weak, then there is a good chance that a revolution in government, and perhaps in society, will occur. The novelty of her analysis came from seeing how this applied in particular historical cases, and thus discovering sources of government strength and weakness which had previously been overlooked by Marxist theory. The comparative method enabled her to develop a slightly more detailed version of the general theory, which fitted the cases she compared. But interestingly she admits at the end that the same general theory has been instantiated in different ways in the revolutions which have occurred this century (1979, pp. 288–92). In some cases the government has been a colonial one, and the revolutionary movement has been funded from abroad.

Skocpol's comparative studies provide some confirmation for the general theory she uses, illustrating the claim that the causes of revolution which the theory sets out are both sufficient and necessary for such a social change. The cases which conform to the theory and with one another suggest that the causes are sufficient; and the cases which differ from it support the claim that the causes are necessary, for where they do not occur, and other things are equal, then a revolution does not occur either. But the confirmation provided by these cases is weak, for the reasons stated before.

Dennis Smith has remarked that Skocpol has not tried to falsify the generalizations she has developed, so that they have not been tested as rigorously as they could be. He suggests that conditions in Germany after the First World War should have produced a social revolution according to her theory, but in fact none occurred (Dennis Smith, 1983, pp. 160–1).

The failure to test theoretical assumptions rigorously has produced some very unconvincing history. The historian's predicament can be explained thus. Suppose an historian believes a certain social fact regularly causes a certain effect, then frequently that theory is confirmed by an analysis of instances, where the instances are examined with only that theory in mind. To test a theoretical assumption, the historian should (1) try to find instances in which the cause did not produce the effect, to see whether it really was sufficient for the effect; and (2) look hard for other possible causes of the effect to check whether it was necessary for the effect, and whether there were other necessary conditions as well. The mere fact that in a number of cases an effect E is preceded by a condition C does not mean that C is sufficient for E, and if the number of cases is small C may not even be necessary for E.

Examples of really woeful explanations have been described by R.J. Holton in his book *The Transition from Feudalism to Capitalism* (1985, ch. 3). He describes three different explanations of the transition in Europe from feudalism to capitalism, each of which rests upon a prior theoretical assumption which seems to have been quite untested, and is certainly quite inadequate.

P. Sweezy and I. Wallerstein adopted what Holton called an '"exchange relations" perspective', pointing out that the manorial system was not suited to producing goods for trade, so that to meet the demand for luxury, manufactured and other goods, a new system of production had to develop. This was the capitalist system, with its more efficient division of labour. Holton doubts that the opportunity for increased trade was enough to bring about the change to capitalism (p. 78), but he explains why Sweezy and Wallerstein thought it was.

> The key to their explanation of capitalist expansion is seen in terms of an underlying tendency of humankind to 'truck, barter and exchange' in pursuit of individual self-interest. When faced with the question why there should have arisen an expansive force for capitalist development external to the logic of feudalism, Sweezy and Wallerstein seem to rely (at least implicitly) on the Smithian 'hidden hand' of economic self-interest to provide the teleological force to resolve problems created by the relatively 'static', 'undynamic' character of feudalism.
>
> (p. 77)

Holton finds their explanation unconvincing because he does not share their assumption that a 'hidden hand' would bring about the changes necessary to maximize the economic interests of the nations involved. If Sweezy and Wallerstein had tested their assumption by looking for cases of delayed development, they might have discovered that changes do not always occur to meet people's perceived economic needs or desires. E.L. Jones has identified a range of conditions which can impede economic growth, including the greed of powerful governments in taking resources for war and consumption, and some very conservative institutions and values (see Jones, 1988, chs 5–8).

The second group which Holton describes is that which adopts 'the endogenous "Marxist" property relations perspective', and includes M. Dobb, R. Hilton, R. Brenner and J. Merrington. These authors explain the emergence of capitalism as a result of contradictions within feudalism, especially the 'fundamental contradiction between the expanding demands of the feudal ruling class for revenue (for such purposes as warfare, luxury consumption, etc.) and the relative inefficiency of feudal production in continuing to meet such needs over the long term' (pp. 80–1). In the West, though not in Eastern Europe, the increased demands made on the peasants caused conflicts which resulted in the peasants achieving considerable independence, and the development in England of agrarian capitalism, later supported by the state. These authors, Holton explains, are convinced of 'the determining role of the material class interests of landowners as the basic driving force of the transition to capitalism'. They see material self-interest as 'a structural compulsion on economic action' (p. 88). Furthermore, 'Dobb, like the later Marx, emphasises a historical teleology, in which humankind is seen as striving to overcome the fetters of unmastered nature and alienating social relations. Both of these are seen as constraining humanity's rich creative potential realisable through production' (p. 81). Clearly, once again, a whole range of important causes have been overlooked. Material self-interest might drive people to economic innovation and expansion, but much more than this is needed to account for the development of industrial capitalism: the existence of natural resources and technology, appropriate government policies, and availability of capital and labour, to name but a few (see Mokyr, 1985).

The third Marxist view of the development of capitalism which Holton describes is that of Perry Anderson. It is quite rich and complex, but one of its main features is Anderson's belief that capitalism emerged from the development of towns in the midst of the feudal order, towns in which ancient Roman law of property was accepted. In these towns he saw the development of an urban bourgeoisie, which was eventually to expand and take political control. Holton remarks that

> it does not seem unreasonable to posit an implicit commitment on his [Anderson's] part to a reading of human history in terms of the development of a social order capable of universalising the legacy of 'classical civilisation' – 'its urban policy and culture' – thereby sustaining what Anderson clearly regards as the cumulative development of rational knowledge.
>
> (p. 99)

Holton believes that Anderson's account of the transition from feudalism to capitalism is too simple. It 'obscures the nature and significance of internal transformations of the rural social structure in western Europe (especially England) in the centuries leading up to the eighteenth- and nineteenth-century industrialisation' (p. 96).

Holton's own position is that 'there is no single pattern of capitalist development within the nation-states of early modern Europe' (p. 146). The evolutionary paradigm inherited from the nineteenth century, he says, has proved inadequate, and no agreed paradigm has yet replaced it (p. 219).

> Instead of the search for a unitary causal force behind the emergence of capitalism, what seems called for is a greater tolerance of causal pluralism, multilinear patterns of social change, analyses of particular unrepeatable historical conjunctures and explanation in terms of contingent rather than historically necessary patterns of social development.
>
> (p. 145)

This does not mean giving up the attempt to explain the emergence of capitalism, and instead explaining the particular events which, taken together, constitute that emergence. Rather it means allowing that the causes of the development of capitalism differed in each country. Holton still prefers structural explanations of the emergence of capitalism, but he has abandoned the search for a single general explanation which will do justice to the processes of change in two or more countries (see pp. 203–5). It is interesting to note that, according to W.H. Shaw,

Marx also allowed for 'different routes to capitalism' (Shaw, 1978, p. 140). In each case he believed it emerged from the disintegration of feudalism, but he wrote that the process 'in different countries, assumes different aspects, and runs through its various phases in different orders of succession, and at different periods' (a quote from *Capital*, in Shaw, 1978, p. 140). I am not suggesting, of course, that Holton shares Marx's belief in historical determinism.

The most successful explanations of social change are those which recognize certain forces at work, furthering and inhibiting particular changes in a society. This approach is explained in the next section. Here I just want to say that comparative methods have been used to discover some general paths to social change, some common kinds of causal process at work. The methods I refer to are not Mill's methods, but just a simple method of comparison, abstraction and generalization. A brilliant example of this is Barrington Moore jr.'s *Social Origins of Dictatorship and Democracy* (1977).

Moore begins with a few assumptions. He acknowledges 'a generally evolutionary conception of history' (p. 427), by which he envisages the outcome of certain movements in history as depending upon environmental factors which assist, deflect or impede their growth. In this book he sets out 'to explain the varied political roles played by the landed upper classes and the peasantry in the transformation from agrarian societies . . . to modern industrial ones' (p. xviii). This sentence reveals the theoretical framework Moore brings to his study. He assumes that there has been a social group, or class, in each society keen to modernize, to develop capitalist institutions, and wonders how the upper and lower rural classes responded to them, and how that response affected the outcome. Clearly Moore was looking for a theory which would cover all cases of industrialization in history, for he examined instances across the world. What he found was that there was not just one path to modernization, but several. In England, for example, the capitalist class was strong, and was joined by the nobility, so that after the Civil War their progress was unimpeded. In France the capitalist class was opposed by the Crown, the nobility and the wealthy peasants, but the support of the cities and the poorer peasants, and the divisions among their opponents, enabled it to acquire remarkable rights during the Revolution. The opposition significantly slowed the process of modernization in France, however. And so it goes on. In Germany and Japan 'the bourgeois impulse was much weaker' (p. xii), and modernization was brought about by the continuing ruling classes, which supported a fascist form of government. In Russia and China the commercial and industrial class was even less significant, and revolutionary changes were brought about by the huge peasantry, which set up communist governments. It was these which then had to modernize the state, making 'the peasants its primary victims' (p. xiii). Having described the particular experiences of these and other countries in Parts 1 and 2 of the book, Moore draws general conclusions about these three kinds of change in Part 3. There is no doubt that the generalizations about these three routes to modernization emerged from Moore's study and comparison of historical cases, and were not known in advance. Notice that each generalization describes the force for modernization and the other forces which either strengthened or opposed it.

Having discovered these general patterns of events, Moore used them for explanatory purposes. For example, he wrote: 'The ways in which the landed upper classes and the peasants reacted to the challenge of commercial agriculture were decisive factors in determining the political outcome' (p. xiv). (And see his 'tentative general hypotheses' on pp. 424–6; and his five 'conditions of democratic development' on pp. 430–1.) Chapter 9, entitled 'The Peasants and Revolution', contains the most intense discussion of causal generalizations in the book, using comparisons repeatedly to set aside or correct them. He is also interested in the effect of social structures in facilitating or retarding tendencies once they are active. At one point Moore draws the following conclusions:

> The general hypothesis that emerges ... hedged with that familiar ritual phrase *ceteris paribus* used by scholars to avoid thorny issues, might be put in the following way: A highly segmented society [such as India] that depends on diffuse sanctions for its coherence and for extracting the surplus from the underlying peasantry is nearly immune to peasant rebellion because opposition is likely to take the form of creating another segment. On the other hand, an agrarian bureaucracy, or a society that depends on a central authority for extracting the surplus [such as China], is a type most vulnerable to such outbreaks. Feudal systems, where real power is diffused into several centers under the nominal authority of a weak monarch, belong somewhere in between. This hypothesis at least fits the main facts in this study.
>
> (p. 459)

Once again it is important to see that the causal generalizations which Moore arrives at gain their plausibility from the very general assumptions about the nature of social conflict and the structure of society which are brought to the study. Moore portrays societies as made up of groups and classes with various rights and privileges and with competing economic and political interests, and explains their history as an outcome of their interactions. The various structures of a society limit what is possible; and the interests of the social groups drive them to act. Each society differs somewhat in the nature of its groups and structures, and so the history of each society is different. But Moore discovers enough similarities between them to frame some generalizations about the nature of the processes of modernization within them. Their plausibility, however, derives from the plausibility of the general assumptions which underlie them.

To sum up, there is no doubt that comparative tests, loosely derived from Mill's methods, are useful in enabling historians to test existing causal generalizations, and, by identifying necessary conditions of social changes, in suggesting new ones. But by themselves, they do not provide much understanding of why social changes occurred. It is only when historians develop a theory of the causal forces which brought them about that a satisfactory understanding is achieved. Such processes are not universal, though certain patterns are common in certain kinds of society.

PROCESS EXPLANATIONS USING THEORIES OF SOCIAL CHANGE

On the basis of observed regularities, sociologists can develop general theories about the causes of social change. Some of the examples discussed in the last section involved simple theories of the sort I am referring to. The conflict theory of society, which Skocpol assumed, is built upon observations of the way in which groups of people in any society pursue their interests, often in conflict with other groups. They compete for funds, for power, and for popularity. In the case of Barrington Moore, he saw society as divided into selfish socio-economic classes, and then drew general conclusions about the way in which the political structure of a society affects the possibility of effective rebellion. He used some fairly general concepts like 'a highly segmented society', 'an agrarian bureaucracy', and 'a feudal system', referring to different political structures. Sweezy and Wallerstein were struck by the way in which groups and individuals 'truck, barter and exchange' with one another in pursuit of economic self-interest. And so on.

General theories of social change can be contrasted with the observed regularities used by positivists in several respects. Theories explain social changes by supposing that certain things, such as a capitalist class or a revolutionary group, have dispositions to act or change in certain ways in certain circumstances, but that the consequent tendencies can be modified by the tendencies of other things affecting the situation. A simple example might help. If a child sits on the end of a see-saw, it will tend to tip in that child's direction. If a heavy stone is placed on the end of a see-saw, it will tend to behave in the same way. One could explain these facts by saying that anything having a weight of more than 1 kilogram placed on the end of a beam which is balancing on a fulcrum at its centre, will tend to tip the beam down on the side of the weight. That generalization describes how balances tend to behave in certain circumstances. Of course, if children of a similar weight sit at either end of a see-saw, it will remain balanced. Physical theory explains that by saying that the force applied at one end, which tends to depress the beam, is offset by the force at the other, which does the same.

Theories focus upon the forces or the tendencies at work in a situation. As the example of the see-saw shows, the manifestation of any tendency, such as the force applied to one end of the see-saw, depends upon other forces at work in the field, such as whether or not there is an equal force or a greater force applied to the other end. In short, the generalizations of theories are formulated for an ideal closed world, telling us what would happen in very circumscribed circum-stances if a certain change were to occur. These laws offer theoretical assertions about the forces at work, but are not intended to predict the manifestation of those forces in the real world, because that depends on the other forces present. Such laws clearly differ from the covering laws which positivists seek, in that they refer to forces or tendencies, and do not predict outcomes in the actual world. (In several publications, Roy Bhaskar has contrasted the old positivist empiricist theory of explanation with what he calls 'scientific realism', in terms of theories of processes of change. See Bhaskar 1975, 1979 and 1986.)

The processes which historians and social scientists try to discover involve the stages in the working out of a tendency, more particularly the impact upon a tendency of other forces which impinge upon it. A balanced see-saw is the product of two forces upon the see-saw, but it is not a process because it does not involve change in time. Giving a child a swing is a process, however, as the force of gravity is repeatedly countered by the push which keeps the swing in motion, until the pusher stops. Similarly, a tendency to political revolution can be stimulated by good propaganda and organization, but can be impeded by a strong government army.

Process explanations begin with whatever event sets a tendency in train. Old structural–functional theories viewed societies as organisms, that is as systems of interdependent parts whose life depended upon maintaining some sort of equilibrium in the system so that it could prosper within its environment. If some event brought about a significant change either to a system or to its environment, such that the successful operation of the system was threatened, then the theory stated that some social change would occur to restore the system's equilibrium so that it could cope with the change. Thus John Foster has argued that the ruling classes in nineteenth-century Britain extended the franchise to the working classes, after their strikes and demonstrations for better conditions had threatened to disrupt the economy. By giving the workers a vote, it was possible to channel their grievances through existing political parties, removing their disruptive effect (Little, 1991, p. 98).

It is now acknowledged that groups and organizations within a society often act to preserve their viability, though society as a whole seldom does so. But even when a group or organization clearly needs to adapt to a change if it is to flourish, the necessary adaptation does not always take place. As Talcott Parsons himself pointed out, there are always people with a vested interest in the *status quo* who will resist change, so that change will not occur until they have somehow been defeated (see Strasser and Randall, 1981, pp. 170–1). There may be other reasons why a social system fails to adapt, besides this one. It may just be too weak or disorganized to do so. So threats to the viability of social systems are not sufficient to ensure the occurrence of a social change. Nor are they necessary. Sometimes systems change in order to grow, to take advantage of new opportunities, and not in response to any threat.

Chalmers Johnson has discussed process explanations with great insight in the second edition of his book *Revolutionary Change* (1983). His own original theory was rather like those described in the last section, setting out the normal stages of the process which produces a certain kind of social change, in his case political revolutions. Johnson based his theory upon a Parsonian theory of the nature of social systems. He explained how events, be they exogenous or endogenous, can upset the equilibrium of a social system by changing the 'synchronization' between its values and its political structures. When routine methods of adjustment fail to restore the equilibrium, and the power of the government to enforce its authority is weakened, then a revolutionary insurrection may result. Using this theory, carefully elaborated, Johnson identified the social causes of a range of events from simple rebellions to total revolutions.

In the second edition of his book, however, Johnson said that theories which describe the normal stages of a process of change, which he called 'conjunction theories', are inflexible. The main elements of the conjunction theory of revolution, he said, included 'alienation, recruitment, ideological conversion, protest, and structural conduciveness' (p. 182). The trouble with conjunction theories, he said, is that they fit only a few cases. As we saw in the last section, Barrington Moore found several routes to modernization; and R.J. Holton remarked that 'there is no single pattern of capitalist development within the nation-states of early modern Europe' (Holton, 1985, p. 146).

Johnson echoes Holton's plea for a more flexible approach to the explanation of social change. Process explanations, as he describes them, do not attempt to describe a general invariable sequence of events which produce a certain kind of outcome. Rather, they identify the particular process which brought each about, going back to the initial impetus for change, and noting all the forces which assisted or impeded that movement. In this way, Johnson said, they allow for the influence of contingencies, which theories of a normal sequence of change do not include (Johnson, 1983, pp. 185–7). To avoid confusion we should distinguish general process explanations, which employ a theory about the normal process by which certain events come about, and particular process explanations, which identify the particular forces which produce a particular outcome, without any suggestion that the process was a typical or normal one.

I would add that despite their flexibility, particular process explanations do not operate in a theoretical vacuum. To identify the origin of a particular historical process, and to judge the influence of various forces upon it, historians must use their general knowledge of cause and effect. And some of this will be specialized knowledge, such as Skocpol discovered by her investigations of the causes of social revolutions. She showed that the strength of a regime depends, not just upon its support among the population at home, as some Marxist theories had supposed, but also upon its international relations, and upon the power and efficiency of its own bureaucracy and police.

The importance of theory for an understanding of the origins of revolution is illustrated in another well-known theory of the general causes of rebellion, that presented by Robert Gurr in *Why Men Rebel* (1970). His theory is derived from a simple psychological theory: 'the basic frustration–aggression proposition is that the greater the frustration, the greater the quantity of aggression against the source of frustration' (p. 9). The frustration which causes political violence, he says, is caused by 'relative deprivation', that is by 'a perceived discrepancy between men's value expectations and their value capabilities' (p. 13). He goes on to explain that people value their own welfare, their power in the community and their interpersonal relationships. People tend to become aggressive if they cannot have the things they value. He sees Johnson's theory as describing just one way in which people's values are not satisfied by society, so that rebellion follows (p. 55). Gurr points out that although relative deprivation inclines people to violence, they will not in fact act violently unless they believe such action to be justified and likely to be successful. (There have been several different theories about the origins of revolutions and rebellions: see Zagorin, 1973, pp. 23–52 for a review of some of them; also Berkhofer, 1969, ch. 13.)

The difficulty of finding true descriptions of a general process of social change can be illustrated again and again. (See Percy S. Cohen, 1968, for a description and discussion of these.) Consider, for example, the conflict theory developed at some length by Ralf Dahrendorf (1959). His theory is that the distribution of authority (legitimate power) in a society results in some groups having authority over others, with the result that it is in the objective interests of one group to maintain that situation and of the others to change it, to acquire more authority for themselves. That clash of interests may produce conflict, and the conflict may produce social change of some sort. But Dahrendorf admits that conflict is neither necessary nor sufficient for social change. He remarks that some social changes can be explained by 'integration theory' rather than by conflict theory. The introduction of the position of personnel manager into many industrial and commercial enterprises can be explained as 'functionally required by large enterprises in an age of rationalization and "social ethic"' (Dahrendorf, 1959, p. 162). The positions are responses to a need, not to a conflict. Likewise it is clear that a conflict of interests will not always be sufficient to produce active social conflict and consequent social change. Interest groups will not conflict unless they are organized (see pp. 242–3). And conflict will not result in social change if those defending the status quo have greater power.

Here is another example of the difficulty of identifying universal processes of social change. Emile Durkheim, in *The Division of Labour in Society* (1964), tried to find the conditions which would transform a society which is held together by repressive laws, in some sort of tyranny, to one in which the various social units do not behave in a uniform way but are interdependent and have contractual obligations with one another, thus achieving a measure of social solidarity. He described the change as a process in which each stage is sufficient for the next. The first stage, he said, is that in which an increase in population and in economic competition produces division of labour within the society. In his words: 'all condensation of the social mass, especially if it is accompanied by an increase in population, necessarily determines advances in the division of labour' (p. 268). With an increase in the division of labour comes the next stage, an increase in the number of rules governing the relationships between people, some defending rights of property and person, and some governing behaviour in families, the conditions of contracts, and the administration of government, all of which regulate co-operation between people. For as labour becomes more specialized, people become more dependent upon one another. As Durkheim says: 'The different parts of the aggregate, because they fill different functions, cannot easily be separated' (p. 149). 'Contractual relations necessarily develop with the division of labour, since the latter is not possible without exchange, and the contract is the juridical form of exchange' (p. 381).

But Durkheim admitted that the process which he described as inevitable does not always take place. For example, 'Though normally the division of labour produces social solidarity, it sometimes happens that it has different, and even contrary results' (p. 353).

He noted that there can exist unresolved conflicts between members of society (p. 354); people, especially in large-scale industry, can lose sight of their dependence upon others in a joint enterprise (p. 356); people can feel unsuited to their task and resentful of those who put them there (pp. 375–6); and finally, if people are underemployed, their behaviour is often poorly adjusted to the needs of the community (p. 389). Clearly the process he had outlined is not sufficient to produce social solidarity. (Durkheim's theory has been criticized at many points. See for example Percy S. Cohen, 1968, pp. 227–9.)

An important difference between positivist regularity theories of explanation and structural process theories is that the former provide just lists of causes which together make an outcome likely, whereas structuralists describe a process of change which, they believe, brought it about. Their theories show how the causes relate to one another, and contribute to the outcome. And while positivists also list the conditions which might falsify a generalization, good social theories describe the effects of these conditions on the process of change. In his discussion of the Industrial Revolution in Britain, R.M. Hartwell (1967) complained that historians in the past have been content to identify 'variables of growth', such as increased capital and other resources, and improved productivity as a result of inventions, but have not been 'concerned with the process of growth, with how the variables interact to produce growth' (p. 10). In particular Hartwell wanted to know whether one leading sector of the British economy grew first, stimulating others to do so too; or whether the growth in the economy was the aggregate effect of several sectors growing at once because of general causes (p. 14). These were the possibilities which current economic theory suggested to him.

Here is Hartwell's summary of the particular process which initiated the British Industrial Revolution in the second half of the eighteenth century. Notice how he applies common economic theory, describing the process of change in theoretical terms, indicating the relations between the causes and the tendencies at work. He would go on to illustrate the generalities later on.

Growth was prompted by the increasing supply of factors [raw materials and labour], by the changing technology and by the increasing demand [resulting from a growth in population]. Investment plus invention increased productivity in industry, created further employment and tended to push up wages. However, since interest rates remained low, and wages rose only slowly, there was neither a capital nor labour shortage to inhibit enterprise. Although demand remained buoyant, the costs of enterprise remained relatively low, and investment was encouraged. The turning-point came in the eighties, when the mounting pressure of demand, both real and potential, created pressures on industry to further increase productivity. This resulted in a series of notable technical breakthroughs which so reduced the price of industrial goods that not only was domestic demand greatly increased, but English goods were cheap enough also to invade, even over tariff and transport barriers, the mass market of Europe. The industrial revolution had begun.

(ibid., p. 28)

Allan Thompson (1973) has taken the discussion further. He objects that the models of development used by Hartwell and others are too simple. They fail to recognize the importance of social and cultural conditions in the process of industrialization; and they ignore the interaction which took place between stages of economic growth and the circumstances which continued to stimulate it (ch. 1). For example, growth of foreign trade in the eighteenth century undoubtedly contributed to industrialization. But it did so because it created wealth, and opened up opportunities which, given their culture and society at the time, stimulated the British to further economic development (pp. 8–9).

More recent economic histories of the industrial revolution show how the search for adequate models of the process of growth has proceeded. An essay by N.C.R. Crafts (1981) reveals the following facts. The models have become much more precise and complex, and are formulated with an eye to quantification: all the variables they relate are quantifiable, given the relevant statistics. There is a preference for 'richer models, that is, models in which more variables have their values determined within the model itself and in which interactions can be considered' (p. 9). And, finally, in several cases there remains considerable uncertainty as to which of two or more possible models is the correct one. For instance, W.A. Cole thinks that the increase in population growth after 1740 increased the demand for goods, which stimulated innovation and economic growth. Thomas Malthus, on the other hand, had seen the growing living standards as an incentive to population growth, which in turn reduced the rate of development. Crafts remarks: 'A case can be constructed for either argument in logic, although based, of course, on different assumptions. Since economic history does not have the controlled experiments of the laboratory and since no way has yet been found to refute either argument conclusively, either can still be entertained' (p. 12). He goes on to contrast two more theories, one which sees the economic growth as driven by an increase in supply, and the other the Keynesian view that it is the result of higher levels of demand (p. 13).

There is an interesting difference between process explanations of a political revolution and these process explanations of the Industrial Revolution. A political revolution is usually the immediate effect of a collective action, motivated by an ideology, and planned by leaders. It can be understood as the working out of a particular purpose, rather like histories of ambitious individuals. Certainly social facts impede and facilitate the progress of the movement, but the resulting explanation does not usually look like a piece of social theory. By contrast, the Industrial Revolution involved the development of a number of industries, with certain aggregate effects on wealth and standards of living. It is not entirely clear what drove the changes, or how some factors affected the process. Much more investigation of cause and effect is needed. The explanation of the Industrial Revolution is a very general description of the various stages of the process, in all their economic complexity.

Given the variety of causal processes noted above, should the attempt to provide a general account of social change be abandoned in favour of a description of each unique process? I think not, for two reasons. First, although no general process of social change is universal, many are very common. Barrington Moore, after all, found several very common processes of modernization. Once a general process has been identified, instances of it can be explained in terms of that general theory, though of course they will not be explained in great detail. Second, in developing general theories of a kind of social change, historical sociologists identify some very important general causes, often structural causes, which regularly tend to produce such changes. Rudé, for instance, demonstrated the importance of effective revolutionary leadership in accounting for the success of political revolutions; Skocpol discovered that the power of the existing regime, not just its popularity, was important in determining their success. The discovery of such general causes of social change helps historians to explain them.

William H. Sewell criticized Skocpol for not appreciating the importance of 'ideology' in explaining the occurrence of revolutions. He pointed out that the ideologies of the revolutionaries directed the form of the change which they brought about. For example, one cannot explain why 'private property was consolidated in France and abolished in Russia' as a result of the French and Russian revolutions respectively, without referring to the different ideologies of the revolutionaries (Sewell, 1985b, p. 59).

In her reply to Sewell, Skocpol admits the importance of agents' intentions in understanding the nature of revolutions.

> Perhaps it was unfortunate that I was so preoccupied in *States and Social Revolutions* with reworking class analysis in relation to a state-centered understanding of revolutions. As a result, I did less than I might have done to rework in analogous ways an alternative strand of theorizing about social revolutions – one that sees them not as class conflicts but as ideologically inspired projects to remake social life in its entirety.
>
> (Skocpol, 1985, p. 88)

She goes on to mention Michael Walzer's theory which describes revolutions 'as "conscious attempts to establish a new moral and material world and to impose, or evoke, radically new patterns of day-to-day conduct"' (p. 88). Walzer, she says, distinguished a revolutionary class, which revolted against an old regime, and an 'ideologically inspired vanguard', which attempted to establish a new one.

What Skocpol should have added is that in her original book she was looking for a general theory of revolution, not one which would account for differences between particular revolutions. There was no need for her to consider their particular ideologies. Moreover, she remains confused about the theoretical basis of her original work. She says it proceeded 'as if some grand intentionality governs revolutionary processes'. She added: 'social structures . . . are not themselves actors. They are, as Sewell rightly says, both enabling and constraining' (p. 87). But she had not assumed 'some grand intentionality', nor assumed that social structures are actors. She had assumed conflict theory, that groups in society compete for power, and that when the governing power is sufficiently weak, a competing group will depose it. That theory works to explain many revolutionary movements. One does not need to refer to the particular ideologies which inspired them.

The conclusion to be drawn is that there are two kinds of process explanations. One is designed to account for a general kind of social change, not a particular instance, and it remains at a level of generality. Thus Johnson and Skocpol developed general explanatory theories for general kinds of revolution. These theories are vital for identifying the relevant social variables which influence the outcome. Then there are explanations of particular events, which can refer to specific aims and actions, contexts and outcomes.

While the work of historical sociologists is vital in identifying general structural causes of social change, historians normally want to explain particular instances of such changes in their uniqueness. As has just been said, to do this they must not only take note of the general structural parameters which inhibited or favoured the possibilities of certain outcomes, but also the particular plans and circumstances which produced the unique features of the change being explained. To understand the Russian Revolution of 1917, for instance, it is important to know Lenin's theory, as stated in *The State and Revolution*, of how the working classes could acquire control of the state. There he explained how the existing state apparatus had to be destroyed, and how the soviets in Russian cities could be used to impose a proletarian dictatorship. He said that a transition period would be necessary, during which classes would be eliminated, before full democracy would be possible. The particular form taken by the Revolution is largely explained by knowing Lenin's particular intentions as its leader.

There is another important reason why explanations in terms of social structures have often to be supplemented by information about particular events. Sometimes the structural facts make a certain kind of outcome highly probable. It was highly probable that the revolutionary Bolshevik Party, so capably organized and led by Lenin, would replace the government of the Tsar, which was crippled by the First World War. However, sometimes the structural facts do not so clearly determine the outcome, which depends also upon contingencies. In that case, to provide an adequate explanation of the outcome, showing why it turned out as it did, the historian has to describe those contingencies which made the difference.

A useful example of the importance of contingencies in explaining some social changes is provided by James M. McPherson, in the Epilogue to his *Battle Cry of Freedom*, where he considers explanations of why there was a northern Union victory in the American Civil War. The fact that the Union armed forces outnumbered those of the Confederacy two to one, and that the Union had much greater economic and logistic capacity, he said, does not explain the outcome, for countries have defended their independence successfully against greater odds, where local loyalty and knowledge and determination to resist invasion largely offset the superiority of the forces against them. Consider the success of North Vietnam against the United States. As for internal divisions, they occurred on both sides, as did a mixture of good and bad leadership. The outcome, said McPherson, depended upon contingencies, more particularly the tides of battle. Victory gave heart to the victor, and that, in his opinion, made all the difference (McPherson, 1988, pp. 854–8). McPherson gives the impression that structural explanations are of no value at all, but that of course is not the case, as he is certainly aware. Had one side in the War enjoyed every structural advantage over the other, in men, equipment, determination, knowledge and co-operation, then a few foolish decisions and military failures would have had but momentary significance. Contingencies are only important in accounting for an outcome, making one outcome more probable than any other, when the structural facts are not sufficient to decide it.

The search for generalizations which explain social changes as a more or less inevitable outcome of a conjunction of conditions, either simultaneous conditions or a certain sequence of events, has proved virtually fruitless. Very few such generalizations can be found. The positivist covering-law model of explanation has proved useless. What can be discovered, however, are generalizations about dispositions things have to produce certain effects in certain circumstances, and these can be used to discover the causal forces at work in any situation, and to account for certain outcomes as a function of these forces.

The forces are often weak, so this form of explanation does not always show the outcome to have been very probable. It does require, however, that the forces were necessary to produce the final effect in the circumstances, or at least that in their absence the probability of such an outcome would have been much less. Comparative methods are of particular value as means of checking general hypotheses about what causal forces were necessary to produce certain kinds of outcome.

11 Should we privilege the individual?

There are two lines of argument favoured by some philosophers of history today which conclude that in explaining social changes in the past, and even in just describing what happened in the past, we should focus upon individuals and their particular behaviour. The first of these arguments has often been called an argument for methodological individualism. That theory says that social changes are brought about by individuals, and so should be explained as the product of individual actions. It denies that social changes can themselves be causes of other social changes. The second line of argument is derived from the work of Jean-François Lyotard, particularly that translated and published under the title *The Postmodern Condition: A Report on Knowledge* (1984). Lyotard attacks all theories of social change, and even theories of knowledge, as 'meta-narratives' which are not really true, and should be ignored. Instead he advises historians to write small narratives of historical episodes, which have no general significance whatever. Both these lines of argument are interesting, but in the end neither is persuasive.

METHODOLOGICAL INDIVIDUALISM

The last chapter concluded by allowing that social changes could sometimes be explained by referring to social causes, and to generalizations stating that such causes tended to produce such effects. There is a widely held view, however, that explanations of social change should describe only those individual actions which brought them about.

The assumption underlying this position is as follows. It is generally agreed that all social facts supervene upon facts about individuals. Thus social organizations depend upon the beliefs, attitudes and practices of individuals; social authority does too; social roles are defined by people's practices and expectations; social classes are just classes of individuals, and so on. Analogies would be that all mental events supervene upon brain events; and all changes in an organism supervene upon the behaviour of its cells. At the bottom of the hierarchy are presumably physical forces which supervene upon nothing. It follows that a social change is brought about by a change in individual behaviour. Some have drawn the conclusions that (1) the cause of social change lies in individual actions; and (2) causal explanations of social change should be in terms of individual decisions and actions.

Michael Taylor, for example, has criticized structural explanations for not explaining enough.

I take it that good explanations should be, amongst other things, as *fine-grained* as possible: causal links connecting events distant in space-time should be replaced wherever possible by chains of 'shorter' causal links. . . . Structuralist and other holistic theories, where they take a causal form, are typically coarse-grained in this sense: they relate macrostates directly to macrostates without supplying a 'mechanism' to show how the one brings about the other.

(Taylor, 1988, p. 96)

Taylor here refers to Jon Elster's assertion that when it comes to macro social events, 'to explain is to provide a mechanism' at a micro level, in terms of intentions as well as other causes. 'A mechanism provides a continuous and contiguous chain of causal or intentional links', Elster said (see also Elster, 1989, pp. 3–13). Taylor objects to Skocpol's explanations saying that although she correlated certain social structures with group behaviour, she did so 'without the intervening links showing the effect of social structure on the individuals and the interactions between individuals', so that 'this is, I submit, at the very best an incomplete explanation' (p. 76).

Raymond Boudon called the social changes which are brought about by individuals 'aggregation effects', pointing out that they are not always intended.

Sometimes, the effects of the aggregation of individual actions or behaviour can be perceived intuitively, as when for one reason or another everyone is led to believe that the price of a product is about to go up. This leads to increased demand and, according to circumstances, either a shortage of the product or a price rise. These phenomena are aggregation effects.

(Boudon, 1986, p. 56)

Many aggregation effects are surprising even to the social scientist. Boudon lists eleven which are quite unexpected (pp. 57–8).

It is true that social changes supervene upon individual actions, but that does not imply that social changes cannot be causes, as has been commonly assumed. Here are four arguments which have been given for denying that social changes can be causes, none of which is compelling.

First, there are people who deny the reality of social facts, and so cannot accept them as causes of social change. This position has been stated in a character-istically dogmatic way by Paul Veyne in *Writing History* (1984).

Abstractions cannot be efficient causes, for they have no existence. . . . Only substances with their accidents [non-essential properties], concrete beings with their ways of being, exist and can be actors in a plot. . . . France does not make war, for she does not really exist; there are only Frenchmen, of whom war may be the accident. No more do there exist forces of production; there exist only men who produce. There exist only the corporal things or people, the concrete, the individual, the specific.

(p. 110)

For Veyne, then, it would be nonsense to say, as Skocpol did, that 'the incapacitation of the central state machineries of the Old Regimes' was a cause of their demise (Skocpol, 1979, p. 41), for according to Veyne such a social fact did not exist.

I suspect that Veyne would restrict reality to things he can perceive, to people and other physical objects. But even physicists admit the reality of unobservables, such as fields of force. Undoubtedly entities at levels above the basic fields of force are supervenient upon entities at levels below them. One can accept the truth of this proposition and still allow the reality of things at every level. After all, that is what we all do all the time. We do not deny the reality of cells because they supervene upon molecules, or of organisms because they supervene upon cells. People get worried about the reality of mental and social entities because they think the real should be confined to the physical. But why should it? We can ascribe predicates to objects at every level which do not apply to the individuals on which they supervene. Perceptions can be red and blue, though brain states are grey. Similarly, a social organization may be large, wealthy and influential, though none of its members is. This is a good reason for affirming its existence. If we allow the reality of facts at the social level, then they can certainly be causes and be referred to in explanations of social change.

A second reason which has been given for denying that social changes can be causes is that generalizations relating social changes are never entirely true. Daniel Little declares that 'in the social sciences . . . we often do *not* find the strong types of regularities and laws that would make us confident in the causal connectedness of social phenomena' (Little, 1991, p. 197). Consequently, he is unwilling to accept explanations which rely upon such social regularities alone. Little is aware that generalizations about the causes of social change normally give no indication of the detailed behaviour of the people who bring them about. For instance, if in a certain kind of society, an increase in unemployment produces an increase in crime, that fact, which can be gleaned from statistical records, gives absolutely no information about the individual behaviour which has, or could, make it true. But, says Little, unless we have a rough idea of the kind of individual behaviour which would make it true, we should not rely upon it. 'A putative explanation couched in terms of high-level social factors whose underlying individual-level mechanisms are entirely unknown is no explanation at all' (p. 196).

Little is far too sceptical about the truth of social generalizations. Certainly it is difficult to produce accurate social generalizations, but with suitable quali-fications one can often formulate tendency statements which are true. Interestingly enough, Little himself provides an example of this. He considers the Marxist belief 'that exploited groups eventually support popular movements aimed at assaulting the class system'. This is not always the case. Their response depends upon their political convictions, their leadership and organization and upon their resources. So Little says the true generalization is as follows: 'Exploited groups with strong political cultures and ample organizational resources tend to be politically active, tenacious, and effective' (p. 198). Certainly this is a more detailed, a more qualified generalization than the original Marxist one. But it is a social generalization nevertheless, and not a narrative of individual responses to a situation. One does not have to imagine how it is instantiated at an individual level to accept its truth.

Third, there are some like Anthony Giddens who regard social facts as objective, implicit in social practices, but deny that they produce any changes except as they are thought of by individuals. They influence change as ideas, they say, but are not real causes in their own right. Giddens allows that social facts certainly seem to be real when one experiences them as a constraint upon behaviour. He has shown how important this experience was in Durkheim's defence of the reality of social facts (Giddens, 1984, pp. 169–74). The prices of goods, the laws of the land, the power of policemen, all these seem objective enough when one experiences the constraints they impose. Giddens allows that physical constraints are real. But he considers the sanctions of the law to be no more than threats which people take into account in deciding how to behave. Structural constraints, it seems, are just ways of behaving imposed by some authority, which many others will accept and co-operate with, regular patterns of response which influence our deliberations as to how we should act (pp. 174–80). What commonly moves people to act, according to Giddens, is knowledge of how others regularly respond to various situations. Giddens says that social structure consists of the rules and resources (material and symbolic) which influence actions, especially those which conform to regular social practices, or affect social relationships (pp. 16–24). These rules and resources are often implicit in social practices, rather as the rules of a language are implicit in its use. Social practices are both influenced by social structure (constrained and enabled by it), and they also reproduce it, in as much as they utilize it, just as the rules of language are reproduced, in a sense, when they are used. (These latter points, about the relation between rules and practices, were earlier developed by Pierre Bourdieu in *Outline of a Theory of Practice* (1977).)

Notice that Giddens' theory is not a purely idealist theory. The rules and resources which we become aware of by watching other people's behaviour are not simply ideas in our head. They really are implicated in people's behaviour, and in that sense are external to us. But Giddens believes they do not have a real external existence with causal power (p. 25).

> Structural constraints do not operate independently of the motives and reasons that agents have for what they do. They cannot be compared with the effect of, say, an earthquake which destroys a town and its inhabitants without their in any way being able to do anything about it. The only moving objects in human social relations are individual agents, who employ resources to make things happen, intentionally or otherwise. The structural properties of social systems do not act, or 'act on' anyone, like forces of nature to 'compel' him or her to behave in any particular way.
>
> (p. 181)

It is because of his conviction that social rules and resources effect change only by being considered by individuals as they deliberate about what to do, that

Giddens espouses methodological individualism. A consideration of people's reasons and motives, he says, is necessary to the 'causal explication' of the influence of social facts: 'there is no such thing as a distinctive category of structural explanation, only an interpretation of the modes in which varying forms of constraint influence human action' (pp. 212, 213).

Giddens' theory of social change has been quite popular in recent years. Philip Abrams expressed a similar idea in these words: 'sociologically, society must be understood as a process constructed historically by individuals who are constructed historically by society' (Abrams, 1982, p. 227). In other words, structural change is mediated by individual actions, and they are conditioned by society. Similar views have been expressed by Alain Touraine, Christopher Lloyd and others (see Lloyd, 1986, pp. 311–21).

Now occasionally this pattern of social change is correct. The thought that the Australian electoral office has the right and power to fine electors who do not vote doubtless moves many to the polls on polling day. But sometimes this is not how social causation works. In societies where an increase in unemployment causes an increase in crime, it is not the thought of an increase in unemployment which causes more people to commit crimes. Certainly a rise in unemployment is symptomatic of changes in many people's lives, changes which might incline some of them to various kinds of criminal behaviour. In other words, there is no denying that social change is mediated by individual behaviour, just as the action of rainwater in rusting an iron roof is mediated by the interaction of molecules of water and iron. This fact does not imply, however, that there are no causal relations at a macro-level. Certain properties of communities can be liable to change in certain ways in certain circumstances, just like properties of individuals. Individuals are liable to feel pain if they put a hand in a fire. Communities too are liable to feel pain, metaphorically speaking, when unemployment increases, for then the rate of crime in that community tends to increase. The crime rate is a property of the community which is liable to change as the rate of unemployment changes, just as the more iron is exposed to water the more it will rust.

The fourth argument against social causes is one given by Lloyd in a recent defence of a theory like Giddens'. His theory is captured in the following extract:

> social structures are the emergent ensemble of rules, roles, relations, and meanings that people are born into and which organize and are reproduced and transformed by their thought and action. It is people who generate structures over time and initiate change, not the society itself, but their generative activity and initiative are socially constrained. . . . There is a duality of causal power in this model, with humans having structuring power and structures having enabling and constraining power.
>
> (Lloyd, 1993, pp. 42–3)

Lloyd seems to go further than Giddens in affirming that social structures have some causal powers, notably those of conditioning human thought and practice to some extent. But he denies that social facts can cause social changes, for the following reason: 'an inanimate force cannot be a prime mover. Surely the prime social force can only be the mentalities and powers of people *qua* social people' (p. 178).

If Lloyd means that a state of affairs, such as a social structure, cannot cause a change because it is itself unchanging, then he is correct. Social changes are produced by events, by other social changes, not simply by structures themselves. It is an *increase* in unemployment which causes an increase in crime. It is unfortunate that Lloyd says 'an inanimate force cannot be a prime mover', because that suggests that only animals and humans can cause changes, which is clearly not the case. The sun can burn skin and melt chocolate, yet it is not an animate force. Causes always include events, changes of one kind which bring about changes of another, but the event can be a social change, not just an individual one.

Thus none of these reasons for denying that social changes can be causes of other social changes succeeds.

A major challenge to methodological individualism has been presented recently by Philip Pettit in *The Common Mind* (1993). Pettit agrees with Giddens that social facts are supervenient upon individual behaviour and material resources, but points out that many generalizations about social structures provide information which is additional to facts about the individuals involved. Suppose in some communities (without sunny beaches!) an increase in unemployment caused an increase in crime. Individuals commit crimes for a variety of reasons, and summing those up would not yield this generalization. Being unable to get work often produces conditions conducive to crime: an incentive to get money or to register a protest against society or to add excitement to life; and an opportunity, since there are few demands made on the lives of the unemployed. The generalization relating changes in the rates of unemployment and crime provides interesting information, additional to the summary of the individual facts which made it true (pp. 129–31, 258–9).

Structural explanations are explanations which rely upon generalizations like this. They need not make any reference to individual deliberation and action. Indeed one reason for favouring structural explanations, which Pettit mentions, is that we often have no idea of the individual actions involved, but do know the social facts which produced a social change.

Pettit thinks that individual actions bring about social change, but a major achievement of his book is to show that even so, often one social change can be adequately explained by another. Pettit explains why the relevant generalizations are true by saying that in such generalizations the antecedent condition makes it probable that individual actions will occur which will produce the social consequent. Increased unemployment will make it probable that more people will have the incentive and opportunity to commit crimes, resulting in an increase in the crime rate (p. 252). So structural regularities, he argues, are quite compatible with an ontological theory which says that social changes are mediated by individual actions. So structural explanations are not inconsistent with ontological individualism, as Giddens and others have assumed. Pettit calls his position 'ecumenical', as he allows that both structural and individualist explanations are acceptable (p. 218).

One reason why Giddens and Pettit come to such different conclusions about structural explanations is that they focus upon different kinds of social regularity. Giddens, like Bourdieu, envisages human social behaviour as guided by rules and practices ('social systems'), and reproducing these patterns by conforming to them (Giddens, 1984, p. 25). Now it is plausible, up to a point, to imagine that the way in which rules and practices affect human behaviour is by being known and followed by members of the community (pp. 22, 90). Pettit pays little attention to these cases, which would fall under his heading of 'social regularities causally continuous with intentional regularities' (Pettit, 1993, p. 121), and which pose no interesting problems. Pettit is interested in social regularities in which the antecedent points to circumstances which either motivate certain characteristic responses, or inhibit or facilitate them. The generalization relating increased unemployment to increased crime is one. Another which he analyses is that urbanization leads to a decline in religious practice. He explains that this is so because 'with urbanisation there is likely to be a shortage of churches, a break with the seasonal basis of liturgy, and a lessening of peer pressure to attend church' (p. 261). Giddens did not consider structural generalizations of these kinds, or he might have been more sympathetic to structural explanations.

I agree with Pettit that social changes can be explained both by describing the deliberation and actions of the individuals involved, and also by reference to structural generalizations without any necessary reference to individuals at all. The only difference I have with him concerning this point is that I allow that changes in society can be real causes, whereas he does not. Pettit declares himself to be 'a causal fundamentalist' (pp. 151–2), one who believes the only real causal work is done by events at a subatomic level. Social changes, he says, are 'causally relevant' to the events they help to explain, and they 'program for' the real causes, i.e. make it probable that there will be real causes which will bring about real, micro-physical effects upon which the social effects are supervenient. But he offers no analysis of causation (pp. 32–3) and no argument to defend this position. On my account of causation there can be real causes at every level of reality, physical, biological, psychological and social.

None of the arguments for methodological individualism, then, is persuasive. Furthermore, social changes can cause not only changes in properties of a community, but also changes in individual behaviour. For social changes often trigger individual responses. Theda Skocpol pointed this out in a critique of the action approach to an explanation of social change. Revolutions, she said, are responses to political oppression, made in situations where revolutionary action has a chance of removing it. Indeed it is some crisis in the power of the government of a country which usually sets a revolutionary movement in train. 'Revolutionary situations have developed due to the emergence of politico-military crises of state and class domination. And only because of the possibilities thus created have revolutionary leaderships and rebellious masses contributed to the accomplishment of revolutionary transformations' (Skocpol, 1979, p. 17). People with a desire for freedom will not act until they see a chance of success, and they will not succeed unless the social conditions are favourable.

It might be thought that such explanations of human behaviour should begin with the agents' perception or belief about the historical situation, rather than with the situation itself. After all it is that belief which in these cases moves people to act. This is true, but the change in belief is caused by social change, and is incomprehensible without it. The people's disposition to act is only triggered once the appropriate social conditions come into existence. Indeed once those conditions exist, then assuming the people's revolutionary desires, one can predict that action will very probably follow.

To conclude, social changes can be said to cause other social changes in two ways. The first is when people perceive a social change and respond to it in a more or less uniform or co-ordinated way, given their common interests, principles or desires. Revolutionary movements are caused in this manner. The second is when the social change triggers the disposition of some property of a social entity to change in such circumstances. Thus in any capitalist economy inflation tends to flatten out when general wage increases are kept small.

Clearly explanations of social change which portray them simply as consequences of collective actions, which themselves are simply the result of the agents' beliefs, desires and dispositions, would be very misleading. Some might wish to deny that social facts influence human behaviour and human history in important ways, but in fact they do.

Before concluding this section, an important point of theory should be made. So far I have discussed causal explanations of social change, arguing that social events can be causes of social change, but allowing that social change is always supervenient upon individual actions. It is interesting to note that contrastive explanations of social change can frequently be given which refer to states of affairs that are not supervenient upon individual behaviour. Such explanations could not possibly be replaced by explanations in terms of individuals and their actions. Thus, to explain why one army beat another on the battlefield, or why one firm beat another in the market-place, it might be enough to say that the victor had greater resources, a better management structure, superior communications, and a more effective strategy. If one were to confine explanations of social change to descriptions of individual actions, such explanations would be impossible.

·LYOTARD'S CRITIQUE OF 'GRAND NARRATIVES'

Throughout this book frequent reference has been made to general concepts, to classification and generalization. Generalizations are very common in history, and are vital for purposes of synthesis and causal analysis. Generalizations attribute a certain predicate to an individual or class of subject, and if they are fairly precise, historians can establish their truth. For example, Durkheim said that the rate of suicide within groups (the subject of his generalization) 'varies inversely with the degree of integration' of those groups (the predicate). To check the truth of this, one would have to know more precisely what he meant by 'integration', and if possible get some idea of the degree of dependence, whether large differences in social integration made a small difference to the rates of suicide or a big difference.

One would also need to know the scope of the generalization, whether it was intended to apply just to modern France, or to more countries and periods. Once these things had been established, then it would be possible to see whether it was true.

In recent years Jean-François Lyotard has launched an all-out attack upon generalizations, or 'metanarratives' as he calls them. In the Introduction to his book *The Postmodern Condition* he wrote: 'I define *postmodern* as incredulity towards metanarratives' (Lyotard, 1984, p. xxiv). His attack has taken two forms. First, he has trivialized methods of verifying knowledge, thus undermining its credibility. This critique applies to knowledge of the particular as well as of the general. Second, he considers some well-known historical generalizations, and shows that they are all false, concluding that no historical generalizations are true. I shall consider his criticisms in turn.

In *The Postmodern Condition*, Lyotard describes the various disciplines as playing language games. Each game has its own rules, and he would say that this book has set out the rules of historical understanding. These rules, he argues, cannot themselves be legitimated by any other language game, and no game can provide an independent legitimation of its own rules. This applies even to science: 'science plays its own game; it is incapable of legitimating the other language games. . . . But above all, it is incapable of legitimating itself, as speculation assumed it could' (p. 40). Even 'philosophy is forced to relinquish its legitimation duties, which explains why philosophy is facing a crisis wherever it persists in arrogating such functions and is reduced to the study of systems of logic or the history of ideas where it has been realistic enough to surrender them' (p. 41). History and science might claim that their conclusions are legitimated by the evidence which supports them, but evidence is only relevant to their conclusions if and how the rules of the game say it is. In the end, Lyotard thinks, legitimation is accorded *de facto* to those performances which produce results which people like. Those who adopt methods which yield welcome results are given the research grants and the academic positions (pp. 46–7).

Bill Readings, in his account of Lyotard's thought, neatly contrasts three approaches to knowledge of the world. The classical positivist, he says, sees knowledge as a function of what it describes and refers to, its referent, the things in the world which the positivist says it is representing. The modernist focuses instead upon the person who produces the knowledge, seeing it as a product of her culture and interests, aimed at achieving consensus within her community, and perhaps power within it as well. The postmodern person attends to the narratives the person tells to justify the knowledge they produce, and perhaps the narratives they tell to justify those narratives. These narratives are stories about how they learned the procedures for producing knowledge, procedures which have been followed and by which the knowledge is justified. The postmodernist sees these narratives as stories about the language game the person is playing. They do not succeed in legitimating that game, but just tell how the person came to be playing it. There is no need, therefore, to respect the knowledge and understanding which people produce, since it cannot ultimately be legitimated.

To test the truth of a generalization, an historian must examine all the relevant detailed facts about the subject of the generalization, or at least a representative sample of them, which can be inferred from the evidence available to her (see McCullagh, 1984, ch. 6). Lyotard would say that the forms of inference which historians use to draw their conclusions from evidence, and to justify them, are merely procedures which they have been taught as part of the language game of being an historian. In other words, he implies they cannot be relied upon to yield true descriptions of the past, descriptions of events whose occurrence is independent of any historical inquiry or historical writing. I admit that there is an element of conventionality about the forms of inference we respect in our culture, but deny that this fact implies they cannot tell us facts about the world. When we test the conclusions about the present world drawn by means of these forms of inference, they are normally confirmed in our experience. If a friend describes a city he is visiting, and we infer that certain buildings, bridges and parks exist in that city, we find that when we visit it they are there. Our forms of inference may not be perfect, but they very often yield descriptions of the world which we can confirm in experience. Our forms of legitimation are not invalid simply because they are conventional and we talk about them.

In the past, historians have written history to illustrate general ideas of historical change, 'grand narratives' as Lyotard calls them. Readings provides a list of the themes which grand narratives have had in the past:

> Thus the Encyclopaedia will free humanity from superstition through enlightenment leading to universal knowledge; the dialectic of history will reveal the Hegelian trans-historical Spirit; Marxism will free the proletariat from bondage by means of revolution; democracy will reveal human nature as the people become the subject of a universal history of humanity; or the creation of wealth will free mankind from poverty through the technological breakthroughs of free-market capitalism.
>
> (Readings, 1991, p. 65)

All of these grand narratives have been discredited, proved false, says Lyotard. Progress in history has been disrupted by the actions of dictators, often acting in the name of the progress which they prevent.

When Lyotard reflects upon the grand narratives of history, especially those which have promised freedom and prosperity, the possibility that someone will promote them as true and then base a dictatorial government policy upon them fills him with 'terror'. 'The nineteenth and twentieth centuries have given us as much terror as we can take' he writes. Yet people still hanker after totalitarianism. 'Let us wage a war on totality; let us be witnesses to the unpresentable; let us activate the differences and save the honor of the name' (1984, pp. 81, 82).

In Lyotard's opinion, there are no generalizations about historical change worthy of respect. History should not be written to remind us of such generalizations any more. 'That is to say, narratives are to be understood metonymically rather than metaphorically' (Readings, 1991, p. 68). Instead of a number of narratives illustrating the same 'truths', Lyotard advocates writing what he calls 'little narratives' of particular events, so that one asks what happened next, and then supplies another narrative. Each narrative is to be seen as presenting just a few figures of the much richer course of events which the historian has in mind but cannot adequately represent. 'The breakdown of metanarratives positions culture as a patchwork of little narratives. For Lyotard, a scepticism has led us to understand culture as discontinuous and fragmentary; cultural representations are too disparate to permit a universal point of view' (Readings, 1991, p. 65).

Lyotard, then, advocates the telling of little stories, 'because they are short, because they are not extracts from some great history, and because they are difficult to fit into any great history' (1989, p. 132). Many historians today prefer to tell 'little stories', which focus upon the activities of individuals, rather than upon generalizations and abstract social structures. The everyday world of individuals is more familiar, and their attempts to cope with the contingencies of life often resonate with our own. It is easy to empathize with individuals as they struggle through life, and it gives us a vicarious pleasure to do so. A lively presentation of the fortunes of individuals is much more fun to read than a dry account of social abstractions. It sells better too.

Even so, it is hard for curious historians to resist generalization, for they want to know whether the particular episodes they have examined had any general significance. Carlo Ginzburg's celebrated study *The Cheese and the Worms* (1980) would seem to be a perfect example of what Lyotard was recommending. It is a study of confessions of a sixteenth-century Italian miller, Menocchio, to an ecclesiastical court about his religious and other beliefs. The subject seems entirely inconsequential. But even in this case, Ginzburg is fascinated by the sources of the miller's ideas, and discusses the general relations between the high and low cultures of the time, with an eye to the theories of Gramsci and others on the subject.

Lyotard has failed to notice that even purely narrative histories provide explanations which depend upon general theories of cause and effect. Only chronicles are structured with absolutely no reference to a general theory of historical change. Ginzburg assumes that when Menocchio's ideas resemble those in books he had read, he had probably acquired those ideas from reading those books, though his reading of them did not always mirror what they said (pp. 33, 108). Some of his ideas were also gleaned from conversations with farmers bringing grain for grinding at his mill (p. 119), and perhaps also from discussions with his local feudal lord (p. 120). Ginzburg is depending on commonplace causal generalizations in making these statements, such as that people often acquire ideas from books and conversations on matters which interest them.

However, even little stories about the world fail to represent the world truly, according to Lyotard, for our concepts can never capture the complex, unique character of things in the world. Descriptions of the world, like paintings, do not depict the very complex reality of the things to which they refer, or represent them accurately. Rather Lyotard regards them as acts of figuration, in which the writer is aware both of the complexity of the subject being referred to and of the general figures or terms in which it is represented (Readings, 1991, pp. 57–62). Readings expresses it thus:

> Post-modernity is the recognition that History as 'giving voice' to the past would be inversely split between the event of writing history, the making present of the voice of the past, and the writing of the historical event, the representation of the past which relegates it to the status of what is to be repeated (*re*-presented).
>
> (p. 60)

In his essay 'Answering the Question: What is Postmodernism?', Lyotard develops this analysis of figuration by referring to Kant's concept of the sublime, and the mixture of pleasure and pain which accompanies the attempt to portray sublime subjects (1984, pp. 77–82). Sublime subjects can be known, conceived, but not adequately represented. Any attempt to represent them by means of familiar concepts produces a feeling of 'nostalgia', he said, a mixture of pleasure and pain: 'the pleasure that reason should exceed all presentation, the pain that imagination or sensibility should not be equal to the concept' (p. 81). The representation of the sublime follows no rules, as works of beauty do. The act of figuration is simply that, an act, which always seems inappropriate. It does not present the reality, but just 'alludes' to it.

It is worth noting that F.R. Ankersmit in the Introduction and final chapter of his recent book *History and Topology. The Rise and Fall of Metaphor* (1994) has repeated and developed Lyotard's themes. In particular he develops the notion of nostalgia in connection with apprehension of the sublime, and applies it to historians' attempts to capture their sense of the past. Like Lyotard, he advocates writing the history of episodes, 'to reflect the episodic character of historical experience', with its 'fragmented', 'contingent' and 'isolated' nature, remarking that 'the microstorie [sic], the history of mentalities, and *Alltagsgeschichte*, with its interest in the insignificant details of daily life, best satisfy these requirements within the compass of postmodernist historiography' (p. 211).

Lyotard's arguments all involve a fallacy of equivocation, in one way or another. Let me consider his three main points. The first is that grand narratives, general theories of historical change, have all been proved false, and are manifestly so, given the power of powerful organizations to disrupt the normal processes of history. Enlightenment and Marxist theories of progress, for example, have proved quite wrong, falsified by the actions of despotic states this century. Therefore, there are no general truths of historical change worthy of respect, upon which to structure historical writing. The equivocation is on the notion of generalization. He convincingly shows that all grand theories of historical change are false, but then assumes that all theories of historical change are false including the much more limited generalizations which historians discover to be true of particular societies. The latter are often quite credible, and provide perfectly acceptable frameworks of historical interpretation and explanation, as illustrated in previous chapters. There is no need to confine historical writing to the portrayal of episodes having no general significance whatever.

Second, Lyotard correctly states that our descriptions of the past cannot capture all the particular details of which the historian is aware, and can only indicate them in general terms. Strictly speaking that means an historian cannot represent the past in all the detail he knows it to have, far less in all the detail it does have, and perhaps could be discovered to have. But that does not mean, as Lyotard supposes, that he cannot represent it accurately at all. Even quite general descriptions have their truth conditions, and are true of any instance which satisfies them. Figuration is not merely a present act. The figure is meant to represent the past, and may do so correctly, even if not in all its detail. To set aside completely the representative function of history as of little significance, as Lyotard does, is to deprive it of an important educational function.

It might not be possible to legitimate the procedures for establishing the truth of historical descriptions without circularity (there are good inductive grounds for thinking induction reliable!), but that does not imply that they are of no value to us in discovering what the world is like, and in planning to act in it successfully. To call the rules of induction the rules of a language game is to trivialize their significance, unwarrantedly.

This leads to the third point. We should all fear totalitarianism, for the terror it produces. But that does not mean we should avoid seeking and testing limited generalizations about causal processes in particular societies, which will illuminate our history. Imagine the terror of living in a world without any idea of the causal processes at work in it. The sort of knowledge Lyotard advocates, confined as it is to knowledge of particulars which have no general significance at all, would leave everyone a prey to the forces of nature and society, with no general knowledge with which to predict and control them. By illustrating processes of change in the past, historians alert readers to possibilities in the present. Herbert Butterfield once said that people who enjoy liberty are in danger of taking it for granted, and should be aware of the struggles by which it was achieved and defended. For there is a 'possibility that liberty may be lost through mere carelessness, at a time when a king or a statesman is stealing a march on the rest of the country' (Butterfield, 1971, p. 20). General knowledge of the functions of our traditions and institutions is essential for a proper appreciation of their value.

THE VALUE OF THE PARTICULAR

Why do people generally prefer to read history of particular events rather than study general patterns of historical change? I suggest that it is because they find in particular events expressions of emotion and spirit which resonate with their own, whereas an understanding of causal processes is rather a matter of practical concern.

First there is the obvious point that we all have basic drives to which we are committed, particularly the desires for sexual pleasure, power and social acceptance, and we obtain a voyeuristic delight from watching others trying to acquire those powers in their own lives. A brief analysis of popular films and TV series demonstrates this fact. Just compare the ratings for eggheads discussing the ills of society with the ratings of passionate dramas! So with history, people love an exciting story, where they can identify with the leading characters in their pursuit of power and fortune, knowing they will generally succeed in the end. Alternatively, they enjoy seeing how others suffered from injustice as they believe that they, or their friends, are suffering today.

J.H. Hexter discussed the ways in which the rhetoric of history is affected by the desire to make past events lively and vivid for today's readers. Historians often sacrifice precision for colour, he says. 'They deliberately choose a word or phrase that is imprecise and may turn out to be ambiguous, because of its rich aura of connotation. Without compunction they sacrifice exactness for evocative force' (Hexter, 1968, pp. 18–19). Herbert Butterfield has also remarked on the skill needed to bring history to life.

> The truth is that to delineate a scene; to depict a personality; to portray a political crisis in all its urgency; to narrate a series of events, and to reconstruct the past in a manner that will enable people really to enter into it and feel the situation properly – these things not only require the art of literature in order to give form to the conception which the historian is seeking to communicate; they require something of the imagination of the literary man to shape them in the first place – to turn a bundle of documents into a resurrected personality and to see how a heap of dry facts, when properly put together, may present us with a dramatic human situation.
>
> (Butterfield, 1951b, p. 232)

To give human shape to a bundle of facts is to reconstruct an episode, or even to devise a plot along the lines Hayden White described, to bring out the tragedy, comedy, or romance of the events that occurred.

So far I have mentioned strong universal human drives. Some people have more particular preoccupations, perhaps with personal ambition, with the challenges of art or religion, with scientific discovery and technical inventions, for example, and are fascinated by the stories of others who shared their enthusiasms, albeit in a different setting, in the past. Once again, the spirit of past enthusiasts resonates with the particular enthusiasm of the reader, so that the history is enthralling to read.

Finally, there are people whose lives have expressed what I call spiritual forces of intrinsic value. The pursuit of truth, beauty and goodness has always been recognized as noble. It requires setting aside one's own interests, and the realization of values which are universally respected. We respect artists and musicians who create things of beauty, we admire scientists who discover truths about the world and the universe, and we salute people who have struggled to maintain and increase justice and community in the world. In honesty we are moved more by the works of beauty than by the lives of those who created them; by the discoveries of scientists than by the experiments required to prove them; and by the achievements of justice and community in our own day, than in the past. Nevertheless, we admire those who have worked to realize these values in the past.

We also admire the qualities of character which are required to create those noble goods with success. The people who achieve them have often to overcome a variety of obstacles, personal, intellectual, professional, and social, and they display courage, integrity and patience which inspire us to emulate them. These are not qualities of intrinsic value, because we do not admire them in villains. They are necessary for a good life, however, and we are encouraged by those who display them in that context. Butterfield, reflecting the opinion of G.M. Trevelyan, summed it up with these words:

> it is wrong to neglect the internal study of the art of Leonardo da Vinci, the work of Dante, the spiritual achievement of St. Francis, the intellectual system of Aristotle or the whole Renaissance art of living. These things represent triumphs of the human spirit, and if we pass over them we are neglecting the very things most fitted to be studied as ends in themselves.
>
> (Butterfield, 1951b, pp. 235–6.)

The study of particular events in the past is not motivated by nostalgia. Nostalgia is a desire for an idealized past, or future, in contrast with an ordinary or unpleasant present. We are always nostalgic about 'the good old days', for an imagined society of peace, goodwill and social harmony, and for familiar objects and practices which seemed to guarantee contentment. The historical past is not nearly as comfy as that. The study of it does not drive us into an idyllic world to escape the present, but into the harsh realities of past life, which helps us in facing the realities of the present.

There is no doubt that by representing human struggles and achievements in the past, history can entertain and encourage us in the present. But precisely the same can be said of good fiction, in novels and films. The good ones portray the difficulties of life as well as its successes, and teach us something of how to survive in society. So is there a value peculiar to history?

In my opinion, the unique value of history lies in explaining the origin and value of all the social institutions, cultural practices and technological advances we have inherited. Many were created to meet the particular needs of a community, and have been of value in meeting those needs for some time. Some have been superseded, some unwisely neglected. Some institutions and practices have been very unjust, and continue to be so. History is the only discipline devoted to the study of these things, our social, cultural and technological inheritance, and is vital for our proper appreciation of it.

It might be thought that the functions of institutions and practices in the past cannot be a guide to their value in the present because circumstances affecting their utility have changed. Thus whereas governors appointed by the Crown exercised important leadership in the development of the British colonies in Australia for several decades before representative government was established, thereafter their role has steadily diminished to one which is now largely formal, ceremonial and symbolic. A knowledge of their early importance seems hardly useful in assessing their value today. The answer is that in studying the value of institutions in the past, it is indeed vital to recognize the conditions which enabled them to function as they did, in case those conditions exist today or have changed. Governors were indispensable in the absence of any other administrative authority in the early history of the colonies, but became of less importance once a parliamentary system of government was established.

In his book *'Lessons' of the Past*, Ernest May has carefully studied the influence of history on several important issues in American foreign policy, and has shown how useful careful analysis of past cases can be in judging the value of policies in the present. For instance, America's decision in 1964–5 to bomb North Vietnam was largely influenced by what was believed to have been the success of such bombing in North Korea in 1952 and 1953 in bringing about peace. May notes:

> There were many previous occasions when bombing was employed for political purposes – by Mussolini in Ethiopia, the Nationalists in the Spanish Civil War, the Japanese in China, Hitler against Britain, the World War II Allies against the Axis powers, and by the United States in Korea. Most of the time, it had been unproductive. In a few instances, however, bombing contributed to the desired political ends.
>
> (p. 127)

Most countries had their resolve stiffened by bombing. In May's judgement, only the bombing of Italy and Japan during the Second World War was probably effective in bringing peace, and the bombing by the United States in Korea might have been effective as well (p. 128). In each case, it produced a change of government, with the new government opting for peace. After studying how bombing affected the governments of those countries, May draws some conclusions about conditions under which bombing could bring peace with North Vietnam.

> On the basis of previous experience, it could have been inferred that the desired decision would come only if, at many levels in the North Vietnamese bureaucracy, pessimism developed about the war in the south. It could also have been inferred that such pessimism would be most likely to develop first, as in Italy and Japan, within the foreign affairs and intelligence bureaucracies, for it would be there that the disparity between North Vietnamese and American resources would be most clearly recognized.
>
> (pp. 139–40)

May's book is replete with examples of ways in which a knowledge of history did help or could have helped in the formation of American foreign policy. He is always aware of the importance of relevant circumstances in deciding whether an analogous case applies to the present or not. He is critical of many decisions for not taking sufficient notice of historical precedents, or for not judging their relevance accurately.

If historians are to reveal the value of our institutions and traditions, I believe that they should deliberately investigate the good and bad consequences of those institutions and practices. Whether historians should be responsible for comparing past situations with present ones is hard to say. Perhaps they should just produce the data for politicians to use today, though their training would make them well qualified to pick out the relevant similarities and dissimilarities. Historians could stop short of making moral judgements, I suppose, by just displaying the way institutions have worked, and for whose advantage, leaving the reader to draw the obvious conclusions.

Like many others, I am particularly interested in discovering institutions and traditions which increase or diminish people's concern and respect for one another. Ferdinand Tönnies, in his book *Gemeinschaft und Gesellschaft*, translated as *Community and Association* (1974), investigated a common shift in European societies from co-operative communities acting with a natural common will, to associations in which relationships are largely contractual, protected and often changed by the state. Tönnies explained the change as a result of feudal society being displaced, through the growth of trade, by an urban industrial society. My interest is in the forces at work in modern states, some encouraging competition and exploitation, others promoting justice, that is respect and compassion for all. Democratic institutions seem to favour justice, promising government by the people for the people, but they fail when instead they provide government by a majority for that majority at the expense of the rest. Legal systems seem to favour justice, promising justice for all, but they fail when the costs they involve mean they provide justice only for the rich. Liberal ideologies seem to promote justice, arguing that everyone should be as free as possible to lead whatever life they choose, but they fail to do so when they provide no protection for the weak against the strong. Christian traditions have motivated great movements of justice and compassion, but they fail to do so when the Church's leaders put their own power and comfort ahead of their vocation. These commonplace generalizations, so important to the understanding of our society and to the planning of its reform, are derived from the study of history.

A critical stance towards the past inevitably involves generalization. One detects the good and bad features of our institutions by seeing what differences they generally made in the past. Are democratic societies generally more peaceful and co-operative than others? Does the separation of the powers of the legislative, executive and judicial branches of government generally protect individual liberty? Is economic growth encouraged more by investment than low inflation? The questions go on and on, and are vital to societies. To answer them we need a general knowledge of history. Knowledge of little narratives, of individual episodes in their peculiarity, is not enough.

Conclusion

It has been a shock for us to learn that we do not perceive the world just as it is, and that our knowledge of the world is inescapably framed by the concepts and language of our culture. It is little wonder that these two discoveries have led many philosophers to deny that we can possibly know anything about the world beyond us. I hope to have shown a sense in which we can.

In the first chapter I proposed a sense in which historical descriptions can be true or false which, I argued, is consistent with everything else we believe about our knowledge of the world. That was the correlation theory, which states that a description of the world is true if it is part of a coherent account of the world, and if the observation statements implied by that account could be confirmed by people of the appropriate culture and with the appropriate interests. This shows how the truth of a description depends upon the way the world is, while allowing that it also depends upon the rules of the language of the description, and upon the concepts of the world which those rules refer to. This is not a naive theory of historical realism that the world is as we perceive it, such as we all accept in our day-to-day lives, because physical and cultural facts about perception do not allow us to regard that theory as strictly true.

Is this theory of any use? Can we prove any historical descriptions true in the correlation sense? Ultimately we cannot. Those perceptions of data which we judge to be true, because they seem so reliable, might not be. Those inferences we draw from the observations of the data are only inductive, and so could be mistaken too, though if an historical description is well supported by data the chances of its being false seem small. And finally, the form of inference used both to interpret perceptions and to draw conclusions from data is often an argument to the best explanation, which cannot be proved to yield truths about the world. However, it has been found reliable in experience, and we conventionally assume it generally produces true knowledge of the world. Given this assumption it is often reasonable to believe the best explanation of perceptions is that they are correct; and to believe that good historical explanations of the perceived data are true.

Knowing that historians want to get as close to the truth as they can, we can understand why they adopt many of the procedures they do. They investigate relevant data carefully, they give priority to descriptions of that data over their preconceptions of the past when deciding what to believe, and they judge alternative explanations of it as carefully as they can.

Knowing that historical descriptions are very probably true justifies us in learning from them what we can which could be of relevance to our lives in the present. In particular we can see the effects of various different beliefs, customs and institutions in the past, to judge their possible value to us in the present.

An historical explanation or interpretation is objective if it can be proved superior to alternative explanations or interpretations according to commonly accepted criteria. When historians compare different explanations and interpretations it becomes clear that they do have criteria by which they judge them.

Historical explanations are judged according to whether they provide the information required by the question they have been designed to answer, and whether the assumptions about the nature of people and societies which they employ are empirically justified. For instance, descriptive explanations are criticized for being incomplete, and causal explanations sometimes do not correctly identify causes, in the opinion of critics.

In practice, historians sometimes have a rather hazy idea of what an adequate explanation requires, so that their explanations are somewhat haphazard, often reflecting their personal interests. The significance of their accounts of the past is then somewhat obscure. It is not clear whether they are providing adequate explanations of something or not. Of course one cannot blame historians for this vagueness. See how difficult it has been for philosophers to find an adequate analysis of causes and causal explanation in recent years. There has not been a commonly accepted analysis of these things for historians to follow.

Interpretations are generally higher-order descriptions of historical subjects, arrived at after reflecting upon the detailed information available about them. Most writers have assumed that interpretations are entirely personal, reflecting the particular interests of the historian. To some extent they are, but they are also subject to certain conventional constraints, so that the range of acceptable interpretations of any subject is much narrower than is generally assumed.

Historians prefer interpretations of historical subjects which are fairly comprehensive and which make many features of them intelligible, both by showing how they are related to one another and by explaining their existence. Above all, however, historical interpretations are expected to be fair, not misleading. This concept of fairness has not been noticed before, yet it is a fundamental constraint upon descriptions of things in the world. Historical interpretations are inevitably partial, relating some but not all of the features of the subject. It is expected that whatever aspects of the subject they do describe, they will do so comprehensively, so as not to provide an unbalanced inaccurate impression of them. Although the concept of fairness has not been discussed, historians generally respect the need to provide fair accounts of their subjects just the same.

Those who deny the possibility of discovering truths about the past have no good reason for distinguishing historical truth from fiction. Historical novels and films which blend fact and fancy are often enjoyable and sell well. However, one cannot respect them as sources of reliable information about the past. It is important to reaffirm the possibility of discovering the truth about the past, so that historians continue to seek it and reveal the glories and horrors of our civilization. Without a knowledge of our history, we cannot understand our present society, nor plan intelligently for the future.

Likewise, those who would confine history to little narratives of particular episodes from the actors' point of view would blind us to the structure of society and to the influence it can have on human experience. Rather than let history educate us, they would use it to escape from the present to a quaint past of other people's passions and beliefs. It is no wonder that such history is being shunned by students, who have more important things to worry about. Let us teach them about the culture, society and institutions they have inherited, and of others which they should be careful to avoid, or which they should try to develop.

References

A. PHILOSOPHICAL AND REFLECTIVE WORKS

Abrams, Philip, 1982. *Historical Sociology.* England, Open Books.

Achinstein, Peter, 1983. *The Nature of Explanation.* New York, Oxford University Press.

Ankersmit, F.R., 1983. *Narrative Logic. A Semantic Analysis of the Historian's Language.* The Hague, Martinus Nijhoff.

—— 1990. 'Reply to Professor Zagorin', *History and Theory* 29: 275–96.

—— 1994. *History and Tropology. The Rise and Fall of Metaphor.* Berkeley, University of California Press.

Appleby, Joyce, Hunt, Lyn and Jacob, Margaret, 1994. *Telling the Truth about History.* New York, W.W. Norton.

Asad, Talal, 1986. 'The concept of cultural translation in British social anthropology', in *Writing Culture. The Poetics and Politics of Ethnography*, ed. James Clifford and George E. Marcus. Berkeley, University of California Press, pp. 141–64.

Austin, J.L., 1962. *How To Do Things With Words.* Oxford, Clarendon.

Barthes, Roland, 1986. *The Rustle of Language*, trans. Richard Howard. Oxford, Blackwell.

Beard, Charles A., 1935. 'That noble dream', reprinted in *The Varieties of History. From Voltaire to the Present*, ed. Fritz Stern, 1956. Cleveland, Meridian Books, pp. 314–28.

Beattie, J.H.M., 1966. 'Ritual and social change', *Man* 1: 60–74.

Berkhofer, Robert F. jr., 1969. *A Behavioral Approach to Historical Analysis.* New York, The Free Press.

Berkowitz, S.D., 1988. 'Afterword: Toward a formal structural sociology', in *Social Structures, A Network Approach*, ed. Barry Wellman and S.D. Berkowitz, Cambridge, Cambridge University Press, pp. 477–97.

Bernstein, Richard J., 1988. 'Rejoinder to Robert L.Woolfolk and Stanley B. Messer', in *Hermeneutics and Psychological Theory. Interpretive perspectives on personality, psychotherapy and psychopathology*, eds Stanley B. Messer, Louis A. Saass and Robert L. Woolfolk. New Brunswick, Rutgers University Press, pp. 114–15.

Bevir, Mark, 1994. 'Objectivity in history', *History and Theory* 33: 328–44.

Bhaskar, Roy, 1975. *A Realist Theory of Science.* Leeds, Leeds Books.

—— 1979. *The Possibility of Naturalism. A Philosophical Critique of the Contemporary Human Sciences.* Brighton, Harvester.

—— 1986. *Scientific Realism and Human Emancipation.* London, Verso.

Black, Max, 1962. 'Metaphor', in his *Models and Metaphor: Studies in Language and Philosophy.* Ithaca, Cornell University Press.

—— 1979. 'More about metaphor', in *Metaphor and Thought*, ed. Andrew Ortony. Cambridge, Cambridge University Press.

Bluck, R.S., 1955. *Plato's Phaedo.* London, Routledge and Kegan Paul.

Bolotin, David, 1979. *Plato's Dialogue on Friendship.* Ithaca, Cornell University Press.

Booth, Wayne C., 1979. 'Metaphor as rhetoric: the problem of evaluation', in *On Metaphor*, ed. Sheldon Sacks. Chicago, University of Chicago Press.

Boudon, Raymond, 1982. *The Unintended Consequences of Social Action*. New York, St Martin's Press.

—— 1986. *Theories of Social Change. A Critical Appraisal.*, trans. J.C. Whitehouse. Cambridge, Polity Press.

—— 1989. *The Analysis of Ideology*, trans. M. Slater. Cambridge, Polity Press.

Bourdieu, Pierre, 1977. *Outline of a Theory of Practice*, trans. Richard Nice. Cambridge, Cambridge University Press.

Braaten, Jane, 1991. *Habermas's Critical Theory of Society*. Albany, NY, State University of New York Press.

Braudel, Fernand, 1972. 'History and the social sciences', in *Economy and Society in Early Modern Europe. Essays from Annales*, ed. Peter Burke. London, Routledge and Kegan Paul, pp. 11–42.

Braybrooke, D., 1987. *Meeting Needs*. Princeton, NJ, Princeton University Press.

Burger, Ronna, 1984. *The Phaedo: A Platonic Labyrinth*. New Haven, Yale University Press.

Butterfield, H., 1951a. *The Whig Interpretation of History*. London, Bell and Sons.

—— 1951b. *History and Human Relations*. London, Collins.

—— 1971. *The Discontinuities between the Generations in History. Their Effect on the Transmission of Political Experience*. The Rede Lecture, 1971. Cambridge, Cambridge University Press.

Cartwright, Nancy, 1983. *How the Laws of Physics Lie*. Oxford, Clarendon.

Case, Arthur, E., 1958. *Four Essays in Gulliver's Travels*. Gloucester, Mass., P. Smith.

Chartier, Roger, 1988. *Cultural History. Between Practices and Representations*, trans. L.G. Cochrane. Cambridge, Polity Press.

Clifford, James, 1986. 'On ethnographic allegory', in *Writing Culture. The Poetics and Politics of Ethnography*, ed. James Clifford and George E. Marcus. Berkeley, University of California Press, pp. 98–121.

Close, A.J., 1972. 'Don Quixote and "the Intentionalist Fallacy"', *British Journal of Aesthetics* 12: 19–39.

Cocks, Geoffrey, and Travis, L. Crosby (eds), 1987. *Psycho/History. Readings in the Method of Psychology, Psychoanalysis, and History*. New Haven, Yale University Press.

Cohen, G.A., 1982. *Karl Marx's Theory of History. A Defence*. Oxford, Clarendon Press.

—— 1988. *History, Labour and Freedom. Themes from Marx*. Oxford, Clarendon Press.

Cohen, Percy S., 1968. *Modern Social Theory*. London, Heinemann.

Collingwood, R.G., 1928. 'The limits of historical knowledge', reprinted in his *Essays in the Philosophy of History*, ed. William Debbins. Austin, University of Texas, 1965, pp. 90–103.

—— 1946. *The Idea of History*. London, Oxford University Press, paperback edn, 1961.

Cooper, David E., 1986. *Metaphor*. Aristotelian Soc. Series, vol. 5. Oxford, Blackwell.

Crapanzano, Vincent, 1986. 'Hermes' dilemma: The masking of subversion in ethnographic description', in *Writing Culture. The Poetics and Politics of Ethnography*, ed. James Clifford and George E. Marcus. Berkeley, University Of California Press.

Culler, Jonathan, 1976. *Saussure*. Britain, Fontana.

Dahrendorf, Ralf, 1959. *Class and Class Conflict in an Industrial Society*. Stanford, CA, Stanford University Press.

Davidson, Donald, 1963. 'Actions, reasons and causes', reprinted in his book *Actions and Events*. Oxford, Clarendon, 1980, pp. 3–19.

—— 1974. 'On the very idea of a conceptual scheme', reprinted in his *Inquiries into Truth and Interpretation*. Oxford, Clarendon Press, 1984, pp. 183–98.

—— 1979a. 'What metaphors mean', in *On Metaphor*, ed. Sheldon Sacks. Chicago, University of Chicago Press, pp. 29–45.

—— 1979b. 'The inscrutability of reference', reprinted in his *Inquiries into Truth and Interpretation*. Oxford, Clarendon Press, 1984, pp. 227–41.

—— 1983. 'A coherence theory of truth and knowledge', reprinted in *Truth and Interpretation. Perspectives on the Philosophy of Donald Davidson*, ed. Ernest LePore. Oxford, Blackwell, 1986, pp. 307–19.

Derrida, Jacques, 1979. 'Living on', in *Deconstruction and Criticism*, ed. Harold Bloom *et al.* New York, Continuum.

—— 1982. *Margins of Philosophy*, trans. Alan Bass. Brighton, The Harvester Press.

Devitt, Michael and Sterelny, Kim, 1987. *Language and Reality. An Introduction to the Philosophy of Language*. Oxford, Blackwell.

Dray, William, 1957. *Laws and Explanation in History*. Oxford, Oxford University Press.

—— 1963. 'The historical explanation of actions reconsidered', reprinted in *The Philosophy of History*, ed. Patrick Gardiner, 1974. Oxford, Oxford University Press, pp. 66–89.

—— 1964. *Philosophy of History*. Englewood Cliffs, Prentice-Hall.

—— 1989. 'Narrative and historical realism', in his *On History and Philosophers of History*. Leiden, E.J. Brill, pp. 132–63.

—— 1994. 'Was Collingwood an historical constructionist?' *Collingwood Studies*, vol.1, pp. 59–75.

Dunn, J., 1969. *The Political Thought of John Locke*. Cambridge, Cambridge University Press.

—— 1980. *Political Obligation in its Historical Context. Essays in Political Theory*. Cambridge, Cambridge University Press.

Durkheim, Emile, 1952. *Suicide: A Study in Sociology*. London, Routledge and Kegan Paul.

—— 1964. *The Division of Labour in Society*, trans. George Simpson. New York, The Free Press.

Eagleton, Terry, 1983. *Literary Theory*. Oxford, Blackwell.

Edel, Leon, 1984. *Writing Lives, Principia Biographica*. New York, W.W. Norton.

Elster, Jon, 1983. *Explaining Technical Change. A Case Study in the Philosophy of Science*. Cambridge, Cambridge University Press, and Oslo, Universitetsforlaget.

—— 1989. *Nuts and Bolts for the Social Sciences*. Cambridge, Cambridge University Press.

Elton, G.R., 1991. *Return to Essentials. Some Reflections on the Present State of Historical Study*. Cambridge, Cambridge University Press.

Eyerman, R., 1981. *False Consciousness and Ideology in Marxist Theory*. Stockholm, Almqvist and Wiksell International.

Farrell, B.A., 1981. *The Standing of Psychoanalysis*. Oxford, Oxford University Press.

Fay, Brian, 1975. *Social Theory and Political Practice*. London, Allen and Unwin.

Fish, Stanley, 1989. *Doing What Comes Naturally*. Durham, Duke University Press.

Fodor, Jerry A., 1981. *Representation: Philosophical Essays on the Foundations of Cognitive Science*. Cambridge, Mass., MIT Press.

Friedländer, Saul, 1978. *History and Psychoanalysis*. New York, Holmes and Meier.

Fuller, Steve, 1991. 'Social epistemology and the brave new world of science and technology studies', *Philosophy of the Social Sciences* 21: 232–44.

Gadamer, Hans-Georg, 1975. *Truth and Method*. New York, Crossroad.

—— 1980. *Dialogue and Dialectic: Eight Hermeneutical Studies on Plato*. New Haven, Yale University Press.

Gallie, W.B., 1955. 'Explanations in history and the genetic sciences', reprinted in *Theories of History*, ed. Patrick Gardiner, 1959. New York, The Free Press of Glencoe, pp. 386–402.

—— 1964. *Philosophy and the Historical Understanding*. London, Chatto and Windus.

Garfinkel, Alan, 1981. *Forms of Explanation. Rethinking the Questions of Social Theory*. New Haven, Yale University Press.

Garfinkel, H., 1967. *Studies in Ethnomethodology*. Englewood Cliffs, NJ, Prentice-Hall.

Geertz, Clifford, 1972. 'Deep play: Notes on the Balinese cockfight', reprinted in *Interpretive Social Science. A Reader*, ed. Paul Rabinow and William M. Sullivan, 1979. Berkeley, University of California Prss, pp. 181–223.

—— 1976. '"From the native's point of view": on the nature of anthropological understanding', reprinted in *Interpretive Social Science. A Reader*, ed. Paul Rabinow and William M. Sullivan, 1979. Berkeley, University of California Press, pp. 225–41.

Giddens, Anthony, 1984. *The Constitution of Society*. Cambridge, Polity Press.

Goffman, Erving, 1971. *The Presentation of Self in Everyday Life*. Harmondsworth, Penguin Books.

Goldstein, Leon J., 1976. *Historical Knowing*. Austin, University of Texas Press.

Goodman, Nelson, 1979. 'Metaphor as moonlighting', in *On Metaphor*, ed. Sheldon Sacks, Chicago, University of Chicago Press, pp. 175–80.

Gough, J.W., 1956. *John Locke's Political Philosophy*. Oxford, Clarendon.

Grünbaum, Adolf, 1985. *The Foundations of Psychoanalysis. A Philosophical Critique*. Berkeley, University of California Press.

Gurr, Robert, 1970. *Why Men Rebel*. Princeton, Princeton University Press.

Hackforth, R., 1955. *Plato's Phaedo*. Cambridge, Cambridge University Press.

Hardin, Russell, 1980. 'Rationality, irrationality and functionalist explanation', *Social Science Information* 19: 755–72.

—— 1982. *Collective Action*. Baltimore, The Johns Hopkins University Press.

Harlan, David, 1989. 'Intellectual history and the return of literature', *The American Historical Review* 94: 581–609.

Hart, H.L.A. and Honoré, A.M, 1959. 'Causal judgment in history and in the law', reprinted in *Philosophical Analysis and History*, ed. William H. Dray, 1966. New York, Harper and Row, pp. 213–37.

Hart, Kevin, 1989. *The Trespass of the Sign. Deconstruction, Theology and Philosophy*. Cambridge, Cambridge University Press.

Harré, R. and Madden, E.H., 1975. *Causal Powers. A Theory of Natural Necessity*. Oxford, Blackwell.

Harré, R., and Secord, P.F., 1972. *The Explanation of Social Behaviour*. Oxford, Blackwell.

Harris, Marvin, 1979. *Cultural Materialism: The Struggle for a Science of Culture*. New York, Random House.

Haskell, Thomas, L., 1990. 'Objectivity is not neutrality: Rhetoric vs practice in Peter Novick's *That Noble Dream*', *History and Theory* 29: 129–57.

Hausman, Daniel M., 1981. 'Are general equilibrium theories explanatory?' in *Philosophy in Economics*, ed. Joseph C. Pitt. Dordrecht, Reidel, pp. 17–32.

Hawthorn, Geoffrey, 1991. *Plausible Worlds. Possibility and Understanding in History and the Social Sciences*. Cambridge, Cambridge University Press.

Heidegger, Martin, 1962. *Being and Time*, trans. John Macquarrie and Edward Robinson. London, SCM Press.

Hempel, Carl G., 1963. 'Reasons and covering laws in historical explanation', reprinted in *The Philosophy of History*, ed. Patrick Gardiner. Oxford, Oxford University Press, pp. 90–105.

—— 1965. *Aspects of Scientific Explanation, and Other Essays in the Philosophy of Science*. New York, The Free Press.

Hexter, J.H., 1968, 'The rhetoric of history', reproduced in his book *Doing History*. Bloomington, Indiana University Press, 1971, pp. 15–76.

Hindess, B., 1986. '"Interests" in political analysis', in *Power, Action and Belief: A New Sociology of Knowledge*, ed. J. Law, Sociological Review Monograph 32. London, Routledge and Kegan Paul, pp. 112–31.

—— 1987. *Politics and Class Analysis*. Oxford, Blackwell.

Jenkins, Keith, 1991. *Re-Thinking History*. London, Routledge.

—— 1995. *On 'What is History?' From Carr and Elton to Rorty and White*. London, Routledge.

Johnson, Chalmers,1983. *Revolutionary Change*, 2nd edn. London, Longman.

Kaplan, Justin, 1986. 'The "Real Life"', in *Biography as High Adventure. Life-Writers Speak on Their Art*, ed. Stephen B. Oates. Amherst, University of Massachusetts Press, pp. 70–6.

Kellner, H., 1989. *Language and Historical Representation: Getting the Story Crooked.* Madison, University of Wisconsin Press.

Kendall, Paul Murray, 1965. *The Art of Biography.* London, Allen and Unwin.

Klein, L.R., 1982. 'Economic theoretic restrictions in econometrics', in *Evaluating the Reliability of Macro-economic Models*, eds G.C. Chow and P. Corsi. Chichester, John Wiley, pp. 23–42.

Kuhn, Thomas S., 1970. *The Structure of Scientific Revolutions*, 2nd edn, *International Encyclopedia of Unified Science*, vol. 2, number 2. Chicago, University of Chicago Press.

LaCapra, Dominick, 1985. *History and Criticism.* Ithaca, Cornell University Press.

Landesman, Charles, 1997. *An Introduction to Epistemology.* Oxford, Blackwell.

Laslett, Peter, 1970. *The Two Treatises of Government.* 2nd edn, Cambridge, Cambridge University Press.

Lemon, M.C., 1995. *The Discipline of History and the History of Thought.* London, Routledge.

Lenin, Vladimir I., 1965. *The State and Revolution: Marxist Teaching on the State and the Tasks of the Proletariat in the Revolution.* Peking, Foreign Language Press.

Lessnoff, Michael H., 1974. *The Structure of Social Science.* Studies in Sociology: 7. London, Allen and Unwin.

Lewis, David, 1973. 'Causation', reprinted in his *Philosophical Papers*, vol. 2, 1986. New York, Oxford University Press, pp. 159–72.

—— 1986a. 'Postscripts to "Causation"', *Philosophical Papers*, vol. 2. New York, Oxford University Press, pp. 172–213.

—— 1986b. 'Causal explanation', reprinted in *Philosophical Papers*, vol. 2, 1986. New York, Oxford University Press, pp. 214–40.

Lipton, Peter, 1993. *Inference to the Best Explanation.* London, Routledge.

Little, Daniel, 1991. *Varieties of Social Explanation.* Boulder, Westview Press.

Lloyd, Christopher, 1986. *Explanation in Social History.* Oxford, Blackwell.

—— 1993. *The Structures of History.* Oxford, Blackwell.

Lukes, Steven, 1970. 'Some problems about rationality', in *Rationality*, ed. Bryan R. Wilson. Oxford, Blackwell, pp. 194–213.

Lyotard, Jean-François, 1984. *The Postmodern Condition: A Report on Knowledge*, vol.10 in the series: Theory and History of Literature, trans. Geoff Bennington and Brian Massumi. Manchester, Manchester University Press.

—— 1989. *The Lyotard Reader*, ed. Andrew Benjamin. Oxford, Blackwell.

McCarthy, Thomas, 1984. *The Critical Theory of Jürgen Habermas.* Cambridge, Polity Press.

McCullagh, C. Behan, 1978. 'Colligation and classification in history', *History and Theory* XVII: 267–84.

—— 1984. *Justifying Historical Descriptions.* Cambridge, Cambridge University Press.

—— 1987. 'The truth of historical narratives', *History and Theory.* Beiheft 26: 30–46.

—— 1990. 'The rationality of emotions and of emotional behaviour', *Australasian Journal of Philosophy* 68: 44–58.

—— 1991a. 'How objective interests explain actions', in *Social Science Information* 30: 29–54.

—— 1991b. 'Can our understanding of old texts be objective?' *History and Theory* 30: 302–23.

—— 1993. 'Metaphor and truth in history', *Clio* 23: 24–49.

Mandelbaum, Maurice, 1977. *The Anatomy of Historical Knowledge.* Baltimore, The Johns Hopkins University Press.

Mannheim, K., 1960. *Ideology and Utopia*, trans. E. Shils and L. Wirth. London, Routledge and Kegan Paul.

Marcus, George E. and Fischer, Michael M.J., 1986. *Anthropology as Cultural Critique. An Experimental Movement in the Human Sciences*. Chicago, University of Chicago Press.

Martin, Rex, 1977. *Historical Explanation. Re-enactment and Practical Inference*. Ithaca, Cornell University Press.

—— 1994. 'Collingwood and von Wright on *Verstehn*, causation and the explanation of human action', *Collingwood Studies, vol.1: The Life and Thought of R.G. Collingwood*, ed. David Boucher. Swansea, R.G. Collingwood Society, pp. 143–62.

Marx, Karl and Engels, F., 1888. *Manifesto of the Communist Party*. Moscow, Foreign Languages Publishing House, 1959.

Mascall, E.L., 1966. *Existence and Analogy*. London, Darton, Longman and Todd.

Meiland, Jack W., 1965. *Scepticism and Historical Knowledge*. New York, Random House.

Meltzer, Bernard N., and Petras, John W., 1972. 'The Chicago and Iowa schools of symbolic interactionism', in *Symbolic Interaction: A Reader in Social Psychology*, ed. Jerome G. Manis and Bernard N. Meltzer, 2nd edn. Boston, Allyn and Bacon, pp. 43–57.

Merton, Robert K., 1967. 'Manifest and latent functions', in his book *On Theoretical Sociology*. New York, The Free Press, pp. 73–138.

Mill, John Stuart, 1949. *A System of Logic, Ratiocinative and Inductive*, 8th edn. London, Longman.

Miller, David, 1976. *Social Justice*. Oxford, Clarendon.

Moore, F.C.T., 1982. 'On taking metaphor literally', in *Metaphor: Problems and Perspectives*, ed. David S. Miall. Sussex, Harvester, pp. 1–13.

Murphey, Murray G., 1973. *Our Knowledge of the Historical Past*. Indianapolis, Bobbs-Merrill.

Nagel, Ernest, 1961. *The Structure of Science. Problems in the Logic of Scientific Explanation*. London, Routledge and Kegan Paul.

—— 1977. 'Teleology revisited', *The Journal of Philosophy* 74: 261–301.

Novick, Peter, 1988. *That Noble Dream: The 'Objectivity Question' and the American Historical Profession*. Cambridge, Cambridge University Press.

Oakeshott, M., 1933. *Experience and Its Modes*. Cambridge, Cambridge University Press.

—— 1962. *Rationalism in Politics and Other Essays*. London, Methuen.

Olafson, Frederick A., 1979. *The Dialectic of Action. A Philosophical Interpretation of History and the Humanities*. Chicago, The University of Chicago Press.

—— 1987. *Heidegger and the Philosophy of Mind*. New Haven, Yale University Press.

Passmore, John, 1987. 'Narratives and events', *History and Theory* Beiheft 26: 68–74.

Pettit, Philip, 1993. *The Common Mind. An Essay on Psychology, Society, and Politics*. New York, Oxford University Press.

Pocock, J.G.A., 1972. *Politics, Language and Time. Essays on Political Thought and History*. London, Methuen.

Popper, Karl, 1979. *Objective Knowledge. An Evolutionary Approach*, rev. edn. Oxford, Clarendon.

Porter, Dale H., 1981. *The Emergence of the Past. A Theory of Historical Explanation*. Chicago, University of Chicago Press.

Putnam, Hilary, 1986. 'The way the world is', in *Realism with a Human Face*, ed. J. Conant. Cambridge, Mass., Harvard University Press, 1990.

—— 1987. *The Many Faces of Realism. The Paul Carus Lectures*. Las Salle, Illinois, Open Court.

—— 1988. *Representation and Reality*. Cambridge, Mass., Bradford, MIT Press.

Ragin, Charles C., 1987. *The Comparative Method. Moving Beyond Qualitative and Quantitative Strategies*. Berkeley, University of California Press.

Randall, John Herman, jr., 1962. *Nature and Historical Experience. Essays in Naturalism and in the Theory of History*. New York, Columbia University Press.

Rayner, J.D., 1980. 'The uses of ideological language', in *The Form of Ideology*, ed. D.J. Manning. London, George Allen and Unwin.

Readings, Bill, 1991. *Introducing Lyotard. Art and Politics*. London, Routledge.

Redhead, Michael, 1990. 'Explanation', in *Explanation and Its Limits*, ed. Dudley Knowles. Cambridge, Cambridge University Press, pp. 135–54.

Rickert, H., 1962. *Science and History. A Critique of Positivist Epistemology*, trans. George Reisman. Princeton, Princeton University Press.

Ricoeur, Paul, 1977. 'The question of proof in Freud's psychoanalytic writings', reprinted in his *Hermeneutics and the Human Sciences*, ed. John B. Thompson. Cambridge, Cambridge University Press and Paris, Editions de la Maison des Sciences de l'Homme, 1981, pp. 247–73.

Roberts, Clayton, 1996. *The Logic of Historical Explanation*. University Park, Pa., Pennsylvania State University Press.

Rorty, Richard, 1980. *Philosophy and the Mirror of Nature*. Oxford, Blackwell.

—— 1989. 'Solidarity or objectivity?' in *Relativism. Interpretation and Confrontation*, ed. Michael Krausz. Notre Dame, University of Notre Dame Press, pp. 35–50.

—— 1991. 'Unfamiliar noises: Hesse and Davidson on metaphor', in his *Objectivity, Relativism, and Truth: Philosophical Papers*, vol.1. Cambridge, Cambridge University Press, pp. 162–72.

Rosenberg, Alexander, 1976. *Microeconomic Laws, A Philosophic Analysis*. London, University of Pittsburgh Press.

Roth, Paul A., 1988. 'Narrative explanations: The case of history', *History and Theory* 27: 1–13.

—— 1991. 'Truth in interpretation', *Philosophy of the Social Sciences* 21: 175–95.

Runyan, William McKinley, 1982. 'Why did Van Gogh cut off his ear?', reprinted in *Psycho/History. Readings in the Method of Psychology, Psychoanalysis, and History*, ed. Geoffrey Cocks and Travis L. Crosby. New Haven, Yale University Press, 1987, pp. 121–31.

Ryan, Alan, 1965. 'Locke and the dictatorship of the bourgeoisie', *Political Studies* 13: 219–30.

—— 1970. *The Philosophy of the Social Sciences*. London, Macmillan.

—— 1978. 'Maximising, moralising and dramatising', in *Action and Interpretation. Studies in the Philosophy of the Social Sciences*, ed. Christopher Hookway and Philip Pettit. Cambridge, Cambridge University Press, pp. 65–81.

Sahlins, Marshall, 1976. *Culture and Practical Reason*. Chicago, University of Chicago Press.

Schmaus, Warren, 1991. 'Whither social epistemology?' *Philosophy of the Social Sciences* 21: 196–202.

Schürmann, Reiner, 1985. 'Symposium: The philosophy of Michel Foucault; "What Can I Do?" in archaeological-genealogical history', *The Journal of Philosophy* 82: 540–7.

Scriven, Michael, 1966. 'Causes, connections and conditions in history', in *Philosophical Analysis and History*, ed. William H. Dray. New York, Harper and Row, pp. 238–64.

Shaw, William H., 1978. *Marx's Theory of History*. London, Hutchinson.

Simmel, Georg, 1977. *The Problems of the Philosophy of History. An Epistemological Essay*, trans. Guy Oakes. New York, The Free Press of Glencoe.

Skinner, Quentin, 1969. 'Meaning and understanding in the history of ideas', *History and Theory* 8: 3–53.

—— 1974. 'Some problems in the analysis of political thought and action', *Political Theory* 2: 277–303.

—— 1978. *The Foundations of Modern Political Thought. Volume 1: The Renaissance*. Cambridge, Cambridge University Press.

—— 1979. 'The idea of a cultural lexicon', *Essays in Criticism* XXIX: 205–24.

—— 1988. 'A reply to my critics', in *Meaning and Context. Quentin Skinner and his Critics*, ed. James Tully. Cambridge, Polity Press.

Skocpol, Theda, 1984. 'Emerging agendas and recurrent strategies in historical sociology', in *Vision and Method in Historical Sociology*, ed. Theda Skocpol, Cambridge, Cambridge University Press, pp. 356–91.

Smelser, Neil J., 1976. *Comparative Methods in the Social Sciences*. Englewood Cliffs, N.J., Prentice Hall.

Smith, Dennis, 1983. *Barrington Moore. Violence, Morality and Political Change*. London, Macmillan.

Smith, Peter H., 1982. 'A view from Latin America', in *The New History, The 1980s and Beyond*, ed. Theodore K. Rabb and Robert I. Rotberg. Princeton, Princeton University Press.

Spence, D.P., 1988. 'Tough and tender-minded hermeneutics', in *Hermeneutics and Psychological Theory. Interpretive perspectives on personality, psychotherapy and psychopathology*, ed. Stanley B. Messer, Louis A. Sass and Robert L. Woolfolk. New Brunswick, Rutgers University Press, pp. 62–84.

Stone, Lawrence, 1992. 'History and post-modernism', *Past and Present* 135: 189–94.

Strasser, Hermann and Randall, Susan C., 1981. *An Introduction to Theories of Social Change*. London, Routledge and Kegan Paul.

Stretton, Hugh, 1969. *The Political Sciences*. London, Routledge and Kegan Paul.

Taylor, Michael, 1988. 'Rationality and revolutionary collective action', in *Rationality and Revolution*, ed. Michael Taylor. Cambridge, Cambridge University Press, and Paris, Editions de la Maison des Sciences de l'Homme, pp. 63–97.

Thomas, David, 1979. *Naturalism and Social Science. A Post-empiricist Philosophy of Social Science*. Cambridge, Cambridge University Press.

Thompson, John B., 1984. *Studies in the Theory of Ideology*. Cambridge, Polity Press.

Tilly, Charles, 1978. *From Mobilization to Revolution*. Reading, Mass., Addison-Wesley.

—— 1981. *As Sociology Meets History*. New York, Academic Press.

—— 1984. *Big Structures, Large Processes and Huge Comparisons*. New York, Russell Sage Foundation.

Tönnies, Ferdinand, 1955. *Community and Association*, trans. Charles P. Loomis, 1974. London, Routledge.

Tosh, John, 1984. *The Pursuit of History. Aims, Methods and New Directions in the Study of Modern History*. London, Longman.

Tourangeau, Roger, 1982. 'Metaphor and cognitive structure', in *Metaphor: Problems and Perspectives*, ed. David S. Miall. Sussex, Harvester.

Van Fraassen, Bas, 1980. *The Scientific Image*. Oxford, Clarendon.

Van Parijs, Philippe, 1981. *Evolutionary Explanation in the Social Sciences. An Emerging Paradigm*. Totowa, N.J., Rowman and Littlefield.

Veeser, H. Aram (ed.), 1989. *The New Historicism*. London, Routledge.

Veyne, Paul, 1984. *Writing History. An Essay on Epistemology*, trans. Mina Moore-Rinvolucri. Middletown, Conn., Wesleyan University Press.

White, Hayden, 1974. 'The historical text as literary artifact', *Clio* III: 277–303.

—— 1975. *Metahistory. The Historical Imagination in Nineteenth-Century Europe*. Baltimore, The Johns Hopkins University Press.

—— 1992. 'Historical emplotment and the problem of truth', in *Probing the Limits of Representation: Nazism and the 'Final Solution'*, ed. Saul Friedlander. Cambridge, Mass., Harvard University Press, pp. 37–53.

Wilson, John, 1983. *Social Theory*. Englewood Cliffs, N.J., Prentice-Hall.

Windschuttle, Keith, 1994. *The Killing of History. How a Discipline is being Murdered by Literary Critics and Social Theorists*. Sydney, Macleay Press.

Wise, Gene, 1973. *American Historical Explanations. A Strategy for Grounded Inquiry*. Homewood, Illinois, The Dorsey Press.

Wittgenstein, Ludwig, 1968. *Philosophical Investigations*. Oxford, Blackwell.

—— 1969. *On Certainty*, ed. G.E.M. Anscombe and G.H. von Wright, trans. D. Paul and G.E.M. Anscombe. Oxford, Blackwell.

Young, Robert, 1990. *White Mythologies. Writing History and the West.* London, Routledge.

Zagorin, Perez, 1973. 'Theories of revolution in contemporary historiography', *Political Science Quarterly* 88: 23–52.

B. HISTORICAL WORKS

Allen, William Sheridan, 1989. *The Nazi Seizure of Power.* London, Penguin.

Aron, Raymond, 1958. 'Causes and responsibilities', in *The Outbreak of the First World War. Who Was Responsible?*, ed. Dwight E. Lee. Boston, D.C. Heath.

Bailyn, Bernard, 1967. *The Ideological Origins of the American Revolution.* Cambridge, Cambridge University Press.

—— 1970. *The Origins of American Politics.* New York, Vintage Books.

Benn, Caroline, 1992. *Kier Hardie.* London, Hutchinson.

Boritt, Gabor, and Forness, Norman O. (eds), 1988. *The Historian's Lincoln. Pseudohistory, Psychohistory, and History.* Urbana, University of Illinois Press.

Bourdieu, Pierre, 1976. 'Marriage strategies as strategies of social reproduction', in *Family and Society*, ed. Robert Forster and Orest Ranum, trans. Elborg Forster and Patricia M. Ranum. Baltimore, Johns Hopkins University Press.

Boyce, D.G., 1990. *Nineteenth-Century Ireland. The Search for Stability.* Dublin, Gill and Macmillan.

Boyer, Paul and Nissenbaum, Stephen, 1974. *Salem Possessed. The Social Origins of Witchcraft.* Cambridge, Mass., Harvard University Press.

Bullock, Alan, 1952. *Hitler, A Study in Tyranny.* London, Odhams Press.

Burckhardt, Jacob, 1944. *The Civilization of the Renaissance in Italy.* Oxford, Phaidon Press.

Burke, Peter, 1974. *Tradition and Innovation in Renaissance Italy. A Sociological Approach.* London, Fontana/Collins.

Burn, W.L., 1968. *The Age of Equipoise. A Study of the Mid-Victorian Generation.* London, Allen and Unwin.

Butterfield, Herbert, 1957. *George III and the Historians.* London, Collins.

Cannadine, David, 1984. 'The present and the past in the English Industrial Revolution 1880–1980', *Past and Present* 103: 131–72.

—— 1991. *The Pleasures of the Past.* New York, W.W. Norton.

Caplan, Jane, 1978. 'Bureaucracy, politics and the national socialist state', in *The Shaping of the Nazi State*, ed. Peter D. Stachura. London, Croom Helm, pp. 234–56.

Christianson, Paul, 1976. 'The causes of the English Revolution: A reappraisal', *The Journal of British Studies* 15: 40–75.

Clark, G. Kitson, 1962. *The Making of Victorian England.* London, Methuen.

Clark, J.C.D., 1985. *English Society 1688–1832.* Cambridge, Cambridge University Press.

Clendinnen, Inga, 1987. *Ambivalent Conquests. Maya and Spaniard in Yucatan, 1517–1570.* Cambridge, Cambridge University Press.

Cmiel, Kenneth, 1990. *Democratic Eloquence: The Fight over Popular Speech in Nineteenth-Century America.* New York, William Morrow.

Crafts, N.C.R., 1981. 'The eighteenth century: a survey', in *The Economic History of Britain since 1700. Volume 1: 1700–1860*, ed. Roderick Floud and Donald McCloskey. Cambridge, Cambridge University Press.

Craven, Avery, 1957. *The Coming of the Civil War*, 2nd edn. Chicago, University of Chicago Press.

Darnton, Robert, 1984. *The Great Cat Massacre and Other Episodes in French Cultural History.* New York, Basic Books.

Davis, Natalie Zemon, 1975. *Society and Culture in Early Modern France.* Stanford, Stanford University Press.

Deane, Phyllis, 1965. *The First Industrial Revolution*. Cambridge, Cambridge University Press.

Dening, Greg, 1980. *Islands and Beaches. Discourse on a Silent Land. Marquesas 1774–1880*. Honolulu, University Press of Hawaii.

Doyle, William, 1988. *Origins of the French Revolution*, 2nd edn. Oxford, Oxford University Press.

Eley, Geoff, 1990. 'Edward Thompson, social history and political culture: The making of a working-class public, 1780–1850', in *E.P.Thompson, Critical Perspectives*, ed. Harvey J. Kaye and Keith McClelland. Cambridge, Polity Press.

Elton, G.R., 1955. *England under the Tudors*. London, Methuen.

—— 1962. *The Tudor Revolution in Government*. Cambridge, Cambridge University Press.

—— 1964. 'The Tudor Revolution: A reply', *Past and Present* 29: 26–49.

Ensor, R.C.K., 1936. *England 1870–1914*. Oxford, Clarendon.

Erikson, Erik H., 1972. *Young Man Luther. A Study in Psychoanalysis and History*. London, Faber and Faber.

Ernst, Joseph, 1976. '"Ideology" and an economic interpretation of the Revolution', in *The American Revolution. Explorations in the History of American Radicalism*, ed. Alfred F. Young. DeKalb, Ill., Northern Illinois University Press, pp. 159–85.

Fawtier, Robert, 1964. *The Capetian Kings of France, Monarchy and Nation (987–1328)*, trans. Lionel Butler and R.J. Adam. London, Macmillan.

Fehrenbacher, Don E., 1987. *Lincoln in Text and Context*. Stanford, Stanford University Press.

Finley, M.I., 1963. 'Generalizations in ancient history' in *Generalization in the Writing of History*, ed. Louis Gottschalk. Chicago, University of Chicago Press, pp. 19–35.

Fitzpatrick, Sheila, 1982. *The Russian Revolution*. Oxford, Oxford University Press.

Freytag, Gustav, 1862. *Pictures of German Life in the XVth, XVIth and XVIIth Centuries*, trans. Georgiana Malcolm, London, quoted in *The Thirty Years' War*, Theodore K. Rabb (ed.), 2nd edn. Lexington, D.C. Heath, pp. 3–7.

Friedmann, Harriet, 1988. 'Form and substance in the analysis of the world economy', in *Social Structures, A Network Approach*, ed. Barry Wellman and S.D. Berkowitz. Cambridge, Cambridge University Press, pp. 304–25.

Gardiner, S.R., 1889. *The Thirty Years' War, 1618–1648*, 8th edn. London, Longman, Green and Co.

Gathorne-Hardy, G.M., 1950. *A Short History of International Affairs 1920–1939*, 4th edn. London, Oxford University Press.

Geertz, Clifford, 1972. 'Deep play: Notes on the Balinese cockfight', reprinted in *Interpretive Social Science. A Reader*, ed. Paul Rabinow and William M. Sullivan. Berkeley, University of California Press, 1979, pp. 181–223.

George, A. and J., 1956. *Woodrow Wilson and Colonel House: A Personality Study*. New York, John Day.

Ginzburg, Carlo, 1980. *The Cheese and the Worms. The Cosmos of a Sixteenth-century Miller*, trans. John and Anne Tedeschi. Baltimore, The Johns Hopkins University Press.

Goldhagen, Daniel Jonah, 1996. *Hitler's Willing Executioners. Ordinary Germans and the Holocaust*. London, Little, Brown and Co.

Goodwin, A., 1953. *The French Revolution*. London, Hutchinson's University Library.

Hampson, Norman, 1963. *A Social History of the French Revolution*. London, Routledge and Kegan Paul.

Harrison, J.F.C., 1971. *The Early Victorians, 1832–1851*. London, Weidenfeld and Nicolson.

Harriss, G.L. 1963. 'A revolution in Tudor history? Medieval government and statecraft', *Past and Present* 25: 8–38.

Hartwell, R.M. (ed.),1967. *The Causes of the Industrial Revolution in England*. London, Methuen.

Haskins, Charles Homer, 1957. *The Renaissance of the Twelfth Century*. New York, Meridian.

Hexter, J.H., 1961. *Reappraisals in History*. London, Longman.

Hiden, John, and Farquharson, John, 1983. *Explaining Hitler's Germany. Historians and the Third Reich*. London, Batsford Academic and Educational Ltd.

Hill, Christopher, 1955. *The English Revolution, 1640*, 3rd edn. London, Lawrence and Wishart.

—— 1958. *Puritanism and Revolution, Studies in Interpretation of the English Revolution of the 17th Century*. London, Secker and Warburg.

—— 1972. *The Century of Revolution, 1603–1714*, 2nd edn. London, Sphere Books.

Holmes, George, 1969. *The Florentine Enlightenment 1400–1450*. New York, Pegasus.

Holton, R.J., 1985. *The Transition from Feudalism to Capitalism*. Basingstoke, Hampshire, Macmillan.

Huizinga, J., 1955. *The Waning of the Middle Ages. A Study of the Forms of Life, Thought and Art in France and the Netherlands in the Fourteenth and Fifteenth Centuries*. Harmondsworth, Penguin Books.

Isaac, Rhys, 1982. *The Transformation of Virginia 1740–1790*. Chapel Hill, University of North Carolina Press.

Jones, E.L., 1988. *Growth Recurring. Economic Change in World History*. Oxford, Clarendon.

Jones, J.R., 1993. *Marlborough*. Cambridge, Cambridge University Press.

Larner, Christina, 1984. *Witchcraft and Religion. The Politics of Popular Belief*. Oxford, Blackwell.

MacDonagh, Oliver, 1981. *The Inspector General: Sir Jeremiah Fitzpatrick and the Politics of Social Reform, 1783–1802*. London, Croom Helm.

McPhee, Peter, 1993. *A Social History of France, 1780–1880*. London, Routledge.

McPherson, James M., 1989. *Battle Cry of Freedom. The Civil War Era*. New York, Ballantine.

Magnus, Philip, 1954. *Gladstone, A Biography*. London, John Murray.

Mandler, Peter, 1990. *Aristocratic Government in the Age of Reform. Whigs and Liberals 1830–1852*. Oxford, Clarendon.

Martin, A.W., 1980. *Henry Parkes: a Biography*. Melbourne, Melbourne University Press.

Matthew, H.C.G., 1986. *Gladstone 1809–1874*. Oxford, Clarendon.

Mauss, Marcel, 1966. *The Gift: Forms and Functions of Exchange in Archaic Societies*, trans. Ian Cunnison. London, Cohen and West.

May, Ernest R., 1973. *'Lessons' of the Past. The Use and Misuse of History in American Foreign Policy*. New York, Oxford University Press.

Megaw, Isobel, 1949. 'The ecclesiastical policy of Stephen, 1135–9: a reinterpretation', in *Essays in British and Irish History in Honour of James Eadie Todd*, ed. H.A. Cronne, T.W. Moody and D.B. Quinn. London, Frederick Muller, pp. 24–45.

Middlekauf, Robert, 1982. *The Glorious Cause, The American Revolution, 1763–1784*. New York, Oxford University Press.

Mokyr, Joel, 1985. 'The Industrial Revolution and the new economic history', in *The Economics of the Industrial Revolution*, ed. Joel Mokyr. Totowa, N.J., Rowman and Allanheld.

Moore, Barrington, jr., 1977. *Social Origins of Dictatorship and Democracy. Lord and Peasant in the Making of the Modern World*. London, Penguin Books.

Namier, L., 1963. *The Structure of Politics at the Accession of George III*. London, Macmillan.

North, John, 1936. *Gallipoli, A Fading Vision*. London, Faber and Faber.

Obeyesekere, Gananath, 1992. *The Apotheosis of Captain Cook. European Mythmaking in the Pacific*. Princeton, Princeton University Press.

Palmer, Robert R., 1963. 'Generalizations about revolution: A case study', in *General-*

ization in the Writing of History, ed. Louis Gottschalk. Chicago, University of Chicago Press, pp. 66–76.

Parker, Geoffrey, 1979. *Europe in Crisis, 1598–1648*. Glasgow, Fontana.

Pelling, Henry, 1965. *The Origins of the Labour Party 1880–1900*. Oxford, Clarendon.

Perroy, Edouard, 1962. *The Hundred Years War*, trans. W.B. Wells. London, Eyre and Spottiswoode.

Pipes, Richard, 1990. *The Russian Revolution 1899–1919*. London, Collins Harvill.

Porter, Roy, 1990. *English Society in the Eighteenth Century*, rev. edn. London, Penguin.

—— 1991. 'Bodies of thought: Thought about the body in eighteenth-century England', in *Interpretation and Cultural History*, ed. J.H. Pittock and A. Wear. London, Macmillan, pp. 82–108.

Royle, Edward and Walvin, James, 1982. *English Radicals and Reformers, 1760–1848*. Lexington, University Press of Kentucky.

Rozwenc, Edwin C. (ed.), 1972. *The Causes of the American Civil War*, 2nd edn. Lexington, D.C. Heath.

Rudé, George, 1959. *The Crowd in the French Revolution*. Oxford, Clarendon.

—— 1964. *The Crowd in History. A Study of Popular Disturbances in France and England 1730–1848*. New York, John Wiley.

—— 1976a. 'The study of revolutions', reprinted in *The Face of the Crowd. Studies in Revolution, Ideology and Popular Protest*. Hemel Hempstead, Harvester-Wheatsheaf, pp. 72–9.

—— 1976b. Review of *The Rebellious Century 1830–1930* by Charles Tilly, Louise Tilly and Richard Tilly, *American Journal of Sociology* 82: 449–51.

—— 1980. *Ideology and Popular Protest*. New York, Pantheon Books.

—— 1981. *The Crowd in History, 1730–1848*, rev. edn. London, Lawrence and Wishart.

Russell, Conrad, 1990. *The Causes of the English Civil War*. Oxford, Clarendon.

Sahlins, Marshall, 1981. *Historical Metaphors and Mythical Realities*. Ann Arbor, University of Michigan Press.

—— 1995. *How 'Natives' Think. About Captain Cook, For Example*. Chicago, University of Chicago Press.

Schoenbaum, David, 1967. *Hitler's Social Revolution. Class and Status in Nazi Germany, 1933–1939*. London, Weidenfeld and Nicolson.

Scott, Martin, 1964. *Medieval Europe*. London, Longman.

Sewell, William H., 1985a. *Structure and Mobility. The Men and Women of Marseilles*. Cambridge, Cambridge University Press.

—— 1985b. 'Ideologies and social revolutions: Reflections on the French case', *The Journal of Modern History* 57: 57–85.

Shils, Edward, and Young, Michael, 1953. 'The meaning of the coronation', *The Sociological Review*, n.s.1: 63–81.

Skocpol, Theda, 1979. *States and Social Revolutions. A Comparative Analysis of France, Russia, and China*. Cambridge, Cambridge University Press.

—— 1985. 'Cultural idioms and political ideologies in the revolutionary reconstruction of State power: A rejoinder to Sewell', *The Journal of Modern History* 57: 86–96.

Stachura, Peter D. (ed.),1983. *The Nazi Machtergreifung*. London, Allen and Unwin.

Steinberg, S.H., 1966. *The 'Thirty Years' War' and the Conflict for European Hegemony, 1600–1660*. London, Edward Arnold.

Stevenson, John, 1979. *Popular Disturbances in England 1700–1870*. London, Longman.

Stone, Lawrence, 1972. *The Causes of the English Revolution 1529–1642*. London, Routledge and Kegan Paul.

Strachey, Lytton, 1942. *Five Victorians*. London, The Reprint Society.

Taylor, A.J.P., 1954. *The Struggle for Mastery in Europe. 1848–1918*. Oxford, Clarendon.

Tepperman, Lorne, 1988. 'Collective mobility and the persistence of dynasties', in *Social Structures, A Network Approach*, ed. Barry Wellman and S.D. Berkowitz. Cambridge, Cambridge University Press, pp. 405–29.

Thompson, Allan, 1973. *The Dynamics of the Industrial Revolution*. London, Edward Arnold.

Thompson, E.P., 1968. *The Making of the English Working Class*. Harmondsworth, Penguin.

Tilly, Charles, Tilly, Louise and Tilly, Richard, 1975. *The Rebellious Century 1830–1930*. London, J.M. Dent and Sons.

Trevor-Roper, Hugh, 1984. 'The European witch-craze of the sixteenth and seventeenth centuries', in *Religion, the Reformation and Social Change and Other Essays*, 3rd edn. London, Secker and Warburg.

Trotsky, Leon, 1980. *The History of the Russian Revolution*, trans. Max Eastman. New York, Pathfinder.

Turner, Victor, 1974. *Dramas, Fields and Metaphors. Symbolic Action in Human History*. Ithaca, Cornell University Press.

Walter, James, 1981. 'Studying political leaders from a distance: the lessons of biography', in *Reading Life Histories. Griffith Papers on Biography*, ed. James Walter, Nathan, Queensland, Griffith University, pp. 29–38.

Ward, John William, 1970. 'Looking backward: *Andrew Jackson: Symbol for an Age*', in *The Historian's Workshop*, ed. J.P. Curtis, jr. New York, Knopf, pp. 205–19.

Westfall, Richard S., 1985. 'Newton and his biographer', in *Introspection in Biography. The Biographer's Quest for Self-Awareness*, ed. Samuel H. Baron and Carl Pletsch. New Jersey, The Analytic Press, Lawrence Erlbaum, pp. 175–89.

Williams, Penry, 1963. 'A revolution in Tudor history? The Tudor State', *Past and Present* 25: 39–58.

Wright, Arthur F., 1963. 'On the uses of generalization in the study of Chinese history' in *Generalization in the Writing of History*, ed. Louis Gottschalk. Chicago, University of Chicago Press, pp. 36–58.

Names index

The names in this index include the names of authors quoted; the names of those who ideas have been discussed; and the names of people who were the subject of historical inquiry, mentioned in the text.

Subject index